EMORY

THE SECRET GUIDE TO

DARK PSYCHOLOGY

5 Books in 1

PROVEN PSYCHOLOGICAL MANIPULATION,
MASTERS OF EMOTIONAL BLACKMAIL,
DARK MIND CONTROL IN NLP,
DARK SEDUCTION AND PERSUASION,
GASLIGHTING GAMES

CLAIM YOUR FREE GIFT

This bundle comes with a free bonus item.

Head straight to the last chapter to quickly claim your gift today!

BOOKS

Proven Psychological Manipulation Techniques

Guiltless Guide into the Psychology of How Cunning People Get What They Want. How to Play Secret Dark Games to Seize Control and Always Win

Emory Green

TABLE OF CONTENTS

INTRODUCTION

There's something that's brought you to this book. There's a reason that you're here.

...The only way to identify that impulse is to understand who you are as a person. You've gotten where you are today through hard graft, good practice, and by leaving no stone unturned. You've built a life for yourself—am I correct? You're not afraid to put in the effort. You impact those around you, and you know that you do; however, there's something you still want to know. It's an itch you need to scratch.

As a problem solver, decision-maker, and naturally inquisitive person, you are hoping to shine a flashlight into the dark corners of human behavior and endeavor, and I hear you loud and clear. Your hobbies are an extension of your passions; they are what drive and define you. Digging away at something, questing, and unlocking the puzzle are what keep you active. You've set yourself this challenge, so you can move forward.

Perhaps you worry that others will undercut your achievements and take them away from you, leaving you with nothing. Is that what makes you sweat at night? Am I close? You fear you might wake up one day and discover that all you've built has been undermined because you didn't keep your eyes wide open; you've told yourself you need to keep vigilant to enemies that could be around you.

Therefore, you want to understand what's lurking just below the surface and in the murkiness of the world.

Are there certain things you can't help but puzzle over? There are definitely folks and forces who exert dominance, which you can't understand. You ask yourself: why do they have power, control, money, and security? Why do they seem to have everything they want? Other people jump when they whistle—what got them to their position of command? What games and tricks have they played and conjured? What is the secret to their art?

These people are **manipulators**. They achieve and succeed, regardless of the wellbeing of others, and they always have an advantage over everyone else. You see them around often; they're the ones with the smiles on their faces.

But how do they do it? What's their secret? You are sick of being left on the outside and you want to be firmly in the know because you understand that that's the only way to protect your business, family, and sense of wellbeing from external influences.

That's why you've reached for this book.

No matter your background, ethnicity, identity, experiences, or career, you've made the right choices, which is to be applauded. Let us move forward together. Rest assured, I am here to provide the detail and perspective that you need.

The trouble is that most psychological studies often steer clear of the subject of manipulation due to the controversy, among other reasons. The subject may touch upon persuasion, coercion, exploitation, slavitude, and mind control, which are all sensitive topics—manipulation is rarely used as a force for good, and it can make for scary reading! But you can't help being fascinated, can you? I know I can't. Like you, I refuse to shy away from the unknown. Who we are as a species, what we do, and why, are all subjects that occupy my thoughts.

That's why I've made manipulation the focus of my research, and why I've written this book. It is the first part of an in-depth Dark

Psychology series, in which I look closely at human nature and pervasive personality traits: the good, the bad, and the ugly. Elsewhere in this series, I will be exploring gaslighting, emotional blackmail, dark persuasion and dark neuro-linguistic programming (NLP) extensively. Here, we will examine manipulation in its many shapes and forms.

Manipulation—getting other people to do things—is as old as the hills, and we've been talking and writing about it for just as long. The very first book of the Bible shows us Satan, as the serpent, using temptation for ulterior motives. Within ancient Greek and Sanskrit texts also dramatize explicitly the connection between willingness and those in power. Shakespeare made poetic case studies of manipulators and manipulation, and modern dystopias—*Orwellian nightmares*—painted a picture of fake news, propaganda, and distortion of information could send chills down our spines.

Manipulation everywhere, and we experience it every day: in the shape of governmental press releases, political campaigns, advertising slogans, and in "subtle" requests for favors from loved ones, colleagues, and strangers. Often clouded in fiction and masked by intrigue, manipulation is a sneaky customer that works best when we are aware of it the least.

This book will give you all the information you need to see the subject clearly. Knowledge is power, and everything has an explanation! Preparation is key; if you want to stay a step ahead, you need to have a handle on what's going on in the world and outsmart the rest. You are accepting of others—that's in your DNA—but that doesn't mean you shouldn't try to understand others' intentions better. Well-equipped, you can stop anyone taking advantage of you, so you won't be a victim. No one is going to scam you, get you to do something detrimental to your welfare, or hold you back. It is vital that you understand that. Reading insights and experiences here in this book will help make your ambitions a reality.

I have worked as a psychologist for over twenty years. In that time, I've also provided consultancy for big enterprises, offering cognitive, behavioral, and motivational guidance. As such, I've liaised with CEOs and top-tier business leaders, and encountered more than my fair share of genius minds! I have seen how they play the game—some play it well, some badly, some fairly, some not so well. I've learned that the most successful, admired, and respected, all share a detailed knowledge of manipulation; therefore, I made it my goal to discuss this topic with them, investigating ethical tactics and approaches. I want to let you in on those secrets now.

My insights, interests, and knowledge have helped a wide range of associates, and their achievements, gratitude, and sense of security all indicate how effective my approach has been. Once you have completed reading this book, you will also be proof of its success. You will see and feel it in yourself, and others will sense it around you too.

I can give you this promise: I'm not here just to satisfy your infomania or tickle your curiosity. I want to change the way you think, behave, and operate, for the better. I want to avoid hyperbole, fluff, and grand and insubstantial claims, as they have no place here. This book will deliver facts. Primarily, it will answer a lot of the questions and uncertainty you may have about this subject while providing a solid foundation of the knowledge you require to progress.

Balancing science and radical new theories, this book will give you the tools you need to avoid dark core personalities before it's too late. These are the malevolent types: those with narcissistic personality disorder, antisocial personality disorder, and Machiavellianism. I will explore these characteristics in more detail later in the book. For now, be warned—you will want to steer clear of these people. I certainly want to help you spot manipulators fast, from a distance and up close. You will learn to identify their methods, scams, and coercive techniques.

Be prepared to read a fascinating overview of the different sides of human behavior, as we examine the darker side of human nature. I will offer a new way of looking at psychological manipulation. You will get a stronger understanding of how the human mind works with how it defends, protects, and asserts itself.

This is how you will be able to outmaneuver others. More than that, you want in on the action, yes? Not as a predator or bully, but to use these strategies ethically. That's how you will sharpen your ability to make proactive judgments, boosting your sense of leadership. You will help your business and personal success grow by motivating and inspiring the people around you. It's all about getting the right balance in your approach, and we will be taking a good look at how that is possible.

You don't need to fear that unknown part of human nature out there in the shadows, and you don't need to be a Jedi from Star Wars to overcome the dark side! There are powerful forces that don't have the good of the rest of humanity at heart. You mustn't make yourself vulnerable to that.

By exploring all facets of human nature—the light as well as the dark—we can better understand the whole. That is the way to fulfill our potential. You want that, don't you? You want to trust your instincts and avoid being bamboozled. You're nobody's fool and feel secure in that fact. So, step forward and cast aside ignorance. Be prepared to face what might be uncomfortable to learn but will help you gain a better, smarter life. That is the reason you're reading my book.

Enjoying this book so far? Remember to head to the last page of this book bundle for a bonus bite-sized yet valuable free resource on Conversational Hypnosis. This mini e-book is the easiest way to learn how to be a successful conversational hypnotist. Curious about the benefits it can do to your normal day to day conversations? Get your copy now! This free resource is available for a limited time only

CHAPTER ONE:

The Gray Area — Manipulative Dynamics

Welcome to Chapter One, in which I will be taking you into some very murky territory. Expect to have your eyes opened wide. If we want to understand this subject, we need to start comprehending what defines and constitutes such a complex area of social behavior. I will guide you through this topic carefully and step-by-step so you can have a better and more comprehensive understanding.

A Starting Point: What is Psychological Manipulation?

I am confident in my assumption that, not only have we all been manipulated at frequent points in our lives, but we have also all been responsible to some degree for manipulating other people too, whether innocently or not. In essence, manipulation is psychologically convincing someone else to feel a certain way, or do a certain something. What exactly is that desire? The reasons for manipulation taking place can be numerous: coveting power, resources, money, or "something extra" are all valid reasons. Perhaps it is connected to status: boosting one's own sense of self-worth and influencing an individual by restricting their autonomy. Maybe it is driven by laziness—an unwillingness to do the work—or wanting additional strength. It might be about yearning for control or gratification. Ultimately, it is all about *gain*. It can certainly come in many different shapes and forms, whether that be:

- Sexual
- Commercial
- Political
- Financial
- Social
- Emotional

Don't, for a moment, think that manipulation is always showy and aggressive; in most cases it is not. It can be subtle, insidious, quietly persuasive, and, often, underhanded. Under these circumstances, you may not have even realized you have fallen victim to it. Sometimes, you have been backed into a corner so neatly that you may actually believe it is the only option available to you.

The Art of Manipulation in Today's World

The techniques and effects of manipulation are timeless and have existed since the beginning of mankind. However, it has become particularly exploitative in the last twenty years, in so many ways. I want to give you a better understanding of how psychological game-playing operates in the world around you, and for you to see how pervasive it can be.

1. We often hear how we live in a consumer culture, and you may regard that as a good thing or the front of all evil. If I were to delve into it further, we'd have an entirely new book. In any case, Western capitalism is certainly built on the back of **addiction**, which is the premise that products are essentially drugs—from the latest TV show, song, or movie to the newest software update, product upgrade, perfume trend, or set of sneakers. They provide a quick gratification fix, which may wear and need replacing.

Attention spans don't linger, prompting this need for innovation. Therefore, the consumer is encouraged to look for constant stimulus in the form of upgrades. Without that stimulus, the economy collapses, and none of us want that. As such, this is a system that's open to abuse, and anti-capitalists will certainly tell us society is just one big, money-spinning entity, playing on our weaknesses from slot machines to the latest iPhone. We have been encouraged to become spending addicts to keep our way of life afloat.

2.   At the center of this world system is *marketing*; again, it's the subject for a book on its own. The main aspect of manipulation within this topic is **advertising**. In a nutshell, its art—its reason for existence—is to persuade people to buy or do something. Often, that person is persuaded when they haven't even identified a need. In a changing world of new products, the only constant is that businesses are always trying to get us to buy their products. Marketing agencies will devise numerous schemes each year to nudge consumers toward a product or service to ensure self-protecting interests. Those are just the facts—manipulation is mainstream. We are fed logos to recognize, themes and tunes to which we hum along, and catchphrase slogans to echo. All of these advertising tactics appeal to our vanities, self-perception, hopes, and emotional welfare.

3.   **Social media** is a hot topic in psychological manipulation. It may appear fun with various benefits; however, as a parent to teen kids, I can say that the entire environment is built around manipulation. How the in-crowd behaves and what one should say, read, watch, look like, and where to eat or go on holiday are all paraded before us as it never was before. In the past, there were gossip magazines and chatter about the latest trends within social circles; nowadays, that influence is *instant*. Our envy, admiration, and aspirations are encouraged through likes, emoticons, and comments. What we see is held up as cool and desirable, and not having the things that other people have is regarded as serious failures. If we don't keep

up with our streaks and notifications, we're toast. In a busy world, social media can become our closest friend, allowing us to check in at any hour of the day… several hours of the day. It's only natural that we are guided by what social media has to say.

4. If we watch a certain news channel or read a particular media outlet, its views can eventually become ours. There is so much information out there, along with various broadcasters and sources of news, we cannot hope to listen to them all. Therefore, we concentrate on one and, after a while, we may find our political/ethical opinions are being formed by someone else for us. Perhaps, with so much going on, we secretly just want to be told what to think; to be told what's right and wrong. We don't call it **dumbing down**, but that's what it is at heart.

5. There have been many recent discussions about the rise of "**fake news**." Objectivity—or lack thereof—aside, a good meme can have lasting reverberations across society. The internet is certainly harder to police than the more traditional, paper news outlets. A recent study into the British election of December 2019 suggested that 88% of one particular party's online ads were false or misleading. The idea wasn't important, but the end effect was the goal. Therefore, voters—willingly and unwillingly—allowed themselves to be brainwashed, which is the definition of mind control!

6. I want to mention **photoshopping** too. Who hasn't altered the lighting on a picture to get that exact effect we wanted? It's an innocent trick, right? Maybe, but we are *literally* manipulating the image we present of ourselves. There's a load of mental health ramifications about not presenting the real you. More than that, if photos can be doctored, who can say for sure what reality is? Our views, welfare, and security are all open to exploitation on a grander scale now than ever before.

7. We all need money to survive. We all have bills to pay and goods to purchase so we can get by. Some of us might find ourselves in

situations in which we try to take on any work we can get just to keep our head above water. Union and labor rights are not universal, and low wages and zero hour contracts can all combine to exploit workers. If we're asked to do that little bit extra, who—fearful of dismissal and unemployment—dares complain? This problem is not new, and thanks to manipulations within the **global market**, products and services can be made and provided for next to nothing in one part of the world, then sold at a higher tariff in another. Our economic stability, not to mention hopes for equality and fairness, are all prone to serious abuse.

8.   There has been much talk recently about **grooming**, which can technically refer to anyone and any situation, but is usually in relation to kids being targeted online by pedophiles posing as other children. It can also, of course, come in the form of emails or calls from "salespeople." The victim is earmarked, and subtle points of emotional connection are made. Grooming is a modern and particularly unpleasant form of duping. The ground is prepared in advance, the mark is buttered up before a proposal is made, and the advantage is taken to bring about the end goal.

You may recognize some or none of the forms of manipulation above, but let me assure you that they are all prolific. I hope you are realizing by now that, figuratively speaking, manipulation is in the air we breathe. Manipulators surround and walk amidst us, often without us knowing it.

How the Traps are Laid

Some manipulation techniques are open, such as when a buddy asks us outright to go with them on a night out and to also give them a ride, even though we have other commitments. In these cases, we may be happy to go along with the flow. In this situation, we may have been maneuvered into giving someone a ride to an event we don't particularly want to go to, but our friend was honest about it, and it will be fun... right?

Other tactics are expressed through sneaky and deceitful means. For example, if that friend of yours isn't upfront about wanting that ride, but relies on it anyway: *Come along why don't you?* and *You'll love it* turns eventually into *How are you getting there?* and *My car's in for repairs. I think I might have to miss out on that fun party.* Do you see what they've done there? They've got you committed and excited about something. Then, they've asked you a favor without *actually* asking you for it—they make you feel bad about the possibility of you *not* doing it. They've played you for sure, steering you in the direction they wanted you to go in.

These kinds of underhanded techniques can often bring power games into play. *If you don't do this, it means you don't love me* or, in a professional context, *Let me down with that and I have no option but to think you aren't taking this job seriously.* Has anyone ever said this kind of backhanded bullying to you, or have you heard it said to other people around you? In essence, this type of language forces the individual to do something that makes them uncomfortable because they are anxious about the potential consequences; they are being made to feel worried about repercussions. In other words, they are being manipulated.

Perhaps some people see a weakness or "opening" in others, and they purposefully act on that. Otherwise, they sense a subliminal vulnerability, and can't help responding to it.

However, remember that this chapter is titled "The Gray Area," and the following is an example of what I mean. Your mom bakes great cakes and does everything for you to make you happy. You're not even necessarily aware of it, but she's one of those natural homemakers who always puts other people first. No matter if you're feeling low after a break up or you're simply hungry, where do you head? Back to the ranch, of course, for mom's fine cooking! Have you manipulated her into providing you the emotional and practical comfort blanket you want? *Maybe*. But also, *maybe* not. Perhaps she secretly minds and feels worn out by it, but she could also be possibly getting more from the relationship than you imagine—that being, perhaps a sense of being useful and important in the life of her child. That is what I mean by there exists a gray area in manipulation.

Getting Some Philosophical Perspective

The widely respected and published professor of Philosophy Allen W. Wood refers to the different aspects of manipulation as being morally problematic. However, as I have already touched upon, some argue that not all forms of manipulation are wrong. We need not always assume the worst or that a situation is entirely negative. As I say, irrespective of the manipulator's intentions, mutual gain can sometimes come from the arrangements. If that is the case, is there actually any loss? Should the act of manipulation be demonized entirely?

I will look at this topic, and the idea of ethics, in more detail in Chapter Eight. For now, I want to help you understand some of the philosophical and psychological arguments regarding manipulation.

I am often asked whether manipulators only operate deliberately or if their manipulation is done subconsciously without them realizing it. Take that friend I mentioned earlier, who asked you along on a night out, then needed a ride. Are they still manipulating you, even if they didn't mean to? What if they asked you along without thinking about how they were getting there, or if they mentioned their own transport woes without purposefully planning to take advantage of your generosity? In this case, Marcia Baron, Rudy professor of Philosophy at Indiana University, asks the important question: is conscious intent needed for manipulation to be at play? This subject has been constantly debated, and the only answers we have are subjective, ethical, and philosophical (not concrete).

Indeed, among other perspectives, manipulation could be merely a question of managing and motivating people effectively. All bosses, parents, and teachers could be considered manipulators under a specific light, as good management and persuasion are key in those cases. Some manipulators, naturally, are more positive than others, as you have probably experienced. Abuse of the position is common; however, let's think beyond the negative for a moment.

In healthy, constructive relationships, we influence one another all the time, from lifestyle choices to good books to read. Negotiation and debate are the fuel of social interaction; compromise and listening to others can help us develop as rounded people. Diets are also aimed at improvement, so let's not necessarily make a villain out of the companies that try to promote vitamin-rich eating and their products to us. What about charities or NGOs using their persuasive skills to alert us to a certain situation and ask for our help? There's also the question of a child having a destructive tantrum or a person with depression contemplating suicide. Talking that person out of that state of mind and convincing them of a different point of view— *manipulating* them—is obviously a good thing to do. In these instances, what is lost (free will) could be argued as outweighed by what is gained.

We are going to discuss later, in Chapter Three, the arch manipulator Niccolò Machiavelli. A Renaissance man throughout the definition—a philosopher, diplomat, writer, polyamorist, and pragmatist from C15/16th Italy—he could always be relied upon to coin a phrase and defend an action. Although he never actually said *the end justifies the means*, he espoused that philosophy. The expression boils down to mean that whatever techniques or routes you take to get what you want; they are all acceptable in the pursuit of that goal. Though celebrated enough to have various philosophies still followed today, he was more infamous than famous, with his own interests at heart. His words are usually applied to shady statecraft and are rarely used as a compliment. However, what he speaks of is **consequentialism**. Nearly 2,000 years ago, the Greek politician

Demosthenes summed up this term neatly as: *Every advantage in the past is judged in the light of the final issue.* Therefore, by implication, it's allowable to manipulate someone if the aim is (arguably) good, and/or that the latter benefits in some way.

The C18th German philosopher Immanuel Kant would not agree. Throughout his writing, he was clear that people shouldn't be used as a means to further other people's objectives, even if those intentions are considered good, noble, or for the benefit of the majority. No bad action is excusable. He believed in a supreme principle of morality, known as the Categorical Imperative. We have a moral duty to do right and must pursue it ethically at all times.

Where this runs into problems is how morality operates at the individual level. Is there an unequivocal right or wrong? It's easy to see why most people would say that pressuring, tempting, deceiving, exploiting, and coercing a drug addict to get them off life-destroying drugs is a moral form of manipulation, but would everyone agree? Let's reverse the situation slightly—a patient requires drugs and blood transfusions to survive; however, their religion tells them that using those mediums is morally unacceptable. Say you are a doctor and you are of a different religious outlook. What level of manipulation and persuasion is allowable to ensure the patient survives? Demosthenes may have been tempted to say any amount. Kant would be more inclined towards saying *none at all.*

The complication here is that no one ever agrees within the philosophical subject of morality. Good-intentioned manipulation on one side may appear as selfish bullying on the other. For one side to change their mind-, the other may have to employ even more persuasion.

Back in ancient Athens, there was a population of teachers known as **sophists**. They could be hired to speak on your behalf in legal cases or instruct you in the art of good oral ability. The emphasis was not necessarily on the truth of what was *being* said, but on how it *was* said. Socrates, the "father" of Western philosophy, hated his contemporaries, the sophists, because they were interested in winning an argument at the expense of everything else. They manipulated people's opinions so they could be seen as correct. Lawyers and politicians throughout time have made use of this approach—persuasive techniques known as **rhetoric**. Today, we refer to such tactics—sophistry—as clever but false arguments designed to impress others so we can get what we want.

We despise our opponents for using rhetoric, but applaud it when our heroes do. The British wartime Prime Minister Winston Churchill was a great orator. Despite many professional failings and a number of considerable personal faults, he is regarded as a statesman because of his level-headed approach and energizing attitude in the face of fascism and Nazi invasion. He turned the popular tide, rallied an alliance, and used his verbal skills to keep democracy alive. Nowadays, it's tempting to say that such oral proficiency is an overused exploitive trick; it can fall into the hands of demagogues hoping to stoke prejudices to further their own desires.

The French psychologist and sociologist Gustave Le Bon, writing towards the end of the C19th, analyzed the dynamics of the 1789 French revolution as a form of crowd-manipulation and propaganda. His *Mob Psychology* is unequivocal in its suggestion that if you repeat a catchy message enough times, persuade influencers to espouse your cause, and repeat the same message for yourself, then people at large will champion it in their masses. That is open to moral disabuse, of course, as it can lead to widespread manipulation. In the modern era, there seems to be no escaping that, and I imagine Le Bon would have a lot to say about advertising and social media's ability to distort reality.

In those terms, how can we ever know right from wrong? How can we even comprehend our own minds? We are being manipulated constantly, without even registering it. None of the information we receive, news we hear, gossip we pick up, or history we have learned reflects truth; only one version of it. In effect, we are conditioned—and weakened—by other people's subjective opinions continuously. We are easy prey, and not everyone means us well.

CHAPTER TWO:

Welcome to the Dark Side

Are you ready to explore the most unpleasant aspects of human nature? In the previous chapter, we discussed the dynamics of manipulation. Next, I want to look at what leads certain people to abuse other people's trust, welfare, and safety. To do that, we need to have a clear understanding of an area of psychology that is not for the faint-hearted.

The Journey Begins: What is Dark Psychology?

What makes some people bad? It's a discussion that obsesses philosophy and social psychology, and has done so since the beginning of time.

You will hear some folk say that a certain child was always destined to be rotten. In years gone by, my grandma was often pointing out some kid on the block and saying: *mark my words, honey, he'll be a bad'un.* That kind of thinking encapsulates the belief that some people are just born evil.

In his dystopian *Minority Report*, later made into a motion picture with Tom Cruise, Philip K. Dick delves into the psychological traits of criminals. The story explores the premise that crimes can be foreseen before they happen, with the implication that some people are predisposed to commit them. Nowadays, science suggests that certain chemical imbalances may be motivators for antisocial behavior—so, is it really all in the genes? If so, is it incurable? To what extent do social factors play a part?

Arber Tasimi addresses this question head on. A postdoctoral graduate from the Department of Psychology at Stanford University, about to take up a position as assistant professor of Psychology at Emory University in Atlanta, Georgia, he specializes in examining the moral inclination of babies. He asked the question: at what age do we start to comprehend the idea of right and wrong before language, culture, and social factors impact? In essence, his studies are all about looking for core values.

Tasimi carried out a range of tests with 13-month-old infants to see if an attraction toward evil would be identified within them. His studies required using puppets to act out stories with a clear good character and a clear bad character. After the show, both the morally-minded and the evil puppets would offer the kids a cracker. Tasimi was interested in patterns of the kids' preference to whichever cracker they chose. Fundamentally, he asked if they were influenced by good or evil; what did they gravitate toward? He planned to roll out this study a step further and introduce puppets with shades of grey; in other words, do these "lesser bad" characters receive any particular preference from the kids who previously only favored the good puppet? This extra step delves further into discovering whether children can see the difference between various degrees of wrongdoing.

Dr. Delroy Paulhus, professor of psychology at the University of British Columbia in Vancouver, made it his mission to tackle the subject of scales of badness. He refused to accept that there is always just *good* on one side and *bad* on the other. Fascinated by "everyday evil," he believes that there is an awful lot of gray in between. As part of his in-depth research into the subject, he undertook a range of psychological tests to establish an individual's propensity toward hurting or exploiting others. His aim was to strengthen his understanding of the features within different people's dark personality—egoism, Machiavellianism, moral disengagement, narcissism, psychological entitlement, psychopathy, sadism, self-interest, and spitefulness.

His findings led him to conclude that there is likely a spectrum that spans different levels of inclinations toward bad behavior, and that we are all somewhere along that spectrum.

This research embraces the premise that we are *all* potentially capable of violence, malice, evil, and deviancy. Some may tend more toward darkness, whereas others toward light, but we can be both good and bad at the same time. There is a dichotomy inside our minds, spirits, and hearts. In many ways, the latest offering in the Star Wars franchise *The Rise of Skywalker* addresses this exact issue! To explain: the film looks at the battle between benign and malicious impulses within an individual person's psychology. It examines how we attempt to avoid temptation and try to do good deeds, but can still ultimately end up being seduced by self-regarding desires.

Dark psychology does the same job and asks the same questions, but more academically. Essentially, it is interested in the in-depth study of that internal battle. It poses vital questions such as: *why do some folk delight in cruelty and causing discomfort to others? Why do they commit antisocial behavior?* At heart, it seeks to understand why some people are inclined to prey on others.

Anthropologists would argue that the capacity to be a predator was built into our DNA since the dawn of time. How else did we survive on the rocky plains? We hunted other animals, so the idea of regarding other creatures as prey has become natural. We carry that in our blood still, but now that we are safely at the top of the food chain with pre-packed nourishment, those impulses are hungry for other means of expression. As such, we tend to have a *craving* for praying on each other, not as a source of food, but as a requirement to satisfy a psychological need.

This historic, genetic fingerprint we all share is the reason various individuals across all cultures and societies have the tendency to victimize other people. Naturally, most of us don't act on that—or else there would likely be complete civil disorder and anarchy—but some do feed their impulses, making it their pastime or, in some cases, almost an occupation.

Bret Easton Ellis' terrifying novel *American Psycho*, later made into a movie, explores in blood-splattering detail how some people can develop a real taste for and addiction to inflicting pain on others. This tips over into unrelenting psychopathic tendencies, and the individual can become hell-bent on bringing upon the destruction of others. However, let's not assume that is the case for everyone who acts on their dark instincts; there isn't always a physical context to these impulses. We're not always talking about sexual abuse or murder when we refer to human predators. This criminal behavior can also manifest in less gory terms of cheating, deception, and exploitation, as we will see in the coming chapters.

In most cases, according to the guiding principles of dark psychology, the abusive behavior has a purpose or a distinct goal in mind. However, studies have shown that perhaps not all predators have a specific reason for doing what they do, like for power, material gain, vengeance, or sexual satisfaction. There is a small percentage of individuals who act manipulatively just for the sake of it, and there may be no specific cause, explanation, or purpose to their actions. We will explore this idea more in Chapter Six when we discuss Shakespeare's Iago and Othello. The key question that should be asked is: do manipulators have an essential disconnect from the world around them? Do they act the way they do because of a lack of empathy or an inability to comprehend the gravity their actions have on others' wellbeing?

We will examine all the dark personalities mentioned in more detail in the next chapter. We will look at what prompts different people to feed on violence, perversion, humiliation, and spite to a fatal level. For now, we can say that dark psychology seeks to understand this abyss within certain individuals.

Good and Evil — Revealing the Worst of Human Nature

I am keen to share with you two studies that address where an individual stands with morality, specifically in terms of inclination toward good and bad. They will help you grasp better the complexity of the subject we are exploring.

1) **Radical Evil.** I mentioned the German philosopher Immanuel Kant in Chapter One, and his belief in moral integrity. We will now delve a little deeper into his thinking. In the first two chapters of his *Religion within the Boundaries of Mere Reason*, published in 1793, he describes in detail what he believes constitutes evil. He observes that obedience to moral law isn't automatic, even though we are all born with a predisposition toward good, and he claims this predisposition can falter.

It is his belief that we have three core or basic aspects of who we are as a person. These are:

A. **Personality**, which is fueled by rational thought, understanding, and reason.

B. **Animality**, which constitutes our sexual drive, survival instincts, preservation of self, and social skills. He recognized that this aspect of our being could often be degraded shamefully by lust or appetite, but he did not necessarily see it as a reason for our undoing.

C. **Humanity**, which is driven by an impulse towards calculation, ambition, and comparison.

Kant argued that evil occurs when this basic principle becomes corrupted because egotism, competitiveness, and self-love have flourished. He did point out that self-regard was not necessarily a bad thing when related to caring about our wellbeing, but it could lead to arrogance where selfish wishes dominate.

The breeding ground for this corrupted principle is general society, in which we see up close other people seeming to be doing much better than us. Once this core aspect of our being is infected—which Kant stated is both a self-inflicted *choice* and an innate *impulse* within us—there is an initiated unwillingness to follow moral codes, along with eventual failure to do so.

This inclination toward championing ourselves corrupts all other behavior and leads to depravity, where an individual's preferences become paramount, and they would use other people as puppets to their desires. It is the source of all other wrongdoing and, as such, is referred to as **radical evil**. Under this inclination, a person's whole character is eventually stained. As far as Kant was concerned, there was no sliding scale—a person was either wholly good or entirely evil.

He did offer some hope, however. Kant was unequivocal in saying that each individual human is responsible for their own sin. This is in direct contrast to the commonly held Catholic belief of all pervading original sin—brought on the whole of mankind by Adam and Eve—and the more predetermined thinking of some of Kant's fellow Protestants, who said God had already earmarked some souls for salvation and others for damnation.

Kant believed evil could be reversed, and he called on corrupted individuals to undergo a revolution. This revolution, simply put, was a significant change of heart within the self toward virtue and a complete restructuring of priorities through applied endeavor and committed persistence. In theory, these practices would help reform character.

His philosophy offered the ability to choose to be good. People with good morals can opt for holiness as a governing maxim. All their actions, thoughts, and relationships would then be ruled by that principle and remain consistent to it. This eliminated vice and stopped an individual lapsing back into old, bad ways.

It was Kant's firm hope and belief that we could all act as moral agents as part of an ethical commonwealth of God's kingdom on earth. This change was his solution to combat the darkness.

2)   **The D Factor** is another concept that tackles this inclination to manipulate others and do wrong. In October 2018, Ingo Zettler, professor of Psychology at Copenhagen University, and his German colleagues Morten Moshagen from Ulm University and Benjamin E. Hilbig from the University of Koblenz-Landau published their research on this subject in the Psychological Review.

Their findings map what lies behind dark impulses: an individual's capacity for evil. The researchers coined the phrase the **Dark factor of personality**, or **D**. It takes the work by the English psychologist Charles Spearman, who underpinned his work with wide-ranging statistical analysis, as its inspiration. In 1904, he developed the **g factor**. His belief was that there was a level of *general* intelligence within individuals; in other words, if you excelled in one type of cognitive test, you would likely be strong in others too. As such, he pioneered a measure of cleverness! Zettler suggested the same could be true of someone's tendency toward evil. This theory asserts that the dark aspects of an individual's personality correlate.

Four different tests were carried out on over 2,500 people, aimed at establishing how individuals justified certain actions or how they avoided guilt and shame when putting their interests before others. A person's propensity towards aggression, competition, selfishness, and impulsive behavior were also monitored, along with how superior they considered themselves to be in relation to those around them.

The main method of the research was via questionnaires, posing statements such as *I will say anything to get what I want,* or *I would find it exciting to hurt people.* Subjects would have to rate how much they agreed or disagreed with those statements.

The aim of the exercise was to measure the levels of certain dark personality traits, as identified by Dr. Paulhus and his colleague Kevin M. Williams in their research in 2002—these dark personality traits include self-interest, sadism, among others. The researchers did statistical analysis on the results to determine each participant's overall D level. Zettler's theory being that these traits overlap to a certain extent, revolving around the central idea of D. Therefore, this D factor expresses itself to different degrees in different people, with some particular traits potentially being more dominant depending on the individual.

As such, this research gives us the startling suggestion that there is something connecting the schoolyard bully, casual liar, unfaithful partner, internet troll, corporate deceiver and murderer. In other words, if a person enjoys manipulating others, then they might also sway toward sadism and other darker personality traits.

If you're interested, you can go and take the test yourself online. When you continue with this book, be warned—the next section will be discussing the characteristics that this study investigated.

CHAPTER THREE:

Dark Personalities We Love to Hate

Our popular culture is awash with pushy villains in television programs and movies. The business pages within magazines celebrate corporate manipulators, and our interest in gossip ensures wall-to-wall awareness of A-lister, self-centered shortcomings. It seems as if there is no escaping the shadow of dark personalities. Who are they, and what spurs them on? In this chapter, I want to take a little time helping you get to know the enemy and the different traits that characterize those types.

Journey to the Dark Center

As I've discussed, no one—neither poet, priest, police, nor philosopher—can decide or agree whether there is one defining factor for why people manipulate others, and why some are more evil than others.

It is this concept that fascinates Dr. Paulhus at the University of British Columbia. I have discussed already in the previous chapter his research into dark psychology and the spectrum of human behavior. In 2002, he and his colleague Williams published findings that set out to identify and name core aspects of personality, which I would like to take a closer look at here.

As I mentioned in Chapter Two, nine key traits make up the dark personality: **egoism**, **self-interest**, **psychological entitlement**, **spitefulness**, **sadism**, and **moral disengagement**. With these nine traits, Paulhus and Williams identified three core types: **narcissism**, **Machiavellianism** and **psychopathy**. These trio of traits are what Paulhus terms the **dark triad**.

You will have heard these expressions before in earlier chapters and, perhaps, on your own beyond this book; however, they are terms often thrown around without people really understanding what they mean. I want to go through them carefully now, giving you the facts and avoiding emotive language like monster or fiend.

These dark personalities are certainly a menace, no matter how you try to spin it. They have been likened to parasites or vampires; in other words, they are feeding off you. They invade your space—mental, physical, emotional, and spiritual—and leech your energy. The bonus-culture and reward-led environments we inhabit only increase their appetite, as they try to get ahead at the expense of others. As we will see in the case studies in Chapters Five and Six, these dark personalities are concerned ostensibly about themselves. What others think or feel doesn't matter; it barely even registers with these personality types. Other points of view are only an encumbrance that gets in the way of achieving goals, which is something that all dark personalities have in common.

They also tend to share characteristics such as aggression, risk-taking, substance abuse, negative humor, depression, anti-social behavior, and histrionic attention seeking, which may manifest itself in self-harming. At the root, there is, what has been identified as, a resilience to chaos. In fact, those who display dark character traits typically thrive on disorder, disorganization, and disarray.

A roll-call of the most famous faces in history would include many names from a list of manipulators, controllers, and dark personalities. Based on that list, to make your mark and get yourself heard, it's likely you would have to put yourself on the D scale somewhere. You might not be surprised to know that the fascist demagogue Adolf Hitler displayed dark personality characteristics, but would you be shocked to learn that freedom fighter and inspirational orator Martin Luther King Jr. is also included? You'd expect to see Julius Caesar, conqueror of Gaul, on the list—but Diana, Princess of Wales and the people's princess? She too had personality traits we may consider on the dark spectrum.

Let us examine these different characteristics individually.

Six Dark Traits to Make You Shudder

Egoism, this is the impulse to put oneself first, at the expense of others. The word has enjoyed an interesting etymological journey, which helps encapsulate its psychological hold over us. It is formed from the ancient Greek verb *to be* or, more specifically, its first person conjugation *I am.* In Latin it means simply *"I,"* whereas in modern French, *egoisme* means *selfish.*

For millennia, philosophers have debated the essential need within ourselves to protect our identity and desires; it is how we all function on a daily basis. Both Charles Darwin and Sigmund Freud have written extensively about this subject, and how our perception of the "I" within us defines everything we do. In a sense, serving the ego is a basic component of human survival; if its demands aren't met, we cannot prosper.

In healthy, well-balanced individuals—who factor in the competing needs or overall aims of the community around them—the excess of the ego remains in check. Problems occur when someone places their objectives as paramount. Typically, they will find it hard to consider the wishes or emotional requirements of others. As a general rule, individuals with a high ego tend to have a number of short, monogamous relationships: moving on when a partner's needs become too demanding. A frequent expression they would use might be: *She was bringing me down, so we split up*, or *He lost her job and*

31

he became very clingy; I didn't want anything to do with that. Avoiding discomfort and ensuring personal happiness are what matters. Blame is frequently the weapon of someone with a high ego, and you should expect a complete lack of commitment from them!

Closely connected to this trait is **self-interest**. This is when a person's thinking is focused primarily—if not *exclusively*—on promoting their own social or financial standing. They will regard a situation only in relation to what they can win or lose from it. Life is a game of slides and ladders, in which they are competing against others. In most cases, the person in question may often brag or show-off their successes, achievements, and possessions because everything is viewed through a prism of material gain. You would often hear them say: *what do I get out of this?* A wider problem might typically be viewed solely in terms of the ramifications it has for the individual, such as: *Her car broke down, she wanted a lift; it cost me $5 in gas*, or else: *It's cool because I was given the project; he completely lost his mojo after his wife ran off with that other dude!* Other people's upsets form a backdrop only, and their weaknesses can often be exploited to bring personal advantage.

Most of us suffer from these first two dark traits, at least to some degree. They are incredibly common, and they make us human. We will delve further into how we can moderate these impulses in relation to a more ethical form of self-assertion and manipulation in Chapter Eight. Left unmonitored and allowed to run rampant, these selfish aspects within ourselves can result in us using other people as pawns and playthings.

Fundamentally, this can be indicative of a superiority complex that prompts certain individuals to believe they are better than others and, therefore, deserving of special treatment. This is referred to as **psychological entitlement**. Some people—either as a result of a high IQ, wealth, great bone structure, or the product of a spoiled childhood—believe the world owes them something. These are the types of people who will often be heard talking about what they deserve, what's not fair, and what ought to have happened in a given situation if there was any justice. Frequently on their lips is the expression *How dare they!?* They may commonly be anxious, impatient, or stressed, as they encounter a reality that refuses to meet up with their expectations. Disappointment has become a way of being for these people, and they ceaselessly express it.

Watch out, for a release valve of this frustration in a controlling type can often express itself as **spitefulness**. This often springs from a deep-seated insecurity and desire to put others down, so they will also feel as low and as depressed. Manipulators with dark personalities will invariably display a malicious impulse to inflict harm on other people through their words or actions. Typically, they love a good feud or grudge match, as they relish the opportunity to dig at others vindictively. The ideas of revenge and punishment are buzzwords in their vocabulary, and they certainly celebrate other people's misfortune. As such, you can often hear them gloating or gossiping about other folk's failings. *They got what was coming to them,* is a usual motto, and it certainly defines their outlook. Don't expect them to like many people, because they don't. They tend to be always angry and full of invective.

This trait is closely linked to **sadism.** This is when an individual actually receives sensory pleasure from inflicting on or witnessing others' mental, emotional, and/or physical discomfort. These dark types enjoy humiliating other people with actual bodily pain or through mental anguish and torture. This may be related to power and dominance, or to fill what they perceive as a void within themselves. These people thrive on drama and disharmony, along with angst, injury, and upset.

As discussed, the wider implication of others' suffering—their pain, hurt, and emotional damage—will rarely impact someone with a dark personality at their core. This is because, more often than not, the individual is also suffering from **moral disengagement.** Quite simply, these types do not see the wrong-doing in any action. Whether

33

you call it sin or immorality, they are incapable of regarding unethical behavior as abhorrent. As such, they operate without a sense of guilt, regret, or any notable feeling. *So what?* or *It's not my fault* guide their everyday thinking. They will not take any responsibility at all, whereas other people or factors at large are always to blame for what happens around them.

The Fearsome Triad: Narcissist, Machiavellian, and Psychopath

At the center of these dark characteristics, Paulhus and Williams identified an intersection of the three darkest, most toxic traits. They called these a triad, representing the most negative and damaging aspects of human nature.

There is some criticism from other academic circles that their work perhaps oversimplifies the state of the human mind. The accusation is that convenient labels and banner headlines have been affixed, which paints personality with a broad brush stroke rather than highlights individual nuances. Some even question whether Paulhus' results are conclusive—in one example, other psychologists question whether they carried out their research on a wide enough range of subjects. No matter how they did their research, Paulhus and Williams have still introduced us to the elemental archetypes that underpin a dark psychology. Distilled, they stand as totems for the guiding principles within a controlling psyche:

- Vanity
- Cunning
- Aggression.

Let us explore them together.

1) *Narcissism.* Put simply, this is when an individual thinks much too highly of themselves, usually in terms of their looks,

achievements, and attributes. You know the type—they're always checking out their reflection in the window over your shoulder.

Their vanity and ego give them pleasure at the expense of others. Controlling, needy, and always hungry for praise and perfection, they are poisonously destructive when it comes to relationships, friendships, and corporate team environments.

You may have heard of Narcissus; he was a proud man of Greek myth. Artists have been fascinated about him, most notably the Latin poet Ovid who wrote about the young hunter over 2,000 years ago. Narcissus thought no one was good enough for him, no one could be as great as him, and no one could reach to his level. He was always putting other folk down and criticizing them in comparison to himself. Unsurprisingly, that made other people miserable, and his relationships didn't exactly soar. One day, he saw his own reflection and experienced an instant, all-consuming lust. There are different versions of what happened to him next, but none of them are happy nor fulfilling.

Many young men and women suffer from a similar tendency of self-aggrandizement today. It is a condition that only gets worse with age, and the realm of fantasy is certainly their favored territory.

In case you are in any doubt on how to spot one, these are a few other features that characterize someone with high levels of narcissism:

- They are self-absorbed and convinced their opinions, and often background and race, are superior. This manifests itself as arrogance and a belief that they can do whatever they want because they are amazing.
- A positive but unfounded self-image, which will often see these types position themselves as experts or heroes in a given situation, despite no corroborative evidence.
- Affirmation is key. They will use "soft" tactics like flattery, gifts, and emotional bribery to get people to do things for

them. They will also punish others or compliment themselves if they believe they are not getting enough attention.

- They prey on the kind-hearted, lovestruck, and generous.
- They are hypocritical, so they rarely do what they advise others to do because they think there is one set of rules for them and another for others. They will often criticize others for the very things they do themselves.
- They will try to tear others down and devalue them, as no one can reach the highest levels of perfection in their eyes. They can become fixated on objects of disdain and will be impassioned in their abuse of their enemies.
- They are hypersensitive to any perceived criticism. Their disappointed sense of entitlement often leads them to suggest they are a victim.
- Jealousy is a tool for them and they love to set up people to compete against each other for their attention (bosses are highly skilled at this). They like to pretend they're more popular than they are.
- It's true that they act as crowd-pleasers. They often have a wide circle of acquaintances; although, they rarely have any deep attachments. Their sense of friendship and commitment are fluid, and they are always falling out with people.
- They are typically attracted to good-looking, popular achievers or admirable types who would reflect well on them. They hope these people will validate them through support and encouragement.
- They become bored easily, particularly by routine.
- Financial irresponsibility pervades their lives.
- A failure to deliver on promises is common. Shifting the goalposts has become second nature. They have built their lives on lies and excuses, and they constantly seek to explain away their failings.

Do you know someone in your life who is like this? Perhaps you recognize a coworker or friend or maybe even your partner. Beware if so and do not fall for their tricks. I will give you more guidance about that in Chapter Seven.

Nobody knows exactly what prompts this condition. Maybe it stems from feelings of abandonment and insecurity as a child, with the individual being prompted to look for validation. All we can be certain of is that manipulation becomes a coping device for narcissists, as these individuals hunger for attention from others. That spotlight becomes the meat they feed on.

Examples you might recognize in public: Narcissists tend to favor creative industries in terms of careers, and we can certainly identify a number of them in music, acting, and reality TV. These people would likely be those who hog the stage at other people's award ceremonies or divas who demand champagne chilled to the right temperature in their dressing room refrigerator.

2) ***Machiavellianism***. These people hunger more for power and material gain than anything else. They will use cunning and calculation to achieve their desires through ruthless plotting and manipulation of people. *It doesn't matter what it takes* could well serve as a guiding principle for these individuals.

The condition is named after Niccolò Machiavelli, the Renaissance man I mentioned briefly in Chapter One. In 1532, *The Prince* was published posthumously, based on his notes and writing from twenty years earlier. It was a study of statecraft and strategies for success unconstrained by conventional morality. There is much critical debate as to whether Machiavelli intended what he was writing to be a criticism of sharp practices—a warning against them—or whether he was advocating for their use out of admiration. In any case, *The Prince* became one of the first self-help books on how to get ahead in business!

Machiavelli has certainly received a bad press over the centuries, connected in popular culture with all things self-serving and diabolic and depicted as rising from Hell in the stage plays of the Elizabethan dramatist Christopher Marlowe.

In the 1960's, social psychologists Richard Christie and Florence L. Geis studied Machiavelli's writings, then asked people how much they agreed or disagreed with certain phrases. They used these findings to work on the **Machiavellian scale**, which determined deceitfulness and callousness in whoever took the questionnaire. This research was published in 1970 as the **Mach IV test**, and places someone as a high or low *mach* depending on how close they are to this dark core personality trait.

Signs of Machiavellianism include:

- Someone who justifies what they are doing simply because they want it.
- Considerable ambition in terms of career and power; they want to get ahead rather than just get by.
- Interested in money, material possessions, and status symbols in general.
- Outwardly confident.
- Always working on schemes and ploys to get what they want in any situation, which would usually involve exploiting other people's weak spots. Peoples are always seen in terms of their utility rather than as individuals; for example, they may form friendships based on what that friendship could offer them, including the other party's contacts or what they own.
- Patience is an overriding emotional marker, as impatience simply threatens to upset their well-laid plans. Famously, the 16th Japanese military leader Tokugawa Ieyasu cited patience as a necessary attribute to subdue joy, anger, grief, fear, and hate; only then could goals be achieved. It's similar to the maxim about good things coming to those who wait.
- We will see more about their flexibility in the case studies found in Chapter Five, but an individual in this category knows that they will need to switch sides on occasion to move

fluidly through life, unimpeded by past commitments or beliefs.

- Untrusting. Anyone could be out to shaft you at any second. If life is a game of chess, a Machiavellian individual would need to stay one step ahead at all times, with their next move and strategy in sight.
- They believe consequences are for wimps and morals get in the way. A lack of scruples helps these people attain greatness, or so they believe.
- Emotions are seen as impediments to success, so the fewer emotional connections the better. That would mean no genuine partners or friends.
- Other people are simply a vehicle to get a high mach type for where they want to be.
- They often study and observe others. Machiavellian individuals are perceptive, though other people's emotions may make them uncomfortable because the latter may complicate things and provide obstacles.
- They tend to see things practically rather than fantastically; however, that is not to say they won't lie and deceive when necessary.
- They do whatever needs to be done. As social chameleons, they will adapt to a situation to get what they want from it.
- They use both soft and hard tactics to achieve their aims. For example, they may sabotage other people's endeavors, seeing everyone as potential competition.

Examples you might recognize in the public eye: The corporate and political environments are awash with high machs, from the CEO who will use whatever means to get ahead—even if that means jettisoning their friends along the way—to the political leader who espouses populist causes to advance their career.

3) ***Psychopathy***. In 1941, the psychiatrist Hervey Cleckley developed a checklist identifying those with strong psychopathic

tendencies, and we would do well to pay it considerable attention. In essence, these individuals are unstable and operate often violently and life-threateningly. Those exhibiting psychopathic character traits are more likely to end up in jail than other people. Unlike those with *sociopathic* tendencies and who would lock themselves away—causing damage through antisocial practices—individuals with psychopathic tendencies more frequently cross the line, luring other people into their web to inflict maximum damage. No one wants to end up alone in a room with one of these dark controllers, unless you're one yourself.

The tendency loiters at the far end of the D scale, but it is actually a lot more prevalent than we might think. In the 1970's, Canadian psychologist Robert D. Hare took Cleckley's studies further, looking for shared characteristics. He identified that a startling amount of CEOs—not to mention psychologists and psychiatrists—display psychopathic traits.

Although the American Psychological Association (APA) doesn't recognize it as a diagnosable disorder, more a characteristic of other disorders, there has been a lot of recent debate about what causes psychopathy.

Are they just bad'uns as my Grandma used to say, or is their condition a result of social conditioning: if a child has been raised in a particularly harsh, abusive, or competitive environment, they are likely to develop a psychopathic psyche. There are those, as I mentioned earlier, who suspect some genetic causes. Scans and studies have indicated that the brains of these individuals are hardwired differently from other people's, and that there is a disconnect between the neurotransmitters and emotional receptors within their brains. The range of chemical imbalances and social conditioning point toward a nature versus nurture argument, as a result of brain trauma as a child or as a long-term reaction to drugs. Could psychopathy even be inherited? If so, then there are several ethical questions about finding fault and appropriate punishment in society to consider. In this book, we are more concerned with how psychopathy manifests itself: the effect rather than the cause.

Both Cleckley and Hare observed that psychopaths tend to display recurring characteristics. These include:

- They are cold-hearted and unconcerned about the feelings of others, yet utterly charming. This trait can manifest itself in glib and superficial small talk in social gatherings.
- Despite the smiles, they often have a lifeless voice and eyes.
- They are quick to size others up and label them. They find the vulnerability of others quickly.
- They blame others for their own actions, often saying things like they made me do it. Crucially, no remorse is shown for their own actions.
- Similarly, there's no empathy or understanding of other people's plight
- Narcissistic impulses toward self-aggrandizement.
- Uses hard tactics to get what they want; for example, threats. They also like to goad and wind people up, usually through physical harm and nasty games.
- As both a child and adult, pleasure is taken in harming others cruelly and sadistically. It is widely reported, for example, that the serial killer Albert de Salvo, otherwise known as the Boston Strangler, would torture animals as a child.
- Has unpredictable mood swings and is prone to a bad temper. When they get very angry, they can turn just mean.
- Tend to be sexually promiscuous, which is often coupled with fantasies of a sado-masochistic nature.
- Persuasive.
- Those with strong psychopathic tendencies rarely get anxious and don't perspire under pressure. In 2012, the controversial neuroscientist Nils Birbaumer undertook a sweat test that led him to conclude that these individuals may be less attuned to

emotions than other people (displaying less guilt, shame, embarrassment, and fear).

- Have no qualms in breaking the law; they may know right from wrong, but they don't care.
- View people and things as disposable. Nothing tends to have a value for long. As such, these dark controllers will rarely stay in any job for a long time.
- High tolerance levels to strong odors and graphic images that other people might find unpleasant or revolting.
- Impulsive, with no long-term goals or signs of planning for the future.

Examples you might recognize in the public eye: Our cinemas and TV screens are rife with these individuals, from Scar in *The Lion King* to the Oscar-worthy *Joker* and *The Shining*'s Johnny. There is a real-life hall of infamy too, littered with instantly recognizable names, including Countess Elizabeth Báthory de Ecsed, who terrorized Hungary in C16th and took vanity to new levels by drinking her victims' blood harness their youth; and the cruel Hamilton Howard Fish, who renamed himself Albert after a dead sibling. In the 1920's, Fish raped and ate his victims, and then taunted their relatives in sadistic letters. The hall also includes the diabolically manipulative cult leaders Charles Manson from 1960's California and the delusional Jim Jones, who saw himself as deity gathering followers around him, 918 of whom he manipulated into killing themselves in 1978. Let's not forget the handsome but heartless charmer Ted Bundy, who famously didn't feel any guilt, despite extreme acts of torture, murder, and necrophilia, notching up more than thirty victims. We could also talk about list the sado-masochistic, bondage-inspired BTK killer, otherwise known as Dennis Radar, who would show off, playing games with the media until his eventual capture in 2005.

But enough of these famous serial killers. I don't want to give too much time to them or shine too much attention on these twisted murderers who have deliberately walked in darkness. There is nothing sexy, enticing, or inspiring about these evil people. Let them stay in the dark shadows, as they do not deserve our attention any longer.

There is a great deal more yet for us to explore together in the chapters still to come. I have discussed in detail various dark personalities; next, we will be looking at how they operate.

CHAPTER FOUR

Hidden Arts Uncovered — How Manipulation Works

We all understand that the world can be a bad place and there are nasty predators out there, but this awareness is completely toothless if we cannot recognize the where, how, and why of it all. The aim of this book, as I have said, is to give you a comprehensive understanding so you don't fall prey to the dark ploys of malicious forces.

In this chapter, I will be giving you invaluable insights and tools so you can call out manipulative strategies. Only then will you be able to stop exploitation or use it for good, as I will go on to explore in Chapters Seven and Eight. Let's take this step by step.

How to Spot Evil: The Tricks of the Trade

Someone can use a number of inter-connected techniques to get what they want from you. I want to give an overview so you can become aware of these persuasive tricks and techniques.

1. **Temptation** can be used as an effective weapon. For example, take a colleague who needs help with a report—they know you like sweets, and they turn up on your front door with a whole dish load of brownies with notes for that report under their arm. Be in no doubt: you *are* being manipulated, even if they do not appear to be

physically harming you. What you like and enjoy is being dangled in front of you, like a carrot for a horse, in return for something else (whether you want to give back to them or not). Your choice here is fairly free, and you are getting something out of the situation, unless you don't actually get to eat the brownies for some reason.

2. Closely connected to the first point is **exploitation**. In this case, someone takes advantage—for their own benefit or gain—of what might be seen as a weakness in you, either in your emotions, financial situation, or physical attributes. Don't always assume when we say exploitation that we are referring to poorly paid workers slaving away in terrible sweatshop conditions. Far at the other end of the scale is the example I gave in Chapter One about your kindly mom baking for you. You could have a debate about her situation and whether she is being exploited—but capital is being made of that impulse within *her*.

3. **Deception** may also be used in various cases. Someone may not be honest about their intentions when trying to get you to do something about which you may be feeling ambivalent. That Kickstarter campaign you signed up for that is urging you to donate case may be a front for fraudulent activity. In another example, your kid could be telling you she needs money for the bus, but she actually plans to use the money for a new shirt.

4. Things can take on a darker note **pressure** is involved. In this case, undue influence is exerted by someone in order for them to get their goal. It can be ostensibly innocent. Maybe you are being pushed, cajoled, or nudged through a daily barrage of emails about going on a skiing holiday with a friend. They say you're letting them down and being a scaredy-cat if you don't go. Be under no illusion—this is a form of bullying. It can take a more serious turn, in which a degree of wheedling or false flattery is involved. Pressuring can also become quite aggressive: *you will do this, won't you?* with an implied *or else* at the end.

5.   **Coercion** is yet another step further on from that, and can start with psychological manipulation and develop into physical abuse. It is when you are being forced or threatened to do something against your will. Blackmail or violence may be used, giving you no choice in the end. Obviously, if you find yourself in these situations, you should seek out assistance from law enforcers or legal professionals.

In all of the above examples—whatever the merits of each individual situation—the manipulator's interests are almost always put before those of the person being manipulated, regardless of any potential two-way benefit that the victim may perceive.

A Map to Help You: The Specific Ploys You Need to Keep an Eye On

As mentioned, we have all probably been manipulated to do things at one time or another; sometimes, it may have been in our own interests or resulted in us doing something we actually enjoyed. Also mentioned, manipulation isn't always at the expense of others, but, sadly, it is still more often used for more sinister reasons, as we looked at in the previous chapter. People become the pawns of others, and neither you nor I want to find ourselves in that position.

Here is an eight-point detailed guide to the specific approaches and behavior traits you need to watch out for at all times.

1. FLATTERY:

False compliments and attention are both sweet and poisonous. As the 18th Anglo-Irish philosopher Edmund Burke remarked: *flattery corrupts both the receiver and the giver.* In other words, no good can come of it! In its different manifestations, it is a powerful weapon in the manipulator's armory.

- **Charm**. We can't help but lower our guard when someone is polite and full of smiles. Watch out for potential deception beneath their smooth manners and sweet-talk. Charm is the favored approach of the dark triad.

- **Stroking the ego**. If someone tells you that you're an expert, beautiful, and clever, you are very likely to want to believe it as true. If told these things, we will also feel receptive toward the person doing that stroking. People seeking favors often try the same technique and take advantage of us when once we're happy.

- **If only…** Advertising thrives on appealing directly to our ambitions and vanities. We're flattered that the ad is aimed at us; at least, we want to believe that it is. With advertising done right, we will believe that could also look great in those jeans on that model, and that we could also be as cool as that A-lister driving that car, sporting that watch, or wearing that scent.

- **Love bomb**. This weapon is all of flattery on overdrive. In this case, we would constantly be told how wonderful we are, given gifts and rewards, are complimented, and held up to others as a beacon of awesomeness. These affirmations can come from a slippery boss, exploitative partner, friends, and parents too. The result leaves you lulled into a false belief that this other person values and appreciates you. It would be a no-brainer, then, when they ask you to go that extra mile for them, and of course you will—you want the praise and you've gotten used to it. More than that, you don't want to let them down and sink in their estimation. Be under no illusion: it's merely a ploy for them to get what they want out of you.

- **Reaffirmation**. The expert in this field will use devaluation and reaffirmation as a perfect ruse. They'll withdraw their compliments and drop you suddenly—or raise the risk of it—only to pick you up again shortly after, full of praise. Toyed with, you can only crave the attention and become putty in their hands. Like an addict, you will do anything to ensure you get your fix of flattery and approval.

- **Allegiance and alliance.** Politicians, marketing executives, and salespeople love to pretend they're on our side. They'll study linguistics and use colloquialisms and jargon that would make us think they're one of us, and they will adapt their body language to appear approachable. They want us to think they are our buddies. False friends and deceitful colleagues at work might say they have our back, only to talk us down behind the scenes. If we think we've got someone's support, we're more than likely to trust them, and the results include us giving them something when they ask for it.

2. LIES.

Those who seek to deceive us won't be straight with the truth. You can count on that. They will:

- Twist facts to suit themselves.
- Withhold the full picture to disguise their wrongdoing.
- Present a certain image that isn't the whole truth.
- Deny any alleged wrongdoing.
- Contradict themselves as a result of being tangled in their falsehoods and inconsistencies.

They may do this as an automatic survival technique to avoid detection, or they may be employing dishonesty deliberately, calculating that it will unsettle you. They count that, at a disadvantage and unsure of where things really stand, you will be easier to manipulate.

3. DISORIENTATION.

In combat, foxing your adversary is key. Why should anything be different in the dark world of manipulation? This tactic to confuse and wrong-foot comes in many forms:

- **Moving the goalposts.** Maybe you've been told that if you do something, there will be a certain result, but once it's done, there's another target on the horizon. A prime example is the boss who tells you that you'll get a promotion if you give up your holiday to complete a project. Another case in point is the on/off partner who says they'll commit when you both get steady jobs, but then insists on other criteria when the time comes around. These are just a few examples of someone moving the goalposts on you. In these cases, you are constantly waiting for something that is never delivered, and your patience and optimism are being abused.

- **Mood swings.** This can be as a result of a chemical imbalance in the brain; however, some predators can deliberately tailor their erratic behavior to unbalance you. If someone is all smiles one day, then surly the next, it is easy for you to become more anxious and crave their sunny side. Here, you have become easier to control.

- **Blame.** Just when you think someone is at fault, they turn around and say you're the one doing wrong. *You're so bossy,* they might say when you're just realizing they're ordering you around. The upshot is that you don't know your left from your right, nor up from down. More than that, if you start defending yourself, they can avoid further scrutiny. Clever, huh?

- **Switcheroo.** This technique is along similar lines as the last and involves sullying and criticizing others for the crimes the manipulator has mastered themselves. *He's such a liar,* liars will say. *Lying is so awful, watch out for people who do it!* The effect is that, psychologically, you would trust that person. You think to yourself that they couldn't be so brazen a hypocrite as to call out the very thing that *they* are doing, could they? The answer is: yes, they could. We will see more of this concept in our case studies later in Chapters Five and Six.

- **Turning the tables.** This is very sneaky, as reversing the situation completely can make the wrongdoer appear to be the wronged, with the wronged seeming to be wrongdoer. It is a particularly toxic technique, which involves laying the blame for malicious actions at the victim's door, often with the self-pitying howl: *It's your fault I'm this way.*

- **Acting innocent.** Have you heard someone say: *Who, me? How could you ever think that? I would never do that!* If so, it is more than likely that someone is trying to manipulate you. Genuine innocence rarely requires a protest in favor of innocence. Slippery types enjoy refuting evidence to the contrary by insisting, shocked that you would question their morality how unlikely it is they could ever do wrong. The end result is that you can't help question your judgment.

- **Playing the victim.** Perhaps the manipulator takes things a step further and pretends to have been the victim instead? We touched on this in Chapter Three—a pushy partner might say they're feeling under pressure at work and, keen to sympathize, you might become a pushover in other areas and cater to their every need. On an evening out, if your self-proclaimed "broke" buddy harps about their bad luck, you'll soon find you're buying all the drinks without even thinking twice about it.

- **Guilt trip.** An extension of the previous tactic, this is a tool often used by charity companies, abusive partners, and so-called friends alike. It is a form of emotional blackmail. If we feel responsible or bad about something, we are more likely to respond by doing what someone asks us to do. Few of us want to feel selfish or without compassion. *Look at this, isn't it terrible? You have the power to fix it, so why don't you?* A problem has been created that we are the solution to, and our unwillingness to rectify the "situation" means its continuation is our fault. Another classic in the canon is: *Why won't you do this? Don't you care about me? I'm always doing stuff for you!* This statement forces you into a corner, effectively making you have to choose between bending to the person's will or feeling the guilt.

- **Minimizing.** People hoping to deceive you will often minimize the impact of their actions. You might complain that something isn't what you want and you're not happy with it, and their response would be to downplay your concern. You're made to think you're being hysterical or unreasonable and, as such, you're being pressured to accept the unacceptable.

- **Acting the joker**. Who hasn't responded strongly against a questionable demand, only to be told that you're overreacting and failing to grasp a particular sense of humor? *I'm only joking* is the practiced retort of malevolent types. Seasoned manipulators might deliberately act in a confusingly, clownish, or bizarrely to get you off their scent, or else make you question your own judgment—leading us to the next dangerous point.

- **Gaslighting**. Creating doubt is an automatic assault rifle in the hands of a manipulator. They want you to become unsure of what's true and what's not. Your memory and judgment are called into question, and once it takes root, it becomes hard to shake. *You must be imagining it* is frequently bandied around, or: *You promised you would do this, why are you pretending now that you didn't?* The technique is deadly. In extreme cases, the person manipulating you may even want to unbalance your sanity, making you uncertain about reality. In case you're in any doubt about the expression *gaslighting*, it comes from the play *Gaslight*, written in the 1930's by British author Patrick Hamilton, and later made into a successful film with Ingrid Bergman. In it, a nefarious and felonious husband is up to no good in the attic, causing the gas-powered lights in his apartment below to flicker; when his wife notices this phenomenon, he convinces her that she's going mad.

4. DIVERSION

Con artists and magicians often believe the secret to their success is getting the audience to look in the wrong direction. That way, the subtle sleight of hand won't be noticed. Deception can pass undetected while avoiding accountability. In the same family tree, expect to find the following:

- **Shifting responsibility.** This is a tactic you may see quite often. In my case, I was keen to make a complaint about inadequate service, but received the reply: *I would love to help you, but these are the rules.* Or else: *my boss says this is the way it's got to be done.* Abusive partners can blame their antisocial behavior on a range of factors: booze, depression, and tiredness, to name a few. If you swallow the story and allow them to make it anyone else's fault but their own, you are allowing yourself to be conned and exploited.

- **Excuses**. Do not be fooled by these, as abusive people will often seek to explain their wrong-doing as normal. They insist that their behavior is acceptable, so they can create the illusion that it is so.

- **Shaming**. If you confront someone for their wrongdoing, they might attempt to shame you into thinking you've got the wrong end of the stick. As we discussed in Chapter Three, *How dare you?* is often the resort of the dishonest who are deflecting truthful accusations.

- **Evasion**. You will often see this tactic used by cheats, liars, and politicians. Ask these people a straight question or call them out on something, and they will often change the subject. They want to distract you or make you forget the subject you originally challenged. They're hoping of course to get off the hook, so if you are met with vague comments and **generalizations** when searching for a precise answer, chances are, someone is trying to avoid the truth and quite possibly have something to hide.

- **Ghosting** or, as it is otherwise known, the silent treatment, is a damaging tactic. Allow me to share something with you here—I had a boss once who, when he didn't want to answer something (a request for a pay rise or a tricky issue that needed sorting with a client, for example), he would *literally* disappear. My emails would go unreturned and the messages I left on his phone would build up. I could tell he was still alive and active because other colleagues had mysteriously heard from him! It left me confused, anxious, and convinced I'd done something to offend him. Eventually, I would just drop the issue and he'd get his way.

- **Promises of change**. These can often be given by those guilty of toxic behavior when they are putting off a final showdown until another day. It's similar to moving the goalposts, as promises may be made and, in effect, the manipulator is disempowering you by pretending to hear your worries and offering a (false) solution. In most cases, that change never comes.

- **Passive aggression.** Let's be honest—most of us have either done this or encountered it in some way. It's the art of pretending not to want something or angling for an end result while acting as if the subject is the furthest thing from our minds. It can also be a deliberate tactic to approach a desire through indirect means: a friend who is always late can be trying "subtly" to exert their control and sense of importance, for example.

5. UNDERMINING

A perfect tactic of malevolent types is to weaken their target in whatever way they can, exerting their own power, force, and assumed superiority.

- **Aggression.** Someone else's aggression and rage can often force you into submission. This bullying tactic ensures you do as they want, and it's part of the pressuring and coercion I talked about in the previous chapter. Faced with such sound and fury, it's not always easy for you to raise objections.
- **Punishment.** This tactic can come in the form of physical violence or threats with the aim to weaken you.
- **Blackmail.** Maybe you are being threatened with the exposure of some secret or threat of harm to loved ones. If so, remember that this is an *illegal* activity. However big your secret, no one has the right to exert their influence over you in this way.
- **Bribery.** This is part of the temptation ploy we looked at earlier in this chapter. Rewards like sex or other treats are dangled in front of you… or else used as weapons. Whatever the exact situation, the common refrain is: *you won't have to do this if you do that instead.*
- **Imagined Fear.** This is a great one for politicians. *Don't vote that way, or this will happen,* or *Watch out for foreigners,* they may

insist. Soon, we accept anything they say because we crave safety and security. Be warned: parents and partners can also use this controlling device.

- **Sarcasm**. Has your boss or partner ever belittled you in front of others? Have they made sarcastic barbs in response to your actions or comments? If so, they're looking to lower your self-esteem. It's a classic controlling technique that makes them think they look witty, strong, and in-the-know. If you're feeling worthless, you might just be tempted to believe them too and, eventually, you'll come to think of them as always right.

- **Exaggeration**. This is when your views are deliberately misrepresented to make them seem absurdly preposterous, and it is a ploy to make you seem irrational. You might have a small complaint or suspicion about something, which is then twisted and blown out of proportion by the person you are accusing. For example, imagine your partner often gets home late at night and a little worse for wear; therefore, you ask what they're doing. It's a normal and natural request, but they might deliberately blow it out of proportion by suggesting you are being paranoid and accusing them of neglecting you: *What? You're saying I'm about to run off and leave you so I can mastermind a drugs ring?!* In the end, they make it sound like you came across as ridiculous.

- **Smears**. Unpleasant people can often seek to besmirch the name of someone else so they can talk them down and remove them as a potential opponent. It is an attempt to create an advantage over the other person.

- **Fear, then relief**. This one has similarities mood swings and the reaffirmation technique I mentioned earlier; in which praise is given, then removed, only to be returned again. In this case, someone may seek to deliberately scare you—perhaps with an accomplice—only to offer you reassurance and support afterward. Psychologically, having been frightened, you will be craving safety and security, and your ability to make balanced decisions will be compromised. This situation makes you much more malleable.

- **Isolation**. Abusive types will often seek to separate you from friends and family. Have you moved away from your neighborhood at someone else's request? Do you stay in with your partner rather than socialize because they prefer spending time with just you? Be warned: you are weaker alone and easier to control, as we will see in the case studies in Chapter Six.

6. OVERWHELM

Every manipulator wants you to feel uncomfortable. If you are feeling under pressure or out of your depth, you become easier to deceive. Watch out for the following:

- **Jargon**. Salespeople or dubious mechanics often like to pose as experts in the know, speaking quickly with complicated phrases. Making you feel small and ignorant, in contrast to their knowledge, means that you are more likely to accept whatever they say.
- **Statistics**. Always beware of a bar chart. Vox pop polls are a little better, and politicians and marketing folk can make them say whatever they want. It's important not to be swayed by them.
- **Comparison.** It's common to be told that you should think in a certain way because other people do. It is a psychological fact that we often assume the majority are right, even if their views differ from ours. Cheats will use this to their advantage—often inventing allies—to get you on side.
- **Out of your comfort zone**. Most deceivers thrive on their home ground. In unfamiliar surroundings, you are at a disadvantage, which is when you must be at your most wary.
- **Time limits**. I have personally noticed the recent rise online of countdown booking. By that, I mean that little clock at the side of the screen, hurrying us along as we try to make a purchase. It's almost as if we are being urged to make non-refundable mistakes! Similarly, who hasn't been told to buy an item at that exact moment because it's the last in stock, lest the special offer expire that day? When flustered, we cannot be at our most vigilant.

- **Following the herd**. Peer pressure is a vicious yet pervasive problem in society. It runs riot in the schoolyard, office, and gym; gets its oxygen from social media; and advertising gives it the ability to breathe. Manipulators will employ stock phrases such as: *everyone else thinks this/does this/has this, so you should too.* Soon, it's easy to lose sight of our own individual needs because we are so keen to jump on the bandwagon and be part of the in-crowd.

- **Brainwashing**. This is not just the terrain of science fiction and spooky dystopias. We can often be force fed the views of one person, political party, or media outlet so much that we no longer have space for our own opinions. Get told something enough times, without seeing another perspective, and we can lose sight of who we are and what we think, effectively making us easy prey. We will see this technique employed to great effect in the victim case studies that we will look at in Chapter Six.

7. PROBING.

Most manipulators are masters of emotional intelligence and use it for sinister purposes. By that, I mean they employ:

- **Observation**.
- **Questions**.
- **Listening**, which is allowing you to speak first or do most of the talking.

Their aim is for you to reveal your weaknesses, access points, and preferences. Once they have a handle on those, they can use them against you for their own gain.

8. ESCALATION

It is quite common for someone to be taken advantage of on a sliding scale.

- **The foot in the door**. I imagine we have all said: *this isn't a problem now, and it will only be if I let it get out of hand, which I won't...* Only to turn around a few months later and discover the situation is actually *escalating*. Crafty manipulators will start small, then build big. They're hoping we will just gradually acclimatize and become blind to exploitation because we have gotten used to them asking favors of us and making demands at a less serious stage.

- **Stage-managed reciprocity**. Have you been in a situation in which someone does you a favor, then expects another, much bigger one, in return? Stage-managed reciprocity is a really low trick that involves someone giving away a little to get a lot back further down the road.

- **Pushing the boundaries**. This one is another form of the previous point; to coin a phrase: give someone an inch and they will take a mile. Manipulators continue to take until they are *stopped*.

What a catalog of calculation! When used for ill, all the above is a veritable recipe for toxicity. It's hard not to feel a little breathless after casting an eye over those machinations; yet, they are active techniques that appear and are woven right into our lives. They exist in our homes, on campus, in high offices of state, on the streets, on billboards, and in the places we work. Read on to see how they manifest themselves in everyday examples, right under our noses.

CHAPTER FIVE:

Confessions From the Boardroom — Sharp Practices in Action

Look no further than the workplace to see some concrete examples of manipulation at play. I'm talking about coworkers who pretend to have your back but secretly talk you down in an attempt to block your rise and facilitate their own promotion. I'm also referring to those wily bosses who prod, cajole, and coerce to maximize their productivity and profit.

To run a company successfully, you certainly need a number of characteristics that differentiate you from other people—this includes not sweating under pressure, using charm, risk-taking, and having management skills. Without a doubt, a boss needs to be in touch with their dark side too.

There are many manuals out there that can teach you how to get ahead in business. Determination and excellent motivational skills come to the top of the list of what an entrepreneur needs if they want to soar. Certain darker elements—ruthlessness, game-playing, and persuasion—aren't always included and, if they are, they're often skimmed over quickly. However, it's these kinds of elements that many recruiters actually look for when recruiting. It's often those who adopt a cutthroat approach to business who achieve the most, and it's unfortunately the people with antisocial tendencies tend to rise the quickest in goal-led environments.

We will be exploring a couple case studies that examine closely the dynamics of manipulation within a business environment. The first is the largely inspirational, but no less ruthless, Steve Jobs, former CEO of Apple. The second case study is about a slighter darker type who will remain anonymous for the time being.

Enjoying the Heights of Success; Tactics of a Genius

By this point, Apple has become one of the biggest and most successful companies in the world, and the catalyst behind that success was Steve Jobs. It is no exaggeration to say that he was a very powerful and skillful manipulator.

It wasn't always that way—as a young man and first establishing the company in 1976, it could be argued that his behavior tended toward the reckless. There was a largely self-destructive aspect to his egocentricity, without any focus or discipline attached. This was a man who didn't seem to care about the consequences or how overtly he could upset the feelings of those around him. As such, he handled situations carelessly and made powerful enemies who would wind him up when he was unprepared.

Jobs left Apple in 1985. Whether the decision was voluntary or forced upon him is a subjective question that historians will probably debate for years to come. In any case, what is of interest to us here is his return in 1996, and his elevation once more to CEO the following year.

The transformation in his character and business techniques was staggering. It's the kind of thing authors of entrepreneurial self-help books could write several volumes about!

Jobs returned with the perfect strategy needed to succeed, as if he had become an expert on how to get exactly what he wanted and achieve great things. As you are likely aware, those great things were certainly achieved!

Some of those practices Jobs employed during his second stint at Apple bear a striking resemblance to the methods of arch-manipulators that I discussed in the previous chapter. They embody classic techniques of persuasion, low-level bullying, and misdirection, combined with a huge amount of focus. We will be going through them now, as they really are the tactics of a true genius. Whether you call them seductive ploys and dark tricks, or part of a brilliant master-plan, they had profoundly successful material results, seeing as Apple became the world's most valuable company within ten years of his return.

It's easy to wonder if Jobs was just being himself, acting with more maturity than he had prior to 1985, or if he sat down and sketched out a route-map for achieving his goals. Looking at the precision and scale of his achievements, it's tempting to say the latter.

Then what was his approach? I will take you through a twenty-point, fact-packed guide of the Steve Jobs recipe for triumphant accomplishment:

1. **Working hard and building respect**. Let's not ignore the fact that, at heart, Steve Jobs was a dedicated and nose-to-the-grindstone kind of guy. He certainly wasn't the type who coasted with his feet up, letting others do the hard work. Jobs contributed an around-the-clock commitment, from early until late. He didn't shy away from taking on different responsibilities and was willing to multitask when necessary. Maybe this came naturally to him, or he knew it was what was needed to earn the respect and trust of others. People were more willing to listen to him and do what he wanted because they saw him as the real-deal, prepared to walk the extra mile himself. Living by that example set the bar high for his coworkers, prompting them to give the same amount of dedication.

2. **Figure out what's not cutting the ice**. Jobs made it his goal to look unflinchingly at where business models, services, and products weren't working. He wanted to understand the how and

why of failure. Honest and upfront about shortcomings, he wouldn't attempt to sugarcoat the issue if he thought a product wasn't fun, interesting, or efficient enough.

3. **Improve and be creative**. Once a problem was detected, it had to be resolved. It's easy to forget sometimes that, at the heart of Jobs' success, was quality. He wasn't a grand illusionist nor an emperor with no clothes: he delivered fantastic products that revolutionized the market. He saw gaps and deficiencies, and he rectified them. As such, Jobs strove hard during his second stint at Apple to gather a team that could deliver quicker start up times, a faster turnaround of products, and more innovation after innovation.

4. **Remain fluid**. We touched on this in Chapter Three—it isn't quite the same as being flexible, which suggests a certain amount of compromise and collegiate sharing of ideas. Jobs was arguably a lot more elastic and wily than that! He attempted the approach, highly favored by politicians, of not letting what he'd previously said or thought hold him back. Just because he'd criticized something in the past did not mean he wouldn't praise it in the present if it now suited his purposes. He was capable of reversing positions seamlessly, and he took advantage of most people's short attention spans. It would be easy to claim that what was said before was right, but because of changing circumstances, he knew when a different position should be adopted. This was the perfect way to keep ahead of the game: adapting to change and learning from experience without appearing weak.

5. **Give the impression of always being right**. Combined with the previous approach, Jobs was also willing to adopt other people's positions if and when it suited him. On some occasions, he'd even propose someone's idea back to them and claim it was his so he could take the credit. Not only did this tactic give others the impression that he was always right, but it also cemented his strength and power. In psychology, there's a term known as

source monitoring, which explains how our brains often retain information but may blank when trying to figure out where that information came from. When we're busy, it's natural to drop data that seems less important than the main kernel itself. Jobs used this psychology to his advantage.

6. **Don't believe in compromise**. As I mentioned above, Jobs did just that. He demanded loyalty and insisted that the best way was always *his* way, until he changed his mind.

7. **Enthusiasm**. There were no half measures, as far as Jobs were concerned. Those working alongside him would often say he was a little crazed and full-on. He enjoyed talking at length about products to investors or potential customers, which he called *pitching with passion*. It's hard not to find such energy irresistible; it's easy to get swept along because you want to see such a dynamic vision rewarded. As such, half the battle was won because mindsets and hearts had been conquered.

8. **Sunny outlook**. Enthusiasm is also partly the guiding principle behind maintaining a positive view toward the future. It seems to be a universal truth that people don't like hearing bad news, so creating a spin and positive outlook will make people WANT to hear and believe you. Jobs was a master at this tactic.

9. **Talking-up**. With the previous point in mind, Jobs also embraced the idea of talking-up. He often pitched and promoted himself, just as much as what he was trying to sell, whether it was a product, service, idea, or vision. He would then repeat that message. Gustave Le Bon called this technique *mob-steering*!

10. **Exceptional marketing**. Talking-up went hand-in-hand with his amazing marketing skills. Jobs knew it was crucial to promote his products—even when he'd criticized them when not at the company! —and get that message out there, fast and wide, as inventively as possible.

11. **Creative advertising**. Beyond exceptional marketing, Jobs knew he would also require catchy and colorful advertising. It was all about convincing people they needed to have Apple products because these products were the best and most cutting edge.

12. **Brand recognition**. Apple thrived not just with its products and advertising, but also in how people were able to quickly identify it. The logo has become iconic, for example, and has become quite recognizable across the world.

13. **Build a fanbase**. All this advertising and recognition has allowed Apple to build a fanbase. This isn't just about your potential customers needing your product; it creates in them a *desire*. There was—and still is, to a certain extent—a positive image connected to having an Apple product. Jobs knew that allure of must-want and must-have was (and still is) a powerful tool.

14. **Doing down the enemy**. Jobs also knew that weakening his competitors would also greatly benefit his company. He used fiercely emotive and negative language toward competitors, which helped create a mindset and get people onside with his ideas and visions.

15. **Ruthlessness**. Jobs often fired people who presented themselves as obstacles or objections for him and his company. He wanted nothing to do with failure, reservation, or anything that wasn't can-do. If you wanted to succeed in his orbit, you needed to embrace enterprise the Steve Jobs way!

16. **Using a position of power**. He was certainly not afraid to use this strategy. As such, when he first returned to Apple, he adopted a "back me or sack me" kind of approach, knowing exactly how vital he was to the company. Ultimately, it came down to: *do this, or I walk; don't do that or you walk*. He certainly exerted his influence and commercial appeal to get what he wanted.

17. **Flattery**. His power was combined with giving people the approval they needed to be motivated and mobilized. It was that smooth-tongued flattery we talked about in the previous chapter—and no, it wasn't always sincere! He would continue to praise so his team would crave and expect it. When they didn't get it, they were unsure why and would crave reaffirmation, looking for ways to earn the compliments again and prompting them to work harder. In short, everyone wanted to be his friend, which is a powerful position for any boss to be in.

18. **Evasion**. If there was something Jobs didn't want to happen, he'd ignore and simply fail to address it. Perhaps he was playing a game of chicken and waiting to see who would buckle first. It's a classic technique of a manipulator: as we saw, it was also that ploy of evasion I was talking about earlier in Chapter Four that was favored by my former boss.

19. **Go with your gut**. Jobs rarely saw the value in commissioning research studies or protracting a decision. If something felt right, he'd go for it. This helped give the impression of being in the know and a natural-born expert that people wanted to follow.

20. **Seize the moment**. Despite advice to the contrary, he went public with Pixar shortly after the buzz and box office gold of Toy Story's success in 1995. He brought the same sense of exuberant spontaneity to Apple. Even doubters couldn't help but admire his confidence, which was how he got people to do what he wanted. It was a gamble, but fortune favors winners, and he won big.

It's hard not to see Jobs' path to glory as pre-planned, and business gurus certainly take a leaf from his book. In any case, the quick, all-important takeaway we can learn from Jobs' success story is undeniable: with goals and a sense of focus, manipulation can bring about significant results.

One may smile, and be a villain — **The Inside Story of a Master Manipulator**

You may recognize part of my subtitle here. It's from William Shakespeare's iconic play *Hamlet*, and comes at the point when the protagonist, the prince of Denmark, realizes his cheery uncle is responsible for his father's murder. It's an expression that has come to describe perfectly someone's ability to act pleasant, yet carry out dark and manipulative deeds. I want to take a look at a billionaire success story who has taken this approach to heart, who is now one of the most powerful people in the world. Let's call him, for reasons of anonymity, B.

B's rise has been spectacular. He went from a lowly pen-pusher to one of the richest, most influential CEOs on the planet, in charge of a multinational organization that provides people-focused services and products around the globe.

But how did he do it?

I'll give you a clue: it's the **image** he has created for himself in a world where spin and style often trump substance. He's been so successful at this that politicians are known to have followed his example in the way they operate and present themselves.

Sure, his background was one of white privilege. He'll criticize the elite now in his role as man of the people, but his own roots were pretty cushy—the best schools, finest advantages, and greatest opportunities had all been laid at his feet. He was certainly born with a silver spoon in his mouth and with the right contacts, funds, and influence to get far ahead. However, he's still been very good at covering his tracks along the way.

The success of his business depends on him being an **everyman**: approachable, one of us, and a warrior against injustice and entitlement. Such is the role that he plays, and he tells us now that Ivy League types are the enemy because they're out of touch and don't care about us or our needs. He criticizes other business leaders and organizations, saying they're aloof and designed only to serve the top 1%. See what he's doing there? He's using that *switcheroo* tactic I described in Chapter Four. We all seem to conveniently forget that B is actually the *very* enemy he describes because he has cleverly set himself up as its foe!

Integral to this everyman act is adopting idioms and **colloquialisms**, which B drops into his speech whenever he can with a *buddy* here and a *y'all* there. We think he understands us when he's telling us about his products and services, and anyone who has heard him speak can be easily dazzled by the speed he rattles through his sentences; he's hoping that we won't get the time to scrutinize the exact details of what he's saying.

Crucially, B has harnessed the language of aspiration throughout his career. Since the early days of his business success, he has given us the idea that he is fueled by **vision**. He pushes a utopia, in which we will all be richer and happier, if only we embrace what he is offering, and the sunny uplands of material comfort are ours if we buy what he sells. It's a seductive message—we want to believe it, even if we see faults or pitfalls in some of the services and products he promotes. B has masterfully managed to create an environment in which consumers are willing to give him the benefit of the doubt because they want so badly the dreams he promotes to be true.

B's marketing strategy is clever and, throughout his endeavors, has been set up to position his products as good for the planet in some way. By buying them, he suggests that we are contributing to a good cause and leading to our material gain, which appears to be a win-win for us. It's quite a smart strategy—we spend our cash, boost his profit, and believe we're doing something **positive**. The Machiavellian psychology behind that is incredible.

It's quite clear that B's key and distinguishable characteristic has been to play the fool and pretend to be everyone's friend consistently throughout his career. We all know the type: they smile, joke, use extravagant expressions that make us laugh. They may also bumble and bluster, taking occasional pratfalls along the way. The reason? They hope to charm and **disarm** us. *This person can't be a threat*, we think. *They're too outlandish to be deceptive. Look, have you seen the way they dress and brush their hair!?* It's a clever technique because they can then operate like a snake in the grass without us suspecting or ever realizing their true nature. Besides, if we like them, we're prone to forgive them for most of their actions. Giving the impression of being harmless and likeable is a valuable tool for manipulators, and B has taken that to heart.

As such, he has managed to get away with the most incredible things to get ahead and make his business more profitable. It's the secret to his ever-amassing riches. We can expect B to be **ruthless** when he wants, but we often fail to notice or think that he is because he plays the clown so frequently and so well. It's a perfect tactic of distraction. He sacks dissenters by implying they are weak, stuffy-nosed, and "not with the program." He pulverizes business competitors with aggressive, crowd-pleasing, and hugely emotive lingo. More than that, he ridicules objections to his proposals by suggesting that other people just don't get his vision, or that they are scaredy-cats lacking in gumption and moral fiber.

That's right—throughout his career and his rise to the top of the boardroom, B has been constantly minimizing the complaints of his adversaries. He says bluntly that they're wrong or too dumb to see the benefits of his suggestions. It has been difficult for others to form alliances against him because no one wants to be seen as pathetic, stupid, or making a mountain out of a molehill. B's **reductive** approach has proved a masterstroke in neutralizing his opposition.

Talking down those in his way has never been a problem for B in his steady rise. Hoping to oust an internal competitor, B was widely reported to frequently comment on her weaknesses: her insomnia and lack of decisiveness in an effort to find compromise. When she made deals and negotiations, he'd criticize them as being half-baked and damaging for the company. Her popularity hemorrhaged, and nothing stood in B's way to take the top spot.

What I've always found interesting about B is his ability to have one rule for himself and another for others. For example, he managed to secure a pay rise for himself, whilst the rest of his coworkers were on a pay *freeze*. He argued he was a wealth-generator and insisted his colleagues needed to work as hard as him and be as successful, to get a pay hike too. Surprisingly, this didn't lead to mass mutiny, but an increased work ethic. He used blame and disorientation tactics to completely **outfox** his critics. The focus was on other people's productivity rather than the hypocrisy of his actions.

Early in his career, B was keen to **set the bar low initially**. He would under-promise on delivery times or capabilities, directly at odds with what his research teams were telling him privately. It was a deliberate tactic; when the product was released "earlier than expected" or exceeded expected specifications, B was in a perfect position to spin the outcome as a significant coup. This helped boost the idea of both him and the company as go-getting and can-do, with the customer's satisfaction as paramount.

Another technique that observers noticed is that, during B's rise, he would **make a problem so he could be seen solving it.**

A major deal was being negotiated between his organization and another. For a moment, it looked as if B's bargaining position was weak, and his critics were ready to pounce and oust him. He told us all, through a series of interviews and press releases, that the other company was putting up obstacles to the deal, and that he would refuse to negotiate unless they shifted position. He claimed that what they were offering was detrimental to his organization and its shareholders, and that he certainly wasn't afraid to walk away from the deal. The message was clear: if the deal failed, it would be other people's fault (because B loved to play the innocent). Calamity seemed close and, if his company teetered, the entire economy could have been at risk.

Investors, consumers, and business insiders were on tenterhooks, and the tension became almost unbearable.

A short while later, B returned to the negotiating table, citing some negligible and almost invisible shift in the other's side position—a completely imaginary shift. The deal he secured for his organization was arguably less of a win than that of his CEO predecessor had lined up prior to her removal. That didn't seem to matter; by this point, shareholders were relieved that any deal had been struck at all. B's role as savior and competent champion was secure.

Self-image is important for this billionaire's success, as I've said. Part of maintaining that image is **hogging the limelight** and isolating any competitors. In the early days of B's rise, he was the head of a team looking at squaring seeming impossible circles in terms of innovational capability, production line efficiency, and operational costs. A colleague who was lower down the pay chain managed to identify an opening with a supplier that would help speed up delivery times with lower expenditure. His solution to the issue was in sight, but B's response was to move the colleague to another team in a backwater department—citing performance issues—then reinvigorate the project to glory. Nowadays, all that anyone remembers is that B made the impossible possible.

Rest assured, B has never been afraid to **take the credit for what works and shift the blame for what doesn't.** It's a crucial ploy in painting himself as a success story and has helped him build his billions.

The one consistency throughout a long, turbulent career has been B's ability to build himself up as a brand. B talks up his achievements whenever he can, and this heightened sense of **self-worth** appears seductive to us. After a while, it's easy for us to be bedazzled and believe the hype. If we're told something often enough, it becomes a kind of truth. Masters of deception and exploitation—CEOs, politicians, salespeople, advertisers, emotional abusers, and criminals alike—all understand the importance of that.

We have seen that B has not been afraid to deceive, lie, and manipulate his way to the top. He has utilized sharp practices skillfully to ensure he becomes a lucrative winner, but at what cost to fair play and those who stood in his way? The damage is untold, but our materialistic world and history both seem to reward the strong. No wonder B retains a bullish, unrepentant attitude.

He has consistently displayed behavior that, in other fields, may have likely seen him serving a prison term. I can't help asking myself, how can someone like that look at themselves in the mirror? Do they ever reflect on the collateral damage that they have caused? They have been motivated by profit and gain, but are they not bothered by what has been lost?

CHAPTER SIX:

Damage Done — The Victims of Manipulation

I've shown you the techniques manipulators employ: the good, bad, and downright dark. I've also shown you a glimpse of evil and the real faces behind the masks. We've explored narcissism, Machiavellianism, sociopathy, and psychopathy, and I have detailed numerous corporate successes of calculating types in the business world. In essence, we have looked at the deadly reach of exploitation and power-hungry ploys, and what underpins them psychologically.

We can all see the dark thrills that certain machinations can bring some people. Tricks, games, and stratagems deliver triumph and satisfaction for a select and slippery few. However, now I want to ask an important question: what about the other side of these ploys and those who *don't* come out on top?

For every scheming winner, there are often many losers in the game. We must never forget that.

We will now spend some time looking at some specific victims of manipulation. One is fictional, though still recognized globally as Shakespeare's Othello. The other is real, with her identity protected and anonymity preserved.

Brought Low by a Beast: A Broken Heart; How Manipulation Ruined Love

I want to tell you about a young woman who came to me for some advice when reeling from the fallout of serious relationship problems, which she could feel were pulling her under. As this is a sensitive case, I will simply call her A.

It all started ten years prior, when she met a boy, perhaps similar to most stories we've seen or read before. These stores often have the same end too. Despite the universal similarities—repeating themselves across history, continents, households, and lifestyles— that's not to underplay the devastating effects that may be unleashed by these unhappy relationships. Those effects are personal and individual, causing profound and long-term damage, as we shall see.

Like many of us, A thought she had found love. She was in her mid-twenties, young, beautiful, and full of initiative. Hope and opportunity were all before her, and she had the energy, wits, and passion to achieve whatever she wanted. She met her new partner at a party—we will call him Nick. They connected instantly as he told jokes and flirted, and she was instantly charmed. He offered her excessive albeit delightful comments compliments that turned her head. Perhaps he seemed a tad more interested in talking about himself, but he, more or less, asked the right questions when he needed to. He seemed open and honest, and he was keen to share and sought her opinion.

Nick was a little older, but that didn't matter. It made him seem more experienced and mature. He was on the rebound: the victim, he said, of an emotionally abusive relationship. A's heartstrings were tugged as he told her what had led to his previous relationship's breakdown. His former partner had cheated on him with his best friend; the two of them had run off together, leaving him broken and in debt and in need of repair.

Who couldn't resist such an invitation? A's sympathy and understanding were unstinting, and things developed from there pretty quickly.

The romance was a whirlwind of passion. Nick was kind and attentive, and he was always complimenting and treating A when he could. He showered her with gifts: flowers, perfumes, jewelry, outfits. *You look great in this,* he'd tell her. *I like it when you're in red.* The attention he gave her was incredible. *I want you all to myself,* he told her. He certainly made her feel special. She was the center of his life; he, hers.

They traveled, partied, and went on adventures. At first, he would pay his way and share the cost 50/50. If he drank a bit more than her or his tastes were a little more extravagant, that didn't matter to A. She enjoyed his company, and she earned more than him, so she didn't mind chipping in to cover his costs.

On these trips, he would let his guard down further—or perhaps it was A. She was sure it had been him, though. He opened up about the difficult relationship he had with his family, telling her how his overbearing dad was envious of his bond with his wonderful mom and how his siblings were all horrible to him. He told her about his controlling and exploitative boss who didn't appreciate his talent. Over late night drinks, Nick railed against all the lies his ex-wife had told, which had prompted their divorce.

Divorce? You were married!? A queried. *That's right,* he insisted, a little irritated. *I told you this before.* He hadn't of course. Why did it matter anyway, he demanded; A wasn't going to get all sniffy about it, was she? If there was one thing that Nick thought was pathetic, it was the jealous types! After their talk, A believed her concerns were minimal and pushed them aside.

With problems at work and that promotion he was hoping for not going through, Nick found it a struggle paying his rent. He was always telling A how he was broke and how his apartment was falling apart.

Whenever he was around A's place, he was happy, and he would always talk up the wonders of her apartment. Soon, as if it was an idea that had come naturally, A found a solution to Nick's worries—why didn't he just move in with her? So, he did. Within this arrangement, it only seemed natural that she pay the bills, since they *were* in her name. She wasn't going to be a nag about it. When he got his pay raise through, he would start paying his share.

But the promotion never came, and Nick left work shortly after, citing creative differences. He had a new idea, which was a project he needed space to develop. If only they had a place with better light, a yard, or a balcony maybe, then his creative juices could flow. *You want me to flourish, don't you?* he'd ask A. Soon after, they moved to a new condo, all at A's expense.

Mind if I use your car? he'd say. *I need to get around for job interviews and stuff to pitch my ideas.* So, she lent him the keys, with the fines and unpaid parking tickets soon building up, all under A's name. She paid for them as soon as it was clear Nick had no intention of doing so; although, he did promise to pay her back.

He talked big about his plans and how he planned to treat her soon, as the gifts had stopped coming, birthdays and anniversaries forgotten. *I've just got a lot on my mind*, he said. *You understand, don't you, honey? You won't bust my balls about this, will you? I'm so low as is!*

It had taken a lot out of him, he explained, being fired. She was shocked to hear that: Fired? She'd thought he had quit. *Yes, fired,* he groaned, annoyed and upset. *you know this: why rub my nose in it?* She wondered if that explained the empty bottles of cheap liquor she kept finding in the garbage, and why he often appeared disheveled when she came back from work.

They rarely went out because he couldn't afford it and she hated leaving him. He'd often beg her to stay with him—*I don't know what I might do to myself if left alone,* he'd say. Soon, A was isolated from her friends and her family. When they called to ask about her, Nick would answer the phone, always ready with an excuse: she was tied up with work or couldn't go see them because she was worrying about money.

For sure, cash was a concern. She wanted a child, but that didn't interest him nor could they afford another mouth to feed. A was paying for both of them, and he'd started to borrow from her, building up debts that he asked for help from her to cover. She would find charges on her credit card she couldn't quite explain, and when he crashed her car and left it a wreck, he said he'd get her a new one once he was back on his feet.

A could feel herself getting desperate. She felt de-energized and as if life was being slowly sucked out of her. She didn't think she could leave him because she was sure she loved him. What kind of person would she be if she left a man who was down like he was? He wasn't *abusive*. He still occasionally gave her compliments that would light up her world, and there was still passion in the bedroom!

Slowly but surely, things got steadily worse. Nick would often disappear for a day or two, either to clear his head or see a buddy. There were always discrepancies and little things she couldn't quite put her finger on with the stories he told. The iPhone she bought him, among other presents she got for him, started disappearing. *I'm not myself,* he'd say. *I'm always losing stuff; don't make me feel worse about this than I already am.*

Whenever they did go out, Nick would often be found over the other side of the room flirting with other women. The check-out girl at the local store one time complained to A that he'd chatted her up and made inappropriate suggestions; however, Nick dismissed all of these claims as fantasy. A was just being needy and cruel, he insisted. Left disoriented from his assertions, A was inclined to believe him.

I'm sure, by now, you can recognize many of the traits and tactics we discussed in Chapters Three and Four in Nick's behavior. Despite all the hardship, A was still unwilling to leave him. She wasn't sure she'd ever find anyone else who loved her as much and doubted that she could love anyone better. She convinced herself that all relationships had their ups and downs. Nick may have been and was becoming increasingly erratic, but he still seemed like a decent man at heart, though perhaps just a little unlucky? She didn't want to upset him or add to his worries.

Then, Nick went missing for a week. Frantic, A tried calling everyone she knew. Eventually, his buddy's girlfriend—we will call her Zoe—came to see her. *He's not coming back,* Zoe explained. *I overheard him chatting with the guys, and I didn't like what I heard. I gave him an ultimatum, you see. Either he told you or I did.*

A could feel her whole body go cold. *Tell me what?*

That's when A learned the heartbreaking truth—Nick had been having an on/off fling with the neighbor from their previous place for five years. He'd gotten the girl pregnant and demanded she terminate the baby, which she did; however, the girl got pregnant again, and she wanted to keep it this time. Nick had been moaning to his buddies that he didn't know what to do; when Zoe overheard, she insisted that he tell A the truth.

Nick never did have the guts to face her, however.

A dumped his belongings outside, changed the locks, put the apartment on the market, and quit her job, moving back home to her family. In the following months, everyone she knew had some story to tell her about Nick: how he would make sexual passes, be seen with other women, talk A down, and sell her belongings to buy drugs. The list was *endless*, and she couldn't help but wonder why she hadn't spotted all of it herself. More than that, what more information had everyone been withholding from her? It was a thought that was quickly replaced by the realization that she wouldn't have believed them, even if they had.

It was a lucky escape from Nick, I told her, but she opened up to me that she was frustrated that ten years of her life had been wasted with a conman. It was ten years that she would never get back. She had been brainwashed and sold a fantasy; one that she had been willing to accept to her own detriment. Without question, the situation had left her feeling:

- Foolish and humiliated.
- Devalued.
- Doubtful of her own worth.
- Unable to "fall for" or commit again, in case a new partner also abused her trust.
- Distrustful of others, believing them to be guarding secrets from her.
- Lonely.
- Suspicious of compliments.
- Angry and gravely upset.

As we can identify from Chapter Three, Nick was a cheat, liar, and self-serving egomaniac with considerable dark personality traits. The actions of this arch-manipulator with undeniable sociopathic narcissism certainly resulted in significant loss to A. He benefitted at her expense and left her completely diminished.

She was ultimately better off without him, and over time—with help and a lot of courage—she grew stronger. However, there is no doubt she was a victim of dark manipulation and in a bad place for a very long time. Being victimized is not fun.

Now, Forever, Farewell the Tranquil Mind

Let us now look at another case study with even more unsettling outcomes. You may know well the story of William Shakespeare's flawed general Othello already. If you do, you will no doubt agree with me that it is hard not to be startled by Othello's fall; he is perhaps the most iconic albeit tragic example of the devastating dangers of dark manipulation.

If you haven't heard about his miserable fate, or are unsure of the details, let us take a moment to peruse his story.

Shakespeare's magnificently complex and dark tale of malice, manipulation, jealousy, and despair was written for the stage in 1604 and first published eighteen years later in 1622. It remains, to this day, a powerful examination of victimization, if not one of *the* most moving and perceptive stage plays in history. The art of manipulation is clearly on display, and we see, in painful detail, their deadly effects.

War-hero Othello, a man of color, married the young, white, and gorgeous Desdemona, the daughter of a member of the ruling elite Brabantio. It was love, and they genuinely adored each other. However, the prospects for them were not so sunny, and their relationship met with a great deal of prejudice, spite, and resistance along all sides. Being older than her and subject to a lifetime of racist abuse and putdowns, Othello couldn't help but suspect that he was, in some way, unworthy of her or was deserving of failure. He certainly knew that that was what other people, including Brabantio, thought. Even so, Othello hoped his past achievements could win the day, but he was left unfortunately and fatally open to negative suggestions.

That was where his bitter colleague and so-called friend Iago stepped in.

Iago stands at the center of this play, weaving a malicious web of deception against nearly every other character for unclear reasons, driven by that deep and inexplicable darkness that lies within certain people, as we examined in Chapters Two and Three. Displaying triad characteristics, he appeared to operate for his own pleasure, more than out of a desire for material gain or his own advancement. He suggested that he had a thirst and motivation for revenge, having missed out on promotion to a younger man, Cassio, whom Othello has advanced in the military ranks. He also voiced a wild, unsubstantiated suspicion that his wife Emilia had slept with Othello, but admit that he didn't even know if it was actually true. These shifting reasons only seek to explain his actions after he set out to bring Othello down.

The poet Samuel Taylor Coleridge, while studying the play for a series of lectures about two hundred years later, remarked that there was a "motiveless malignity" to Iago's actions. In other words, the only encouragement the man needed was merely the act of frustrating and destroying people itself. Yes, my Grandma would have definitely called him a bad'un!

He remarked that another one of Iago's victims—Roderigo, a young fellow in love with Desdemona and whom Iago used to bankroll his slippery lifestyle—only hung around Othello to "serve his turn on him." He adds: "In following him, I follow but myself." (Shakespeare, 1622, 1.1.58). As an audience, we should be in no doubt that Iago is up to no good, and he admitted that he was "not what I am." Despite his hatred for Othello and evident racism, he gave out a "sign of love" by pretending to have Othello's back. When we see Iago with the general, he acted as a confidante and, crucially, a helping hand by offering him advice and suggestions for flourishing in his relationship with Desdemona.

Othello was open about his loving feelings for his new bride. Initially, he was convinced that his service to the state and accomplishments would keep him in good stead, but he hadn't counted on the grand puppet-master Iago, who was pulling everyone's strings behind the scenes. Iago stirred hatred against his friend by talking Othello down at every opportunity and inflaming bigotry.

More than that, Iago was skilled in the psychological study of his victims and knew exactly what buttons to push. Othello was absolutely convinced his friend was honest, though such thoughts would be his undoing, as Iago remarks: "the better shall my purpose work on him" (Shakespeare, 1622, 1.3.389). Iago could see clearly that Othello had a "free and open nature" and thought "men honest that but seems to be so" (Shakespeare, 1622, 1.3.397-398). All this meant that the general could be easily fooled. As such, Iago's awareness of Othello's weaknesses, fears, and anxieties allowed the former to wreak terrible damage.

It did not take long for Iago to falsely implicate Desdemona as not *really* being in love with her new husband. Worse, he insinuated that she and Cassio are having an affair. He painted a vivid picture of adultery, which fed Othello's insecurities and jealous nature. Cunning to the core, Iago did his best to cut Othello off from any other support network, causing him to fall out and make enemies with whoever may have been previously on hand to help him see sense. It was certainly a master-stroke, putting a wedge between the general and Cassio.

Iago's techniques are straight from the arch-manipulator's playbook. He told lies, dropped hints, and employed generalizations and evasions. He exploited situations to his own ends, laid traps, and proved skillful in deception. At one point, he played innocent and created a perfect smokescreen, saying sweetly: "men should be what they seem" (Shakespeare, 1622, 3.3.130).

Iago was certainly adept at delivering false accusations and fake news: "look to your wife" he said, which Othello lapped up—the character of the woman he trusted, his beloved partner, was now spotted. Viciously, Iago twisted the metaphorical knife further, telling Othello that he shouldn't expect anything else from mixed race relationships. He hit Othello at his most vulnerable spot, voicing the general's fears that had been bubbling beneath the surface since Othello first entered that racist environment.

Weak, alone, distrustful, and self-doubting, Othello was now where Iago wanted him to be: poison running rampant in his veins. From this moment on, Othello is completely disorientated; he literally does not know what to think and is troubled by contradictory beliefs. He admits: "I think my wife be honest, and think she is not" (Shakespeare, 1622, 3.3.390).

This was when Iago upped the ante expertly by providing doctored evidence. It was a perfect trick to plant Desdemona's treasured handkerchief—a gift from her husband—in Cassio's room. Othello's response was volcanic: "my bloody thoughts, with violent pace/ shall ne'er look back" (Shakespeare, 1622, 3.3.464-465). The woman he once loved and adored was now damned in his eyes, and he then promoted Iago, replacing Cassio. Iago, surely, now had everything he wanted. He could have stopped there, but he *didn't*.

The ploys, machinations, subtle game-playing, and insidious schemes continued, and Othello, brave soldier and defender of freedom, was no match for Iago's tricks. What followed was a sad, rapid loss of sanity and reason. As Desdemona remarked: "my lord is not my lord" (Shakespeare, 1622, 3.4.121). The rhythm and syntax of the protagonist's speech became disordered, graphically displaying the unraveling of Othello's mind.

The rest of the play is gore-soaked, as Othello loses everything, bit by bit. He killed Desdemona, saying "I have no wife/ O, Insupportable." He loses his own identity, remarking of himself: "That's he that was Othello" (Shakespeare, 1622, 5.2.285), and, ultimately, takes his own life.

What is remarkable about Iago's evil is that he barely lifted a finger when bringing about the terrible outcomes he desired. Rhetoric was his weapon, with his insinuations and falsehood prompting Othello to do all the legwork. As such, Othello became the author of his own undoing and the ruin of those he loved- the most.

Othello's response was undeniably violent and abusive toward innocent bystanders, which cannot be condoned. His actions cannot be downplayed, not even by saying that he was horribly tricked into taking this destructive path. He was very much at fault too. I say this because I do not want to excuse Othello's reactions, but we can pity him all the same.

Was he just unlucky, or was there something that made him particularly vulnerable and open to Iago's ploys? The short answer to that last question is yes. Great drama doesn't usually spring from someone being in the wrong place at the wrong time; however, a stinging a lack of luck can be.

Before we move on from this sorrowful story, let us take a look at what made Othello such a prime mark for exploitation:

- Vulnerable, despite his physical strengths.
- Isolated.
- Trusting in false friends.
- Inferiority complex coupled with pride, which is a dangerous mix.
- Insecurity.
- Anger.
- Suffered from jealousy and compared himself to others.
- A lack of self-awareness.
- Low emotional intelligence.
- Unable to properly communicate his feelings.
- Open to suggestion.
- Naivety.
- Allowed others to talk him down.
- Only saw what he wanted to see.

That the general was ripe for victimization should, in no way, allow the scheming Iago off the hook, nor does it mean that our antihero completely deserved what befell him.

The takeaway here is that Othello's inner nature, combined with external conditions, can explain perfectly why he becomes susceptible to manipulation, and why he did what he did. We should find much food for thought in that, and I am eager to explore the issue further, in more specific detail, without delay.

CHAPTER SEVEN:

Are You on the Radar?

The tactics we examined in the previous chapters are pervasive and used often by manipulative bosses, lovers, and friends; they are the tools of false-hearted narcissism, Machiavellianism, and psychopathy. Any one of us could fall prey to one or all of the exploitative tricks that have been mentioned.

That's right—in theory, no matter how well-equipped, we could all potentially become a mark or victim in waiting.

However, not all of us will end up being manipulated. In this chapter, I want to look at why certain folk are manipulated while others aren't and discuss the damage that can be caused. I also want to give you some crucial guidance for making sure you're not someone whom others can take advantage of so easily and often.

In Plain Sight: What Makes Us Susceptible to Manipulation?

Let's be honest—it's not as if there is a telltale sign that some of us wear on our forehead saying: *take advantage of me.* In the case studies I gave in the previous chapter, neither Othello nor the young woman A invited exploitation or deserved it. However, they may have subconsciously flag that they were particularly prone to manipulation. Are you and I doing the same without even realizing it?

I will take you through a range of personalities that tend to be susceptible to manipulation. I have identified fifteen core types:

Shrinkers

There are many people out there who are not huge fans of conflict and confrontation. In some cases, that's good—it's not always healthy entering into aggressive situations. If you are constantly wary of the negative emotions that can arise whenever you say *stop* or *Hang on, that's not right,* then you may be easy prey to people who want to nudge you into doing what they want.

Pleasers

We all know the kind of person who likes to make other people happy; maybe, we are one of them ourselves. There is nothing wrong at all with wanting to bring a smile to the world. It is an immensely admirable quality, so we shouldn't sneer at the everyday saints amongst us. Stereotypically, they're moms! If you know someone who is always doing favors, these are the people you will probably call when your car breaks down in the middle of the night on the highway. However, they can come in many shapes and forms. Who knows their exact motivation: do they get a sense of self-worth from being needed, are they craving approval, or are they just inherently altruistic? Either way, they find it hard to say *no*. Unfortunately, they are prime targets for both low-scale and heavy-duty manipulation.

Innocents

These are the people who might be described as gullible and naïve. They just cannot imagine that people would be deceitful in a given situation. Be warned: these types don't come with a label that says *sucker.* As I said, they could even be you or me without us knowing it. Innocents are in denial. They can be the lovestruck: people who won't accept that the focus of their adoration is up to no good. Otherwise, innocents are what I call kind-hearted individuals. They're decent, easily exploited people. Perhaps you are prone to giving people the benefit of the doubt—imagine some guy approaching you on the street, He says he's lost his wallet, and he wants you to help by giving him money for the bus so he can get home to his kids before they get in from school. What are you going to do: trust him or assume the worst? You don't want to deny him charity, but watch out. Too much of this attitude and you could become seriously out of pocket.

Doubters

This kind of person constantly questions their own opinion and tastes, believing that someone else will always know best. No, someone else may not necessarily know best! This impressionable attitude often comes from an inferiority complex and complete lack of confidence, meaning it can easily be exploited.

The Vain

I touched on this in Chapter Four when we talked about manipulators who stroke our ego. Who hasn't been flattered into doing something they didn't want to do? *Hey, you're so good with your tech. Could you fix my Wi-Fi?* Yep, we've all been there!

Careless

There are those who simply don't really pay attention to what's going on. They have their head in the clouds or are too busy and preoccupied with other stuff to notice when they are being manipulated. Perhaps they are impulsive and don't like to dwell too much on something because that kills spontaneity. Maybe, but that can still lead to exploitation.

Submissive

Perhaps it is part of your inner personality to allow yourself to be reliant, and you may crave the protection and the security of being dependent on someone else. What they say goes because it makes you feel safer. Otherwise, you assume that you don't deserve any better than your current situation—this is as good as it gets, and you reckon you should accept it.

Self-harmers

This is when a person masochistically welcomes the idea of being dominated by another person and actually receives (sexual or sensory) pleasure from it. The sadists that I talked about in Chapter Three would form a perfect—or imperfect—partnership with these people.

The Lonely

Maybe you want to welcome the attention of others, good or bad, because the alternative is silence. You may have been isolated for so long that you find it hard to see things in perspective.

The Old or Infirm

In these cases, the physical or mental weakness of others is preyed upon because they cannot fight back easily.

Lack of self-awareness

Maybe you just don't really know what you want or think. It could be that you don't have the emotional clarity or self-questioning sense of analysis needed to process your feelings. In that case, it would be no wonder that you're easily swayed, if it happens.

Keeping it all in

In this case, people may fail to express themselves or simply lack the necessary communication skills to get their opinion or preference across. If so, the individual may end up being manipulated by others who are acting unintentionally. They don't actually know what you want because you're not saying it clearly enough; as such, your needs seem ignored and playing second fiddle to someone else's desires.

Low maintenance

Do you think it's better just to go along with the flow because it makes it simpler? You never make a fuss or nag, which can be a positive thing that allows you to be open to new ideas and easy company. It certainly means that you're not high maintenance—one of those people who always has to shape an event and invariably has something to say about where to eat, drink, or shop. However, the negative aspect of being pliable is that you can become disengaged. In practice, that means you often seem indecisive, wishy-washy, and easily persuaded; therefore, others can bend you to their will without resistance.

Stuck in a rut

Often when someone is feeling down and fed up with their life, they will try searching for any change they can get. That's because they think that figuratively jumping off a cliff is better than standing still. In this situation, they will be open to a range of suggestions: try this narcotic, try this scheme, etc. Politicians exploit the need for rescue and change all the time; although, those seeing re-election find that a harder challenge when they are the incumbent.

Full of empathy

Maybe you are just too understanding for your own good. You may know that someone is manipulating a situation, but you still attempt to see it from their point of view. You reckon they are acting that way because they are down in the dumps, broke, lonely, or committed to a certain cause. You may feel guilty for not being a "nice" enough person, so you try your best to meet others' needs and wants. Empathy is a vital skill to have, but not when you are using it to make excuses for others' damaging behavior.

Reading through that list, I'm sure you recognize aspects of yourself and other people. As I say, many personality traits can be positive, charitable, and helping make the world a better place. However, left unchecked, they can help dark forces thrive.

Feeling the Pain — The Negative Effects

None of us want to fall victim to darkness, and the harm caused by exploitative techniques is unquantifiable. They can gradually corrode or chip away in small yet intrinsic ways, insidiously causing psychological damage. Underhand tactics can certainly have a variety of long-term negative effects on self-image, the world, and other people. Alternatively, as we saw with Othello in Chapter Six, they can have huge and dramatic repercussions, including loss of life, livelihood, or possessions.

I don't want to dwell too much on this because I would rather help you understand manipulation better, so you can avoid it or harness its positive aspects. However, it is vital that you have a comprehensive overview of how unhealthy various forms of tricks can be.

Here are a few of the main outcomes of being targeted by a manipulator:

- **Low self-esteem**. It's easy to feel worthless when you're aware someone has taken or is still taking advantage of you.
- **Shame and humiliation**. Perhaps you can't stop feeling like a fool for being caught off guard.
- **Guilt**. Maybe you have been made to feel as if something you are doing is wrong, or that you are bad for resisting another person's will.
- **Shut down**. It's easy just stop feeling and go numb to block out all the negative emotions inside and around you.

- **Poor self-care**. Leading on from the previous point, this one happens because being manipulated can have you always putting yourself second.
- **Eating disorders**. In some cases, excessive dominance or critical comments from another can lead you to seek psychological coping mechanisms to regain control of your life.
- **Reduced performance**. How can you fulfill your potential and do your best if you are constantly being drained or distracted from your own needs?
- **Scared of being alone**. Maybe you are fearful that you will be targeted if you are left to your own devices.
- **Damaged relationships** between friends, partners, and family because you ultimately can't feel relaxed, happy, or yourself around someone else who is seeking to bend you to their will.
- **Fear of commitment**. As we saw in our case study of the young woman A, being hoodwinked by a partner can lead to a fear of entering into new relationships, as there is the worry you'll be abused again.
- **Lack of trust** (and its cousin, *paranoia*). It's only natural after being duped or dominated to start assuming everyone is the same.
- **Doubt that what you believe is correct**. This is being dishonest with yourself about your feelings or opinions. Quite simply, you can begin to question whether your current suspicions and thoughts are true.
- **Uncertainty**. I don't just mean about your own thinking, but also in terms of what is the real situation. We discussed this in Chapter Four when looking at gaslighting—it can have serious psychological repercussions if you are unsure of the true nature of reality.
- **Anxiety**. Undue anxiety and depression are the natural outcomes of all the above. Insomnia, mood swings, and self-harming can also follow.

- **Disappointment**. Ultimately, if you've been tricked—whether by a politician, lover, or salesperson—you will probably end up with the opposite of what you were promised. Disappointment can only follow if you don't get the good things you thought were coming your way.
- **Danger**. As I've described when examining manipulators from the dark triad, if you are targeted, you can be incredibly dangerous. It is no exaggeration to say that your life and welfare could be at risk.

What a litany of negativity! There is no way we should accept it because we want the best for our lives, right? So, how do we go about that?

The Great Escape: What to Do in Order to Avoid Manipulative Techniques

I have now given you quite the load of doom and gloom! I don't want to spook you, however—rest assured, it is possible to navigate through the rocky waters of manipulation and avoid its dangers. I want to take you through a practical, twenty-step how-to on ensuring you are not susceptible to manipulation and vulnerable to its negative effects.

Let's take a look.

1. **Ask the inner you**. It is vital that you spend time learning what it is you feel, want, and need. That is the foremost way to guarantee that you are still in control of your situation. Make sure your wishes are being answered.

2. **Trust yourself**. I know this point is easier said than done, but have confidence in your own opinions and strength of character, and rise above any attempts to coerce you into doing what you don't want to do. You know yourself better than anyone, and you shouldn't forget that fact.

3. **Own up to the problem**. Don't explain, excuse, or minimize any behavior that upsets or unsettles you. Identify it as an issue that needs to be handled.

4. **Establish limits**. Work out your boundaries and what you are comfortable with doing. Ensure this line is never crossed.

5. **Look for inconsistencies**. Quite often when someone is trying to pull the wool over your eyes, they will contradict their story. They are probably lying to you if nothing they say is either straight or consistent. You can try keeping notes of conversations that you've had, so you don't find yourself wrong-footed later.

6. **Hold people accountable**. Demand answers and responses. If they seek to avoid answering, act like a broken record yourself. *Let's get back to the issue in hand* is a useful expression you can use in these circumstances.

7. **Check for credentials**. If you are being approached by a so-called expert, demand to see their ID. If someone claims to be your friend or have your best interests at heart, try to find evidence of that from past and current behavior.

8. **Be vigilant**. Keep on the lookout for situations in which you may be vulnerable to exploitation. Be watchful for unusual behavior or activity, and don't accept everything you hear.

9. **Have the whole picture**. Ensure that this is always true, so you aren't hoodwinked or fall for fake news. Do your best to search for critical facts, context, and other perspectives, as getting other opinions can help in your pursuit of truth.

10. **Seek safe, neutral spaces**. Don't put yourself in situations or surroundings in which you are at risk or a disadvantage. Therefore, search for areas that are safe and neutral when dealing with strangers or people who are asking things of you. In doing so, you lessen your chances of being manipulated.

11. **Maintain a support network**. As such, don't allow yourself to be isolated. Keep in touch with people you can trust, including friends, family, and loved ones. You need to know there is someone who has your back and whom you can call on if you suspect someone is taking advantage of you.

12. **Don't play along**. That's right: just move away from an uncomfortable situation or close your ears if the need arises and do not engage. It's important that, as soon as you identify any manipulative behavior, you refuse to give it oxygen.

13. **Shut it down**. I want you to call out manipulation wherever you see it. There's no need to get sidetracked with unnecessary confrontations or accusations, but stay focused on making it clear you do not plan to play anyone's game. Learn the importance of saying, *I am not going to accept that*. If you are being accused of something, as an attempt to undermine or discredit you, calmly respond: *that is not the case*.

14. **Be honest**. There is nothing wrong in calmly, politely, and resolutely saying *I don't want to do that*. In fact, it doesn't matter if you stutter those words out; if that's what you feel, make sure you're heard.

15. **Compromise**. Entertain this idea. If a favor has been asked of you, and you don't mind doing it, but there are some aspects you deem inconvenient, then find some middle ground. However, stick to your guns in regard to those uncrossable lines we mentioned before.

16. **Hide vulnerabilities**. It's great to be yourself and open to share with others. But don't let everyone know you're careless with money or a sucker for sob stories, for example. If you do, you will have given them an easy-to-read guidebook on how to exploit you. As such, keep yourself smart and presentable. It's a sad fact but manipulators—those with more psychopathic tendencies, in particular—target people who look weak and down at heel.

17. **Try something new**. Maybe you are beginning to question why you use a certain brand or always have pizza with your partner on a Friday night. Perhaps you've become known as the desk jockey who always works late. Mix things up a little; otherwise, you may find you are doing things without actually wanting to do them.

18. ...Of course, in some situations, a more rigorous approach is required.

19. **Cut ties**. Sometimes, the only way out of an unhealthy relationship in which you are being dominated is to leave it. In these cases, you need to leave without looking back. However, be aware that this may not necessarily be a long-term solution. You must ask yourself why your guard was low enough to allow for this kind of manipulation in the first place, and you may just be moving out of one damaging relationship only to open yourself up to another one further down the road.

20. **Therapy**. Perhaps the reason you are allowing yourself to be manipulated is because of something inside of you telling you to be. I am not seeking to apportion blame or excuse other people's domineering behavior. You may have a mental health issue, personality disorder, or feelings and impulses that you cannot explain. Seeking the guidance of a professional will help you identify why you make certain decisions. This can be the first step to avoiding situations that leave you at a disadvantage. Equally, you may want to address how you recognize triad traits in yourself and are the one who is the manipulator in certain circumstances; in which case, you need to address it before it gets out of hand. Whichever side of the fence you fall, counseling could be the perfect solution.

21. **Call for assistance**. By this, I mean the police or civic authorities. I touched on this before: if there is any suspicion of coercion or abuse or illegal activity, get the professionals in.

The forces of manipulation are not insurmountable, and they can be stopped. Be warned, however, that there is no magic, bulletproof suit you can wear that will protect you from all ill intentions. I said before about equipping yourself with knowledge; in the words of the 18th English philosopher Abraham Tucker: *forewarned is forearmed*. As such, know your own mind, do your research, and seek the truth before trusting someone fully. Be honest and forthright.

That is how to take out the sting of manipulation. In the next chapter, we will be looking at other constructive ways to move toward the light.

CHAPTER EIGHT:

A Guide to Ethical Approaches

In your everyday life, in terms of your relationships, friendships, social interactions, and working practices, do you motivate or manipulate? Look at yourself carefully and ask yourself: do I influence others positively or negatively?

However "good" a person you think yourself being, the questions above do not always have ready-made and clear-cut responses.

Diagnosing Who You Are, and Establishing Right from Wrong

To determine the impact you have on others—and whether it is energizing or exploitative—you first need to correctly *identify* your actions and interpersonal relationships. Do you engage in methods of gentle persuasion, or is it actually coercion? Are you hoping to influence or trick someone to get what you want? Do you rely on rational debate, interacting with another individuals' facultative reasoning abilities, or do you aim to sucker people by appealing to their emotions and impulses?

In essence, I want to know if you encourage free will in others and seek to keep them open to all options available to them.

These aren't hard questions to answer. I'm willing to bet that if you're honest with yourself, you will admit that your approaches straddle both motivation and manipulation.

Next, I want you to *evaluate* whether your objective in influencing others is ethical. You probably don't think of yourself as evil and see a million differences between yourself and all those dark case studies we looked at in earlier chapters. However, take some time before you respond. The simple guideline you need to follow here is: are you acting to benefit others or serve yourself? Are you following a certain course of action for power and control? Does it look like a game from which you cat get some degree of pleasure? It may not be easy to name your exact motives, but you can tell quickly what ball park they are in, and whether you are hoping to use your influence to achieve positive change.

Be prepared to find yourself in a gray area here. As I have said throughout the course of this book, not everything is necessarily black or white. Consider hypnosis, for example; this technique—manipulating an individual's state of mind and preferences through suggestion—appeals to the subconscious, and it bypasses reasoned thought. In some cases, it is clearly used for selfish ends. This can be seen in the literary example of Svengali, an exploitative and criminal man in George du Maurier's *Trilby*, which outlines a fascinating outlook at seduction and control. In this story, Svengali hypnotizes a young woman and transforms her, through the power of suggestion, into an amazing singer with money-spinning potential. His reasons spring from the dark desire to dominate and gain material recognition, against the woman's wishes. In this case, we have identified and evaluated that the manipulation is wrong because the means and motives are both unethical.

However, hypnosis is frequently used as a method to help people quit smoking. In this case, the objective is positive with health benefits; therefore, it can be identified as deliberately seeking to sidestep preconditioned thought. In other words, it helps fix what the addicted psyche has established chemically, as reason and justification for the action. The means I have observed may attempt to subvert free will and intrinsically restrict certain choices, but further evaluation will surely suggest that the aims can be noble.

Way back in Chapter One, we looked at whether good intentions negate immoral action. I wasn't willing to give an answer then, and I'm not now. In contrast to Kant, I strongly believe you must find your own answer to that question!

If you suspect that your actions are at the expense of others, perhaps you should consider seeking professional help, as I discussed in the previous chapter. You may like to take an online test that will assess your level of pushiness, and whether you are an actual risk to others or if it is merely a tendency you need to self-monitor to ensure a balanced and happy environment around you.

Light in the Dark: A New Moral Understanding

In his seminal work *Ethics,* philosopher Aristotle advocated the importance of living life in accordance with positive values. His thinking toward virtue and *what is right* have remained respected for over 2,500 years. A sense of ethical understanding, he claims, can help guide an individual through the extremes of everyday life, in which moral decisions are made frequently. As far as he was concerned, ***honesty and integrity*** should be our watchwords. When identifying and evaluating your behavior, these principles are the beacons that light your way if you follow an ethical approach.

What does that mean practically, and what does integrity mean in our modern world? To achieve an ethical utilization of your persuasive skills and ability to influence others much easier, you may need to rethink how you see your purpose and goals in life completely. By that, I mean we need to start thinking more about ***WE rather than I***. Processing a situation collectively and adopting a sense of communal responsibility are important for bringing this point home. Consider the wider impact of an action and the maximum amount of people it can benefit; for example, let's say that you regularly get a ride to work with your buddy, and you know two other coworkers are also experiencing transport difficulties. They aren't on your route to the office, and picking them up will add time to your journey. In this case, the greater good—for your colleagues and the planet— is to convince your buddy to do that detour.

In southern Africa, there is a line of philosophy that has been gathering ground since the 1800's, and has gained a strong voice in the last half century during the transition periods between colonization and apartheid, with followers including human rights activist Archbishop Desmond Tutu. It is known as *Ubuntu*, which is Zulu for "humanity." Essentially, it embodies the idea of one-ness: *I am because we are*. As such, its emphasis is on a sharing methodology to produce worldwide harmony.

Therefore, it would be suggested that an ethical viewpoint can be gained in our interaction with others if we start thinking about how we all benefit together. With this approach, it is time to adopt a global approach, thinking wide and big. The C19th British philosopher and economist John Stuart Mill, however, saw a few flaws in this proposal. His argument was that it is impossible—therefore, a futile exercise— to attempt to take on the burdens of the entire world. Thinking about *everyone* can become too vague, and some would argue that complete altruism isn't possible. He argued that it would be far better to adopt the causes of the smaller community around oneself: think about what benefits the team, neighborhood, friendship circle, or family. The United States is still being protected, above the needs of the *me*, but far more manageably.

But how do we change our sense of focus so radically? It has been suggested that positive change is only possible if we apply what has become known as **The Golden Rule**. This is a way of thinking amounts to *treating others as you would like to be treated*. It is not a universally adopted approach, and certainly not so in the business world. Despite that, it has been around as a concept since the dawn of civilization, though the history of empire-building rarely mentions it.

References to this philosophy can be found in our earliest writings, including on papyrus remains of one of the oldest surviving fictional stories, *The Eloquent Peasant*, dating back to Ancient Egypt over 4,000 years ago. The Sanskrit epic *Mahabharata*, composed more than 2,000 years ago, sums up the idea succinctly as the perfect advice that can be given to a king. Only a little later, in Ancient Rome, did the renowned dramatist and philosopher Seneca morally interrogate the ideas of slavery by asserting: treat your inferior as you would wish your superior treat you. Philosophical movements including Confucianism, Zoroastrianism, and humanist thinking, along with various religious scriptures—Judaism, Christianity, Buddhism, Hinduism, Islam, and Sikhism—embrace the idea of reciprocity. It is a school of thought we should keep close to our hearts if we hope to practice ethical approaches in life.

Is Now the Moment to Motivate?

With that in mind, I want to give you a quick five-point checklist to keep in case you hope to pursue an ethical approach in life, working for the good of others as well as yourself. It will help you identify and evaluate when you should exert your influence more clearly.

1. When seeking to motivate, encourage, influence, or persuade, ask yourself: *would I want this* advice or product myself? Put yourself in the other person's shoes.
2. Take that a step further and be honest: will what you're about to say or do help people? Will what you're offering **improve** their lives in a small way or monumentally?
3. If you're unsure objectively, clarify: *do I believe in what I am saying*? Machiavellian types may not, but will probably say they do anyway. If you are hoping to maintain an ethical

approach at all times, then don't publically support something you secretly oppose.

4. Perhaps **seek a second, objective opinion**. If you want to give your coworker advice about avoiding an abusive partner, you can first present the facts unemotionally to someone you trust to see what they think.

5. If you are convinced that you are **serving a need,** then proceed.

Now that the basics are under your belt, it is time to start talking about getting by in a manipulative world.

In Your Hands: The Gift of Positive Prompting

Self-help books offering the promise of relationship and business glory are everywhere. They will give you tips on what you need to do to land that fish, shine, and get ahead. Here, I want to suggest a practical guide on how to succeed ethically when seeking to influence other people's mindsets or actions.

I like to call the power you yield *prompting*, which differentiates it from the negative connotations of manipulation. In essence, it encourages free will. The award-winning economists Sunstein and Thaler discussed this in their 2009 research into ethical "nudges." It involves encouraging someone to choose to do something only after they know the options. In that way, they consent, and you have achieved your goals by bringing about positive change.

My aim is to empower you responsibly with the most effective interpersonal tools available, so you encourage and motivate at all times. Therefore, you can learn to use persuasion for the good.

•   Refuse to support bad, antisocial behavior, either in yourself or others. **Self-control** is key. It is vital you master your own feelings and display emotional intelligence. This idea relates to that Aristotelian theory we were discussing earlier: dominate your personality instead of letting it dominate you, balancing the self and avoiding excessive appetites and emotions such as anger. Put in the effort to be a good person. Being manipulative for selfish reasons takes up just as much energy (think of all that subterfuge!).

- Keep your team clean! Specifically, surround yourself in your workplace, home, and social settings with non-triad personalities. If you are wanting to practice an ethical approach, other people's dark impulses will hamper your efforts. **Avoid toxicity**.

- **Root out problems**. As such, do a frank evaluation of your circle: who is hard to work with or be around? Why? Do they display dark triad characteristics? If so, approach them when they're in a good mood and at their most amenable. Observe their body language: are their hands crossed and are they avoiding eye contact? If so, it may suggest they won't be receptive. If they are meeting your gaze and show emotion on their face, they may be more willing to listen. Shut down lies and don't be swayed by manipulative techniques. Use your own arts of persuasion and promoting to tell them their behavior is de-energizing. Give precise examples and help them identify triggers and solutions. Make it clear they must change their ways within a realistic time limit.

- Be **patient** but also vigilant because not everything you want needs to come to fruition in the short term. Remember to set deadlines for trying new approaches, or to cut ties with someone if promises and commitments have not been met.

- Be determined but never forceful. As such, learn to **be assertive without getting angry or aggressive**. You must be strong but fair. Remain calm and stand your ground. If you feel unsafe in a situation, remember to leave.

- **Be careful how people feel**. The aim isn't to belittle anyone or assert your superior outlook on life—make sure to maintain a light-hearted and blame-free attitude. No one will listen to someone who makes them feel bad.

- If your endeavors are ethical, it is likely that you will see some **reward** for the other person, so make sure you express that. I'd advise emphasizing the positive; for example, take a look at the success rate of something rather than its failure rate. Focus on the greater good and flag up the disadvantages of not doing something. This tactic is known as *consequence ethics.* You are not making any threats or false promises, but you are laying out the facts of the situation to encourage a positive, can-do attitude.

- **Concentrate on what you believe in** and work hard to promote that. Make your message and vision—what you are offering— meaningful. It should be appealing and offering harmony, benefit, and balance. You need to see it genuinely as an opportunity for good things.

- The people you are prompting should be curious to hear more. **Inspire** a sense of a journey and shared learning to whatever it is you are suggesting.

- It is vital in our interactions with others that we earn and establish **trust**. Be true to your words, as your experience, behavior, and knowledge ought to inspire people to turn to you. Equally, if you surround yourself with people whom you trust and vice versa, it encourages an ever-increasing circle of loyalty. *Don't betray that trust!* Once you are caught telling a lie or failing to deliver on a promise, no matter what your role, your credibility and influence are both lost.

- Throughout your dealings with other people, **exercise respect and empathy**. Follow the Kantian principle that people are not things or pawns; instead, they are complete in themselves with valid opinions. You must remember that your interaction with them is a dialog and not a soliloquy. So, listen and maintain eye contact! As I mentioned earlier, whomever you are seeking to prompt must be part of the eventual choice they have to make. All options must be discussed. You are a coach, not a dictator; you should promote independent thought and autonomy.

- **Strong verbal communication skills** are a must. Speak clearly, calmly, and slowly, expressing yourself in accessible language. This was a quality that those manipulators in the case studies we looked at lacked. You may need to read more widely while boosting your knowledge and vocabulary. You might also want to practice in front of a mirror—or video yourself—while studying your body language and voice. That way, you can ensure you don't gesticulate distractingly are avoiding mumbling in monotone, which can be very uninspiring.

- Keep yourself and your surroundings clean and neat, which is vital for making yourself **approachable**. You can try wearing colors that lift your expression, for example; always aim to be presentable and smell good.

- Be positive, cheerful, and confident, while avoiding negativity. Remember what I said about Steve Jobs' **sunny outlook**? Use it here to inspire others ethically.

- Continuous **positive reinforcement**, affirmation, and encouragement are advised, but they must still remain sincere, balanced, and consistent.

- Remember to be **open and transparent, while also being honest and fair**. If you are trying to get a partner to kick an unhealthy habit, needing a favor from a friend, or wanting to motivate a coworker to maximize productivity, then use tact and integrity to explain *why* you are trying to prompt them in a certain way. You should be able to truthfully say: *I am doing this for you.* If not, then *I am doing this for all of us.* You know you are in the shallows if all you can say is: *I am doing this for me.* If that is the case, something has gone wrong with your endeavors.

Shining Examples — Choosing a Mindset

In 2013, Auvinen et al. of the department of Psychology at the university of Jyväskylä in Finland, carried out important research about how leaders could avoid dark-controlling techniques. They looked at how hard or tough messages can be employed through soft means, such as storytelling and collegiate team-based interactions.

At the center of their findings was the CEO, who would regularly use anecdotes to motivate his colleagues. At a difficult juncture of product development, he told them the (fictional) story of a car factory in the early days of the automobile industry. The factory was full of various experimental studies that were based on different fuel technologies, from horse-drawn to pedal-power. The factory burned down, and only one prototype remained; therefore, the workers had to develop that car. It just so happened to be the petrol model that remained, and their invention went on to create global success.

The CEO's humorous tale served the function of getting his team to refocus. The message was clear for those who listened carefully enough—forget about the prevarication and get on with the basics of selecting a prototype that would soar. He could have used other means to get his point across, including a tirade that threatened them all with dismissal, for example. However, he chose something a little more encouraging and heart-warming.

With that in mind, I'd like to share a story about a young man I know, whom we will call C. I've known him since before his career as a theater and film director took off. Back when he was first starting out, he suffered from an almost crippling lack of confidence. To counter this in the rehearsal room, he would often bark out instructions and play the tough guy. He'd lose his temper, shout, and domineer. To win allies, he'd pit actors against each other, getting them to gossip and backbite freely. He wasn't immune to deception either, specifically in terms of bigging up the prospects of the show and which talent scouts might be there to see it.

Needless to say, his behavior won him very few friends. The rehearsal environment was fairly toxic and his productions always lacked that necessary spark to lift them to the next level. He came to me asking for my advice, and I gave it to him. Basing my instruction on the secrets I'd learned in boardrooms around the globe, I taught him about the positive benefits of ethical leadership.

Yeah, right, he said. *Quaint ideas. They don't work in the real world.*

I urged him to listen to the voice of experience and trust the proof of other people's success. Give it a go, I counseled him.

He got his opportunity soon after. He was staging a Shakespeare play—experimental and gender-blind—in a miniscule theater in the back of beyond. The rehearsals had gone well and he'd kept his calm, nudged rather than coerced. During this time, he'd earned a circle of trust, and the results were bearing some modest fruit on stage. The show really could go down a storm, C thought. Then came the first night, and a genuine tempest was raging outside. Within a few minutes to curtain up, there were only two people in the auditorium.

Despairing, the actors refused to go on stage. *It'll be humiliating* they said. Besides, the stage manager pointed out that, under labor and union rules, the performance couldn't go ahead if the audience outnumbered the cast.

C sat down with his actors in a circle on the dressing room floor. *I'm going to level with you,* he said clearly and slowly, meeting them in the eye one by one. *I want you to do this show tonight. I want to convince you why you should.* He had a feeling that, if they didn't get on stage that evening, they might not again; they'd lose the motivation and drive to do it, looking for other excuses to cancel.

First, he listened patiently to what the cast had to say, and took on the chin any criticism they might have had about poor marketing and how they felt let down. He answered their complaints calmly and constructively, and took them through the reasons why he felt they should perform. He itemized the hard work each one of them had put in—from the star to the supporting spear carrier—and entertained them with amusing anecdotes of different mishaps and triumphs during rehearsal. He gave an honest yet positive assessment of their individual performances. He told the shows' first time performer, *You've worked so hard to nail the iambic pentameter. Don't throw all that away.*

He also reminded them that some people had braved the wind and rain to come see the play. What kind of professional entertainer lets its audience down, however small it was? All in all, he urged them not to quit. *You owe it to that couple out there and you owe it to yourselves.*

With an almost Shakespearean sense of rhetoric, repetition, and rousing cadence, C led his troupe forward, enthusing and motivating them all. It was certainly manipulation, but ethical with an admirable goal in sight. It's what we could call expert team management.

As a coda or epilogue to this tale: those two people in the audience gave a standing ovation. More than that, they were critics and their reviews were ecstatic. Full houses followed for the rest of the run, and several successful careers were launched that night!

Reaching the Sunny Uplands

For me, this case study is powerful, entertaining, and a reminder that leadership can transform and be truly from the heart. It can be no less successful because of that. It is what I have been talking about throughout the course of this important chapter; you can embrace ethical practices fairly while shunning the dark and still achieve great things.

I want you to know that it is possible to win fairly.

CONCLUSION

You came to read this book to satisfy your curiosity and understand that nagging question better: why do some people succeed in getting what they want?

You were inspired to read this detailed study of dark psychology and manipulation because of who you are. At the center of your thoughts was the puzzle: *How can I flourish too?* That's because, motivated by your efforts to self-improve, you were unwavering in wanting the best for yourself to function more efficiently, yet fairly, in your workplace, home, and social environment.

That is why you turned to my book, underpinned as it was by my experience as a psychologist and self-help practitioner.

By now, I am trusting that you will know you made the right choice. I promised at the beginning of this book that I would help you to change the way you see things and offer you a new, stronger, and more secure way to operate. Can you feel the benefits already? What a journey we have been through together, and largely jargon-free! I've tried my best to keep the explanations in this book in layman's terms rather than with confusing, technical speak, for your convenience.

Perhaps looking over your shoulder and seeing what you are reading, people may have wrinkled their nose and called you out. They may be thinking that this is a nasty subject matter and certainly not for the faint-hearted, as I've said. *Why do you want to go there?* they might ask. *That kind of stuff is creepy.*

It is certainly, but that's no excuse to shy away. Only through exploration can we discover the tools we need to survive and prosper.

Dramatists, philosophers, and spiritualists have all been asking themselves for millennia: *what defines human evil?* It is the job of psychologists like myself to let everyone know there is no value in painting bad people as cartoon villains, then running behind the sofa to avoid them. The follow-up question should always be: *how can evil be countered?* If we understand the darkness—bad thoughts, feelings, and inclinations—rather than looking the other way, we can combat everything that seeks to undermine us as a society.

Certainly, the research of Paulhus, which looked into tendencies toward dark behavior and why some figures of authority might abuse their position, has been used to great effect by civil and military authorities. His studies into dark psychology have actively helped identify, at the recruitment stage, certain individuals predisposed to seek jobs where they would be in control of vulnerable individuals and seeking to exploit that.

Similarly, Zettler's findings on the D Factor provided mapping that could get us closer to stopping the more violent triad extremes of dark behavior. People with high D ratings operate hidden, though still technically in plain sight. These are still-functioning individuals within society, and the D factor can help us identify, before it's too late, which of them might be tempted to escalate their crimes.

Without question, embracing rigorous research can allow us to prompt innovations in psychological understanding that will improve how we prevent harmful and reckless behavior. That can only be a positive step to take, don't you agree?

I'm sure that you do. After all, you have looked boldly into the unknown, unafraid to listen to what needs to be heard.

Together, we have explored human nature and its dark corners. We discussed the concept of dark personalities and saw a number of case studies, asking ourselves about the differences between right and wrong. We have come to realize that manipulation is everywhere—in the books we read, TV shows we watch, and horrors we hear on the news. By now, you should have the information you need to protect and prepare yourself.

You may have identified that you keep company with manipulators. If so, I have now also given you the tools to identify their techniques and overcome them.

Perhaps, through reading this book, you have come to recognize dark traits within your own personality, which is great! Now you are also equipped to tackle these characteristics and seek the help you need to make something positive of your impulses. I have shown you that there is both truth and deception in all of us. Human nature is so nuanced and profound that it can sustain contradictions. To misquote the magnificent poet Walt Whitman, *we are large, we contain multitudes.*

At the center of this complex spirit of ours is the idea that free will is paramount. That means you can decide how to behave ethically, independent of other people's influences or coercion. You can do it if you try hard enough. With fact-based examples and a sense of perspective, I have given you the knowledge you need to soar. It is up to you to decide how you use that power.

Perhaps you are looking at our ego-centric political leaders, celebrities, and CEOS and yearning for something else—a way to be different. Maybe you have gotten tired of seeing wrong-doing and malice rewarded. This book has taught you that evil doesn't always prosper at the expense of good.

Not only can the dark art of exploitative manipulation be avoided, but an ethical approach to influencing others can be achieved instead, which is great news. There are those who prey on others, and there are those—more fair-minded, self-aware, and objective—who genuinely want to help the greater good. These prompters, as I call them, are aware of how both mass- and micromanipulation work. However, they're too smart to fall into that trap, and too ethical to use those techniques for selfish gain themselves. They encourage us all to progress from what is to what could be.

That is how to avoid the dark shadows and enjoy the light. We can all do it if we so choose.

Thank you for allowing me to share these thoughts with you. If there is one thing I would especially want you to take away from this book, it's that you can create and sculpt the nature of your own success. That's because your mindset is for *you* to shape. So, go blazing into the night; shine bright and long, and your influence on others will be profound.

RESOURCES

Abrams, J.J. (2019). *The Rise of Skywalker*. [Motion picture]. Disney.

Adam, D. (2019, March 12). Does a dark triad of personality traits make you more successful? *Science*. https://www.sciencemag.org/news/2019/03/does-dark-triad-personality-traits-make-you-more-successful

Allers, R. & Minkoff, R. (1994). *The Lion King*. [Motion picture]. Disney.

Arabi, S. (2019, November 1). Recovering from a narcissist. *Psychcentral*. https://blogs.psychcentral.com/recovering-narcissist/2019/10/5-terrifying-ways-narcissists-and-psychopaths-manufacture-chaos-provoke-and-manipulate-you/

Arabi, S. (2016, May 12) The love story of a narcissist and his victim. *Thought Catalog*. https://thoughtcatalog.com/shahida-arabi/2016/05/the-love-story-of-a-narcissist-and-his-victim/

Arabi, S. (2019, April 4). 20 diversion tactics highly manipulative narcissists, sociopaths and psychopaths use to silence you. *Thought Catalog*. https://thoughtcatalog.com/shahida-arabi/2016/06/20-diversion-tactics-highly-manipulative-narcissists-sociopaths-and-psychopaths-use-to-silence-you/

Aristotle. (1943). *The Nicomachean Ethics* (H. Rackham, trans.). Basil Blackwell & Mott. (Original work written 340 BCE).

Auvinen, T., Lämsä, A. M., Sintonen, T., & Takala, T. (2013, August 1). Leadership manipulation and ethics in storytelling. *Journal of Business Ethics*. https://www.researchgate.net/publication/257541869_Leadership_Manipulation_and_Ethics_in_Storytelling/citation/download

Bacon, F. (2012) Meditationes sacrae. In *Wikisource*. https://en.wikisource.org/wiki/Meditationes_sacrae (Originally published 1597).

Bariso, J. (2016, August 23). 10 ways manipulators use emotional intelligence for evil (and how to fight back). *Inc*. https://www.inc.com/justin-bariso/10-ways-manipulators-use-emotional-intelligence-for-evil-and-how-to-fight-back.html

Brenner, A. (2016, October 27). 9 classic traits of manipulative people. *Psychology Today*. https://www.psychologytoday.com/us/blog/in-flux/201610/9-classic-traits-manipulative-people

Brown, F. (2019, December 19) Investigation finds '88% of Tory ads misleading compared to 0% for labour. *Metro*. https://metro.co.uk/2019/12/10/investigation-finds-88-tory-ads-misleading-compared-0-labour-11651802/

Brown, L. (2018, June 12). 10 disturbing signs of emotional manipulation that people are missing. *Ideapod.* https://ideapod.com/signs-emotional-manipulation/

Burke, E. (1790). Reflections on the revolution in France. *McMaster University Archives.* https://socialsciences.mcmaster.ca/econ/ugcm/3ll3/burke/revfrance.pdf

Bussing, K. (2020). 13 signs you're dealing with a psychopath. *Reader's Digest.* https://www.rd.com/health/conditions/signs-of-a-psychopath/page/2/

Carver, J. (2018, October 15). Personality disorders. *Mental Health Matters.* https://mental-health-matters.com/personality-disorders-controllers-abusers-manipulators-users-relationships/

Chinn, K. A. (2017, September 7) Can manipulation be used in a positive way? *Go1.* https://www.go1.com/blog/post-can-use-manipulation-good

Chivers, T. (2017, August 26). How to spot a psychopath. *The Daily Telegraph.* https://www.telegraph.co.uk/books/non-fiction/spot-psychopath/

Chung, K. (2017, October). The dark triad. *Edinburgh Napier University.* https://www.napier.ac.uk/~/media/worktribe/output-1031400/the-dark-triad-examining-judgement-accuracy-the-role-of-vulnerability-and-linguistic.pdf

Coons, C., & Weber, M. (2014, August). Manipulation: Theory and practice. *Oxford Scholarship Online.* https://www.oxfordscholarship.com/view/10.1093/acprof:oso/9780199338207.001.0001/acprof-9780199338207

Coughlan, S. (2018, June 26). Narcissists 'irritating but successful.' *BBC News.* https://www.bbc.com/news/education-44601198

Cukor, G. (1944). *Gaslight.* [Motion picture]. MGM.

Davies, J. (2017, April 5). 20 most common manipulation techniques used by predators. *Learning Mind.* https://www.learning-mind.com/manipulation-techniques/

Demosthenes. (n.d.). Public Quotes. http://publicquotes.com/quote/20328/every-advantage-in-the-past-is-judged-in-the-light-of-the-final-issue.html

Depression Alliance Staff (2018). Famous narcissists. *Depression Alliance.* https://www.depressionalliance.org/famous-narcissists/

Dick, P. K. (2002). Minority report. *Citadel Press Books.* https://d3gxp3iknbs7bs.cloudfront.net/attachments/42055afc4cb3e9c1ed90f1da5a9dd42c9754c9ca.pdf

Dockrill, P. (2018, September 27). Scientists have identified the driving force behind all your darkest impulses. *Science Alert.* https://www.sciencealert.com/scientists-identified-driving-force-behind-all-your-darkest-impulses-personality-traits-triad-psychopathy-narcissism-machiavellianism

Dodgson, L. (2017, July 7). Here's why CEOs often have the traits of a psychopath. *Business Insider.* https://www.businessinsider.com/ceos-often-have-psychopathic-traits-2017-7?r=US&IR=T

Dodgson, L. (2018, June 26). Narcissists are actually really successful, research finds. *Inc.* https://www.inc.com/business-insider/narcissists-more-successful-research-psychology.html

Dodgson, L. (2018, August 6). The 4 types of people narcissists are attracted to, according to a psychotherapist. *Insider.* https://www.insider.com/the-types-of-people-narcissists-are-attracted-to-2018-8

Du Maurier, G. (2009). *Trilby* (E. Showalter, Ed.). Oxford Classics.

Eddy, B. (2018, August 1). 3 steps to identifying a narcissist. *Psychology Today.* https://www.psychologytoday.com/us/blog/5-types-people-who-can-ruin-your-life/201808/3-steps-identifying-narcissist

Elder, L., & Paul, R. (2004). Fallacies: The art of mental trickery and manipulation. *The Foundation for Critical Thinking.* https://www.criticalthinking.org/files/SAM-Fallacies1.pdf

Ellis, B.E. (1991). *American Psycho.* Picador.

Enderle, R. (2017, June). The art of manipulation and misdirection. *TechNewsWorld.* https://www.technewsworld.com/story/84616.html

Eyal, N. (2012, July 2). The art of manipulation. *Forbes.* https://www.forbes.com/sites/nireyal/2012/07/02/the-art-of-manipulation/#2fa6793d5009

Flippin, W. E., Jr. (2012, April 6). Ubuntu: Applying African philosophy in building community. *Huffington Post.* https://www.huffpost.com/entry/ubuntu-applying-african-p_b_1243904

Garvey, J. & Stangroom, J. (2008). *The greatest philosophers.* Capella.

Ginsberg, L. & Huddleston, T., Jr. (2019, March). The psychology of deception. *CNBC.* https://www.cnbc.com/2019/03/20/hbos-the-inventor-how-elizabeth-holmes-fooled-people-about-theranos.html

Grayling, A. C. (2009, November 25). The art of manipulation: When people become mere pawns in a game. *The Independent.* https://www.independent.co.uk/voices/commentators/a-c-grayling-the-art-of-manipulation-when-people-become-mere-pawns-in-a-game-1820853.html

Hanson, E. (n.d.). Kant, Immanuel: Radical evil. *Internet Encyclopedia of Philosophy.* https://www.iep.utm.edu/rad-evil/

Hilbig, B. E., Moshagen, M., & Zettler, I. (2018). What is D? *D: The Dark Factor of Personality.* https://www.darkfactor.org/

Hill, R. (2015, March 2). How to manipulate people: Expert manipulation techniques. *Psychologium.* https://www.psychologium.com/7-ways-to-manipulate-someone-to-do-anything-you-want/

Hirstein, W. (2017, June 8). 9 clues you may be dealing with a psychopath. *Psychology Today.* https://www.psychologytoday.com/us/blog/mindmelding/201706/9-clues-you-may-be-dealing-psychopath

Holland, K. (2018, February 2013). How to recognize the signs of emotional manipulation and what to do. *Healthline*. https://www.healthline.com/health/mental-health/emotional-manipulation

How to detect each of the 9 dark personality types recognized by psychologists. (2018, September 8). Code. https://www.lifecoachcode.com/2018/09/08/the-9-dark-personality-types-psychologists/

Jacobson, S. (2015, January 8). What is Machiavellianism in psychology? *Harley Therapy Counselling Blog*. https://www.harleytherapy.co.uk/counselling/machiavellianism-psychology.htm

Kane, S. (2018, October 8). How to recognize a psychopath. *PsychCentral*. https://psychcentral.com/lib/how-to-recognize-a-psychopath/

Kingsley, J. (n.d.) Styles of leadership — Do you motivate or manipulate? *Jeremy Kingsley*. http://jeremykingsley.com/styles-of-leadership-do-you-motivate-or-manipulate/

Kubrick, S. (1980). *The Shining*. [Motion picture]. The Producer Circle Company.

Lancer, D. (2018, December) Beware the dark triad. *PsychCentral*. https://psychcentral.com/lib/beware-of-the-dark-triad/

Le Bon, G. (2018). *Psychologie des foules* (G.Shinri, Ed). Kuro Savoir.

Lectures 1808-1819 on literature 2: 315. (n.d.). Shakespeare Navigators. https://shakespeare-navigators.com/othello/motiveless.html

Markarian, T. (n.d.) 15 of the most famous psychopaths in history. *Reader's Digest*. https://www.rd.com/culture/most-famous-psychopaths-in-history/

Machiavelli, N. (1981). *The Prince*. (G. Bull, Trans.). Penguin Classics.

Manipulation. (2019, March 26). Good Therapy. https://www.goodtherapy.org/blog/psychpedia/manipulation

Marlowe, C. (1990). *The Jew of Malta* (T.W. Craik, Ed.). New Mermaids.

Mcardle, R. (2018, January). Modern mind control: Public opinion manipulation in our online world. *Enigma*. https://www.usenix.org/node/208126

Murphy, B., Jr. (2015, December 7). 11 psychological tricks to manipulate people, ranked in order of pure evilness. *Inc*. https://www.inc.com/bill-murphy-jr/evil-psychological-tricks-to-manipulate-people.html

Noggle, R. (2018, March 30). The ethics of manipulation. *The Stanford Encyclopedia of Philosophy*. https://plato.stanford.edu/archives/sum2018/entries/ethics-manipulation

Nuccitelli, M. (2020) iPredator inc. DMCA take down policy. *iPredator*. https://www.ipredator.co/ipredator-inc-dmca-policy/

Orwell, G. (1987). *1984*. Penguin.

Personality traits in victims. (2020). The Sociopathic Style. https://sociopathicstyle.com/personality-traits-in-victims/

Phillips, T. (2019). *Joker*. [Motion picture]. Warner Bros. & DC Films.

Pinola, M. (2012, October 19). Three of the easiest ways to manipulating people into doing what you want. *Lifehacker*. https://lifehacker.com/three-of-the-easiest-ways-to-manipulate-people-into-doi-5953183

Psychology Behind. (2017, October 30). Psychology behind the art of manipulation. *Medium*. https://medium.com/@PsychBehind/psychology-behind-the-art-of-manipulation-d9e0bdd6d8d3

Rauthmann, J. F. & Kolar, G. P. (2012, November). How "dark" are the dark triad traits? Examining the perceived darkness of narcissism, Machiavellianism, and psychopathy. *Personality and Individual Differences, 53*(7), 884-889. https://doi.org/10.1016/j.paid.2012.06.020

Robson, D. (2015, January 20). Psychology: the man who studies everyday evil. *BBC Future*.https://www.bbc.com/future/article/20150130-the-man-who-studies-evil

Sălceanu, C. (2014). Personality factors and resistance to the manipulation of advertising. *Science Direct*. https://www.sciencedirect.com/science/article/pii/S1877042814022939

Sarkis, S. (2019, June 19). Know the "dark triad" to avoid workplace chaos. *Forbes*. https://www.forbes.com/sites/stephaniesarkis/2019/06/16/know-the-dark-triad-to-prevent-workplace-chaos/#587b7747555f

Seltzer, L. F., (2014, April 23). The vampire's bite: Victims of narcissists speak out. *Psychology Today*. https://www.psychologytoday.com/us/blog/evolution-the-self/201404/the-vampire-s-bite-victims-narcissists-speak-out

Shakespeare, W. (1984) *Othello* (M. R. Ridley, Ed.). The Arden Shakespeare.

Shakespeare, W. (1986) *Hamlet*. (H. Jenkins, Ed.). The Arden Shakespeare.

Shortsleeve, C. (2018, October). How to tell if someone is manipulating you — And what to do about it. *Time*. https://time.com/5411624/how-to-tell-if-being-manipulated/

Smith, D. (2019, June 2). The Steve Jobs guide to manipulating people and getting what you want. *Business Insider*. https://www.businessinsider.fr/us/steve-jobs-guide-to-getting-what-you-want-2016-10

Stieg, C. (2019, October 31). Narcissists are happier, tougher and less stressed, according to science. *CNBC*. https://www.cnbc.com/2019/10/31/study-narcissists-tend-to-be-happier-tougher-and-less-stressed.html

Stosny, S. (2008, August 26). Effects of emotional abuse. *Psychology Today*. https://www.psychologytoday.com/intl/blog/anger-in-the-age-entitlement/200808/effects-emotional-abuse-it-hurts-when-i-love

The dark triad: Narcissism, Machiavellianism and psychopathy. (2018, June). Exploring your mind. https://exploringyourmind.com/the-dark-triad-narcissism-machiavellianism-and-psychopathy/

The golden rule. (2020, February 16). In *Wikipedia*. https://en.wikipedia.org/wiki/Golden_Rule

The Mind Tools Content Team. (n.d.). Understanding the dark triad. *Mind Tools*. https://www.mindtools.com/pages/article/understanding-dark-triad.htm

Thomas, J (2019, June 6). The dark triad in the workplace: How to manage difficult personality types. *Toggl*. https://blog.toggl.com/dark-triad-in-the-workplace/

Throne, I. (2015, November 19). Seven terrifying dark triad men from history. *Dark Triad Man*. https://darktriadman.com/2015/11/19/seven-terrifying-dark-triad-men-history/

Tracy, N. (2012, July 24). Effects of emotional abuse on adults. *Healthy Place.* https://www.healthyplace.com/abuse/emotional-psychological-abuse/effects-of-emotional-abuse-on-adults

Tucker, A. (2013, January). Are babies born good? *Smithsonian Magazine.* https://www.smithsonianmag.com/science-nature/are-babies-born-good-165443013/

Tucker, A. & Mildmay, Sir H. P. St. J. (1805) *The light of nature pursued.* Philosophy, *2.* https://books.google.je/books?id=4GorAAAAYAAJ&printsec=frontcover#v=o nepage&q&f

University of Copenhagen. (2018, September 26). Scientists define the 'dark core of personality.' *Science Daily.* https://www.sciencedaily.com/releases/2018/09/180926110841.htm

Vyasa, (1989). *Mahabharata* (C. Rajagopslschari, Trans.) Bharatiya Vidya Bhavan.

Weller, C. (2014, March 6). What's the difference between a sociopath and a psychopath? (Not much, but one might kill you). *Medical Daily.* https://www.medicaldaily.com/whats-difference-between-sociopath-and-psychopath-not-much-one-might-kill-you-270694

West, D. (2016, Jun 23). How does Iago manipulate Othello? *Studymoose.* https://studymoose.com/how-does-iago-manipulate-othello-essay

What is psychological manipulation? (2019, July). Band Back Together. https://bandbacktogether.com/master-resource-links-2/abuse-resources/psychological-manipulation-resources/

Whitman, W. (1855). *Song of Myself.* Poets.org. https://poets.org/poem/song-myself-1-i-celebrate-myself

Yarrow, K. (2016, September 29). The science of how marketers and politicians manipulate us. *Money.* http://money.com/money/4511709/marketing-politicians-manipulation-psychology/

Zivaljevic, A. (n.d.) Positive manipulation theory. *Mix Prize.* https://www.mixprize.org/sites/default/files/media/posts/documents/Positive%20%20Manipulation%20Theory.pdf

Masters of Emotional Blackmail

Understanding and Dealing with Verbal Abuse and Emotional Manipulation. How Manipulators Use Guilt, Fear, Obligation, and Other Tactics to Control People

Emory Green

TABLE OF CONTENTS

INTRODUCTION

Are they difficult, or are they toxic? I'm talking about relationships with people close and dear. No matter how close-knit relationships are, some can be quite challenging. But, some might even have transformed into a toxic relationship without you being aware of it.

However, you can determine if your relationships are healthy or toxic.

A healthy relationship requires sincerity and compassion from both ends. It helps the two involved to evolve and grow into confident and kind personalities. But what if you start feeling suffocated and controlled in a relationship? What if your needs don't matter in a relationship you rely on? Worst of all, you don't feel safe and supported to express your feelings. That makes up for a toxic relationship. Such a relationship can tear down your self-esteem to the bottom.

However, it's not easy to identify a toxic relationship. Even more so, when those relationships are dear to you. You rely on them for all your emotional support. They are the backbone of your emotional well-being. Yet, they have turned poisonous.

It's not easy to identify toxicity in relationships because the people around you, the ones you love the most, may use tactics. Tactics to manipulate you in a way that seems harmless, though they aren't. They may use them to manipulate you and get what they want. In short, they may blackmail you emotionally. But why can't you easily identify that you are being emotionally blackmailed? Simply because the blackmailers use covert techniques to manipulate you.

They may make their demands seem reasonable, or make you feel selfish, or use a person of influence to intimidate you.

Ultimately, you feel pressured to give in. It becomes difficult for you to stand up for yourself, your needs, and your opinions. As a result, you endure the toxic relationship for fear of losing your loved one. The relationship and the blackmailer take over you, over your mind, intellect, and feelings. You feel frustrated, but there's nothing you can do.

Well, that's what you think and feel until now. However, there's always a ray of hope amongst the darkest of holes.

Your ray of hope is right here. It's in the secret I'll reveal in this book. A secret that helps you understand.

Understand what emotional blackmail is, what is the mindset of these blackmailers, what drives them towards emotional blackmailing, why they behave the way they do, and what shapes up the personality of these blackmailing vampires. Once you know this, I guarantee you can easily safeguard yourself from getting emotionally manipulated.

Also, if you gain an insight into the covert techniques these blackmailers use, you'll easily identify the fingerprints of emotional blackmail. How these blackmailers use words and phrases that fog your mind; how they compel you to think that they are right and you are wrong. You'll identify the methods used by blackmailing vampires to take advantage of you to get what they want.

Finally, I'll give you simple and practical steps to change this dynamic and pull yourself from the clutches of emotional blackmail. Following these tips will help you defeat emotional blackmail and regain your lost power over those who manipulate you.

How could I tell you this secret? Am I a relationship guru?

Well, ascribe it to my experience, observation, and study exploring the depths of dark psychology and covert manipulation, emotional manipulation, and blackmail. I have been exploring the tactics of motivation, persuasion, manipulation, and coercion that people use to get what they want.

My own experience led me to do so. I had been the victim of the severest form of emotional manipulation in my younger years. I have witnessed emotional abuse in a very intense form. It enslaved me with feelings of guilt for years. My heart pounded with the stigma of seeing emotional manipulation in front of me, yet staying silent about it.

Nevertheless, I got an opportunity to explore. To see and to understand what makes emotional blackmail so powerful. What is it that makes it the trickiest and prevalent form of manipulation to know and understand, especially in our close-knit relationships?

I also learned about the powerful tools, the tactics, the subtle techniques these blackmailers use to reign over our emotions. How they use our weakness against us to manipulate and get what they want.

In this book, I'm going to reveal all that I learned. If you are in a similar predicament, I don't want you to be a victim for one day longer.

Do you feel yourself being torn apart to the core, that this is being caused by one you love the most? Do you find others seizing control over your emotions? Then, you are definitely being targeted by all sorts of manipulative and coercive tactics people use to take advantage of you. But no more!

Reading this book will not only make you aware of such manipulative tactics, but also puts a sword in your hands. A sword, a powerful weapon that you can use to safeguard and protect yourself from the emotional savagery of such people.

What I'm going to reveal between these pages will empower you to define your boundaries, and will give you mental resilience to stop being taken advantage of. Not only will you feel strong, but you'll be mentally and emotionally prepared to handle such vampires and lead a peaceful life.

Understanding the techniques of those blackmailers will also help you in some self-introspection. What I mean is you'll be able to assess your own tactics in various walks of life – work, family, romantic relationships, and friendships. You can avoid the trap of being a blackmailer yourself.

Don't get me wrong when I say that. But, it's so extremely easy to fall prey to these tactics that we might even use them ourselves unknowingly. We might not only be on the receiving end of such methods, but we might also be an offender.

That's why I began tracing those methods that transform us or others from 'being human' to 'being a blackmailing vampire.' My intention in writing this book was - and still is - to pull as many people as possible from the grasp of emotional blackmail and help them lead a joyous life.

And I'm experiencing the realization of that intention every single day when I proudly bring freedom to hundreds of people by exposing these tricks.

Imagine! Imagine your life without that emotional blackmailer. No guilt, no shame, no fear, and no doubts. No more hurting or apologizing for things you didn't do. The very idea feels great! Doesn't it?

Now, turn that imagination to reality by traveling through the pages of this book that teaches you A-Z about emotional blackmail. It will remove all haze and fog from your mind and reveal the truth about your relationships. You'll be able to see your loved ones, not just for who they are, but also their intentions.

And once you see the truth, it sets you free. Free from the guilt, shame, and obligations you have been carrying for long.

So, are you ready to learn the truth of your relationship?

Before moving forward, answer this question: Is your relationship just difficult, or is it toxic? The sooner you answer, the better. Otherwise, it might be too late to fix a relationship that may blossom into something good, or too late to run from a captive relationship. The decision is yours, whether you want to be stuck with a dark relationship for your life, or take advantage of the lessons I teach in this book to build healthy relationships.

If you choose the second one, you'll come to know the genuine happiness and freedom that awaits you.

Enjoying this book so far? Remember to head to the last page of this book bundle for a bonus bite-sized yet valuable free resource on Conversational Hypnosis. This mini e-book is the easiest way to learn how to be a successful conversational hypnotist. Curious about the benefits it can do to your normal day to day conversations? Get your copy now! This free resource is available for a limited time only

CHAPTER ONE

Emotional Blackmail in Black and White

What is emotional blackmail?

By definition, emotional blackmail is an act of controlling the person with whom you have an emotional connection. This control is by using tactics that make him/her feel guilty or upset. Put simply, when any person uses your feelings (in a negative way or against you) to control your behavior or seek what he wants, it's called emotional blackmail. You can be emotionally blackmailed by your spouse, parents, children, siblings, friends, colleagues, or anyone close to you without realizing that you are being manipulated.

But why am I using the word 'emotional blackmail' and not just 'blackmail'? That's because the two are different.

Blackmail vs. Emotional Blackmail

What comes to your mind when you think of blackmail?

Probably, a movie where the villain blackmails the hero or an employee who blackmails his boss to get things in his favor.

OR

You might observe some examples of blackmail in your daily routine. A school kid threatens his classmate that he'll beat him up if the classmate complains about him. A co-worker knows some private information about his colleague and threatens to reveal it in exchange for a small fee.

To sum up, blackmail is usually associated with criminal activities, or forcefully persuading someone to give something, or follow the blackmailer's way, in return for not exposing the information that might be harmful or compromising about that person.

Yes, you understand the idea of blackmail, but what about the concept of emotional blackmail? Do you understand it as well as blackmail? Are you able to tell when it is happening to you?

I'm asking this because it's important to grasp the meaning of emotional blackmail; to understand its relevance in interpersonal relationships and society. Understanding the method is also the first step in eliminating its effectiveness, its power over you.

As previously defined, an emotional blackmailer uses your feelings against you; to control your behavior the way they want or to seek their intended objective. So the threat here is not tangible. Your feelings are used against you in emotional blackmail.

Let's get clearer with a few examples.

The husband gets caught cheating on his wife, yet he spins the circumstances, making his wife feel guilty and inadequate. He uses drama to emotionally blackmail her, and feel sorry about doubting her husband.

This situation is commonly seen in the corporate world. When one person climbs the ladder of success higher than the other person, even if they deserve it, they receive emotional blackmail for achieving so much. This may rob that person of joy, pride, and self-esteem.

One partner joins a fitness program and achieves great success with their fitness goals. The other partner may emotionally blackmail them and make them feel guilty for not spending time with them.

Strategies of emotional blackmail

An emotional blackmailer uses three main emotions against you – fear, obligation, and guilt coined into an acronym, FOG by Susan Forward, one of the USA's leading psychotherapists. For a blackmailer to be successful, he/she must know about your fears, the deep-rooted ones like fear of isolation, humiliation, or failure. The most interesting part is that these fears might be unique to you. No one else perceives them as a threat from the blackmailer except you. This gives a chance to the blackmailer to threaten you to isolate you, ridicule you in front of others, or expose your past failure if you don't succumb to his desires.

Obligation is yet another favorite tactic used by these addicts. They justify their addiction by blaming others. Instead of taking up the responsibility for their wrong behavior, they project it onto others. For example, a habitual drinker may threaten his wife by saying, "If you kick me out of the house, I'll be forced to drink more." The innocent wife believes and hopes that her husband will stop drinking if she obeys him, but it's just a trap she falls into.

Guilt-tripping is used by blackmailers to make their target feel guilty about causing some negative outcome to the blackmailer. The end result might not even be that negative, but the blackmailer presents it in such a way that the target feels pain and guilt.

The idea behind using these three emotions to control a person is that they are negative emotions, and nobody wants to experience such feelings in their life. Consequently, they give in to the demands of the blackmailer to avoid experiencing these negative feelings.

Legal definition of emotional blackmail

Emotional blackmail is a form of emotional abuse that is not legally right. That's because the blackmailer can:

- Threaten to endanger your life.
- Threaten to kill himself if you don't obey his wishes.
- Control you by using money.
- Threaten to end the relationship with you.
- Manipulate you in such a way so that you feel compassionate for him/her.
- Make you feel guilty.
- Demoralize you.
- Hurt you or make you suffer in some form.
- Deprive you of love, care, and appreciation.
- Make you feel selfish and inconsiderate.

Very tactfully and cleverly, the blackmailer makes you believe in his demands. However, the more you give in, the more the threats intensify. The only way out is to identify that you are being emotionally blackmailed. This gets easier if you know the common statements used by these emotional blackmailers to manipulate/threaten you.

Here are a few examples:

- If I ever see you with that man, I'll kill him.
- I will kill myself if you stop loving me.
- My friends and family agree with me that you're being unreasonable.
- I'm going on this vacation – with or without you.
- You can't say that you love me and still be friends with them.
- You're stopping me from spending money on myself.
- I was late for work because of you. It's your fault.
- I wouldn't be overweight if you cooked healthy food for me.

- It's your fault I'm unsuccessful in my career.
- I'll wind up in the hospital/on the street if you don't care for me.
- If you don't do this, you won't see your kids again.
- I'll make your life miserable.
- I'll destroy your family.
- You're not my son/daughter anymore.
- You'll have to feel sorry about it.
- I'll cut you out of my will.
- I'll get sick if you don't love me.
- If you can't buy me this, you're a worthless mom/dad/lover/husband.

By now, you have understood what emotional blackmail is, but it's also important to understand the mindset that drives people to use these strategies.

Why do people behave this way?

People often resort to emotional blackmail because it gives them control over other people's thoughts and feelings. They don't know how to get it another way and resort to emotional manipulation. Emotional blackmailers are very good at making their victims feel powerless and confused. They mistakenly think that by making others feel helpless and vulnerable, they'll feel powerful and good about themselves. In other words, emotional blackmail is their way of dealing with their emotional insecurities. Insecurities that might stem from an emotionally abusive childhood.

If you look into the history of these individuals, you'll often find them on the receiving end of emotional manipulation as a child. This makes it very hard for such people to know what is normal and what is not. They can't understand what a healthy relationship is and how to build one themselves. They had been bought up seeing emotional blackmail from parents, and consider that it is the right way to get things done. They find a remedy for their insecurities in repeating the cycle themselves.

Emotional blackmailers share some common personality traits:

1. Lack of empathy

It's usually not too hard for us to imagine ourselves in the other person's shoes and feel his agony, his pain, and empathize with him. But that's not so with emotional blackmailers. They can't have real empathy with others. Either they can't imagine themselves in the other person's shoes, or even if they do, it's from a position of distrust. They think that the other person is going to harm them, and thus, they are justified in manipulating them.

2. Low self-esteem

Low self-esteem? In emotional blackmailers? Are you serious?

They are capable of robbing others of their self-esteem via emotional manipulation. So how could they have low self-esteem?

I know it sounds a bit weird, but that's the truth. As explained previously, emotional blackmailers are often emotionally insecure and have low levels of self-worth. Instead of finding ways to raise their self-esteem, they believe in lowering that of others to feel good. Low self-esteem also means such people struggle to form close relationships. They might have just one close relationship and look up to it to give all the things they are missing elsewhere. This is their dependency on a relationship, and if they feel they are going to lose it, they resort to more intense emotional blackmail.

3. Tendency to blame others

Emotional blackmailers never take up the responsibility for the problems in their relationship or a failure in their careers. They always hold others responsible for their pain and suffering. Such logic makes them feel justified in threatening others to get what they want.

Chapter Summary

1. Emotional blackmail is a form of abuse where the blackmailer tries to control the other person's feelings and behavior.
2. The blackmailer uses fear, obligation, and guilt to manipulate the victim.
3. Such people lack self-esteem and empathy and blame others for their bad relationships.
4. To know if you are subject to this in your relationship, ask yourself these questions:
5. Does my partner say or do things to make me feel guilty for actions that aren't wrong?
6. Does my partner point out negative things related to my success?
7. Does my partner seek a way to bring my mood down?
8. Does my partner frequently make me feel fear, obligation, or guilt?

If you answer 'Yes' to these questions, you're definitely being emotionally blackmailed.

In the next chapter, you will learn….

- Six Progressive Steps in Emotional Blackmail.
- Common Types of Emotional Blackmailers.
- Warning Signs and Characteristics of Emotional Blackmailer.
- Blackmailer Personalities.
- Key Characteristics and Emotions of Victims.
- How to change the dynamics of blackmailer and victim transaction.

CHAPTER TWO:

The Blackmailer and the Victim Transaction

Are you feeling empowered with the knowledge gained so far? Well, you must be because now it's easy for you to pin-point the instances of emotional blackmail in your life. However, there's a common misconception people have about this situation. They tend to label every person who tries to control them as an emotional blackmailer. But common sense tells us this is not true.

If the person wants to be loved, valued, supported, or appreciated by you, he might act in a controlling way. And his wants are absolutely legitimate. Also note that demands will be made on you in any relationship, if not all the time, at least sometimes.

And it's very common to disagree with someone's demands at first, and then come to a mutual agreement, or comply with the other person's wishes even if you don't like to. But, you may do it for the love of your relationship and the other person.

The problem is not in his *'wants'* but how he goes about getting what he wants. Does he threaten you or become insensitive to your needs in doing so? Then, you can justifiably say it's a case of emotional blackmail, otherwise not.

Let's understand this with an example!

Ahana wants an iPhone from her Mom, but Mom refuses. Now, Ahana may try to get it in two ways. She may persuade her Mom by saying, "But, Sara's mom bought her an iPhone." This is clearly not an emotional blackmail. But, if she grabs a knife and threatens to kill herself if her Mom doesn't buy her an iPhone, we are in a very different place, and it's an emotional blackmail without a doubt. So the problem here is not the iPhone, but the method used to try and obtain it. It's that which helps us to analyze whether it's emotional blackmailing or not.

Moreover, if it always comes about that someone is giving in to the other's demands, then the situation has reached one of emotional blackmail.

An emotional blackmail is sometimes a transaction, perhaps even an unconscious one, between the blackmailer and the victim. The blackmailer is the *'controller'* who suffers from a dysfunctional psychological state, and who tries to control another person's emotions. The victim is the *'controlled'* who provides a reassuring reaction to this psychological state.

This transaction has 6 parts, as detailed below.

6 progressive steps in emotional blackmail

Susan Forward and Frazier identify these six stages of emotional blackmail:

Step 1: The demand

The blackmailer tells the victim (that's you) about what they want and adds an emotional threat to it. "If you don't do this, I'll kill myself."

Step 2: Resistance

Of course, you may well decline to bow down in front of the blackmailer's demands. So, initially, you resist the demand.

Step 3: Pressure

The blackmailer can't accept 'No.' So, he builds pressure upon you to give in. They don't care about how you'll feel. They are only concerned with what they want and try to grab it by hook or by crook. In consequence, they deliberately try to make you feel scared and confused by using any of their covert strategies. You begin to wonder if your initial resistance was reasonable. That's where you become weak, and they latch on to your weakness.

Step 4: A threat

A threat is the emotional blackmail itself with a statement, "If you don't do as I say, then I will…"

Step 5: Compliance

You give in to the blackmailer's threat even though you don't feel happy about it.

Step 6: Setting of a pattern

The emotional blackmail is over, but only for now. Expect a heavier demand with a much bigger threat the next time. This is because the blackmailer has identified your weak area, and he knows he can use it against you to get what he wants.

The most prevalent example showcasing these stages of emotional blackmail might even be your child. How often do you get an unreasonable demand from your son/daughter? I'm sure it's uncountable. You resist initially, may even scold your child, but ultimately give in because your child threatens you by saying,

"Mom/Dad, you don't love me. Otherwise, you would have bought me this."

Result: You melt like butter and fulfill the demands without a second thought.

Can you see what your child did here? They sensed that by threatening you repeatedly with such statements, you would obey their commands and get them what they want. In short, they devise an easy way to manipulate you emotionally and have their way.

Common Emotional Blackmail Types and their Language

We can classify the emotional blackmailers into four different types:

1. Punishers

Punishers threaten to directly hurt the person they are blackmailing. They use the strategy of fear to punish you if their demands are not met. The punishment might be physical, or a financial penalty, or stopping you from seeing your friends, or withdrawing their affection, or ending their relationship with you if you don't do what they say.

A typical remark might be: "Do as I say or else I'll beat you."

2. Self-punishers

Self-punishers threaten to harm themselves as a form of blackmail and put the blame on you. They hold you responsible for doing what they do to themselves. They do so to trigger fear and guilt in you and compel you to do what they ask for.

For example, "If you don't buy me that gift, I'll kill myself."

3. Sufferers

Sufferers don't threaten you directly but will show they are sad/upset because of you. They'll blame you for their emotional state and expect you to comply with their wishes to make them feel better. Sufferers use the tactics of fear, obligation, and guilt to manipulate you.

For example, a husband says to his wife, 'You can go out with your friends if you want, but I'll feel sad and lonely if you do."

4. Tantalizers

Tantalizers also don't give direct threats, but they lure you with a promise of something better if you do what they want. Your spouse may say, "I'll buy you that necklace if you stay with me at home this weekend." However, they rarely keep their promise.

Warning signs and characteristics of an emotional blackmailer

Below are the warning signs of emotional blackmail in a relationship:

- If you frequently apologize for things you aren't doing, such as the other person's negative emotional state or outbursts.
- If your partner insists on their way and no one else's, even at the expense of other people's needs and emotions.
- It seems to be only you who is complying and making sacrifices.
- If you feel you're being threatened. If you feel intimidated into obeying the other person's demands.

As said, emotional blackmail is a vicious cycle, and as a victim, you may be inclined to apologize, plead, cry, and give in to the demands of others. But, you'll find it difficult to stand up for your needs, or address the issue directly, or communicate with the blackmailer about his inappropriate attitude. You are not able to set clear boundaries to help others know what is acceptable to you and what is not.

All this happens because you aren't aware of the characteristics of emotional blackmailers. Unless you are, you can't spot if the other person is manipulating you or not.

Any person engaging in emotional blackmail demonstrates the following characteristics:

- Insists you are crazy/unreasonable in questioning their demands.
- Tries to control what you do.
- Ignores your concerns.
- Avoids taking responsibility for his actions.
- Always blames others for their behavior.
- Gives you empty apologies.
- Uses fear, obligation, threats, and guilt to get their way.
- Not willing to compromise.
- Justifies their unreasonable behaviors and requests.
- Intimidates you until you obey their demands.
- Blames you for something you didn't do to earn your compassion.
- Threatens to harm you or themselves.

Blackmailer personalities

There's no exact prototype of emotional blackmailers, yet they demonstrate certain common characteristics.

Such people often have narcissistic tendencies or an inflated sense of self-importance. They think they are the best at everything and brag about it. Everything in their lives will center around themselves, and if this is threatened, they are prone to extreme anger, frustration, panic, or depression. Blackmailers often exhibit emotional immaturity; they're not in touch with their feelings or don't know how they exactly feel. They are likely to be people who have been on the receiving end of emotional blackmail in their early lives and have noted that it is an effective tactic.

Blackmailers have a tendency to want approval from others, often due to low self-esteem. They will create a scene out of every little issue. Although highly critical of others, they usually can't accept advice or criticism.

Some of these traits are easily visible, while some, like emotional insecurities, fear, and pain, may lie deep within their psychology.

The inner world of the blackmailer

Emotional blackmailers are cowards in a real sense. They hate to lose and can't tolerate frustration. Their frustration is connected to deep-rooted fears of loss and deprivation, and they experience it as a warning to take immediate action to avoid experiencing intolerable consequences.

Such people believe they can compensate for the frustrations of the past by changing their present. The possibilities of emotional blackmail rise significantly during crises such as separation or divorce, loss of a job, illness, and retirement, etc., any of which might undermine the blackmailer's' sense of self-worth.

It's not the crisis that makes them emotional blackmailers, rather their incapability to handle such problems. Often, you'll observe that people who are incapable of processing these issues in their life were either overprotected, or have had everything in their childhood. This gave them little opportunity to build their self-confidence and ability to handle any kind of loss. At the first hint of deprivation or loss, they either get angry or panic, and resort to blackmail to avoid experiencing that feeling.

Usually, blackmailers focus unconditionally on their desires and needs. They are least interested in other people, or how their pressure affects you. For them, each interaction with you is a make-or-break relationship scheme. If you agree to what they want, they'll stay or else withdraw from the relationship.

Blackmailers know what the relationship means to you and its importance. Therefore, they use tactics to create a potential split in the relationship. They know and realize that you won't let the relationship go. That makes you vulnerable to their manipulation.

Most blackmailers have an I-want-what-I-want-when-I-want-it attitude. And the urgency to have what they desire obscures their ability to see the consequences of their actions.

The most prominent thing to notice in a blackmailer's psyche is that they sound like it's all about you. In fact, they'll talk in a way to make you feel like it's all about you, but in reality, it's not about you at all. It's only about the blackmailer and his desires. Blackmailing flows from insecure places inside the individual doing it. Most of the time, it has to do with the blackmailer's past, rather than his present. It has to do with the blackmailer's needs, rather than with what the blackmailer says about your doings.

It takes two to blackmail

Just like it takes two to tango, it takes two for the blackmail to succeed, or even happen. The blackmailer alone can't do anything without the active participation of the victim. Unless you give the permission for the blackmail to occur, it can't happen.

Sometimes you are aware of the problem, yet you can't resist it because the blackmailer's pressure sets off a series of programmed responses in your mind, and you act out of an impulse. For example, if the blackmailer threatens to kill himself if you don't obey his commands, it doesn't leave much room for any discussion. You are immediately gripped with the fear of losing that person. You are inclined to give in, lest he takes that suicidal step. So, the blackmailer didn't even leave a space for you to think or ponder. You are bound to react impulsively.

Blackmailers are aware of your "hot" buttons. The moment you resist, the blackmailer's fear of deprivation kicks in, and they use your hot buttons to change your decision and get what they want.

So why can't you resist? Why do you play a victim to other's schemes? It's because of the characteristics that make you vulnerable.

Key characteristics and emotions of victims

Not only the blackmailers, but even victims of emotional blackmail, feel insecure, unvalued, and low about their self-worth. They doubt themselves to a damaging degree.

Victims of emotional blackmail exhibit common traits that make them vulnerable. They seek other people's approval all the time. They are afraid of anger and desire peace at any price. They often display excessive compassion and empathy. Victims of blackmail like to take the responsibility of other people's lives upon themselves. They experience high levels of self-doubt and are scared of being abandoned in any relationship they embark upon. They personalize things and generally have low self-esteem.

When you exhibit these traits repeatedly or in an extreme manner, it dooms you to the status of the 'preferred target' of an emotional blackmailer. Emotional blackmailers take cues from how you respond to daily situations or their behavior, and use them against you.

The impact of emotional blackmail

These relationships may or may not be life-threatening, but it robs the victim of his self- integrity. The victims start questioning their sense of reality. The effects of emotional blackmail on victims can be regarded as:

- Low self-esteem.
- Think poorly about themselves or believe they are of no value.
- Distorted thinking about themselves.
- Vicious cycle of blackmail and low confidence.
- The victim may even betray others to please the blackmailer.
- Feeling isolated and lonely.
- Distrust in relationships.
- Anxiety and depression.

How to change the dynamic?

After knowing the traits of the blackmailer, and yours, that makes you susceptible to emotional blackmail, it's time to spring into action. To work out how you can change this dynamic and stop being treated in this fashion.

What is necessary to stop emotional blackmail?

You must start looking at the situation in a new way. It's crucial to detach from the emotions of the blackmailer. Detachment doesn't mean becoming without feeling, but don't get distressed by their emotions. You must realize that you are being treated in a way that is not appropriate. Once you've grasped that, commit to taking care of yourself; don't allow this abusive treatment to continue. Consider the demands that are being made and how they make you uncomfortable.

Don't be tempted to give in to the pressure of the blackmailer. Set your boundaries. Take time to consider the situation from all angles, and think about the alternatives before making a decision. Have a clear vision of what you hope to achieve by changing your mindset and ways of handling the relationship.

Give due respect to your own needs first.

How to respond to emotional blackmailers?

Once you change your mindset to approach the blackmailer differently, it's time to learn the specific answers to their blackmailing statements. However, the result won't be there at the first instance. You have to practice saying these answers until they seem natural to you. Blackmailers will bombard you with visions of the extreme negative consequences of not obeying them. They'll try pressuring you to change your decision. But hold your ground.

Below are the specific ways to respond to their catastrophic statements:

1. They say: I'll land up in the hospital if you don't care for me.
    You say: That's your choice!

2. They say: You won't see your kids again.
    You say: I hope you won't do that, but I've made my decision.

3. They say: You're not my child anymore/I'll cut off my will/I'll make you suffer/You'll be sorry.
    You say: I know you're angry/upset right now. Why don't we talk again on this subject when you're less upset? Threats/suffering/tears won't work anymore.

4. They say: You're being selfish.
    You say: You're entitled to your opinion.

5. They say: How could you do this to me after all that I've done for you?
    You say: I know you won't be happy about this, but it has to be this way.

6. They say: Why are you spoiling my life?
   You say: There are no villains here. We just want different things.

7. They say: Why are you acting like this?
   You say: I know you're disappointed by this, but it's not negotiable.

Susan Forward suggests three tactics - a contract, a power statement, and a set of self-affirming phrases to stop emotional blackmail.

Contract

A contract is a list of promises you will make to yourself to stop being a victim of emotional blackmail. Take time every day to read the contract out loud to yourself.

Examples of promises:

I promise myself to no longer let fear, obligation, and guilt control my decisions.

I promise to learn and apply the strategies in this book to stop getting emotionally blackmailed.

Power statement

Create your power statement in response to that of the blackmailer, and repeat it over and over again when threatened by the manipulator. For example, "I won't do this." or "I'm not doing this." Power statements are succinct and have impact. They challenge your doubts and limiting beliefs about your capability of handling such people.

Self-affirming phrases

By giving in to the demands of the blackmailer, you may feel guilt, embarrassment, hurt, fear, shame, anxiety, anger, resentful, powerless, hopeless, etc. The only way to stop feeling these negative emotions is to start changing your thoughts. Develop some self-affirming thought-patterns to repeat whenever negative thoughts strike your mind. Ask yourself: Is the demand being made on me making me uncomfortable? Why? What part of the demand is ok and what isn't? If I comply, what will be the consequences?

Always remember SOS before responding to a demand:

STOP – take time to think about it.
OBSERVE – your reactions, thoughts, emotions, and triggers.
STRATEGIZE- analyze the demands and the potential impact of complying. Consider what you need and explore alternative options.

Since blackmailers are highly defensive, they can comment on your phrases and often escalate conflicts. Try to stay away from escalating statements, and stick with non-defensive communication such as:

- I can see that you are upset.
- I understand you are frustrated.
- I'm sorry you're angry.
- I can understand how you might see it that way.
- Let's talk about it when you feel calmer.

Handling silent blackmailers

It's easy to respond to the blackmailers who throw open threats or blackmail verbally, but what about those who sulk in silence? What can you say or do when they say nothing? This silent treatment is far more subtle than an overt attack. Sometimes, it feels nothing works with a silent blackmailer. However, if you stick to the principles of non-defensive communication, and follow these do's and don'ts, you can tackle a silent blackmailer as well.

Do's

Remember that the blackmailer you are dealing with is inadequate, powerless, and afraid that you may hurt or abandon them.

Confront them when they feel more ready to hear what you have to say. Consider writing a letter to them.

Reassure them that you'll hear their feelings without retaliating.

Be tactful and diplomatic. This assures them you won't exploit their vulnerabilities.

Say reassuring things like "I know you're angry right now, and I'll be willing to discuss this with you as soon as you're ready to talk about it," Then leave them alone. You'll only make them withdraw more if you don't.

Tell them openly that their behavior is upsetting you, but begin by expressing appreciation. For example: "Mom, I really care about you, and I think you're one of the smartest people I know, but it really bothers me when you clam up every time we disagree about something and just walk away. It's hurting our relationship, and I wonder if you would talk to me about that."

Don't be deflected from the issue you're upset about. Stay focused.

Expect to be attacked when you express a grievance. The blackmailer will experience your assertion as an attack on them.

Let them know that you know they're angry and what you can do about it.

Accept the fact that you'll have to make the first move most of the time.

Let some things slide by.

Don'ts

Expect them to make the first move towards resolving the conflict.

Plead with them to tell you what's wrong.

Keep after them for a response (which will only make them withdraw more).

Criticize, analyze, or interpret their motives, character, or inability to be direct.

Willingly accept their blame for whatever they're upset about to get them into a better mood.

Allow them to change the subject of discussion.

Get intimidated by the tension and anger in the air.

Let your frustration cause you to make threats you don't mean (e.g., "If you don't tell me what's wrong, I'll never speak to you again").

Assume that if they ultimately apologize, it will be followed by any significant change in their behavior.

Expect major personality changes, even if they recognize what they're doing and are willing to work on it.

Emotional blackmail is a painful and dysfunctional form of abuse that can tear you apart. You might feel stuck in a toxic relationship with such an abuser. But, if you hold on, and use the above tactics to respond to their threats, it will help you stop and prevent emotional blackmail in your relationships.

Chapter Summary

1. Every person who makes a demand on you in a relationship is not an emotional blackmailer.
2. It's not the demands that make a person an emotional blackmailer, rather how he goes about fulfilling those demands.
3. An emotional blackmail is a transaction between the blackmailer and the victim. The blackmailer is the *'controller'* of the victim's emotions.
4. Emotional blackmail starts with placing a demand by the blackmailer to which the victim resists. However, the resistance is short-lived as the blackmailer threatens and pressurizes the victim to comply with his wishes by using the tactics of fear, obligation, and guilt. This sets a pattern for repeated pressure on the victim.
5. Emotional blackmailers can be classified into four categories - punishers who threaten to hurt the victim, self-punishers who threaten to hurt themselves, sufferers who blame the victim for their bad emotional state, and tantalizers who lure the victim with false promises.
6. All emotional blackmailers exhibit some common characteristics - narcissistic tendency, low self-esteem, fear of losing and abandonment, deep anger, panic, frustration, and depression, emotional immaturity, and lack of accountability.
7. Emotional blackmail can't happen unless the preferred target of the blackmailer accepts the threat and gives in.
8. Certain traits make you susceptible to emotional blackmail by others - low self-esteem, seeking approval from others, being extremely compassionate, extreme pity for others, fear of isolation, and taking on other's responsibility on your shoulders.

9. Emotional blackmail may be life-threatening or can torment the victim mentally and emotionally.

10. The only way to stop being emotionally blackmailed is to change your mindset and your approach towards the blackmailer. Setting clear boundaries, and using non-defensive communication goes a long way in handling emotional blackmail successfully.

In the next chapter, you will learn....

• The FOG - Tactics used by emotional blackmailers.

• Projection of emotional blackmail: blame, guilt, and shame.

• The emotional tools of blackmailers.

CHAPTER THREE

Blackmailing Basic Tactics

After knowing the traits of emotional blackmailers and of your tendencies that make you susceptible to manipulation, it's time to dive deep into the tactics used by these blackmailers.

Do you know who popularized the term 'emotional blackmail'?

The leading therapists and psychologists, Susan Forward and Donna Frazier. They also introduced the concept of fear, obligation, and guilt, or the FOG. Let's know more about this FOG!

The FOG

FOG is the technique emotional blackmailers use and rely on for success. That's because their victims feel scared of them, obligated to them, or guilty of not doing what they've asked. The blackmailer knows these feelings of their victims, and soon captures their emotional triggers to allow his blackmailing to work. FOG represents the combination of three strategies that manipulators use to blackmail their victims. They can use either one, or all three, unless the victim succumbs to their demands. It stands for fear, obligation, and guilt.

Being aware of these tactics used by the emotional blackmailers will help you not to behave in a manner they want. It will help you escape manipulation and exploitation at the hands of such a person.

The three techniques used by blackmailers are:

They use your fears (F)

What's fear?

It's an emotion, a feeling that we experience when we anticipate that something bad will happen, like the fear of losing our loved ones. However, this fear also protects us from danger. Unfortunately, some people use this fear to manipulate you and make you comply with their demands. To blackmail you emotionally, the blackmailers use different kind of fears, such as:

- Fear of the unknown.
- Fear of isolation.
- Fear of making someone upset.
- Fear of confrontation.
- Fear of tricky situations.
- Fear of your physical safety.

Example: The husband knows that his wife is having an extra-marital affair with another man. He has caught them together red-handed. Yet, he can't ask his wife to stop seeing the other man because he **fears** that if he does, the wife will leave him.

They use your sense of obligation (O)

A relationship is a commitment. You are morally bound to the person with whom you are in a relationship. That's your obligation. But, when the same person uses this sense of obligation to manipulate you, to press your emotional triggers, and force you to comply with their wishes, it becomes an emotional blackmail.

For example, your partner may pressure you, and ask for what they want by reminding you of all the things they have done for you, or the sacrifices they made. This makes you duty-bound to do what they want, even if you don't like it.

They make you feel guilty (G)

If you don't comply with the blackmailer's demands, even when they use your sense of obligation, they'll use their next tactic, which is guilt-tripping. The blackmailer will make you feel guilty for not keeping up your promises as per the obligation. They'll make it seem like you deserve to be punished. For instance, you may be guilt-tripped for being happy when your partner is feeling low; you are being emotionally blackmailed.

FOG technique resides in the dark. It stems from emotions and not logical thinking on the part of the blackmailer.

However, as discussed in the last chapter, it takes two to blackmail. If you refuse to play hostage to the fear, obligation, and guilt used by this person, install personal limits, take care of yourself, and don't get blinded by your emotions, you can prevent yourself from being captivated by the blackmailer's demands.

Once he fails to captivate or manipulate you, he's less likely to try these tactics again.

What makes you hostage to the blackmailer's FOG technique?

Besides the traits that make you a victim of emotional blackmail, you fall prey to the FOG technique because of these reasons:

The need to please people - You end up giving in to the emotional blackmailer so that the other person is not angry with you. Since you are vulnerable at this point, you feel that the unjustified and unloving treatment you receive is right. You feel guilty of making the other person angry.

Wearing you down - Constant compromise in a relationship, giving in to someone's demands that don't align with your own needs and desires, can wear you down. This makes you more susceptible to emotional manipulation by FOG technique.

Fear of anger and retaliation - Most people fear other people's anger and retaliation. This fear is a powerful driving force towards becoming a victim of emotional blackmail.

Emotional manipulation by people suffering from BPD

BPD stands for borderline personality disorder. It's a mental health disorder that impacts the way the patient thinks and feels about himself and others, causing disturbance in day-to-day life. People suffering from this mental illness have self-image issues, difficulty in managing their emotions and behavior, and an intense fear of abandonment. In short, they can't tolerate being alone.

Signs and symptoms of BPD include:

- An intense fear of abandonment, so much so that the person can take extreme measures to avoid real or imagined separation.
- Having unstable intense relationships. For example, the patient may idealize someone at one moment, and then suddenly believe that the person doesn't care for them.
- Self-identity issues and seeing yourself as bad or as if you don't exist at all.
- Moments of stress-related paranoia and loss of contact with reality.
- Impulsive and risky conduct, such as gambling, reckless driving, spending sprees, binge eating, or drug abuse, or sabotaging success by suddenly quitting a good job or ending a positive relationship.
- Suicidal threats, often in response to fear of separation or rejection.

- Wide mood swings. Moods can fluctuate from intense happiness to irritability to shame or anxiety.
- Consistent feelings of emptiness.
- Inappropriate, intense anger, such as frequently losing temper, being sarcastic or bitter, or having physical fights.

The struggle with impulsivity and fear of abandonment makes people suffering from BPD resort to emotional manipulation. However, their manipulation is a way to cope with their anxieties and not a malicious plot.

How to deal with emotional manipulation by your loved one with BPD?

Though your BPD loved one has no bad intentions for you, dealing with them can create a lot of pain and emotional turmoil.

BPD author and expert, Randi Kreger has provided five steps to deal with your BPD family member or loved one. She calls her approach "Beyond the Blame System" which is an empathetic and no-nonsense way to deal with emotional manipulation by BPD sufferers.

The 5 steps of her approach include:

1. Caring for self

The first step begins with reaching out to your friends and trusted family members for support. Also, consult a qualified therapist who can guide you on how to deal with your BPD loved one tactfully. Remember not to deal with your BPD loved one when you are feeling tired, hungry, sick, or emotional. First, take care of yourself and eat right. Find ways to boost your self-esteem. Don't take your BPD loved one's behavior personally. They react out of their mental illness, and not to hurt you.

2. Know what keeps you stuck

You might have created a rescuer relationship with your BPD loved one, but it's not healthy for either of you. Perhaps actions like slamming doors, and throwing objects, have been used to control your behavior, which keeps you stuck in fear and trapped in a repetitive pattern with your BPD loved one.

Fear might control you in other ways like fear of their reactions, being afraid of conflicts, fearful of being alone, etc. Know what keeps you stuck in this unhealthy dynamic with your BPD loved one.

3. Communicate to make your point

Approaching the BPD sufferer, and trying to communicate with them, can feel frightening because the interaction was chaotic and conflicting in the past. Your attempts went in vain, and you were overwhelmed.

However, communication is the best and healthiest way of moving forward. When reaching out to the BPD sufferer, always demonstrate empathy, attention, and respect (EAR). When you approach them this way, it stands a better chance of making your loved one calm down and listen to you.

To communicate, be brief, informative, friendly, and firm. Don't be critical or sarcastic, but stick to the positives, and remain firm with your boundaries.

4. Set limits with love

This step may feel hard if you have never set boundaries with your BPD loved one, or if you've never breached them as a result of the FOG. But keep in mind, setting boundaries is essential to your mental health and the health of your relationship.

You have to communicate your boundaries with firmness as well as love. For example, if you chose to go out of the room when your loved one expresses rage, you need to clearly express that you aren't abandoning them. You need to tell them how much you love them and are leaving to help yourself, not to hurt them. You'll return only when they are calm again.

Start small while setting limits with your loved one. Be firm, but fair, and do not waver from your boundaries. Setting boundaries are commitments you make for the sake of both you and your loved one.

5. Reinforce the right behavior

Actions speak louder than words. Don't react impulsively when your BPD loved one expresses outsized negative emotions. Any reaction of this type from your side will reinforce their negative feelings, even if you only respond this way occasionally. Either walk away for a moment or address only positive contributions.

The Emotional Tools of Blackmailers

Manipulation by emotional blackmailers can include overt aggression, narcissistic abuse, and subtle forms of emotional abuse. The typical tools and tactics they use for manipulation are:

Lying

Well, nobody is 100% honest, nor a 100% liar. But, manipulators are habitual liars. They lie even when it's not necessary, not because they are afraid or guilty, but to confuse you and get what they want. Along with lying, they may put you in defensive mode with false accusations. Lying can happen through vagueness of information given, or omitting the real part and telling other things which are true.

Denial

Not realizing that you've been abused or have an addiction are not denials. Denial is to relinquish things you know, such as promises, agreements, and behavior. It also includes rationalizing excuses. For example, the manipulator may act as if you are making a big deal over a petty issue or justify their actions to make you doubt yourself or gain sympathy.

Avoidance

Manipulators avoid being confronted or take responsibility at all costs. They avoid having conversations about their behavior, which might be combined with an attack such as, "You are always nagging me." This traps you in blame, guilt, or shame.

Avoidance can also be subtle when the manipulator tactfully shifts the subject of discussion to something else. He might camouflage it with boasting, compliments, and remarks you want to hear.

Example, a husband may turn the topic of discussion by saying, "You know how much I love you" or "You are so caring and patient."

Evasiveness is another avoidance tactic that blurs the facts, confuses you, and makes you doubt yourself.

Projection - Blame, Guilt, and Shame

These are the tactics of projection. Projection is a defense mechanism used for manipulation by narcissists, BPD sufferers, and addicts. It's a defense where the manipulator accuses others of his/her own behavior. They believe in the motto, "It's not me, it's you." By putting the 'blame' on others, they put the targeted person in defensive mode; that individual now feels guilty and shameful, while the manipulator escapes as innocent.

Sometimes, even an apology may be another form of manipulation. Addicts usually blame their addiction on other people, such as a demanding boss or a spiteful spouse.

By guilt-tripping and shaming, manipulators shift the focus on to you, making you weak and, thus, getting a chance to achieve a win over you. Shaming is a step ahead of guilt-tripping to make you feel inadequate.

Shaming not only demeans your actions/behavior, but you as a person. Comparing is also a form of shaming, like parents comparing their children with siblings or playmates.

Blaming the victim also calls for guilt-tripping and shaming. For example, a wife finds evidence on her husband's phone that he is flirting with another woman. Now, the husband acts outraged because the wife has checked his phone. So he has switched the focus on to his wife, who is actually the victim. By blaming his wife for going into his phone, he has avoided a confrontation about flirting. Further, he may also lie about it or circumvent it altogether.

As a result of this response from the husband, the wife feels guilty of spying, and he will continue to flirt without worrying about the victim's emotions. The real issue of flirting remained unaddressed.

Intimidation

Intimidation is not always direct. It doesn't necessarily include direct threats to the victim each time. It can also be achieved with a look, or tone of voice, and statements like:

- I always get my way.
- I have friends in high places.
- I have contacts with many influencers.
- Do you know the repercussions of your decision?

Sometimes, the blackmailer may also resort to telling a story that evokes fear in you, such as, "She left her husband, and consequently lost her kids, her house, and everything." This is not a direct threat, but given as a warning to the victim that if he/she dares to go against them, they'll pay for the consequences just like the character in the story.

Playing the Victim

The blackmailer may persuade you to give in to their demands by playing a victim themselves. Rather than blaming you, they'll blame themselves to arouse guilt and sympathy in you. They may say, "I don't deserve to be cared for. I haven't given you much care myself, so how can I expect it from you?" This 'poor me' tactic forces you to think they are right, and you are wrong. You begin getting trapped in their manipulation and comply with what they want.

However, your compliance breeds your resentment, hurts the relationship, and encourages continued manipulation.

Once you know the emotional tools and tactics these blackmailers use to manipulate you, it gets easier to identify the instances of similar pressures and tactics in your relationships.

Now, it's time to learn the strategies for dealing with emotional blackmail.

How To Deal With Emotional Blackmail And Stop Being The Victim

The first step to deal with emotional blackmail is to know what emotional blackmail is and how you can recognize that you or someone else is being blackmailed.

Remember the following things when dealing with an emotional blackmailer:

1. **Don't give in to their demands**

Though the situation may sound scary if you're faced with direct physical or emotional threats, giving in to their demands will only encourage the blackmailer to repeat it. It will worsen the situation. So hold onto your ground, be firm, and refuse to comply with the blackmailer's demands. This is even more important if the threat is violence towards you or others. Remove yourself from the situation.

2. **Know that people don't blackmail the ones they love**

The most common misconception in victims about the blackmailer is that the abuser loves the victim and can abandon the relationship if he/she doesn't give in to what they want.

However, this is unlikely to be true. You must recognize that people who truly love you, who genuinely care for you, will never make demands while threatening to harm you or themselves. This will help you detach from the situation, see the reality, and have an option to refuse to follow their demands.

3. **Change the equation**

Sometimes, It won't be possible to control the blackmailer, but you can control yourself. Remove yourself from the situation for a certain period. That shows the blackmailer that he/she has no one to control. Plus, you'll be able to deal with the situation better when you're not doing it under pressure.

Whether it's you or your loved one who falls victim to an emotional blackmail, the foremost thing to know are the signs, so that the victim can be removed from the situation safely. Never take the threats of violence against the victim lightly.

How to deal with projection from blackmailers?

As discussed, projection is a defense mechanism of blackmailers, especially narcissists, BPD sufferers, and addicts. When they project, they defend themselves from unconscious impulses or traits they deny themselves or don't want to acknowledge. They believe that their emotions originate from the other person, while, in fact, it is their thoughts and feelings that are the problem. For example, they may think that the other person hates them while it's they who hate the person.

Projection is behavior that indicates low levels of emotional development or maturity.

How should you deal with projection from manipulators? Set your limits so that you don't react in anger to the projected behavior from blackmailers. Don't judge yourself based on the opinion of other people. Although it can be hard if you're a sensitive person, try not to take the projector's comments and statements personally. Try to empathize with the projector. Most importantly, don't allow anything to diminish your self-respect and belief in yourself.

Chapter Summary

1. FOG or fear, obligation, and guilt are the techniques used by emotional blackmailers for successful manipulation of their victims.
2. The need to please your loved ones, or fear of their rage and retaliation, make you susceptible to emotional blackmail by them.
3. Besides the FOG technique, emotional blackmailers use tools such as lying, denial of their promises or agreements, avoiding confrontation/conversation about their behavior, projection, intimidation, and victim playing to win over you.
4. Projection is a defense mechanism used by narcissists, BPD sufferers, and addicts where they use blame, guilt, and shame to blackmail their victims emotionally.
5. Not giving in to the demands of the blackmailers, setting your limits, and direct, firm communication with them to keep your opinion, are the best ways to deal with emotional blackmail and to stop being a victim.

6. Never hesitate to reach out and ask for support from friends, family members, and psychotherapists to deal with emotional blackmail.

In the next chapter, you will learn....

- Effects of Emotional Blackmail on Kids.
- Difficult parents versus toxic parents.
- Ways to cope with blackmail in a family.

CHAPTER FOUR:

Blackmailing in the Family

The decision-making process in the family is a complex phenomenon where many factors, including emotions, play an important part. Both parents and children use emotions to influence each other and drive decisions in their favor. This is generally natural and healthy.

Healthy families make decisions on negotiation, clearly defined rules, and just authority. Though it's nearly impossible to please every family member in the decision-making process, parents attempt to listen to everyone before making the final decision. Such a discussion removes the hostage situation at home and allows everybody to express their opinions, even displeasure in the open. Thus, the issues are out in front of the family rather than one person's will imposed on the family.

Also, when rules and expectations are clear, the just authority structure is clear, the need for manipulation becomes less, and the family members develop trust in the decision made.

Using emotions becomes harmful when they are used as threats to control another's behavior or intimidate them. Parents may use threats towards children, children may use them against parents, and sometimes, even grandparents enter this cycle of emotional threats.

These emotional threats usually occur through rage, screaming, crying, whining, or complaining. They not only make the situation uncomfortable for the victim, but also forces them to do something which they don't like.

When these emotional threats take place in public spots, it becomes very embarrassing for the victim, which further adds pressure on him to yield. After several episodes of such threats, the victim is forced to give in to avoid creating a scene in public. Here, not only the psychological pressure, but the mere discomfort of that embarrassment creates pressure to give in.

Repeated emotional threats, whether from the parent or the child, creates a hostage situation within the home.

Withholding is yet another form of emotional blackmail seen within the family. The blackmailer may threaten to withhold love, attention, money, or dignity in order to have their way.

Unfortunately, many parents use emotional blackmail as a strategy for bringing up their children. They use fear, guilt, and intimidation to make their children do what they want. And the truth is that they are frequently unaware of its consequences on their children. They don't realize the effect it can have on children and the relationship they have with them.

It seems very tempting and easy to use emotional blackmail, and have children obey their commands, but the consequences are immensely damaging. Children can learn to emotionally blackmail by imitating the example set by their parents.

Why do parents resort to emotional blackmail?

Parents often resort to emotional blackmail because it gives them a way to get children to obey without protest. What they fail to understand is that control is not synonymous with education. Parents can tell the child what to do and how to do it. But, if they threaten them for not doing it immediately, they reduce the decision-making capacity in the child. Consequently, as the child grows up, he/she will be either overly dependent or very rebellious.

Further, using emotional blackmail towards children reveals the adults' insecurity as parents. It shows they have little or no patience and can't respect a young person's way of doing things. It is also the worst way to protect yourself from your child's questions.

How does emotional blackmail affect your children?

Emotional blackmail by parents is a form of manipulation that leaves the child with no choice. They have to obey you, but probably it's short-lived. In the long run, the strategy of emotional blackmail won't work. Worst, the child may start using it against you because that's what he has picked up from you - if you can't have your way by reasonable means, threaten others to get what you want.

Additionally, emotional blackmail may fill your child's heart with resentment, which they can't explain initially but shows up as they grow older. Emotional blackmail also tarnishes the love in parent-child relationships.

Why emotional blackmail doesn't work

Sometimes, emotional blackmail by parents doesn't work because parents use threats that they don't follow up on. No parent will stop loving their child because they don't keep their room clean, so what's the point of threatening that they will?

Many psychologists have proved that these types of threats don't last long and have a very poor outcome. By using threats, you can never make your child learn and understand the real reason for keeping their room clean.

They will never learn that by having a tidy room, they can easily find their possessions. They will never learn the importance of brushing their teeth. And so on.

Most likely, when the threats seem to stop showing their effect on your child, the good habits you wanted to instill will also disappear.

In short, blackmail doesn't teach your child to solve problems or do things because it is best for them. It changes the child's behavior only for a moment, but there's no real or lasting change.

Also, if you threaten your child with a consequence, and fail to carry it out, you lose credibility in the eyes of your child. Your threats become empty.

What are the alternatives to emotional blackmail?

If you wish to tell your child to do something or how to do it, the best way of teaching is to help them or accompany them in doing the task. This is far better than shouting or giving orders from the sofa. For older children, the best teaching method is through your example. If you want them to do what you want, let them imitate your actions and attitude. Give them something positive to imitate.

Children are not robots. Only robots and machines respond to our commands the first time we ask. So you might need to repeat things more than once to make your child do them. If they delay in doing something, it isn't always laziness or a conscious act to make you angry. Children take time to learn and remember things. So let them do it at their pace.

Difficult versus Toxic parents

Difficult parents are very cautious and may cause their child to behave similarly. On the flip side, toxic parents are more inimical to their child's personality development and character formation.

You can't label a parent as toxic if:

- He/she is a bit moody.
- Stresses due to financial, relationship, or family issues.
- They're preoccupied with work.
- Physically and emotionally unavailable for their children.
- Feel resentful and bitter about being trapped in parenthood.

Such a parent is emotionally neglectful towards the child, but they're not necessarily toxic.

Here are some questions to ask yourself about your parent's behavior. If it's consistent and chronic, you might be in a toxic relationship with them.

- Do your parents overreact or create a scene over little things?
- Do they blackmail you emotionally?
- Do they place frequent or unreasonable demands?
- Do they try to control you?
- Do they criticize you or compare you with others?
- Do they listen to you with interest?
- Do they blame you often?
- Do they take responsibility for their conduct or apologize?
- Do they respect your physical and emotional boundaries?
- Do they respect your feelings and needs?
- Do they envy you?

The causes of toxic behavior from parents

The most important reason for toxic behavior from parents is basically the repetition of what they experienced themselves as a child. What they learned and imitated from their parents is now being delivered to their children in the form of abuse.

Since they didn't have enough self-awareness, knowledge, and skills to change those unproductive patterns, they continued with the same style of parenting. Also, receiving toxic abuse themselves as a child may have left them with a personality disorder or a mental health problem, which affects their ability to parent their own children correctly.

People who are parents now, if they had been traumatized in their childhood with emotional blackmail, they may well lack empathy and consideration for the needs of their child. Their child's vulnerability triggers the parent's emotional insecurities, which they can't face, and they punish the child for showing 'weakness.'

On the other spectrum of toxic parenting are those who had seemingly good childhoods, but who were 'pampered' and spoilt. They were overly-indulged and never had to wait for anything they wanted.

Such people grew up believing that their needs came first; their needs are superior to anyone else's needs, and they deserved to have power over others. They think that they should receive special attention, privileges, and rewards because they are superior to others.

Signs and symptoms of toxic parents

Toxic parents put their feelings and needs first. They are self-centered and believe themselves to be the focus of attention. They usually display erratic, unpredictable, and scary behavior. Due to these factors, they can't provide a safe and secure environment for their children.

They can't accept their child might sometimes fail because, in their eyes, this is a negative reflection upon them. Their child's failure makes them feel shameful, and they punish the child for making them feel bad. They feel jealous and envious if someone favors or appreciates their child. Due to envy, they can also turn violent towards the child's beauty or talent.

Toxic parents view their child as an 'object' on whom they can rely emotionally, physically, practically, and financially.

It's difficult, or rather impossible, for the child to please or satisfy this kind of parent. However hard they try, they are unable to please them. The child of such parents feels suppressed and oppressed. Their physical and emotional needs are neglected. Frequently, the needs of the child, even the genuine ones, feel like a burden for the toxic parent. When the child cries or craves care and attention, such a parent will belittle, ridicule, ignore, or punish the child.

Toxic parents are not interested in what their child has to say. The child's feelings and opinions are completely ignored.

Toxic parents create a severe atmosphere of tension and fear at home. Playing mind games with the child is the second nature of toxic parents. They will tell lies, give out mixed messages, to confuse and manipulate the child. They bully their child, mentally and emotionally. The child, being immature and possessing little innate gifts for reasoning, rationality, and logic is unable to question and challenge the parent's motives or behavior. The child can't dare to challenge the parent for fear of the harsh consequences.

Toxic parents exhibit passive-aggressive behavior by ignoring the child's requests and comments. Even if they promise the child something, they never keep the promise.

If you challenge the conduct of toxic parents, they may turn aggressive and violent, or give silent treatment by refusing to talk to the child.

Toxic parents showcase themselves as victims, and try to get others to believe them, and be on their side against the child.

Toxic parents are always in a 'deal' mode. They'll agree to do something for the child only if he/she agrees to their whims and fancies. The toxic parent needs to feel powerful and have control over the child's thoughts, emotions, language, and behavior. They squash the child's authentic emotional expression – even telling the child that they are wrong for having feelings.

Guilt-tripping and emotional blackmail are the favorite weapons to get their child to conform to them. Toxic parents are often highly critical and scrutinize the child's activities using sarcasm, blame and shaming comments. Toxic parents seldom respect their child's personal boundaries and will intrude upon them. They have weak boundaries themselves, and avoid making decisions or giving their child adequate guidance.

Toxic parents play double roles of a martyr and the hater. At one time, they'll say, "How can you treat me like this? After all, I've done so much for you?" On the other hand, they'll switch to "I wish you'd never been born. You have ruined my life."

Toxic parents with two or more children will play them off against one another. Both are treated differently, yet not in a beneficial manner for any one of them.

Toxic parents also may abuse their child physically and sexually.

How to cope with toxic parents?

Let's face the truth. Some individuals are so dangerous, so manipulative, and so draining, you had better stay away from them.

But, what if those individuals are your parents? Is it really possible to cut off all contacts with them?

Nope! Therefore, two mental health professionals - Justin Shubert, founder of Silver Lake Psychotherapy, and Rebekah Tayebi, a clinical therapist and family coach, advise the following methods to cope with this kind of situation.

Determine if your parents are actually toxic

Look, your relationship with your parents can't be rosy at all times. There will be moments of argument where you or the parents make mistakes. Your Mom doesn't like your dress or questions you. She might say something critical which gets under your skin. She might behave the way you don't want a million times, and you feel like punching a hole in the wall.

However, all these things count for a bad equation and not toxic parents.

Toxic is when the parent's needs overtake that of the child for an extended period of time. They have extreme difficulty in regulating their emotions, or even communicating them in the right manner. Consequently, any conversations immediately flare up. Things also get very unpredictable. The psychotherapists advise you to ask yourself: Do you feel like you can breathe when around your parents? OR are you constantly suffocated in their presence because you can't be yourself and feel pressured to do what they want to please them?

Understand that typical boundaries get disrupted with toxic parents

One thing is evident from toxic family systems. The children in the family are attuned to their parents' needs. The typical parent-child relationship is inverted, and there's a lot of confusion on what boundaries to set.

For example, one parent may be in a toxic relationship with the spouse. But, they talk and argue in front of the kids rather than taking the matter behind closed doors. As a result, the kids also get involved in the parental discourse and start taking the side of one or the other parent.

Toxic parents are so absorbed in their own needs, dramas, and addictions, their children never learn how to be themselves.

Choose a go-to phrase to redirect the conversation

It's very easy for children to pick up the dysfunctional behavior of their parents and imitate them. That's why it's crucial to catch the negative patterns in the parents' behavior, and whenever possible, redirect the conversation. You can do this by modeling the type of behavior and boundaries you'd like.

For example, if your Mom's attitude becomes overbearing, you can say, "Mom, I understand it's really hard for you. But, I'm feeling quite escalated now."

So, you validate the feelings of your parents and also tell them what you experience from them. You communicate that you're feeling escalated, bowed down, or anxious, and need a break from the conversation.

Practice these responses ahead of time so that you can use them as your saving mantra to tackle the situation.

The parent may not respect your boundary, but it's much healthier for you to speak like a broken record rather than giving in to their manipulation.

Have a plan of action and a support system to rely on

Sometimes it's safer and healthier to stay with friends than with family. Maintaining a safe distance can give you a space to retreat.

Have an itinerary of activities, so you have to spend the least time possible with your toxic parent.

This helps you place boundaries and decide on:

- How many days do you want to spend with them?
- Do you really want to stay with them or not?
- If you want to stay with them, do you want to bring someone along?
- How much time are you willing to spend with them in a day?
- Do you have a plan of escape if things turn worse?

Thinking about these things in advance will prevent you from falling into the old cycle of victim and regret.

Also, be clear with your support system on how you want the support. Instead of just venting out your situation to a close friend, prepare your friends for what may be coming down the line in the presence of your parents. Tell them clearly what you want from them.

Allow yourself to say "No"

Most kids who grow up in toxic parenting abandon their own needs for the sake of their parents. However, you must remember that it's not wrong to make a space for yourself and commit to it.

Remind yourself that your feelings are as valid as those of your parents, and it makes complete sense to give yourself the space you need. Take care of your feelings at that time and then get back to the family life.

Chapter Summary

1. Healthy families make decisions on negotiation, clearly defined rules, and just authority. On the other hand, when

either parents or children use emotions as threats to control each other's behavior, it creates a hostage situation at home.

2. Many parents use emotional blackmail because it seems to be the easiest way to have children obey their commands without protest. Parents who resort to emotional blackmail are often emotionally insecure themselves.

3. Emotional blackmail in children reduces their decision-making capacity. They'll be either overly dependent on others or rebellious in the future.

4. Blackmail doesn't teach your child to solve problems or do things because it's in their interest. Plus, it changes the child's behavior only momentarily.

5. The best way to teach children what to do and how to do it is by accompanying them in the task or through your example.

6. Toxic parents resort to emotional blackmail because they experienced the same trauma in their childhood.

Tell-tale signs you have a toxic parent are:

- They are self-centered.
- They can't accept your failure.
- They envy you.
- You can't satisfy/please a toxic parent however hard you try.
- They neglect your needs and feelings.
- They play mind games and may call you names.
- They bully you, mentally and emotionally.
- They may be aggressive and violent to you.
- Are highly critical.
- Dealing with toxic parents begins with identifying whether they are actually toxic or not. Learn to say no to their unreasonable demands and expectations. Set your boundaries and assert them. Have friends to support you and rely on if things go awry.

In the next chapter, you will learn....

- Blackmailing in relationships.
- Seemingly innocent things that are emotional blackmail.
- Warning signs of emotional blackmail in love relationships.
- Life after toxic relationships.
- Real love versus attachment.

CHAPTER FIVE:

Blackmailing in Relationships

Seemingly innocent things that are emotional blackmail

Can you differentiate healthy behavior by your lover from toxic manipulation? Unfortunately, it's easy to mistakenly take jealousy, possessiveness, and other unhealthy actions as romance or love. Experts warn that many seemingly innocent things in love can be emotional blackmail. Sometimes, it's hard to tell.

Emotional blackmail is one of the primary ways a partner uses to control the other partner by manipulating their emotions in a way that forces them to give what they want, even outside their will.

It can take place in many forms. One such form is sarcasm. For instance, if you tell your partner or complain to them for being too critical, they'll respond by saying, "I am sorry for being such a bad person."

Instead of using this criticism in a constructive way, the blackmailing partner uses sarcasm as a manipulative response to invalidate their partner's emotions and protect their own.

According to Kelsey M. Latimer, Ph.D., founder of Hello Goodlife, emotional blackmail should never be ignored. It should be taken very seriously as an emotional abuse, and you should immediately tell the person how you feel. Also, get others involved if you feel a sense of danger.

Here are some seemingly innocent things that are actually emotional blackmail:

They want to know everything about you immediately

It's great to have someone wanting to know about you. But, it's not that great if they try to know everything right away, and push you to the point it makes you uncomfortable.

For instance, you should be cautious if they ask you about your finances too early in a relationship. You may assume that they care for money and stability, but they might not be asking for the right reasons. Especially if they push you or make you feel bad for not sharing, it's emotional blackmail.

In such a situation, it's important to set your boundaries. If you don't feel comfortable sharing, don't do it. The person who loves you will respect your boundaries.

They pinpoint your flaws

Expressing your weaknesses honestly is good, but it should never be hurtful. If your lover constantly brings up your flaws, it's an emotional blackmail. Though he/she may bring them up in seemingly harmless ways, it can trigger fear and doubt in your mind.

When you are criticized constantly, you start believing in those words. You start looking down upon yourself. You become a victim of emotional blackmail and feel stuck in a relationship because you are scared that no one else will love you for your flaws.

When the situation reaches this point, it's a clear-cut case of emotional abuse, and you shouldn't think twice about ending such a relationship.

They try to punish you after a fight

It's common to argue with your partner. But, if after the argument, your partner stays out for hours without saying where they are, it's a sign of emotional abuse. They are punishing you for the disagreement by intentionally causing you to worry or feel anxious about them.

Asking for space after the heat is fine. But, if someone intentionally does it to punish their partner, it's an emotional blackmail. When this happens the first time, approach your partner calmly, and explain your mental condition to them. If you are in a healthy relationship, your partner will make sure it doesn't happen again.

They'll test you

A healthy relationship is a balanced relationship. You don't have to go to your extremes to please your partner. For instance, if you've been longing to go on a vacation with your partner, but he insists that he'll only make it happen providing you wear dresses of his choice, that's emotional blackmail. It shows they don't welcome you in their world unless you comply with their demands.

It's a controlling behavior that makes the relationship unhealthy.

They keep an account

If your partner is an emotional blackmailer, they'll go out of their way to do things for you, but none of their actions are selfless. Indeed, they'll bring it up over and over again to remind you of the sacrifices they made for you. They'll use their good deeds to make you feel guilty and have what they want.

They turn to you for everything

It feels nice to be needed by people, but if someone starts making statements like, "You are the only one I can rely upon" or " You are the only one in my life," it should raise a red flag. No one should make you responsible for their happiness or use you as a tool to keep their problems at bay.

They want to be your everything

If you are the whole world for the emotional blackmailer, on the flip side, they expect the same from you. They want you to turn to them for everything you need. In fact, they'll do everything they can to ensure this. Though it seems harmless, it is a trap. When you have no one to turn to except them, they can easily control you.

The important thing here is to stay aware of these red flags in relationships. It's easy to regard these things as innocent and to romanticize them. But, if you find yourself in a situation of such manipulation, confront your partner and tell them how you feel. Use 'I' statements without placing blame on your partner.

Still, if you aren't able to resolve the issue, consider terminating the relationship because relationships dominated by these methods are unhealthy and emotionally exhausting.

Six warning signs of emotional blackmail in relationships

Do you know when that loving relationship transforms into an emotional blackmail? Watch out for these signs:

1. Manipulation of your decisions and choices by reacting negatively to them.
2. You are intimidated until you do what your partner wants.
3. They blame you for things that you didn't do so that you feel guilty and compelled to give in to their demands.
4. Your partner accuses you of something you didn't do.
5. They play a victim and dramatize their suffering publicly until you agree to what they want.

6. Threaten to harm you or themselves to get you to do (or not do) what they want.

People who use these techniques to control you often work in cycles. At times, you'll feel there are periods during which everything is normal. There's no guilt-tripping, or pressure to do things their way. However, such people are insecure individuals. When they start to feel out of control or uneasy about a situation, they begin to increase the pressure of manipulation on you.

If you are a victim of this kind of manipulation by your partner, seek help from a counselor right away. Besides counseling from a therapist, take these three crucial steps:

1. Set clear boundaries for yourself, and don't let the poor attitude of your partner change your mind. Giving in to them only makes things worse.
2. If your partner threatens to harm you physically, leave the location immediately, and call the authorities. Don't stay in dangerous situations simply because you fear losing your personal belongings.
3. Reach out to your friends or family or relatives for support.

However, keep in mind that many people have a certain level of emotional insecurity. And every insecure person won't turn into a monster. Sometimes your partner just needs a simple reassurance from your side. But, when reassurances don't seem enough, and you feel more and more manipulated by your partner, those are the red flags of psychological abuse. So, pay attention to these warning signs.

Are you really in love with your partner?

Love is a complicated thing. It's easy to confound attachment with love. However, here are a few differences between attachment and real love that will help you understand your relationships better.

Love is selfless; attachment is selfish

When you're in love, you focus on making your partner happy. You always think of ways to make sure your partner feels loved and fulfilled. You don't keep a tab on who helps more, or fight over who'll wash the dishes. You neither pressure the partner nor seek to dominate the relationship.

On the flip side, attachment makes you focus on yourself, how they can make you feel happy. You become heavily dependent on your partner and even try to control them for fear of abandonment. You look up to your partner to improve your self-esteem and fill the void in you. You hold them responsible for your happiness and get frustrated if they fail to content you.

Love liberates, attachment controls

True love allows you to be yourself. If your partner loves you, they'll accept you with your strengths and weaknesses, and encourage you to be who you genuinely are. True love helps develop mutual trust and acts as a catalyst for the personal growth of the two involved. When your partner accepts you for who you are and encourages you to pursue your dreams, you'll never feel the need to control their life.

Attachment, on the other hand, fuels controlling patterns. You or your partner may stop each other from spending time with friends or manipulate each other, regardless of one's feelings.

Love is a mutual growth; attachment impedes growth

As said, love develops mutual trust, which, in turn helps in the growth of both the partners involved. It helps both of you become the best version of yourselves. In short, your partner stimulates your growth, and you do the same for them.

Attachment impedes yours as well as your partner's growth. Since you are overly dependent on them to solve your issues, and you try to control them, it impedes their growth as well. Unsurprisingly, this makes it difficult to love each other in a healthy way.

Love is everlasting; attachment is short-lived

Love is eternal. Even if you and your partner breakup, either temporarily or permanently, they'll continue to have a place in your heart, and you'll always wish them the best for their life.

On the other hand, if you were only attached to them, you'll hold resentment for them after the breakup. You'll blame them for betrayal because you considered them responsible for your happiness.

Love makes you egoless; attachment boosts ego

A loving relationship reduces your ego, fosters your growth, and makes you less selfish and more loving. Such a relationship fuels positive changes in both the partners, encourages both to open up about their weaknesses, vulnerabilities, and have communication from the heart.

Alternatively, relationships based on attachment are ego boosters. Attachment generates dependency on your partner, and you feel you can't be happy without them. You depend on your significant half to resolve your problems or help you forget them.

Dealing with emotional blackmail in relationships

If you are dealing with emotional blackmail from a loved one, you'll feel frustrated and trapped. But things can get better if you take the following steps:

Step 1: Recognize emotional blackmail

An emotional blackmailer, even if he/she is someone close to you, gains the upper hand over you because you fail to recognize their tactics. As a result, you give in to their demands and invite further manipulation from them.

Thus, it's crucial to recognize emotional blackmail before you can deal with it. Watch out for threats or punishments if you don't do what they want. The threats can be withdrawal of affection or making you feel insecure in a relationship.

Example: They may say, "If you don't want to move in with me in that house, it's absolutely fine. I knew this relationship wasn't going anywhere." Such a statement will make you feel the need to rush the relationship or risk losing them.

Notice if they threaten to hurt themselves if you don't do what they say.

Example: Your partner may say, "I know you don't love me or care for me; otherwise, you won't refuse to give me money. I am such a bad husband. I don't deserve to live anymore."

Observe when your loved one tries to make you feel guilty for no reason. The blackmailer may try to accuse you of hurting them, even though you haven't done anything. Beware if this guilt drives you to do things for them, it may be an emotional blackmail.

Example: Statements like, "You never do what I want." Or, "My friends say you neglect me" may make you feel guilty.

Take note of the times when they try to make you feel a sense of duty. Being in a relationship, you have a responsibility towards your family, friends, and your partner. However, if your loved one tries to make you accept a sense of duty when you don't, they are trying to manipulate you. Doing it this way, the blackmailer tries to convince you to take on a role or responsibility that isn't yours.

Example: Your neighbor may ask you to babysit her kids for free.

Beware of their blaming strategy. Blaming is a form of emotional manipulation to get you to do what they want. They'll accuse you of things you haven't done.

Example: Your wife lost her job due to her careless attitude. However, she might blame you by saying, "I lost my job because you never bought me better work clothes."

Realize when your loved one puts their needs before yours. This shows that they care only about themselves, and, therefore, they expect you to tend to their needs.

Example: If your partner asks you to leave your work to listen to his issues, but cuts off when you wish to vent about your situation.

Step 2: Set your boundaries

Don't give them what they want

Saying 'Yes' to the demands of the manipulator will reinforce their conduct. Even if their threat seems overbearing, hold your ground, and stay firm. If they continue pushing you, step away to take a few moments for yourself. Ask a friend or a relative for support.

Be empathetic towards their situation but don't give in to their demands. If they threaten to harm you, call the emergency services. If they threaten to harm themselves, call for help and stay with them. Enquire about what they are feeling at the moment.

Don't take their comments personally. Ignore certain things they say to get attention, by continuing your side of the conversation as if they didn't say anything.

Tell them to clarify their intentions

This will help you determine any inappropriate attitudes or actions without blaming or accusing them. It also forces them to state what they want clearly and allows you to address them without worrying about their emotional threats.

Clearly state what you'll accept and what you won't

Setting your boundaries and telling others about it gives them the guidelines about how to behave around you. Tell them straightforwardly that you won't accept any manipulative tactics. Instead, if they want something, they should tell you clearly.

You could say, "I won't listen to you if you scream and shout at me. I'll leave the room. However, I am ready to listen if you speak in a soft, calm tone."

Take their threats of violence seriously

It's important you take their threats of violence seriously and call for help, whether they threaten to harm you or themselves. If they threaten to harm you, remove yourself from the situation immediately and, if need be, call the police.

Don't hold yourself responsible for their feelings and actions

Individuals like this blame you to make you feel guilty, and they act as if you are responsible for their feelings and actions. The truth is they are responsible for their feelings, while you are responsible for yours.

For instance, they may try to blame you for their bad mood and expect you to fix it. Though there's nothing wrong in making someone cheer up, they shouldn't manipulate you for that. Your responsibility shouldn't revolve around that only. You could empathize with them and say, "I am sorry you had a bad day. I can't change that, but I would like to enjoy a nice evening with you."

Follow through if they overstep your boundaries

While setting your boundaries, it's also essential to decide the consequences if anyone breaks them. Emotional blackmailers will try testing your rules. So you have to stand firm and do what you promised to do if they broke your rules.

If you said that you'd call the police if they threatened you violently, then follow through. Doing so makes them realize that your rules are for real, and they'll respect them. Otherwise, neither you nor your boundaries will receive recognition, and you'll invite more manipulation from them.

Take a break from the person if the problem is grave

If your loved one continues to pressure you, it will take a toll on your emotional health. So it's best to protect yourself and spend some time away from them. That will also make them realize that you won't tolerate manipulative or bad behavior.

Step 3: Confront the person

Call them out when they blame you

Tell them that you won't take responsibility for their actions. Ask them to accept the blame for their actions and encourage them to solve their problems.

You can say, "It's not my fault that you forgot your phone this morning. I am sorry you had to stay without your phone in the office today, but you must accept responsibility for your actions."

Express your feelings about their conduct

Since emotional blackmailers are more focused on their feelings, they may fail to realize that they are hurting you. So it's your duty to tell them how their actions affect you, that you are the victim, not them.

Adopt a non-defensive way of communication

If you blame or accuse them in reciprocation, they'll turn defensive and manipulate you more. This makes it difficult to resolve the issue. So adopt a non-defensive way to communicate with them. Such as:

- Don't deny their complaints immediately.
- Take turns to speak.
- Don't accuse them of anything.
- Don't point out their actions to justify yours.

Use "I" statements

When pointing out the way they behave, use "I" statements to keep the focus on how you feel rather than blaming them. This reduces their risk of becoming defensive and pulling away from the conversation.

Ask them to help you solve the problem

This makes them see that you are their friend, not an enemy, and they may transition to your side. It makes them feel safe that you aren't attacking them.

You can say, "I know we've had a tough time communicating with each other. I really want to have a good relationship with you. Do you think we can work together to solve this?"

Step 4: Coping with a manipulative loved one

Recognize your emotional triggers

Your loved ones, especially those closest to you, have a special ability to manipulate you because they know you in and out. They know the emotional triggers they can use to get under your skin. These triggers could be:

- Love can be used to soften you.
- Anger and apathy.
- Criticism to make you feel guilty you aren't doing enough for them.

- Their suffering.
- Helplessness.
- Explosiveness to make you feel scared of them.

Listen to their feelings without changing your mind

Sometimes, your loved one may be in actual distress. It helps to talk it out with them and listen to what they feel. However, you can't necessarily give them what they want. Otherwise, you'll invite manipulation.

Step away from their tantrums

If their actions are out of control, such as throwing a tantrum or crying endlessly, take a break from the situation. They feel that by being so dramatic, they can make you feel bad and manipulate you. It's important to realize at this moment that you are not causing them to behave this way. They are doing it themselves.

Give them the benefit of the doubt when they behave nicely

Unfortunately, emotional blackmail may turn you skeptical towards your loved one, and you begin to doubt their intentions, even when they are not manipulative. Accusing them of manipulation when they aren't doing this, can harm your relationship.

Model good behavior

You can accidentally teach your loved one to blackmail emotionally by doing the same with them, especially children. Instead, set an example for them by behaving the way you would like them to. Have a healthy communication with them, be responsible for your actions, and follow the family rules.

For example, don't try to control your child by saying, "You spoiled my mood. You've made me sad." Don't break their possessions if you feel angry.

Life after toxic relationships

Finally, if all the methods to cope with a toxic relationship have failed, you have to end that relationship. It's natural to feel bowed down after that, and spend a few days grieving. However, some people experience what is called post-traumatic relationship syndrome. It's a mental health syndrome that occurs after experiencing trauma in an intimate relationship. These feelings can prevent you from finding a healthier relationship in the future.

Signs of post-traumatic relationship syndrome

1. Afraid of making another commitment

It's OK, and even healthy, to take time, after a breakup from a bad relationship, before you commit to a new relationship. If you wish to seek another relationship but can't make yourself do it, you may still be under the trauma of the last relationship. You are in self-doubt and experiencing low self-worth. In such a case, seek support from friends or even a counselor to figure out the ways to move past the trauma and learn to trust again.

2. Feeling unworthy or unconfident

If you feel downtrodden and worthless after a break-up, it's a sign of trauma. Such thoughts are a side-effect of harsh words from your ex who could have manipulated you to the extreme and eroded your self-esteem. Though tough to shake, it's possible to get rid of such thoughts with the help of a therapist.

3. Feeling guilty

Once the relationship ends, you'll heave a sigh of relief. But after a few days, you may be surrounded by feelings of guilt and self-doubt. The toxic relationship created such a dependency in you, it's common to wonder, "Did I do the right thing?" or "Was it really my fault?" At this stage, many people get back with their ex to make this discomfort go away. That may be fine in some cases, but rekindling with a toxic ex? Give yourself plenty of time to think over what you went through in that relationship, and whether you genuinely want to get back with them.

4. Feeling isolated and lonely

Yet another feeling that envelops you after the break-up is the intense feeling of loneliness. There's a general sense of wasted time, days, months, and years of life. It can put you in a very vulnerable state. It can also lead to rebound relationships as you struggle to free yourself from these negative emotions.

5. Engaging in another unhealthy relationship

If you don't give yourself time to recover from the toxic relationship, or treat your trauma, or learn about the traits of a healthy relationship, you may immediately fall into another relationship that's equally bad.

6. Difficulty in letting it go

It's common to feel low after a break-up, but all the more difficult to move on from a toxic one. You may focus on things your ex said, try to replay those scenes, or wonder how they could have been different.

It's possible to shift your attention from your ex, focus on the self, and fill your brain with healthier, positive thoughts. Take help from friends or a trained therapist who can help you address the issues you have in letting it go.

7. Having intrusive thoughts

It's OK if you get thoughts about your ex or what went wrong once in a while. But check if you are getting obsessed with such thoughts. This can make you doubt your choice in relationships, and you'll find it hard to trust the process of relationship building. It will be hard to trust your instincts about others. All this leads to distraction, acting impulsively, disturbed sleep, or constant crying and irritability. Consulting a therapist will be the right choice to help you move on.

8. Feeling distrust in new relationships

When you go into a new relationship without healing yourself of the past wounds, it's common to expect those bad things to happen all over again. After exiting a toxic relationship, you can often find yourself reacting to friends, family, or new relationships with suspicion.

Being aware of this tendency is the first step in recovery. You must be aware if you are sensing something negative in new relationships, but also if you're labeling a simple mistake by your new partner as something harmful. This can tar your new relationship.

Talk to your therapist or loved one to help you overcome the marks of trauma and deal with these trust issues.

9. Feeling insecure

The trauma from the past toxic relationship can also make you insecure, and you may find yourself frequently apologizing to the new partner. When you've been in a toxic relationship, you develop coping patterns to keep arguments to the minimum. Most of these coping patterns consist of apologies and saying sorry for your thoughts, feelings, and actions. This conditions your mind to believe that, by apologizing, you can control your partner's reaction. And you continue the same with the new partner to protect yourself from the hurt previously experienced.

10. Feelings of anxiety

Look out for any signs of stress you may have, especially those to do with your relationships. Post-traumatic relationship syndrome mainly stems from the fear and mistrust in relationships.

There could be many other causes of anxiety. So don't jump to any conclusion that you were in a toxic relationship or were traumatized simply due to this feeling of anxiety. If it's in line with what you experienced in the past, it could probably be the cause. Seek treatment from the therapist if necessary.

11. Having flashbacks and nightmares

It's possible to have flashbacks to past moments or wake up in a cold sweat from a bad dream after leaving the toxic relationship. You can experience bouts of anger and sadness, or waves of self-doubt, and take too much of the responsibility for what happened.

Since all this is not healthy for you, it's important to seek help and support as soon as possible. This will help you move past the trauma and create healthier relationships in the future.

How to maintain your grace after a bad break-up?

The most serious consequence of breaking up from a toxic relationship is that you can lose all your calmness and try to hurt your ex the way they have hurt you. However, you can stop all this from happening to you; handle your break-up with grace by following these steps.

Remember not to be in the attacking mode after the breakup. It's natural to feel a desire to get back at someone, but this only sets a cycle of spiteful interactions from which it'll be hard to recover. Instead, acknowledge your hurt and take time to recover from it.

Admit your negative feelings after the break-up and deal with them healthily rather than denying them behind a false mask of strength.

Never use your vulnerability in this period to emotionally blackmail your ex. That will only invite guilt and resentment. You'll have to take responsibility to recover and regain your emotional strength.

Distance yourself from your ex to take time to recover. Avoid their favorite places, mutually favorite places, and meet your common friends separately. Brooding over your relationship will only aggravate your pain.

Respect your ex's secrets and don't reveal them to your friends to take revenge for what they did. Remember, your secrets are in your ex-partner's possession, and they can do the same thing with you.

Don't announce your breakup and negative feelings on social media. Keep away from posting those sad songs, and cryptic status updates, on social media. Don't let your inner state tarnish your social media image.

You might feel guilty and resentful after the breakup. However, don't let this resentment influence your decisions in the present and for the future. In fact, shift your focus from resentment to healing yourself from those wounds.

Find a friend or a support system where you can express your emotions - anger, rage, sadness, vulnerability, etc. Also, find an activity to convert this rage into something positive. It could be something artistic or perhaps going to the gym.

Avoid the outbound gossip about your break-up in your social group. Don't reveal the details to everyone. Keep things confidential by revealing only to a small group of trusted friends.

After the break-up, it's natural for your ex to behave like an ass, refusing to return your stuff, badmouthing you to friends, or other obnoxious behavior. Counteract his behavior with calmness, kindness, and dignity.

Chapter Summary

1. Jealousy, possessiveness, and other unhealthy feelings are often mistakenly taken as romance or love.

2. There are certain things in a loving relationship that seem innocent but might be emotional blackmail. If they want to know everything about you right away, if they point out your flaws that don't exist, if they try to punish you after an argument, if they test you or keep a score of all the good deeds they've done for you, or turn to you for everything, or want to be your everything.

3. You can tell if you are in a loving relationship with your partner or merely attached. When you are in love, you'll reduce your ego, foster each other's growth, be loving, and not self-centered.

4. Alternatively, if the relationship is based on attachment, it will be dominated by ego. You'll focus on how your partner can make you happy, and become overly dependent on them to solve your life issues.

5. To deal with emotional blackmail in relationships, be aware of the warning signs, set your boundaries, be firm with them, and if the situation gets out of control, break-up from that toxic relationship.

6. It's natural to feel bowed down after ending a relationship with a loved one. Accept the help of a trained therapist to overcome the negative feelings, vulnerabilities, rage, and fear that envelops you in that time period.

In the next chapter, you will learn....

- What is codependency?
- Signs you are in a codependent relationship.
- The link with Sociopaths, Psychopaths, and Narcissists.
- Codependent parents.

CHAPTER SIX:

Codependency

What is codependency?

Codependency is a state of depending on other people for your emotional gratification, and for the carrying out of both essential and inconsequential daily and psychological functions.

In short, codependent people are needy, demanding, and submissive. They always fear others abandoning them. Therefore, they cling to them and behave immaturely. Codependents can go to any extremes to safeguard their relationship with their companion. They can even let themselves be abused or maltreated., but will remain committed to the relationship.

Thus, by accepting the role of victims, codependents control their abusers and manipulate them.

Types of codependency

There are 4 types of codependent behavior based on the root cause of their codependency:

Codependency to fend off fear of abandonment

These people can't bear their friends, spouse, or family members to desert them or attain true autonomy and independence. As a result, they are clingy, prone to panic, smothering, and display self-annihilating submissiveness.

Codependency to cope with the fear of losing control

Such people feign neediness and helplessness, and get people to cater to their needs, wishes, and requirements. They are 'drama queens,' refuse to mature emotionally, and force their loved ones to treat them as emotionally/physically invalid individuals. These types of codependents use emotional blackmail, and even threats to secure the presence and compliance of their loved ones.

Vicarious codependents

Vicarious codependents live through others. They sacrifice their own needs, opinions, and requirements for the sake of others, only to get their approval and keep them in their life forever. Also known as inverted narcissists, these people crave to be in a relationship with a narcissist irrespective of how much they abuse them. They actively seek relationships with narcissists and ONLY narcissists. They feel empty and unhappy in a relationship with any other kind of person.

Signs you are in a codependent relationship

It's sometimes hard to know if you are in a codependent situation. However, if you find yourself in a relationship, and you rely exclusively on it for feeling better or happy, you are likely to be in a codependent relationship. The feelings you associate with such a relationship are actually of infatuation rather than love. These feelings are more strongly experienced than the normal feelings associated with seeing or hearing from your partner. It's a state of euphoria.

A codependent relationship is like an addiction. It takes complete hold of you long before you realize it. Consider the following to know if you are in a codependent relationship:

- Do you often apologize or make excuses for your partner's attitude and actions in public or in front of friends and relatives?
- Do you fear to speak about your opinions or concerns in front of your partner?
- Does being around your partner give you feelings of low self-worth?
- Does your partner treat you with disrespect?
- Is your partner jealous of your accomplishments? Does he/she try to demoralize you, or criticize, or make you feel bad about yourself?
- Do you feel like your partner is too dependent on you and can't function without you?
- Does your partner threaten to harm themselves if you try to leave the relationship?
- Is sexual attention interpreted as love or affection by you?

If you answered 'Yes' to any one or all of these questions, you might be in a codependent relationship. However, codependency is often a two-way street. Not only your partner, but also *you* may be the perpetrator of codependent habits.

When you are codependent, you'll suffer from low self-esteem, and exhibit passive-aggressive or controlling psychological states. For instance, rather than telling your partner how you feel about a particular thing, you'll react by ignoring them or lashing out at them. You may also overreact on petty issues or use abusive language to control others.

8 warning signs you're in a codependent relationship

1. You start filling in the gaps

In a codependent relationship, one person starts taking complete responsibility for keeping in touch. If one partner starts pulling back on how much time, energy, and care they give, the other partner instinctively starts filling the gap by working harder to stay bonded.

2. Desire to 'fix' your partner

Codependent personalities are people-pleasers; they thrive on helping others or even think of 'fixing' them.

3. You lose your boundaries

Codependent individuals are over-givers. They continuously feel the need to give to others even at the expense of their own needs. They feel overly responsible for others or care too much for them. However, in the compulsion to give, they often neglect their boundaries and even let others intrude on them.

4. You don't have an independent life

When you become so dependent on someone that you lose who you actually are or the essence that makes you unique, you are in the trap of a codependent relationship.

5. You lose contacts with friends and family

When you start losing touch with your loved ones or those who are important to you, it's a sign of something grave. Your primary focus is on your partner, but it shouldn't be to the point where you're becoming isolated from the people previously important to you. You should be aware of this, and consider it seriously; otherwise, you'll become more and more dependent on your partner. Sometimes, if you decide, you aren't meant for each other, you'll look around for old friends but won't find any.

6. You always have to ask for approval

If you feel you have to get the permission of your partner for daily basic things or you can't make a decision without them, you are very possibly in a codependent relationship. If you had loads of confidence when you entered the relationship, but over time, you began to doubt yourself and became indecisive, you could be in an abusive codependent relationship.

7. Your partner has unhealthy habits

One of the early signs of a codependent relationship is when one person repeatedly engages in unhealthy habits like heavy drinking or binge eating. The other person either joins them or encourages it for his or her own reasons.

Example: Sara knew her boyfriend was pre-diabetic and should stop eating sweets. Yet, she never accepted this because of the good feelings she got from her boyfriend's appreciation of her recipes. So, despite knowing the truth, Sara kept promoting her boyfriend's unhealthy eating so that she could feel good.

8. You always chase reassurance

Ask yourself these questions:

- Do you or your partner always worry that the other person will break off the relationship?
- Does either of you need constant assurance that you are loved?
- Does either of you create tests to get the other person's attention?
- Does either of you flirt with people outside the relationship to evoke jealousy in one another, so that, if one threatens to leave, they can be begged to stay?
- Do you avoid direct conversations about the state of your relationship?

- Do you have difficulty being alone?
- Is your relationship extremely tense, and both of you enjoy the drama of breakups and reunions?

If you answered 'yes' to any of these questions, you are probably in a codependent relationship.

If you are in a healthy relationship, you'll celebrate each other's accomplishments, show respect to each other even if your opinions differ, and feel comfortable expressing your thoughts with each other. You'll feel loved and appreciated, happy in each other's company in public, be respectful of each other's privacy, and trusting towards one another.

On the opposite side, if you are in a codependent relationship, you'll be jealous of their accomplishments, fear speaking out your feelings to the partner, withhold your affection, spy on them, and feel resentful and suspicious about them.

Codependency shares some common symptoms of addiction like feelings of denial, low self-esteem, inability to adhere to or set boundaries, dysfunctional communication, and controlling attitudes.

Understanding the codependency bond with sociopaths, psychopaths, and narcissists

Reading from above, it may almost sound like codependency is a disease. However, it's an emotional and behavioral condition that is stored in your subconscious mind. It affects your ability to have a healthy relationship with others.

Psychotherapists call codependency a 'relationship addiction.' And, just like an addiction, a codependent relationship is based on insecurity, denial, control, and manipulation.

Someone who is a relationship addict may threaten to harm themselves if their partner thinks of ending the relationship with them, or they'll use other forms of emotional blackmail to control their partner. The person trapped in a codependent relationship, or the one who plays a passive role, frequently ends up putting more and more effort into pleasing their partner and sidelines their own needs.

To understand the bond between codependency and sociopaths, psychopaths, and narcissists, it's important to understand these three types of personalities.

Who is a sociopath?

The term 'sociopath' is used to describe a person who has an antisocial personality disorder. Such people can't understand another's feelings. They'll break rules, or act out of impulse, without feeling guilty for their actions. Sociopaths also use 'mind games' to control friends, family, colleagues, and their partners. To label someone as a sociopath, their psychology must show at least three out of these seven traits:

1. No respect for social norms or laws.
2. Telling lies, deceiving others, using false identities, and using others for personal gain.
3. Behave without thinking of consequences.
4. Shows aggressive behavior and gets into fights with others at every occasion.
5. Doesn't consider their safety or that of others.
6. They don't follow up on personal or professional responsibilities.
7. Don't feel guilty for hurting or mistreating others.

Who is a psychopath?

The term 'psychopath' also refers to antisocial personality disorder. Therefore, it's frequently used interchangeably with sociopaths. Both the descriptions are used under an umbrella term of Antisocial Personality Disorder (ASPD).

The common signs of a psychopathic mental state include:

1. Socially irresponsible conduct.
2. No interest in the rights of others.
3. Inability to differentiate between right and wrong.
4. Difficulty in empathizing with others.
5. Tendency to lie.
6. Manipulating and hurting others.
7. Recurring problems with social laws.
8. Disregard towards safety and responsibility.

What is narcissistic personality disorder?

Narcissistic personality disorder is used to describe an individual who is excessively full of themselves. It can be mistakenly perceived as self-love, but it's not a healthy sort of self-love. Narcissistic personalities need constant admiration and consider themselves to be better than anyone else.

They're in love with this inflated or exaggerated self-image that often masks deep feelings of insecurity. They exhibit self-centered behavior, lack of empathy and consideration for others, and excessive need for admiration. This thinking and conduct surfaces in every walk of life: work, friends, family, and love relationships.

Signs and symptoms of narcissistic personality disorder

1. Grandiose sense of self-importance.
2. They believe they're better than everyone else and should be recognized as such, even when they haven't done anything to earn it.
3. They exaggerate or lie about their achievements and talents.

4. Living in a dream world with self-glorifying fantasies of unlimited power, success, brilliance, and attractiveness characterize narcissistic personalities.

5. Narcissists need constant admiration to feed their egos. So they surround themselves with people who will feed their obsessive craving.

6. They expect favors from others as their due, their birthright.

7. They expect others to always comply with their whims and fancies.

8. If you fail to admire or praise them, they'll consider it as a betrayal

9. They view people in their lives as objects to serve their needs and can't empathize with anyone.

10. They feel threatened by people who are confident, popular, or who challenge them in any way.

11. They use bullying, insults, name-calling, and guilt to make others comply with their needs.

Despite all these shortcomings, narcissists often have a charming and magnetic personality. It's very easy for them to attract others by creating a fantastical, flattering self-image. Their apparent confidence and lofty dreams are often seductive enough to mesmerize anyone. Yet, it's wise to be cautious around such people.

If you think narcissistic personas can fulfill your longing to feel more important, more alive, you are very likely mistaken. Generally, it's only a fantasy with 0% reality.

How is codependency related to sociopaths, psychopaths, and narcissistic personalities?

Codependents lack a healthy relationship with themselves. They are prone to put others before themselves. They are so dependent on others for emotional gratification that they sideline their own needs for the sake of keeping the relationship.

Thus, codependent individuals are vulnerable targets for sociopathic, psychopathic, and narcissistic personalities. Since these personalities regard themselves as above everyone else, they use and exploit the codependent individuals without any guilt or remorse.

Codependents and sociopaths/psychopaths/narcissists find each other like the two pieces of a puzzle. When one is extremely giving, and the other is extremely demanding, they make the perfect duo of an abuser and the victim.

Codependent parents

Codependency doesn't necessarily exist between a boyfriend and girlfriend or a husband and wife. It can be between a parent and a child as well. The caregiver nature of parent-child relationships often makes it difficult to detect codependency.

However, here are a few signs that could indicate codependent parents:

Victim mentality in parents

A codependent parent believes that other people, particularly their children, are responsible for the wrongs committed to them in life, and therefore, they expect them to pay the compensation. Thus, they often exhibit guilt-tripping tactics to harness sympathy from their children. Instead of dealing with their life issues and traumas, and seeking a positive solution through counseling or therapy, the codependent parent latches onto the child and asks for compensation.

For instance, a father who could not achieve higher success in sports may demand that his son excel in sports and make up for his loss. If the child denies him, he'll use manipulation and guilt to make them comply.

The codependent parent is never wrong

Two people in a relationship can't be right all of the time. But in a codependent parent-child relationship, the parent is always right; at least the parent thinks so. Even when the child grows up to be an adult, the parent refuses to approach a discussion with openness and thereby avoids the possibility of being wrong. Instead, the parent will try to impose his/her view on the adult child and "correct" the child.

Such a parent never listens to the child's feelings and problems; they never learn about their child's personality, fearing it as a challenge to their authority.

If it's revealed that the codependent parent is wrong, they'll never apologize, or, if they do, they do it insincerely. A codependent parent wants absolute dominance over the child, and any weakness on their part will threaten this dominancy.

The codependent parent is extremely emotional

Crying, yelling, and silent treatment are the favorite weapons of a codependent parent. When they feel they're losing control in a situation or can't have the upper hand in an argument, they resort to crying, screaming, and other forms of intimidation to turn things in their favor.

If you point out their manipulative ways, they'll accuse you of being callous or insensitive. Further, if the child cries or expresses his hurt, the codependent parent gets angrier, often claiming the child's distress is insincere and manipulative.

The codependent parent is a poor listener

The codependent parent doesn't have a hearing disorder; nevertheless, they are poor listeners because they never listen/consider anyone else's opinion. Talking to a codependent parent may feel like 'talking to a brick wall.'

If the argument or the discussion is valid, even if you present irrefutable facts, the codependent parent will deny them and won't be moved in their position. They'll change the topic of discussion from the actual point being made.

The codependent parent imitates your words and phrases

If a child expresses his/her feelings to a codependent parent, the adult will mimic them. For instance, if the child says that the parent is upsetting them, the parent will reciprocate by saying, "You're hurting my feelings."

Whatever concern the child expresses, the codependent parent will turn it and adopt it as their own. If this is pointed out, the parent will ignore it, get angry, or act bewildered and confused.

The Codependent parent has mood swings

The codependent parent rapidly shifts from one mood to another to avoid responsibility and guilt. This especially happens when their manipulation tactics have succeeded in garnering the child's compliance.

For example, a mother rings her daughter in college and screams at her for not phoning often enough. Her manipulative tactics may eventually get the daughter to obey her and call more often. Once the mother achieves this, to maintain her victory and her role as a victim, she may say, "No, it's OK. You need not call me often. You'll only be doing it because I have asked you to do so."

In this case, the daughter will be persuaded to not only call her more but also reassure her that she's doing it out of her own free will.

Codependent parents wants to control at all costs

Control is the end goal all codependent parents desire. They expect love and devotion from their children to make up for the lack in other relationships. Often, the codependent parent will seek to gain from their child the love and attention they didn't receive from their parents.

The codependent parent seeks to gain control even over the adult child. If it becomes clear that they won't succeed, a meltdown often ensues. When the adult child refuses to give the parent what they want, they'll attempt to control with guilt by appearing frail, playing a victim, or using aggressive strategies.

The codependent parent uses subtle manipulation

Examples of subtle manipulation include silent treatment, passive-aggressive comments, denial of wrongdoing, and projection. The codependent parent uses all these forms of manipulation to leave their child confused as to ''Who's the real bad guy?''

Codependent parents are often oblivious to their manipulations. They believe they are doing it in their child's best interest. When you call them out on their manipulation, they get genuinely and deeply hurt and bewildered.

A codependent parent usually manipulates, not because they *want to*, but because they *have to*. That's because they don't know any other way to communicate with their adult child. So, they'll manipulate with finances, emotions, guilt, or any conceivable method to maintain their codependent relationship.

What should you do if you have a codependent parent?

The right way to deal with such parents depends upon the severity of the situation. In some cases, you may have to end the relationship completely. In others, you have to set your rules, carefully impose them, and perhaps look for a family therapist to help you maintain a healthy relationship with them.

Chapter Summary

1. Codependency is the mental and emotional dependency on others. Also known as 'relationship addiction,' it makes you demanding, submissive, and live in fear of abandonment by your loved one.
2. Codependents are vulnerable targets or victims of emotional manipulation because they allow abusers to control them for fear the abuser might leave the relationship.
3. If you rely exclusively on a particular relationship, whether parents, spouse, friend, or lover, to feel better and happy, you are possibly in a codependent relationship.
4. Two partners in a codependent relationship are often jealous of each other's accomplishments, are afraid of speaking about their feelings to each other, or will spy on each other out of suspicion.
5. A codependent relationship is based on insecurity, denial, control, and manipulation.
6. Sociopaths or psychopaths are the terms used for people suffering from Antisocial Personality Disorder. Such people have no concern for social norms and will exhibit socially irresponsible behavior without thinking about the consequences or considering other people's feelings and safety.
7. Narcissists have an inflated sense of ego and believe themselves to be better than everyone else. They crave praise and admiration from others.
8. Both codependent people, and sociopaths/psychopaths/narcissists, have an unhealthy relationship with themselves. One puts others before themselves, while the other puts themselves over others. Both interlock as abuser and victim, just like two pieces of a puzzle.
9. Codependency can also exist between a parent and a child.

10. A codependent parent holds their child responsible for the parent's unhappiness and expects the child to compensate by complying with all their demands.

11. The codependent parent thinks they are always right and tries to impose their views on the child. They use crying, yelling, or silent treatment to gain the advantage in any arguments.

12. Codependent parents are poor listeners and never listen to, or consider, their child's feelings and opinions. They also exhibit rapid mood swings to avoid responsibility and guilt.

13. Codependent parents always wish to control their child, and use subtle manipulation to achieve the same.

14. In mild cases of codependent parents, you should set your boundaries, impose them firmly, and look for a family therapist to help overcome the issue.

15. If the problem is insoluble, it's best to end the relationship with codependent parents.

In the next chapter, you will learn....

- How to avoid emotional blackmail.
- How to defeat emotional blackmail.
- Non-defensive communication skills to stop emotional blackmail.
- Developing boundaries and mental resilience.

CHAPTER SEVEN:

Dealing With Emotional Blackmail

Emotional blackmail is not a pleasant experience, but unfortunately, many of us succumb to it at various stages of our lives. The truth is there are many people out there ready to prey upon you and exploit you for their advantage. It's crucial you know about emotional blackmail, the tactics used, and where you can find these parasitic personalities.

After discussing all this, we come to the most interesting and significant part. That is how to deal with emotional blackmail.

Here's the ultimate guide to deal with emotional blackmail:

Recognize the red flag situations

Red flag situations are absolutely, without any doubt, pointing towards emotional blackmail. Being aware of these situations is the first step to deal with the threat and make it powerless.

Ask yourself if you find yourself apologizing for your actions even though you weren't wrong or at fault? Observe if your partner is ever prepared to take 'No' for an answer. Do you always find yourself giving in to your spouse or partner's wishes at the expense of your own? Perhaps you may have noticed that you always seem to be the one who makes the sacrifices and compromises in the relationship.

Worst of all, does your spouse or partner intimidate or threaten you into complying with their demands?

Know the typical emotional blackmail tactic

People who employ these tactics use Fear>Obligation>Guilt as their favorite way of getting what they want.

At first, the blackmailer tries to make the victim fearful, angry, or disappointed. This makes the target feel obligated to meet the demands. If the victim still doesn't comply, the manipulator instills feelings of guilt in them for not abiding by the abuser's wishes.

All this is done in a very subtle manner to appeal to the victim's sensibilities. They play manipulation in a way that the victim thinks their demands are reasonable, and they should agree to them.

If you feel yourself to be the victim of this FOG technique, ask a close friend or a relative to give you a different perspective on the relationship, and tell you what they see or feel from the outside.

Know if you are vulnerable

People who have trouble saying 'No' are most susceptible to emotional blackmail. If you are one of them, allow yourself to get comfortable with the idea of refusing. Think of the tone and the words you'll use to signify empowerment and say 'No' to other's manipulation in future.

How to stop emotional blackmail?

1. There are times when you need to give priority to your wants, needs, and preferences over those of your partner.

2. Stand up for your truth, views, and opinions, and become more assertive and self-protective.
3. Set clear boundaries of what you'll accept and what you won't. Boundaries shouldn't be overstepped in any circumstances.
4. Realizing your well-being comes first even if you love your partner dearly. Share your personal priorities and make compromises accordingly.
5. Don't give in to the emotional blackmail; it will make the situation worse.
6. If your loved one threatens you with physical violence, immediately leave the situation and alert the relevant authorities.
7. Reach out to your close friends or social support system and seek professional help from a therapist if necessary.

Are you emotionally blackmailing someone?

Besides being the victim, you can also be an offender. None of us are immune to that tendency. Observe your patterns in getting others to do what you'd like. What is your response when someone argues with you or doesn't do what you'd like? Do you implore? Get punitive? Punish through not providing love and affection? Do you take their opposition as a threat to the relationship? Do you respond with remarks like "If you loved me, you would have done so and so"?

If you answer in the affirmative to any of these, you may well be blackmailing others, either knowingly or unknowingly. So you must admit and acknowledge this. This is a way of taking responsibility for your actions and creates a climate of safety and repair for yourself and the other person.

Tell the person you have been manipulating that you are aware of your actions. Saying sorry won't be enough, though. You have to assure the person that you are ready to own your actions and seek to change the way you behave. Ask the person you have hurt what they need from you to feel they can trust you. Find ways to resolve the issues together and move forward.

How to defeat emotional blackmail?

First, read the following checklist to know if you are a victim of emotional blackmail:

- You tell yourself that giving in is OK.
- You believe that giving in is fine to calm the other person down.
- You feel that what you want is incorrect.
- You think it's better to give in now; you'll oppose it another time.
- You feel that it is better to surrender than to offend someone.
- You don't usually make a stand.
- You give away your power.
- You do what other people want, not what you want.
- You accept everything without protest.
- You give up things you like to placate the other person.

If any of these strike a chord with you, you could well be the victim of emotional blackmail. So, now it's time to gather your courage and make changes in yourself. Grab that personal maturity and take the position that will stop you being a victim; take a stand for yourself.

Take a moment to look at your past and see if that complacency is automatic, inherited, or the result of some acquired habit in childhood. It can be difficult and daunting to shift your perspective from being a victim and change the dynamics, but it's well worth it. Reach out for support when needed.

When you are emotionally blackmailed in a relationship, you still have choices. You can let things stay as they are, or work towards a healthier situation, or decide the relationship will have to end. There are tactics, abilities, and life-style changes to alter the situation before you decide to give in or give up.

You need two things to defeat the person who blackmails you emotionally:

- Learn and develop the skills of non-defensive communication.
- Develop your boundaries and mental resilience.

When you decide to shift yourself out of a situation of emotional blackmail, it requires a lot of courage and willpower to tolerate the feeling of displeasing your loved ones. Sometimes, that can bring up past anxieties. Many of our fears are derived from past experiences, even though we mistake them as originating from current events. We mix up our earlier lives with the present, and therefore, when we get hurt, we act according to our past experience. We can and will do anything to protect ourselves from anxieties over other people's reactions.

But, if you separate the present from your past, you'll have more confidence and many more choices for how you respond. Don't see yourself as weak or incapable. Your personal history need not continue to dictate your present. Believe in yourself, and have the strength and resilience to handle change. Despite feeling fearful, allow yourself to go with it.

Along with fear, comes guilt which can be a major contributor to your problems. Just as you allow yourself to cope with fear, you can tolerate this guilt too! Your dignity, self-respect, and emotional health will ultimately thank you for doing so.

Take a closer look at your fears and guilt. Ask yourself the following questions:

- Am I doing anything spiteful?
- Am I being cruel?
- Did I do anything abusive?
- Did I insult someone or wanted to insult them?
- Is what I did humiliating someone?
- Is my behavior insulting?
- Am I being harmful by doing this?

If your answer is an honest 'No' to these questions, then there's nothing you should be guilty of. If it's 'Yes,' then you need to change the way you behave. Changing might seem uncomfortable in the beginning, but try to see this discomfort as a new start in your relationship, as a way to greater maturity.

Many people think that they need to become stronger before they can take constructive steps towards defeating emotional blackmail. The truth is that as you start shifting to a new set of thought and conduct, the sense of your strength will ensue automatically.

Others may feel surprised by your alteration and may react adversely. Allow for this; don't take it personally. Don't back out from changing your determination not to accept emotional blackmail. It won't feel terrific at first, but that's still all right.

The tactics of an abuser thrive on confrontation and escalation. The victim is pushed lower and lower in the power structure. When we are emotionally connected to someone and receive criticism from them, we naturally tend to get defensive. However, defensiveness creates a similar response in the other person. Find non-defensive ways to communicate with your blackmailer, they won't be able to get to you, and you can shift the dynamic.

Remember this mantra! Next time when anybody asks you to do

something you are not happy with, the first thing to do is STOP. Take a deep breath. This helps you pull out of the situation and any habitual ways you might have of reacting defensively.

Instead of a blunt 'Yes' or 'No,' say, "I am unable to take the decision just at the moment; I need to think about this." That will allow you time to calm down, gather your strength, and connect with your thoughts without anxiety and pressure. When you are in balance and can double-check with both your intellect and emotions, you can make a healthy decision.

How to develop the skills of non-defensive communication?

Non-defensive communication is a style of communication that avoids the defensive maneuvers and power struggles that tend to fuel an argument or conflict.

The opposite of non-defensive communication is the 'war model,' which increases the conflict because the focus is on winning the argument rather than solving the problem. Communication under the 'war model' elicits a defensive response that activates the emotional part of your brain that controls the 'fight or flight' response. As a result, the person reacts impulsively and not rationally. This reduces their capacity to communicate effectively.

When we're defensive, we engage in power struggles as a part of the 'flight or fight' response. Sometimes, the person even withdraws and surrenders. This vulnerability makes one susceptible to hurt or attack.

We all have a natural tendency to get defensive to protect ourselves from criticism. When you get defensive while communicating with others, you make it harder for people around you to listen to what you say. It also gets difficult to hear their side of things.

You might have observed this during critical conversations with your spouse, boss, co-worker, or friend. When you get defensive, the other person is likely to respond the same way. The result is ultimately frustration and exhaustion, where neither of you gets what you want.

To avoid this happening, develop your non-defensive communication skills by following these three steps:

1. State your observation

To start your conversation in a non-defensive way, avoid blaming the other person for the problem. Be careful not to make character assassinations about the opposite person. Instead, focus on what you see or hear.

For example, instead of saying, "You didn't iron the clothes," say, "I see the clothes are not ironed."

Or instead of "You are always late," say, "I seem to be the first one to arrive at the office."

When you use "I" statements, you sound less critical and make your listener feel less defensive when compared to the statements starting with "You."

2. Describe your feelings

Follow-up your observation with a comment regarding how that behavior made you feel. This helps the listener relate better to the problem in question. Expressing your feelings here is more than a one-word answer to, "How do you feel about a particular thing?" You must identify your feelings properly and narrate them in detail to relate more effectively to the person you are talking to.

For example, in place of, "You make me angry," say, "I am feeling frustrated and stuck."

3. Request a specific behavior

The most critical part of non-defensive conversation is how to make requests for different attitudes and actions in the future. By making such a request, you let the other person know you aren't holding any grudges or complaints against them. Instead, you wish to work towards a constructive solution to the problem.

For example, "I would appreciate it if you could move those papers off the dining table before dinner."

If you follow the above steps diligently, you can quickly learn the skills of non-defensive communication, and make your conversations successful. By being polite and respectful in communicating, you play the role of a 'bigger person.'

Don't bottle things up. Don't wait to bring up the issue; otherwise, your suppressed emotions will escalate, and you won't be able to keep your conversation productive.

Non-defensive communication takes practice and time to bear fruit. Hang in there with it; it's worth the effort.

Non-defensive communication requires a person to change their core attitude. It obliges them to alter the way in which they ask questions, give feedback, express feelings, and offer opinions. They may well have to change their tone of voice, phrasing, and body language.

Once you follow these steps of non-defensive communication with persistence, you feel empowered. The blackmailer can't successfully attack you or rob you of your powers.

How to stand up for yourself at the workplace without being defensive

In the workplace, not everyone plays fair office politics. You'll find people talking about your work in a way that can negatively impact your reputation. A person may falsely accuse you of something wrong or take credit for your work. Misunderstanding can ensue with people pointing fingers at you.

It's critical you stand up for yourself. You can't afford to stay quiet waiting for the 'truth' to come out by itself. You have to play an active role in standing up for yourself to build or defend your reputation.

Besides standing up for yourself, it's important how you do it. Standing up for yourself is a communication skill that needs practice and time to master. You have to do it without sounding hostile. If you use an aggressive mode of communication, it'll be tough to get people to listen to your side of the story.

Let's say something happened at your workplace. You'll have your perception of what happened, and others will have their view of what happened. The two may not coincide. When you try to forcefully convince others of your perception, you are basically attacking them. You'll be using the classic, "He said, she said" phrases, and you'll sound defensive. The more you insist you're the one telling the truth, the more it implies that the other person is lying. You'll only sound worse. The goal of standing up for yourself is to maintain your poise, show others that you're confident of your work, and they can't easily take advantage of you.

Follow these 4 tips to stand up for yourself without sounding blunt and defensive:

1. Stay cool and use a calm tone

That's hard to do when someone has said bad things about you, but it's crucial if you want to take the best approach to stand up for yourself. Your communication becomes sharp and vengeful when your emotions dominate your judgment. When you act through your emotions, you'll sound defensive and vulnerable without achieving the goal of standing up for yourself in the best way. On the other hand, if you are composed, people are more likely to listen to what you say.

2. Communicate your perspective without blaming others

When someone accuses you of doing something wrong, it's an impulsive reaction to say, "No, I didn't do it. They are lying." Such a statement tends to sound defensive. Alternatively, you can say something like, "I am surprised by this news. I am not sure why you perceived that I did this, but I respectfully disagree." Taking this path, you focus your conversation on your reactions, and the facts pointing towards you, instead of the person who accused you.

3. Be the bigger person

Sometimes people misunderstand what happens, and this leads to miscommunication. They point the gun at you because they fail to understand the situation from your point of view. Instead of pointing fingers at them, be the bigger person, and respond by saying, "This is perhaps a misunderstanding." This way, you'll appear more generous and willing to build healthy relationships at the workplace.

4. Support your perspective with facts

You can't present your case without any facts to prove it. Don't alter them to turn the situation in your favor. Just present the facts that support why you disagree with others without blaming them. It's also important to know when to stand up for yourself. When in a group setting, if someone says you did something which you didn't do, it's not always advisable to make a forceful stand then and there. You can simply say that you are surprised by their accusations, and you disagree. Remember, it could be a misunderstanding. In that instance, you still stood up for yourself in front of the group, but did so without blaming the person and going into details. It shows your poise and communication skills, which will leave a good impression.

How to develop mental resilience?

Life is hard sometimes. When adversity strikes, can you recover quickly? Do you adapt? Or do you feel as though you have no choice other than to go under? If so, that suggests you don't naturally have a great deal of resilience. However, it's not a thing to worry about. There are many ways you can improve your mental resilience. You can learn and hone it through practice, hard work, and discipline.

Our lives can be challenged by different circumstances. That might be a bereavement, losing our job, or the end of a relationship. Despite this, such challenges provide an opportunity to develop into a stronger person.

How to be mentally strong?

Mental strength means being able to cope with stressful situations, problems, and challenges in our lives. It's the occasions when we rise to the challenge, and do our best, even if we're in difficult situations. Building mental strength is fundamental to leading our best life. Just as we exercise and eat the right foods for our physical health, we must also develop our mental muscles by using psychological tools and techniques.

Good mental health helps us have happier lives, have better friendships and social ties, and does wonders for our confidence. It helps us to deal with the difficult situations we may find ourselves in.

In order to have stable mental health, you must work at it. It can take a while to see results, but it can be done. Just as you see physical gains by regular exercise, mental strength is built by developing good psychological methods that enhance our minds and spirits.

For physical health, you must leave behind things like junk food. Similarly, for mental gain, you should get rid of unhealthy habits like self-pity or blaming others.

Building resilience and mental toughness

The American Psychological Association defines Mental Resilience as *"The process of adapting well in the face of adversity, trauma, tragedy, threats, or even significant sources of stress."*

On the same lines, Mental Toughness is the ability to stay strong in the face of adversity, to keep your focus and determination, despite the difficulties you face. A mentally tough individual sees adversity and challenges as an opportunity rather than a threat, and has confidence and a positive approach to deal with them constructively.

The 4 C's of mental toughness

1. Control

Are you in control of your life, including your emotions and sense of purpose? The extent to which you are in control of these elements indicates your level of mental toughness. This control component can be considered as your self-esteem.

The higher you are on the Control scale, the more comfortable you are in yourself. You can control your emotions well, be less likely to reveal your emotional state to others, and you'll be less distracted by other people's attitudes and feelings.

Being lower on the Control scale means you take situations personally and believe you can do nothing about what has taken place.

2. Commitment

This is the measure of your personal focus and reliability. If you are High on the commitment scale, you can effectively set goals and achieve them consistently without getting distracted. You are good at establishing practices and strategies that cultivate success.

On the other hand, being Low on the commitment scale indicates your difficulty in setting and prioritizing your goals or adapting habits indicative of success. You also get easily distracted by other people or competing priorities.

The Control and Commitment scales represent the Resilience part of mental toughness. The ability to respond positively to setbacks requires a sense of knowing that you are in control of your life and can make a change. You also need focus and an ability to establish habits and targets that will get you back on track to achieve your goals.

3. Challenge

Challenge is the extent to which you are motivated and can adapt. Being high on the Challenge scale means you are determined to achieve your personal best and see adversity as an opportunity instead of a threat. You are psychologically agile and flexible. Being Low on the Challenge scale means you see change as a threat and avoid difficult situations for fear of failure.

4. Confidence

Confidence is your ability to be productive and capable. It's your belief in yourself that you can influence others. Being high on the Confidence scale means you believe that you will successfully complete tasks, take setbacks in your stride while maintaining and strengthening your resolve. Being Low on the Confidence scale shows that you easily get upset by disappointments, and believe that you aren't capable, or that you lack ability to influence other people.

The Challenge and Confidence scales represent the Confidence part of Mental Toughness. They represent a person's ability to identify and seize an opportunity and see the situations as opportunities to explore. If you are confident in yourself, you can easily interact with others and are likely to convert problems into successful outcomes.

How to Build Resilience?

Resilience can be improved through concentration, good habits, and hard work. There are many strategies for the same. However, you need to identify the way that works best for you. Your level of mental resilience is not something that is decided upon by random factors. It can be improved throughout your life.

So here are the different strategies and techniques to improve your mental resilience:

1. Developing new skills

Learning new skills is an integral part of building resilience because it helps to build confidence in your ability to learn and grow. These inner and outer qualities can be utilized during challenging times, and also increase your self-esteem and ability to solve problems. You can invest in learning new activities through competency-based learning.

Also, if you can acquire new skills in a group setting, there's nothing like that. It gives you an added advantage of social support, which also helps in building resilience.

2. Setting your goals

Develop the ability to set out what you want to achieve, measuring out the steps by which you will get there, and acting accordingly. This will help to develop will-power and mental resilience. These goals can be anything related to your physical health, emotional well being, career, finance, or spirituality.

If you have goals that require you to learn new skills, it will have a double benefit, perhaps something like learning a new language or learning to play an instrument. Setting and working towards goals that have a spiritual dimension, doing voluntary work for disadvantaged people, can be immensely rewarding and helps in building resilience.

This is because such activities provide a more profound insight into life, which is valuable during tough times.

3. Controlled Exposure

Controlled or gradual exposure to anxiety-provoking situations helps people overcome their fears much more quickly. Research studies show that this can build resilience, along with skill-acquisition and goal-setting strategies.

For example, public speaking is a useful life skill, but it also tends to create anxiety in many people. Such individuals could set goals of controlled exposure to acquire the ability to do this. They could begin by speaking in public to a small number of friends. Then, having gained some confidence in doing that, they can then move on to larger audiences.

The American Psychology Association further shares 11 strategies for building mental resilience:

1. Make connections

You can strengthen your resilience through healthy links to family, friends, and community. Building relationships with people in your life who are important to you, and who will help you when times are hard, all these things can be immensely useful in lifting our spirits and encouraging us to feel there is light at the end of the tunnel. Similarly, when you help others in their tough times, it helps you as well.

2. Crises are not Disasters

Even though problems may confront us, it's vital to bear in mind that our reactions are what makes us. If we deal with what is in front of us and look to the future, we can have confidence that things will change for the better. This simple faith can make us feel better and give us the necessary power to deal with the situation.

3. Accept that change is inevitable

Life is, by its nature, prone to constant change. What we might want at one period of our life may have altered a few years down the road. It may be that some objectives may have to be changed. By accepting the factors you can't change, or which are not under your control, it allows you to focus on those subjects that can realistically be dealt with.

4. Move towards your goals

Besides setting your goals, it's also important to make sure they are realistic. Creating small, actionable steps makes your goals attainable. Try for practical realistic accomplishments on the way to achieving the major prize. Try to accomplish things in small increments instead of trying to do everything all at once.

5. Take decisive actions

Instead of running away from problems, or daydreaming that they will go away, resolve to take decisive action to solve them in the best way possible.

6. Look for self-discovery opportunities

Misfortunes in your life create stress but can be a meaningful source of learning and personal growth. Finding out how to cope with a difficult situation, and successfully coming through it, can boost your confidence, improve your spirits, strengthen your relationships, and teach you deeper truths. You can unlock your hidden strengths during these challenging times. Sometimes, it can be a journey that makes us appreciate life all the more.

7. Think positively about yourself

Working towards your goals and improving your confidence helps in preventing difficulties and building resilience. Having a positive view of yourself is also at the core of problem-solving.

8. Keep things in perspective

When things get tough, remember that many people experience similar hardships in their lives. It is, in the end, all part of being human. Don't let yourself see the problem as worse than it is. Make sure you keep one eye on the future when times seem challenging in the present.

9. Maintain a hopeful outlook

When you focus on the negative part of the situation, you can give way to your fears and find it hard to know what to do. Keep your spirits up, and be confident you can solve the difficulty. Work out how you can cope with it, and you will probably surprise yourself.

10. Take care of yourself

Looking after yourself is something that shouldn't be underestimated. It will help you to deal all the better with hard and stressful circumstances. Self-care should include things like paying attention to your feelings, and doing things that help you to feel happier and more content. Taking up hobbies, exercising, engaging in creative pursuits are all extremely useful.

11. Other ways to strengthen resilience

It can be a great idea to undertake a course in meditation or similar mental disciplines. Techniques such as this are certainly of immense help in calming your mind and thereby improving your resilience.

Strategies for building resilience

As said before, the right approach to building resilience will vary between different people. Every individual reacts in their own way to traumatic and stressful life events. Therefore, what might work for one person may not work for another.

Here are some common strategies to employ for building resilience:

Learn from your past

Take a look at your past experiences and sources of personal strength to get insight as to which resilience-building strategies will work for you. The American Psychology Association recommends asking these questions to yourself to judge how you've reacted to challenging situations in the past:

1. What types of events have been most stressful for you?
2. How have those events affected you?
3. Did it help to think of important people in your life when distressed?
4. Who did you go to for support when working through a trauma?
5. What have you learned about yourself during challenging times?
6. Is it helpful for you to assist someone else with a similar experience?
7. Have you been able to overcome obstacles, and if so, how?
8. What makes you feel more hopeful about the future?

Be flexible

Being resilient means having a flexible mindset. When undergoing stressful circumstances and events in your life, it is necessary to maintain flexibility and balance in the following ways:

1. Allow yourself to experience strong emotions, and realize when you have to push them aside to continue functioning.
2. Take the necessary action to deal with your problems and meet the demands of daily living, but also know when to step back and rest/re-energize yourself.
3. Spend time with your loved ones who offer support and encouragement; nurture yourself.

4. Rely on others, but also know when to rely on yourself.

Sometimes, the support of family and friends is not enough. Know when to seek assistance from outside, such as self-help and community support groups, books and publications, online resources, or a licensed mental health professional.

Books, publications, and online resources offer a wealth of information where you can hear/read how others have successfully navigated through tough and challenging situations like yours. These are valuable resources of motivation, inspiration, and ways to deal with stress and trauma. However, make sure you always refer to a reliable source.

Sharing your experiences, emotions, and ideas within support groups can provide relaxation and comfort to you. It will make you feel there's someone to rely on during difficult times.

If other methods prove unsuccessful, it's best to seek professional help from a mental health professional. Talk to a licensed therapist if you can't function in your daily life because of painful life events.

Resilient Relationships

Resilience is also an essential aspect of your relationships. Relationships demand ongoing attention and cultivation, especially during times of adversity.

Certain relationships can survive better than others. That's because they foster resilience in each other.

Seven characteristics of highly resilient relationships

1. **Active optimism**

Optimism is not just hoping that things will get better; instead, it's believing that they will and then taking action. Optimism in a relationship means an agreement to avoid critical, hurtful, and cynical comments, and work together to harness the power of living positively.

2. Honesty, integrity, accepting responsibility for one's actions, and the willingness to forgive

When two people involved in a relationship are committed to recognizing the responsibility of their actions, are loyal to each other, and forgive each other, they are likely to cultivate resilience in their relationship.

3. Decisiveness

Having the courage to take action, even when it can provoke anxiety in a relationship is crucial. Decisive action could involve leaving a toxic relationship. Such decisiveness can promote your resilience.

4. Tenacity

Tenacity is perseverance and ability to hold on in the face of discouragement, setbacks, and failures. Remember, there will always be ebbs and flows, good times as well as hard times, in your relationships. But, how much you can hold on is a testament to your tenacity.

5. Self-Control

In the context of relationships, self-control is the ability to control impulses, resist temptations, and delay gratification. These are desirable qualities that help one to avoid negative practices and promote healthy practices, particularly in times of adversity.

6. Honest communication

Open, honest communication maintains the sense of 'belonging' and connectedness in a relationship. Sometimes, the most difficult conversations are the most important ones to have.

7. Presence of Mind

Presence of mind has many positive implications for you as well as your partner. This awareness leads to calm, non-judgemental thinking, and open communication between the couple. It also enables collaborative thinking and openness to new solutions, rather than blaming and condemning each other.

How to become resilient for life?

If you wish to have strong mental resilience for the rest of your life, start building it right now! Practice the strategies and tips discussed above with perseverance; over time, you will increase your ability to bounce back and adapt to your hardships.

The craziest thing about experiencing adverse events is that the more you flex your resilience muscle, the better you'll be able to respond next time.

Developing your emotional boundaries in relationships

The second way to beat emotional blackmail is to set your boundaries. The most important question that may click in your mind right now is, "Why should I have boundaries? How can setting boundaries save me from emotional blackmail?"

Setting healthy personal boundaries fosters healthy relationships, increases your self-esteem, and reduces stress, anxiety, and frustration. Boundaries help protect you by clearly defining what you accept and what you don't in any relationship.

Boundaries include physical as well as emotional boundaries. Physical boundaries include your body, personal space, and privacy. If anybody stands too close to you, touches you inappropriately, or flips through the files on your phone, they violate your physical boundaries.

Emotional boundaries include separating your feelings from that of others. Taking responsibility for another's feelings, letting them dictate your feelings, sacrificing your needs to please others, blaming others for your problems, and taking excessive responsibility for their difficulties are violations of your emotional boundaries.

When you have strong boundaries, they protect your self-esteem and your identity as an individual, and your right to make choices in life.

Setting boundaries is not sufficient unless you protect them too. But, most of us find it difficult to set healthy boundaries consistently, especially the emotional ones. It's tricky sometimes to even identify when these boundaries get crossed. The reason is the fear of consequences to our relationships by setting them.

The red flags of violation to your boundaries are - discomfort, stress, anxiety, resentment, fear, and guilt. These feelings occur from the sense of being taken advantage of or not being appreciated.

Ask yourself if the following statements resonate with you:

- You can't make your own decisions.
- You can't ask for what you need.
- You can't say No.
- You feel criticized.
- You feel responsible for other people's feelings.
- You seem to take on their moods.
- You often feel nervous, anxious, and worried around those people.

If you have vague boundaries, or none at all, you'll have a weak sense of self-identity, and a feeling of disempowerment in making the decisions of your life. In consequence, you'll rely on your partner for your happiness and decision-making responsibility, thereby losing important parts of your identity; this creates the risk of becoming codependent.

The inability to set boundaries also results from the fear of abandonment in a relationship, fear of being judged, and fear of hurting someone else's feelings.

The first step to building better boundaries is to know what your limits are. Who you are, what you're responsible for, and what you aren't responsible for. You are responsible for your happiness, your behavior, your choices, and feelings. You cannot be held to account for someone else's happiness, behavior, choices, and feelings.

Emotional boundaries and boundary traps

Emotional boundaries fall into the categories of time, energy, emotions, and values. However, beware of the boundary traps in a relationship. Do you recognize any of the following thoughts, or things you may have said?

- I don't have my own identity. My identity comes from my partner, and I'll do anything and everything to make them happy.
- This relationship is better than my last one.
- I spend all my time fulfilling my partner's goals and activities. I have no time to do what I want to do.
- My partner will be lost if I am not there.
- This relationship will get better if I give more time to it.
- Most of the time, the relationship is great, except for a few occasions, and that's enough for me.

How to set your emotional boundaries?

First, commit to yourself to put your identity, needs, feelings, and goals on priority. Healthy emotional boundaries start with a belief and acceptance of how you are at present. Let go of the responsibility to fix others, to be responsible for the outcome of someone else's choices, saving or rescuing others, depending on their approval, and changing yourself to be liked by others.

Prepare a list of boundaries you want to strengthen. Don't just jot them down, but visualize yourself setting them, and assertively communicating them to others. Boundary setting is a process. So start small by setting non-threatening boundaries first, experience success with them, and then move on to more challenging ones.

Here are a few to start with:

- Say no to the tasks you don't want to do or don't have time to do.
- Be ready to help.
- Thank others without apology, regret, or shame.
- Ask for help when required.
- Delegate tasks to your partner or family members.
- Don't overcommit to anything. Protect your time.
- Ask for your personal space.
- Speak out when faced with behavior that infringes on your space.
- Honor yourself and your needs.
- Drop the guilt and responsibility for others.
- Share personal information gradually and in a mutual way.

When you are setting your boundaries and shifting the dynamic in the relationship, you are likely to encounter resistance from the other person. Stick to your guns, and keep on communicating your needs. The 'broken record technique' comes in handy at this moment. Repeat the statement as many times as needed.

Healthy relationships are a balance of give and take. You feel calm, safe, supported, respected, cared for, and unconditionally accepted in a healthy relationship. You are free to be who you are and encouraged to be the best version of yourself.

Similarly, healthy boundaries are also a sign of emotional health, self-respect, and strength. By setting your boundaries, you set high standards for those around you. Expect to be treated the same way you treat them. You'll soon find yourself surrounded by people who respect you, care for you, your feelings, needs, and treat you with kindness.

Chapter Summary

1. To deal with emotional blackmail, you first need to identify the red flag situations of the tactic.
2. If you always apologize to your partner, even for the right actions, if you can't say No to your partner, if you always make sacrifices, or give in to your partner's demands at the expense of your own, you are the victim of emotional blackmail.
3. Know the typical FOG technique or the tactics of Fear, Obligation, and Guilt used by blackmailers to manipulate you.
4. If you find it difficult to say No to your partner or in any relationship, you are vulnerable to emotional blackmail. Get comfortable in refusing the demands that don't align with your best interests.
5. Give priority to your needs, stand up for your truth, views, and opinions to stop emotional blackmail.
6. Set clear boundaries of what behavior you'll accept and what you won't. Make sure your boundaries can't be overstepped under any circumstances.
7. Observe your actions to know if you aren't employing any of those tactics to manipulate others. If yes, admit and acknowledge your manipulative behavior, say sorry about it,

and assure your target that you're ready to change your ways. Make them feel the trust and safety in your relationship.

8. You need two things to defeat emotional blackmail - developing the skills of non-defensive communication, and developing your emotional boundaries and mental resilience.

9. Non-defensive communication is the best way to deal with a blackmailer. It is a way of expressing your thoughts and feelings to others without getting defensive or pointing fingers at others.

10. When you use a defensive mode of communication, the other person also gets defensive in turn. This makes it difficult for them to hear your side of the story.

11. You can communicate in a non-defensive way by stating your observation about the situation, describing your feelings by using "I" statements and requesting different behavior in future.

12. Your mental strength is your capacity to deal effectively with stressful situations and perform to the best of your ability.

13. Mental strength can be developed over time by choosing the habits of personal development.

14. Mental resilience is the process of adapting well to the adversities in your life.

15. Mental toughness is the ability to stay strong in the face of adversity and keep your focus and determination.

16. Control over your emotions, commitment towards your goals, ability to be productive, capable, and adapting to the adversities of life are central aspects of mental toughness.

17. Your mental resilience level is not decided upon at birth; you can develop it through will power, discipline, and hard work.

18. There are different strategies and techniques to build your mental resilience. Choose the one that works best for you.

19. Resilience is also important for healthy relationships. Relationships that foster resilience in each other have better chances of survival than others.

247

FINAL WORDS

A healthy relationship helps you evolve into a better version of yourself. It enables you to grow into a kind and confident personality.

If you feel suffocated and controlled in a relationship; if your needs don't matter, or you feel unsafe to express your thoughts and feelings with that person, your relationship has transformed into a toxic one.

Toxicity can creep into the dearest and closest relationships. It could be between parent and child, your spouse, lover, or a close friend. Toxicity invades a relationship when one person starts manipulating the other to give in to their demands without recognizing or respecting the other's needs.

Manipulation may sometimes seem harmless, but is actually an emotional blackmail, an emotional abuse. That's because the emotional blackmailer uses your feelings negatively against you to get what they want. In short, they control you and your behavior in order to fulfill their demands.

It's essential to be aware of the signs of emotional blackmail. Develop awareness that you are being manipulated. Otherwise, the person will continue to blackmail you, and you'll end up with frustration, anxiety, and low self-esteem. If you aren't aware of the signs of emotional blackmail, you can't deal with it or stop it.

Here are some examples of manipulation used by an emotional blackmailer:

- Threats to endanger your life.
- Threats that they will kill themself if you don't obey their wishes.
- Control you by using money.
- Threats to end the relationship with you.
- Manipulate you into feeling compassionate for him/her.
- Making you feel guilty.
- Demoralizing you.
- Hurting you emotionally.
- Depriving you of love, care, and appreciation.
- Making you feel selfish and inconsiderate.

The blackmailer uses clever and covert techniques to make you believe that his/her demands are reasonable, and you must comply with them. However, the more you concede, the worse the situation gets.

Moreover, the emotional blackmailer gets to know your fears, the deep-rooted ones like fear of failure, isolation, and humiliation, which they use against you to get their demands fulfilled.

But why do some people resort to emotional blackmail?

Emotional blackmail is usually used as a weapon to gain control over someone else's thoughts and feelings. Such people are generally emotionally insecure, possibly due to their experience of similar abuse in childhood. As a result, they can't differentiate what is right and what is wrong.

Since they grew up being emotionally manipulated themselves, they believe it to be the right way of asking for things or obtaining their demands. They mistakenly believe that by making others feel powerless and vulnerable, they'll feel powerful and good about themselves.

Every person who resorts to emotional blackmail suffers from low self-esteem, lack of empathy, and a tendency to blame others for the problems in their lives.

However, it's important to note that it's not '*the wants*' that qualify for labeling the person as an emotional blackmailer, rather how he/she goes about fulfilling those '*wants.*' If he/she threatens you or gets insensitive to your needs, the term 'emotional blackmailer' is justified for them.

Indeed, there are 6 progressive stages of emotional blackmail:

1. In the first stage, the blackmailer tells you about his/her demands and adds an emotional threat.
2. Second, you resist the demand of the blackmailer.
3. Since the blackmailer can't tolerate any refusal, they put pressure on you to comply.
4. They repeat their threat as a consequence of your denial.
5. Affected by negative emotions, you decide to give in to the blackmailer's demands.
6. As a result, a pattern is set where the blackmailer knows your hot buttons and how to push them to get what they want.

The pressure they build upon you for compliance is basically through three tactics - Fear, Obligation, and Guilt, commonly known as the FOG technique.

Most of us have different kinds of fears like fear of isolation, fear of the unknown, apprehension about confrontation, worry about abandonment, fear of tricky situations, etc. Emotional blackmailers know your weak points, and how they can use them to get what they want.

Using your sense of obligation to press your emotional triggers and manipulate you is yet another favorite technique of emotional blackmailers. They can make you feel guilty for not keeping up your promises as per your obligations.

All these tactics stem from cowardice. Emotional blackmailers can't tolerate failure, loss, deprivation, and frustration. The moment they experience these feelings, they spring into action and resort to emotional blackmail to get what they want and remove these negative feelings.

You can classify emotional blackmailers into 4 categories:

1. **Punishers** who threaten to punish you physically, with financial penalties, or ending the relationship with you if you don't do what they want.
2. **Self-punishers** who threaten to harm themselves if you don't comply with their wishes.
3. **Sufferers** who blame you for their low emotional state, and expect you to do what they want to make them feel better.
4. **Tantalizers** who lure you with a false promise of something better if you do what they desire.

Whatever the tactics they use, if you find yourself apologizing for things you aren't doing, or find you're the only one making sacrifices in a relationship, or the other person insists on only their way, or you feel you're being threatened into obeying their demands - you are the victim of emotional blackmail.

However, it takes two to blackmail. Unless you give in to the demands, emotional blackmail can't happen. It may be that your need to please people, fear of their anger, abandonment or conflicts in relationships, extreme compassion and empathy, tendency to take the burden of other's lives on yourself, and low self-esteem make you vulnerable to such individuals.

To change this dynamic and stop being emotionally blackmailed, you must first recognize the red flags of emotional blackmail as detailed in this book. Next, commit to taking care of yourself. Resolve not to let this abusive treatment continue.

Give due respect to your needs first. Detach yourself from the blackmailer's emotions and look at the situation from a different perspective. Don't be tempted to give in to the blackmailer's demands instantly. Pause, take time to evaluate if you should comply or not, and then make your decision.

Use the strategies detailed in this book to develop your mental resilience, and develop the skills of non-defensive communication to talk to the emotional blackmailer.

Finally, set your emotional boundaries and express clearly what you'll accept and what you won't accept. In this way, you can permanently put a stop to emotional blackmail in your life.

RESOURCES

Galinsky, L. (2018, November 13). The Use of Emotional Blackmail in a Relationship. Retrieved from https://goodmenproject.com/featured-content/remember-that-time-you-wanted-a-relationship-for-all-the-wrong-reasons-wcz/

Doll, K. (2019, June 19). 18+ Ways to Handle Emotional Blackmail (+ Examples & Quotes). Retrieved from https://positivepsychology.com/emotional-blackmail/

Emotional Blackmail. (n.d.). Retrieved from https://www.merriam-webster.com/dictionary/emotional%20blackmail

Understanding Emotional Blackmail. (2019, January 14). Retrieved from https://claritychi.com/emotional-blackmail/

Hammond, C. (2017, October 10). What is Emotional Blackmail. Retrieved from https://pro.psychcentral.com/exhausted-woman/2016/08/what-is-emotional-blackmail/

Emotional Blackmail Law and Legal Definition. (n.d.). Retrieved from https://definitions.uslegal.com/e/emotional-blackmail/

Paler, J. (2019, December 6). The toxic cycle of emotional blackmail and how to stop it. Retrieved from https://hackspirit.com/emotional-blackmail/

Emotional Blackmail and How it Harms our Kids. (2018, August 1). Retrieved from https://exploringyourmind.com/emotional-blackmail-and-how-it-harms-our-kids/

Johnson, R. S. (2018, August 16). Emotional Blackmail: Fear, Obligation and Guilt . Retrieved from https://www.bpdfamily.com/content/emotional-blackmail-fear-obligation-and-guilt-fog

Go your Own Way. (n.d.). *Emotional Blackmail.* Retrieved from http://www.goyourownway.org/GOYOUROWNWAY/DOCUMENTS/EMOTIONAL%20WELLBEING/EMOTIONAL%20BLACKMAIL.pdf

What Is Emotional Blackmail and 5 Personality Types That Use It. (n.d.). Retrieved from https://www.learning-mind.com/emotional-blackmail/

Four Types Of Emotional Blackmail Manipulators Use Against You. (n.d.). Retrieved from https://www.aconsciousrethink.com/9824/emotional-blackmail/

Kreger, R. (n.d.). Fear, Obligation, and Guilt (FOG) in High Conflict Relationships. Retrieved from https://www.bpdcentral.com/blog/?Fear-Obligation-and-Guilt-FOG-in-High-Conflict-Relationships-36

abcClub. (2018, August 15). Emotional Blackmail_ Feeling like in FOG (fear, obligation, guilt). Retrieved from https://www.youtube.com/watch?v=jPXUQnTSyeU

Mayo Clinic Staff. (n.d.). Borderline personality disorder. Retrieved from https://www.mayoclinic.org/diseases-conditions/borderline-personality-disorder/symptoms-causes/syc-20370237

Freedom from the FOG of Emotional Manipulation. (2014, May 23). Retrieved from https://www.borderline-personality-disorder.com/borderline-personality-disorder-research/freedom-from-the-fog-of-emotional-manipulation/

Lancer, D. (2019, July 2). Covert Tactics Manipulators Use to Control and Confuse You. Retrieved from https://www.psychologytoday.com/us/blog/toxic-relationships/201907/covert-tactics-manipulators-use-control-and-confuse-you

Four Signs of Emotional Blackmail. (n.d.). Retrieved from https://www.powerofpositivity.com/4-signs-of-emotional-blackmail/

Lancer, Darlene. (n.d.). COMBAT NARCISSISTS' AND ABUSERS' PRIMARY WEAPON: PROJECTION. Retrieved from https://www.whatiscodependency.com/narcissist-abuse-empaths-projection/

Murrah, J. D. (n.d.). Breaking the Cycle of Emotional Blackmail. Retrieved from https://www.streetdirectory.com/travel_guide/7367/parenting/breaking_the_cycle_of_emotional_blackmail.html

Harley, M. (2017, July 24). What makes a parent toxic? Retrieved from https://lifelabs.psychologies.co.uk/users/3881-maxine-harley/posts/18860-what-makes-a-parent-toxic

Avila, T. (2018, November 2). How to Cope with Toxic Parents Whom you Can't Avoid. Retrieved from https://www.girlboss.com/wellness/toxic-parents

Lancer, D. (2018, August 31). 12 Clues a Relationship with a Parent is Toxic. Retrieved from https://www.psychologytoday.com/intl/blog/toxic-relationships/201808/12-clues-relationship-parent-is-toxic

Fellizar, K. (2019, January 23). 7 Seemingly Innocent Things That Can Actually Be Emotional Blackmail In A Relationship. Retrieved from https://www.bustle.com/p/7-seemingly-innocent-things-that-can-actually-be-emotional-blackmail-in-a-relationship-15866011

Centore, A. (2012, November 16). 6 Warning Signs of Emotional Blackmail: Couples Counseling Tips. Retrieved from https://thriveworks.com/blog/6-warning-signs-of-emotional-blackmail-couples-counseling-tips/

Griffin, T. (2019, December 4). How to Deal with Emotional Blackmail. Retrieved from https://www.wikihow.com/Deal-with-Emotional-Blackmail

Steber, C. (2018, April 18). 11 Signs You Are Experiencing Trauma After A Toxic Relationship. Retrieved from https://www.bustle.com/p/11-signs-you-are-experiencing-trauma-after-a-toxic-relationship-8759486

Dodd, G. (n.d.). How To Maintain Your Grace After A Bad Breakup. Retrieved from https://www.bolde.com/how-maintain-grace-after-bad-breakup/

Meurrisse, T. (n.d.). 5 Differences Between Real Love And Attachment. Retrieved from https://www.lifehack.org/317383/5-differences-between-real-love-and-attachment

Vaknin, S. (n.d.). Codependence and the Dependent Personality Disorder. Retrieved from https://www.healthyplace.com/personality-disorders/malignant-self-love/codependence-and-the-dependent-personality-disorder

Psychological Manipulation in Treating Codependency. (n.d.). Retrieved from https://emotional-intelligence-training.weebly.com/psychological-manipulation-in-treating-codependency.html

Hunter, D. (2019, March 12). How Codependency Affects Recovery. Retrieved from https://www.rehabcenter.net/how-co-dependency-affects-recovery/

Blackmoor, L. (2016, December 16). 8 Signs You May Have a Codependent Parent. Retrieved from https://wehavekids.com/family-relationships/8-Signs-You-May-Have-a-Codependent-Parent

Dodgson, L. (2018, February 13). 8 warning signs you're in a damaging codependent relationship, according to experts. Retrieved from https://www.businessinsider.in/strategy/8-warning-signs-youre-in-a-damaging-codependent-relationship-according-to-experts/articleshow/62904771.cms

Jewell, T. (2018, January 11). Sociopath: Definition, vs Psychopath, Test, Traits. Retrieved from https://www.healthline.com/health/mental-health/sociopath

Lindeberg, S. (2019, January 9). Psychopath: Meaning, Signs, and vs Sociopath. Retrieved from https://www.healthline.com/health/psychopath

Smith, M. (2019, December 6). Narcissistic Personality Disorder. Retrieved from https://www.helpguide.org/articles/mental-disorders/narcissistic-personality-disorder.htm

Happe, M. (n.d.). The Relationship between Narcissism and Codependency. Retrieved from https://www.mentalhelp.net/blogs/the-relationship-between-narcissism-and-codependency/

Ramirez, J. (n.d.). A Guide To Avoiding and Dealing With Emotional Blackmail. Retrieved from https://www.ba-bamail.com/content.aspx?emailid=19234

Sattin, N. (2016, September 7). Defeating Emotional Blackmail and Manipulation with Susan Forward. Retrieved from https://www.neilsattin.com/blog/2016/09/55-defeating-emotional-blackmail-and-manipulation-with-susan-forward/

Perper, R. (2014, January 29). Non-Defensive Communication In 3 Easy Steps. Retrieved from https://therapychanges.com/blog/2014/01/non-defensive-communication-3-easy-steps/

Israel, L. (2011, September 7). Powerful Non-Defensive Communication: A New Way to Communicate. Retrieved from https://www.maritalmediation.com/2011/09/powerful-non-defensive-communication-a-new-way-to-communicate/

Camins, S. (n.d.). Setting Emotional Boundaries in Relationships. Retrieved from https://roadtogrowthcounseling.com/importance-boundaries-relationships/

Han, L. (n.d.). How to Stand Up for Yourself Without Sounding Defensive. Retrieved from https://bemycareercoach.com/soft-skills/stand-up-for-yourself.html

Ribeiro, M. (2019, December 5). How to Become Mentally Strong: 14 Strategies for Building Resilience. Retrieved from https://positivepsychology.com/mentally-strong/

Dark Mind Control Techniques in NLP

The Secret Body of Knowledge in Psychology That Explores the Vulnerabilities of Being Human. Powerful Mindset, Language, Hypnosis, and Frame Control

Emory Green

TABLE OF CONTENTS

INTRODUCTION

Have you ever been in a situation in which you felt manipulated or influenced to act, behave, or think in a specific way for reasons other than your own? Perhaps your popular friends persuaded you to do something you didn't fully agree with? Has the sample person at the grocery store ever tried to convince you to buy the food they offered you to sample? Or, what if a supposed utility worker tries to persuade you to buy their services at a cheaper rate even if you are not needing those in the first place? What did they do to convince you? Did you consent? Were you even *aware* that you consented?

Truth is, there are highly persuasive and manipulative people out there who are successful in their ability to use NLP for their own advantage. One good example of people who use NLP successfully are salespeople; a case would be a cable company representative having persuaded you to buy more services that you didn't really need. If you are alarmed about the concept of NLP, wondering how it works or are curious why people are interested in harnessing its power, you've come to the right place. NLP can change your life when you put it into practice, and to have it so, you should be exploring the potentials, truths, and controversies of the most powerful NLP techniques. These techniques have been known to transform lives, decisions, and how people think.

NLP, once mastered, draws a roadmap in your mind that can alter it into something that works to help you reach your goals. Accessing the ability to control your mind and other people's to achieve favorable outcomes, while also aligning your programming and beliefs with success, is essential. Once you understand your own concept of control and how to apply these powerful NLP techniques for your own gains without guilt and limiting beliefs, you will be on your way to living the life you've always dreamed of!

Decades into the profession of business psychology, I have seen patterns of the smartest, most cunning mindsets that would not take no for an answer when it came to winning business and life. I have witnessed large corporate deals between leaders looking for favorable outcomes for their business and career. As a business psychologist who draws success roadmaps for people, political campaigns, and businesses, I give these people my applause every time. It is true that some will do anything for success. This is why, more than the usual, psychology of good motives and purpose is needed to be successful with life, goals, and undertakings. I am also passionate about looking into the less-explored side of winning, which includes darker, albeit highly influential, manipulative techniques for persuasion and always getting what one wants.

However, this book does not assert what is right and what is wrong; instead, it will be giving you helpful insights on the power and potential of NLP, so you can use it effectively in your life, no matter how you plan to use it. One thing is sure—the knowledge you will gain about NLP has no holds barred and is geared toward aligning your actions with known methods and techniques in psychology. This will help you analyze people, control situations, and avoid being controlled by the very same tactics. So, if you think someone is playing with your mind or you are prone to be around people who may manipulate your mind, you will surely be better equipped after reading this book.

People are in awe of the many win-win situations, opportunities, and business deals that can occur without knowing if these may have been sealed and secured through techniques used in NLP. You are about to learn those techniques today. I hope that you will also get your own positive shift in life after reading this book and achieve the results you really want from any situation.

The topics and knowledge in this book are presented comprehensively and directed to be applied toward areas in which these techniques are found to have the best potential for success. This book is also written without judgment towards its readers. Let us extend full respect to our human capacity to understand human vulnerabilities, flexibilities, diverse perspectives, and mindsets. In addition, this book does not cover the usual topics in NLP, but the controversial albeit most powerful techniques that have historically found success.

Many of us may not realize, but NLP techniques are widely used to sway people's perceptions, mindsets, and decisions. It is practically everywhere in sales, business, the workplace, management, leadership, politics, and even in meaningful relationships. Knowing little about it is almost equivalent to becoming an eventual victim of the power falling into the wrong hands. It is your choice between being controlled and being in control of every situation you are in. Time to take that power into your own hands!

More people should be well-read, well-aware, and well-informed about the potential power of psychology, and more than those manipulators inclined to use it deviantly and with unbalanced views. Knowledge is *key!* If you want to create a win-win experience for everyone, then you should be the rightful taker of this power now. Read this book and use all its information to create the world you want for you and everyone in it.

Enjoying this book so far? Remember to head to the last page of this book bundle for a bonus bite-sized yet valuable free resource on Conversational Hypnosis. This mini e-book is the easiest way to learn how to be a successful conversational hypnotist. Curious about the benefits it can do to your normal day to day conversations? Get your copy now! This free resource is available for a limited time only

CHAPTER ONE:

The Mysteries of NLP

NLP Today

NLP, or **neuro-linguistic programming**, has been evolving over time, as more and more people witness its application in various situations of life, whether that be business, familial, social, or personal. NLP, as an evolving science, can be useful because it allows for changes of people's thoughts, associations, behaviors, and even emotions. NLP can ultimately change a person's life, given the power of suggestion, influence, and persuasion through techniques used to help them find more beneficial ways of thinking and taking action. In short, NLP can be practical and advantageous to any situation, no matter how difficult or challenging.

NLP Interpreted

NLP consists mainly of three important components: the mind or brain; language, including both verbal and non-verbal; and individual programming. The first part of NLP—the **mind** or **neuro**—suggests how different states of mind can affect a person's behavior and communication. For example, if my present state of mind is calm, I will be more likely to communicate effectively, in comparison to if I were stressed and upset. How I think and feel can directly affect the outward manifestation of my functioning and behavior.

The second part of NLP is the **linguistic component** or the **language** an individual employs to communicate their state of mind and body. However, most of us only pay attention to the words spoken rather than non-verbal body language. In fact, it would seem non-verbal communication is more a telltale sign of an individual's state than the words spoken. This is because, while it can be easy to choose words during a verbal interaction, non-verbal body language, like your face flushing, can be more of an involuntary reaction than a choice. In other words, reactions and responses usually do not lie, whereas words can.

The third part of NLP is **programming**. Programming can be described as an individual's customary way of reacting, thinking, feeling, and assuming. However, surviving on autopilot isn't always beneficial when it comes to dealing with new challenges and changes effectively. Change is the capacity to modify or transform into something different, which is where programming comes into the picture. This is because, as human beings, we have the capacity to change our habits to be more beneficial for our purposes and goals. It is a better alternative to following outdated information that no longer serves a purpose. NLP can, in effect, transform people into more functional human beings, given self-modification and adaptation.

Modern Views and Controversies of NLP

Modern views of NLP suggest neuro-linguistic programming is applicable to both businesses and for personal reasons. Businesses can be improved by using NLP techniques cleverly on its employees, buyers, and investors, while an individual can enhance their personal situation by applying NLP techniques to the people in one's life. However, the controversies surrounding NLP stem from the belief that it's a form of brainwashing, hypnosis, and even mind control to get people to do what one wants. This may suggest that people can also be unknowing victims of NLP, such as in modeling, mirroring, and anchoring. For example, when a person skilled in using NLP mirrors or models your use of linguistics and language, the NLP user will create a sense of rapport and trust, thus allowing them to lead the interaction eventually in their favor. In addition, the use of NLP techniques, such as anchoring, can be just as effective in changing subjective experience. This is because, when a skilled NLP user uses anchoring (physically touches the unknowing person), specific states of mind can manifest in the latter, convincing them to act at the NLP user's discretion. This can either lead to positive or negative outcomes, depending on the use of NLP in the situation.

Foundations of NLP

The practice of NLP began in the 1970s with its foundations rooted in psychology, linguistics, and even computer programming, by the means of family therapist Virginia Satir, Gestalt therapist Fritz Perls, and hypnotist Milton Erickson. It was also studied by a group of noteworthy people including linguistic professor John Grinder and computer programming student Richard Bandler. Bandler, Grinder, and others observed that, when therapists like Satir, Perls, and Erickson used particular communication patterns with their clients, more results were achieved in comparison to traditional methods of therapy. For example, when they used modeling—a show that the NLP practitioner values the client through the use of similar predicates, like spoken language—the individual became more prone to letting their guard down and allowing themselves to be led toward more beneficial outcomes.

The foundations of NLP are built on the ability to read an individual through verbal and non-verbal cues. Eye movements, for example, can give away a person's preferences for using feelings, words, or pictures when learning or accessing information. This action allows the NLP user to gauge or estimate such things as the individual's next thought or state of mind. Furthermore, the supporting principles of NLP include building rapport, a full awareness of one's senses, thinking of the outcomes, and a flexibility to adapt to change by implementing new ways of doing things (Bundrant, 2019). The NLP user can then influence any associated behavior, thoughts, and even the emotions by using supporting principles of NLP.

Real World Relevance of NLP

The real world relevance of NLP is that it can be used to create successful people and outcomes that benefit, not only the individual, but also everyone associated with them, whether that be employees, colleagues, friends, or family. For example, competing businesses can apply NLP techniques to train their managers and supervisors, which would then teach those employees how to be successful through such practices. In fact, NLP is used widely today because, as businesses become more competitive given the prevalence of the Internet, customer interactions are becoming highly valued. Customer interactions have more influence than an impersonal email from a food delivery service online, for example. It is the influential and persuasive interactions between a business and customer that can determine the fate of the business' success. Therefore, the practice of NLP can increase successful outcomes for all parties involved due to the power of suggestion, persuasion, and influence toward buying a product or service.

Power of NLP

NLP can change lives with repeated practice of reprogramming belief systems, thinking patterns, and outward manifestations of behavior. It can change how you view your present situation to how you react and respond to it. NLP can change the individual's subjective experience of reality, whether that be for better or for worse. More specifically, NLP can influence people on a massive scale with the power of subliminal messaging and interjected layered meaning through powerful NLP techniques like NLP hypnosis and the use of non-specific language to elicit action. For example, the advertising you see everyday can influence you to spend more money than you usually would, due to some of NLP's covert techniques. This, of course, has me wondering if individuals in general even realize such things as the power of consumerism, thanks to neuro-linguistic programming. NLP can literally change the direction of your life by affecting surrounding people on a deeper level due to NLP's prevalent presence. A lot of people likely employ NLP techniques without them realizing it; for example, with the use of emojis in instant messaging to keep a certain mood within the message.

NLP Training

People who take NLP training can become better communicators, more adept at interpreting the nonverbal signals, and more proficient in mastering thoughts and feelings. People also take NLP training to achieve success, whether that be personal or professional. In addition, NLP training can correct less-than-useful behaviors in individuals, such as addiction. It can also elicit information from others by allowing the user to communicate efficiently using learned NLP techniques. NLP training is used for an endless list of reasons.

Levels of NLP training include NLP Practitioner, the NLP Master Practitioner, the NLP Trainer, and the NLP Coach, where NLP Practitioner is the beginning level of instruction and NLP Coach is the top level of training available. Once an individual successfully learns one level of NLP training, that person is allowed to graduate to the next level of NLP proficiency. NLP training becomes successive and more in depth as it progresses from one level to the next.

Specifically, the **NLP Practitioner** starts by learning the NLP basics. In addition, the NLP Practitioner learns to apply NLP techniques to everyday situations. When the NLP Practitioner applies the newly learned NLP techniques and tools to their life, the individual can start to learn how NLP is useful to others as well.

The **NLP Master Practitioner** learns more advanced, detailed, and in-depth NLP models and techniques, such as modifying values and belief systems that can pertain better to work, family, and life. In addition, the NLP Master Practitioner also learns improved techniques in communication, including quantum linguistics, which is a system of language that suggests that the human nervous system is powered by the mind's self-talk and created visual images (Miller, n.d.). Furthermore, the NLP Master Practitioner would also learn about **Meta Programs**, which include leading NLP techniques like linguistic negotiation. Taking the master course is critical to changing and improving in all areas of life.

The next level of NLP training is the **NLP Trainer**. By this point, the NLP Trainer should have mastered all critical and advanced NLP techniques and tools. In addition, the NLP Trainer has learned to present themselves with utmost confidence to their audience as they successfully train others in using persuasive and influential skills on a large scale. These training strategies include understanding and analyzing the processes of groups, so they can become influential speakers and presenters. Once the NLP Trainer has mastered these techniques, they should be able to present them successfully to an audience.

The final level of NLP training is the **NLP Coach**. The NLP Coach is now competent in NLP and life coaching via pretalk, information gathering, transformation, and integration (International Neuro-Linguistic Programming Center, n.d.). In addition, the NLP Coach is flexible and can alternate between various NLP models and techniques during a coaching session. The NLP Coach is capable of directing and guiding the client toward a more successful and beneficial outcome, which is the point of NLP.

Harnessing the Power of NLP

Some reasons people would want to harness the power of NLP include personal empowerment and improvements within business. If an NLP user can motivate people to think, act, and behave in a certain manner that aligns with the former's interests and goals, then they can control and manage people effectively for personal and professional gain. However, a good percentage of NLP users want to help people overcome whatever has been hindering them in their personal lives, whether it be depression, phobias, or bad habits. NLP has the power to change the course of our lives through reprogramming people to be more functional and efficient members of society.

However, harnessing the power of NLP requires the individual to not only master NLP techniques, but also master themselves. In other words, an NLP Practitioner cannot be efficient if they don't practice, because harnessing NLP requires more than words; it requires action on the NLP Practitioner's part for a more believable and effective application. To accomplish this, the NLP Practitioner's body language must match the words chosen to impart the message to the client; otherwise, the client will be less likely to view the former as convincing or credible, affecting the outcome of NLP practice. In other words, the NLP practitioner must be able to control and manipulate their person first before trying to accomplish doing so with others.

It would seem that harnessing the power of NLP is a lot like harnessing one's natural resources, such as the mind or body, to make them more effective.

Dark NLP

In some cases, NLP users employ the techniques to control and manipulate others and their situations to the former's advantage and the latter's expense. For example, someone with narcissistic tendencies can get inside the mind of their victim by using the same NLP techniques that benefit people, but more disruptive and covertly, such as feigning interest in the victim to garner their obedience and subservience to a specific agenda. In other words, **dark NLP** can also be used for malicious intents. In the wrong hands, dark NLP could potentially harm a population because those people could be programmed to inflict destruction instead of promoting more helpful intentions and goals.

NLP's Power to Persuade, Influence, and Manipulate

NLP can persuade, influence, and manipulate people into thinking, feeling, and behaving in ways unaligned with their best interests. For example, when an NLP user speaks words in time to the natural heartbeat of the other person (a mind control technique), the mind of the recipient becomes more suggestible (Kumar, 2016) and, therefore, swayed more easily to the will of others. Another mind control technique they could use involves using more suggestible "**hot words**" because they are connected with the preferred senses the recipient uses most. For instance, words and phrases such as *feel this*, *hear this*, and *see this* can induce a more impressionable state of mind.

More Controversies and Criticisms on the Dangers of NLP

There is much controversy surrounding the use of NLP with the various mind control techniques that were mentioned in the previous sections. One criticism of NLP is that it messes with the recipient's head more than it improves their life. NLP users, like Richard Bandler, have made it their life mission to get inside the other person's thoughts, feelings, perceptions, and beliefs by practicing the art of mind control. Yet, people question its authenticity and validity because NLP has often been framed as a pseudoscience or black magic—not an actual field of scientific study. Other controversies stem from how, although NLP may be framed as a pseudoscience, it is still applicable in most facets of life, from professional development to personal growth. These claims come from the results NLP has produced. Be that as it may, NLP is still evolving with much to be discovered.

Chapter Summary

In this chapter, you have learned all about NLP, or neuro-linguistic programming, in addition to some of its main tools and techniques. You have also learned many reasons why people want to harness and train in NLP techniques. Equally important is dark NLP because of its potential in controlling and manipulating people through mind control. To refresh your memory, here are some key points from this chapter:

- NLP is neuro-linguistic programming through the mind, language, and habitual ways of thinking, feeling, and behaving (programming) can alter subjective experience.
- NLP can be useful for business and personal reasons, given the power of suggestion, persuasion, and influence.
- The foundations of NLP include building rapport, a full awareness of one's senses, thinking of the outcomes, and flexibility to adapt to change.
- The real world relevance of NLP is that it can be used to create successful people and outcomes that benefit not only the individual, but also everybody associated with them. This can include employees, colleagues, friends, or family.
- NLP has the power to change lives with the repeated practice of reprogramming belief systems, thinking patterns, and outward manifestations of behavior.
- People who take NLP training can become better communicators, more adept at interpreting nonverbal signals, and better at mastering their own feelings and thoughts.

- Levels of NLP training include NLP Practitioner, NLP Master Practitioner, NLP Trainer, and NLP Coach.
- Reasons for harnessing the power of NLP include personal empowerment and improvement for successful business.
- Dark NLP employs techniques for controlling the mind and manipulating the individual and the situation to their own advantage—at the recipient's expense.
- NLP can also persuade, influence, and manipulate people into thinking, feeling, and behaving in ways unaligned with the recipient's best interests.
- NLP is not without controversy and criticism.

In the next chapter, you will learn all about crossing dangerous boundaries when using NLP.

CHAPTER TWO:

Crossing Dangerous Boundaries

NLP Ethics

The use of NLP is controversial because many of its techniques can be covert and manipulative to the recipient. This is because most of the time the recipient isn't aware that they are being manipulated. For instance, the use of mirroring to elicit acquiescence, trust, and rapport from the individual is questionable because it tricks the individual into thinking the NLP user is similar to them, thus letting their guard down. This tactic and similar kinds of NLP techniques can cross dangerous boundaries because of the chance that the recipient was anchored to a relatively harmful or destructive state afterward. An even scarier and alarming result would be the possibility that the natural programming of the individual was reconstructed unnaturally.

What Is Ethical and Not Ethical in Using NLP?

It's curious to think whether the practice of NLP is ethical, given its purpose to influence and guide others without their knowledge nor the exposure of a hidden agenda. This could be considered an act of subterfuge because the NLP user employs deceit to accomplish their objective. The recipient can also be viewed as potentially being used as a means to an end. This idea is inherently unethical because the recipient is less in control of their own faculties and decisions when under the influence of NLP, given having been "programmed" subconsciously.

Knowing this information, people who practice NLP should be careful with its use and application, so as not to harm the recipient. The highest standards and ethics would have to be applied, similar to doctors promising to cause no harm to the individual under the Hippocratic oath. Practicing NLP ethically is using it without the intent to harm, control, or otherwise disadvantage others. One's moral compass, whether professional or personal, must be applied to avoid mistreatment of the recipient. In addition, it is more acceptable to practice NLP on yourself to improve your situation more than it is to practice it on others without their consent or knowledge. Subliminal messaging and NLP programming are everywhere—in self-help classes, advertising, business, and even politics.

Are NLP Impositions Ethical?

Advertising, business, and politics are infamous for imposing their views, thoughts, and beliefs onto the recipient. However, a person who professionally engages in NLP practice must steer clear of imposing personal views, values, and beliefs on a suggestible individual because the latter would be more likely to adopt or subscribe to the NLP Practitioner's views when they need an anchoring point for change and unfamiliar territory (InspiritiveNLP, 2008). For example, when my son was deployed to Africa by the Marines for six months, I needed context to deal with not knowing if he or I would survive that experience. I went to see a professional to deal with it, and the professional did not impose her beliefs, values, or views into my person and, as a result, I felt more uninhibited to be myself in discussing my emotions associated with my son being deployed.

However, deployment of NLP techniques is more ethical if the recipient is profoundly aware of what is going on and has given permission ahead of time. This permits the NLP Practitioner to practice their craft ethically and morally, with the intent of improving or bettering the client's situation. Due to the power being entrusted in the NLP Practitioner's hands, they have a responsibility not to abuse the implicit trust granted to them. It is an obligation to the client for the NLP Practitioner to embody integrity when engaging in NLP practice and application with the client. Clearly, similar values and moral principles must guide the conduct of the NLP Practitioner too.

NLP Presuppositions

NLP practice and application include many assumptions that help guide, structure, and define this evolving science into a more ethically accepted line of work. For example, the NLP presupposition of respecting the other person's worldview or model infers that the NLP Practitioner takes into consideration worldviews other than their own. Every worldview or model from which the individual operates should be as worthy and valid as the next. It is important to pay attention to this because, in some cases, the NLP Practitioner may develop their own preconceived ideas about the client based on that worldview, which isn't ethically correct or fair to the recipient.

In fact, it would seem having preconceived notions, ideas, or presuppositions may suggest an inflexibility on the NLP Practitioner's part, leading to another presupposition of NLP practice. According to Goodman, when NLP Practitioners become inflexible in their thinking and communication with the client, rapport isn't as easily forthcoming from the latter (2018). The client may even become resistant to the NLP Practitioner's attempts to build that rapport. Furthermore, ethics starts to enter the conversation because it brings with it an obvious inequality within the equation. It implies an expectation that the client needs to accept all communication from the NLP Practitioner, while neglecting any expectation that the NLP should listen to the client's thoughts and ideas at all. In short, communication and interaction needs to go both ways between the client and the NLP Practitioner because the relationship needs to build a connection of understanding. Despite this give and take, presuppositions can clearly characterize and type what can sometimes be an already unequal balance of power and influence.

Another important presupposition of NLP is that all behaviors have positive intentions because they are the best possible choices at the time, given the availability of resources. In short, we do the best we can with what we have within any given time frame. The behavior is characterized as positive because there is always something useful to be gained (Goodman, 2018). In addition, the behavior is never fundamentally "wrong" due to the aforementioned reasons; however, there is a difference between positive and what is morally acceptable, along with what is negative compared to that which is considered wrong. For instance, if there is something useful to be gained from the practice of NLP, does this infer that the NLP Practitioner's conduct is always positive and ethically acceptable? Clearly, there are presuppositions and assumptions in NLP that seem to be at odds with its actual practice when the tables are turned on the NLP Practitioner and their line of work. This idea contradicts the veracity of NLP practice because of the imbalance of power, persuasion, and influence between the NLP Practitioner and the individual.

Despite this, influencing each other's mind and body leads into the NLP presupposition that one will affect the other because they are interconnected. More specifically, when we change our line of thought, our bodies manifest outward what is going on inside our minds. Likewise, how we behave can also modify our innermost feelings and thoughts. The **mind-body connection** can affect our subjective experience of reality, which is useful to NLP practice and application. This is because, if the NLP Practitioner can modify one's natural state or programming after having learned more about how they operate, then the mind and the body can become more in tune with each other, ultimately benefiting the client. The NLP Practitioner can also benefit from the client's mind-body connection because the former can influence the client even more once the latter's mind and body are synchronized.

Some other NLP presuppositions include (Goodman, 2018):

- We are always communicating.
- We already have all the resources we need, or we can create them; therefore, there is no such thing as unresourceful people. There are only unresourceful states of mind.
- The system (person) with the most flexibility (choices) in their behavior will have the most influence on the system.
- People work perfectly.
- Accept the person, change the behavior.
- There is no failure, only feedback.
- Choice is better than no choice.
- All processes should lead to integration and wholeness.
- If you want to understand, act.

These NLP presuppositions are quite valuable to NLP application because they also help guide and direct its real world implementation.

NLP Applications

NLP as an evolving science can be used for various purposes. One of those purposes includes self-improvement into the best version of ourselves. For example, NLP can help a person achieve an optimal state of health by reprogramming them to adopt consistently healthier exercise and eating habits. Perhaps less than healthy habits like smoking could also disappear with a persuasive influence from the NLP practitioner. In the case that an individual wants to communicate better with a loved one, there are many NLP-based self-improvement classes they can take to optimize that situation, among others as well.

In addition, NLP is used for professional and business purposes, such as in teaching how to become a better manager, colleague, or leader through NLP techniques. For example, a manager could learn to communicate better with employees to elicit improved productivity on the job. On the other hand, an employee could potentially improve their mindset so they can understand and work with fellow employees more efficiently. In short, NLP is mostly used for professional and personal enhancement.

However, NLP is also sometimes used to control people on a large scale through content/context reframing at seminars and gatherings. For example, the individual employing NLP on the crowd would reframe the situation as being more optimal than it really is, so they can distract the large group of people from their actual message, usually brainwashing or persuading them into believing whatever ideology, such as Hare Krishna. Another example could be in a large business seminar about improving relationships with customers. With these, the skilled NLP user may indoctrinate the large group into accepting without question the beliefs, values, and perceptions. One method the NLP user would use to accomplish this is to induce a heightened state of suggestibility through layered and subliminal messaging, so they can reframe the situation as more positive or optimal.

In terms of **layered meaning** and **subliminal messaging**, advertisements may also try to trick the consumer into buying their products or services by using certain NLP techniques. For example, using vague language allows the advertiser to trick the consumer into believing that they have more options to choose from because vague language allows for more interpretations of the advertiser's message (Evolution Development, 2019). This emanates from the Milton Model from Milton Erickson, who purposefully used vague language with his clients to allow more room for interpretation. It is this ambiguous language that can make the consumer buy into the product or service, given the supposed freedom of choice presented. NLP practitioners can also present choices to their clients through purposeful, non-specific language.

NLP is also used in politics, especially during election time, when the candidates start airing advertisements directed at the voting populace. Some politicians even go so far as to use **hypnotic trance words** so the voter becomes more likely to feel a sense of rapport with the politician. For example, according to Basu, some words are similar to an anchored trance effect, since they impact us with a meaning we would ascribe through our thoughts, feelings, beliefs, and experiences (2015). When an influential politician repeats these words back to the people, the people then become more motivated than before. This can also affect the voting populace by making them more oblivious to the effects of political maneuvering.

Cults and Manipulators Use and Abuse NLP

Manipulators and cults will use and abuse NLP by overrunning an individual's sense of identity and agency by pushing an unstated agenda with the intention of total mind control, obedience, and subservience. This mind control can be dangerous to the welfare of the individual because thinking or acting independently becomes next to impossible. This impossibility stems from the individual being taught to *depend* on the cult leaders and group for their sense of identity, meaning, and/or purpose. The individual suffers detrimental consequences because that lack of identity allows for easier manipulation and mind control through mass hypnosis. In other words, NLP application among similar techniques by a destructive cult or a manipulator does not help the individual, but instead, harming them. These actions are unethical and dangerous.

Clearly, there is the potential to cross dangerous boundaries when practicing NLP. For instance, the recipient may no longer be able to function effectively in life due to their subjective reality and consciousness having become less functional. Marriages can break down, job loss can occur, and less-than-optimal psychological conditions like depression may even surface after a weekend with NLP enthusiasts. According to Tippet, cult-like groups can use mass

285

hypnosis to bring about a subjectively altered state of mind for the individual by inhibiting the latter's faculties and inducing emotional responses (1994). For example, when I went through Army basic training, the drill sergeants would yell commands to follow, which induced an emotional response, thus attempting to break down the new recruit into submission. It is an effective technique that produces obedience and subservience in the individual because, after following their commands for so long, emotional and physical exhaustion can hinder the original sharpness of the recruit's faculties. Such techniques can be harmful to the recipient because their individuality no longer exists in these circumstances, having been overrun by cult-like techniques reminiscent of hypnosis and NLP. Case in point, after I was honorably discharged from the military, it took some time for me to acclimate back to everyday life again.

As we've seen, NLP and similar techniques can be dangerous to not only the individual, but also the group, which is why NLP techniques need to be practiced and applied with the utmost care and awareness. NLP practitioners must take this responsibility to heart, due to the trust that has been given and sometimes elicited from the client. I believe this quote sums up the situation fully:

Nearly all men can stand adversity, but if you want to test a man's character, give him power

Abraham Lincoln

Chapter Summary

In this chapter, you have learned about the ethics of NLP practice. You have also learned about how the presuppositions of NLP can help guide the practice, while also considering their ethical implications. Furthermore, you have learned about how NLP has been used in other ways beyond self-help. Lastly, we went over the importance of considering how NLP can be abused by organizations such as cults.

To refresh your memory, here are some of the key points from this chapter:

- NLP techniques can cross dangerous boundaries, given its covert and manipulative nature.
- In order to keep NLP ethical, it should be used without the intent to harm, control, or otherwise disadvantage others.
- NLP practitioners must not impose their values, perceptions, and beliefs onto the client.
- The NLP practitioner has a responsibility not to abuse the implicit trust granted to them during a session.
- Presuppositions, like respecting the individual, help guide the practice of NLP. Some other presuppositions include (Goodman, 2018):
  - There are no resistant clients, only inflexible communicators.
  - The mind and body affect each other because they are connected.
  - We are always communicating.
  - We already have all the resources we need, or we can create them; therefore, there is no such thing as unresourceful people, only unresourceful states of mind.
  - The system (person) with the most flexibility (choices) in its/their behavior will have the most influence on the system.
  - People work perfectly.
  - Accept the person, change the behavior.
  - There is no failure, only feedback.
  - Choice is better than no choice.
  - All processes should lead to integration and wholeness.
  - If you want to understand, act.
- NLP is used for self-improvement, business, advertising, politics, among other areas.

- NLP can be abused by manipulators and cults, who use it to overrun an individual's sense of identity and agency for easier manipulation and mind control.

In the next chapter, you will learn about the fundamentals of control and manipulation

CHAPTER THREE:

Control and Manipulation

Control and Manipulation Interpreted

Having the power to direct, control, or otherwise manipulate people's thoughts, feelings, and behaviors skillfully is a big deal. This manipulation can affect those people significantly and for a long time, depending on the type, depth, and direction of control and manipulation used. It is the control and manipulation that can shape and influence lives either optimally or nonoptimally. In this case, the person in control can direct and even determine the subjective experience and reality of the person being controlled. In fact, the implications of the controller's outward behavior, words, and actions can directly affect the person being controlled, due to the latter's interpretation and reactions.

Control and manipulation in the context of NLP can be quite similar, with **control** being the power to direct people's behavior, whereas **manipulation** is the action of controlling something skillfully. The main difference between control and manipulation is that having the power to direct something (control) is not the same as knowing how to skillfully do it (manipulation). For example, I have the power to program my computer (control) efficiently, yet I may not know how to skillfully do that (manipulation) quite yet, given a lack of experience or training. It seems being able to manipulate something adeptly, such as a computer, takes the reality of control to the next level.

Being in Control and Being Controlled

Likewise, being *in control* compared to being *controlled* also suggests different subjective realities. More specifically, being in control is an active state compared to being controlled, which is more passive. For example, a skilled psychologist controls or directs the therapy session actively, whereas the client would allow the psychologist to guide them as the recipient of that expertise. In addition, being in control involves agency and autonomy, whereas being controlled usually does not. If I just allowed things to happen to me, I would be more likely to be controlled by others; however, if I take action, I will be more able to control how I respond to those events. The difference is in the response to the stimuli because the individual can react or choose to act instead.

Avoid Being Controlled

To avoid being controlled by a manipulator, it is important to have a strong sense of identity or self. This is because being aware of your identity allows you to be more in-tune with your values, beliefs, and feelings. Your awareness will then allow you to protect yourself from someone trying to impose their beliefs on you using covert manipulation techniques. Manipulators and other controlling people won't be as likely to take advantage and compromise your core identity when you know yourself and what you stand for. Otherwise, taking advantage of someone is easier if that person isn't fully aware of their identity.

Another way to avoid being controlled is to have confidence in yourself. A lack of confidence can lead to self-questioning, thus making you naturally give others more credibility than they deserve

(Golden, 2016). The resulting self-doubt will allow controlling people to push their beliefs, values, and agenda on you much easier because you are handing more power over to them. This can lead to becoming a pawn for the manipulator because their validation of your self-worth will give you a false sense of confidence. It is also healthier to build confidence in yourself to begin with.

It is also important to avoid becoming overly dependent on other people so you won't be controlled by them. For example, if you depend on your partner to satisfy your every need instead of engaging in self-care regularly, then you may be opening yourself up to that individual's attempts to control you later down the road. In other words, when you neglect to take care of yourself and your needs, you invite others to do it for you through potentially well-meaning albeit controlling interventions (Bundrant, 2011). It can also lead to an unhealthy codependency, given the need for constant coddling; therefore, it is important to learn how you can rely on yourself, so you can avoid this trap altogether.

Furthermore, you will be easier to control if you are not living in the present. In other words, if you are still focusing your attention on past experiences, then those experiences will end up controlling you emotionally and mentally, despite physically being in the present. Living in the past can diminish your critical faculties and your ability to function because that energy will be hijacking your reactions and responses to the present; you will be more fatigued from trying to coexist in both realities and, consequently, you will be easier to manipulate and control.

Internal Control

Being in control is an entirely different experience from being controlled because you are in the driver's seat and can choose for yourself, in contrast to allowing someone else to make those choices for you. Beyond that, being in control allows you to direct and improve the situation to and in your favor. For example, if I can control my reactions to stress with improved coping techniques, I can direct and guide how I respond to them better. This allows the individual to exercise authority over their own autonomy and self-govern their choices. Internal control usually comes with a goal—if that goal is to lose weight, for instance, the individual would adjust their choices and behavior accordingly. If the goal is changed, the behavior is then modified to reach that new goal.

External Control

Applications of the context of control in regards to people and situations suggest that people, in general, aren't as easy to control when their goals change. In this case, they would no longer need to behave or act in the same manner to achieve that goal. According to Carey, what people want can change, thus allowing for the rules of the game to change as well (2015). This makes people and their situations less able to be manipulated and controlled because they no longer need to act or behave the same as before. Therefore, if a change in behavior, thoughts, and feelings can occur as a result, control is no longer applicable to the situation.

Still, controlling and manipulating people becomes less difficult when the main objectives do not change; although, the behavior associated with that goal must change for it to remain effective. We could think of it as there being more than one way to get from point A to point B. For example, an individual can change and manipulate their thinking and still accomplish the same goal by changing the context to reflect the objective and state of mind better. Thus, the main objective of control and manipulation is change itself.

Taking Control of the Past, Present, and Future

Change resulting from skillful manipulation is necessary to take control of the past, present, and future because, otherwise, we could use the past as an excuse to continue poor behavior. On the other hand, thinking in the present can ultimately affect the future. For example, if I continue to eat food when emotionally upset, I will be less likely to eat healthily in the present when faced with new emotional challenges. This can affect my future because, if I become dependent on food whenever I am emotionally challenged, I could gain a lot of weight and/or compromise my health and quality of life. Therefore, repeating past bad habits does not help because they will keep us anchored to that past. If we can change those past behaviors and use more functional coping mechanisms in the present, our present and future outcomes will sway more in our favor.

In addition to repeating past behaviors, people also tend to react more when dealing with past events. For example, if I become emotionally triggered over something upsetting from my past, I may be less likely to deal with it adequately in the present because my emotions would be overwhelming and dampen my ability to act appropriately. I would also have a harder time learning new skills to use in the present when a trigger materializes again. There needs to be a balance of action and reaction to effectively deal with the past, present, and future. Similarly, controlling and manipulating an individual's actions and reactions can benefit both the present and the future.

According to Firestone, the reality of recreating similar dynamics and environments from our past can also color the present and future (2016). This is because, as people, we tend to favor the familiar compared to the unfamiliar; for example, if an individual grew up in a big family with plenty of siblings, that person may recreate that situation by always having plenty of people around, in contrast to learning how to live alone. Recreating the family dynamic or environment may be undesirable, as it can hinder the individual's progress toward adulthood. In addition, manipulating the present to reflect the past isn't always indicative of future events because, although people like to think they have control, reality often suggests otherwise. Case in point—control is an illusion, whereas skillful manipulation is real, given the latter's production of tangible results and outcomes.

Repeating, reacting to, and recreating the past suggests a lack of control and some level of manipulation because, as children, we had little control over the environment and the dynamics we grew up in. Yet, we have more control now with guiding our situation skillfully, due to the differentiation, autonomy, and agency we gained through adulthood. Once we establish that, we can begin to control, guide, or otherwise manipulate important goals into better outcomes ethically. In fact, experiencing better outcomes suggests that the connotation behind control and manipulation is more positive than most would believe.

Consequences of Triggering the Subconscious of Strangers

Once the individual has the power to control, guide, and manipulate their situation more in their favor, that person can then also trigger the subconscious of strangers by using NLP techniques reminiscent of control and manipulation. For example, psychological manipulation through NLP can provoke mental health conditions, such as depression, within the unconscious mind to alleviate them. Some other examples of triggering the subconscious of others include the use of the following NLP techniques and tools (Beale, 2020):

- Affirmations.
- Amplifying good feelings.
- NLP belief change.
- NLP hypnosis and meditation.
- Modeling.

This list is not exhaustive; the NLP toolkit allows for effective manipulation and control of the client, focusing more on producing tangible results compared to traditional forms of therapy. For example, using affirmations will help keep the client on track when their focus drifts from the main goal. **Affirmations**, like belief and mission statements, can also remind the client of their motivation for taking action. In addition, affirmations used correctly can influence mindsets with the use of repetition and reiteration. Therefore, mindful manipulation of thoughts and feelings through affirmation statements can control real life events for the recipients, as it helps them replace negative messages they may have encountered previously.

Amplifying good feelings of clients can also help them strengthen their appreciation of certain events, allowing them to relive those good feelings in vivid detail as well. For example, if I close my eyes and remember the day my son was born, I can envision the sights, sounds, and positive feelings of the moment he was placed in my arms. Nothing compares to holding your firstborn for the first time! The only drawback is that, eventually, the client has to come back to reality and they may have a less-than-positive reaction to coming back. Strangers can benefit from amplifying good feelings, but what if these techniques are misused to control the client maliciously?

In addition, **belief change** is another helpful NLP technique that modifies beliefs to help free up behavior. The philosophy is that, once the recipient realizes their beliefs—even strong ones—are relative and not a scientific truth, those beliefs should have a lesser effect on their behavior. The scary thing is that, if the NLP Practitioner practiced belief change on a stranger on the streets, the stranger's freed-up behavior would be disadvantageous for everyone involved. In this case, behavior becomes unpredictable when beliefs and values do not govern it to some extent. Furthermore, if NLP Practitioners freed up everybody's beliefs through NLP belief change, there would be many people merely doing what they wanted, no matter how chaotic. As implied, this scenario could cause situations akin to anarchy, given the lack of belief systems, thus the lack of control overall.

Nevertheless, practicing NLP hypnosis and meditation is another technique that can trigger the subconscious of strangers. This is accomplished by inducing involuntary control over their faculties while making them highly suggestible to external influences, such as the NLP Practitioner's voice. For example, the client might be able to relax more during the recall of a traumatic life event if the NLP Practitioner uses a specific tone of voice. NLP hypnosis is mainly used to improve the outcomes of NLP therapy, yet when a stranger's subconscious is triggered by hypnosis, they could react negatively to less beneficial influences, thus compromising their identity while hypnotized. Could somebody under NLP hypnosis be responsible for breaking the law? Who is really in control while hypnotized?

Last but not least, the NLP **modeling** technique is also valuable in NLP practice because, by imitating and copying successful methods, it becomes easier to see what works for the individual (Beale, 2020). For example, by imitating and internalizing my mother's work ethic, it will be easier for me to figure out what work ethics work for me within specific jobs and lifestyles. If the client is able to identify with another's success story, then the former will be more likely to want to succeed as well. However, the price paid for modeling another's successful techniques is that the recipient may lose some individuality. The last thing the NLP Practitioner should want is for the recipient to lose their sense of identity and agency. For example, a recipient may lose functioning in their triggered subconscious if they lose their identity.

NLP Mind Control: The Basic Three

The aforementioned NLP techniques can trigger the subconscious of strangers while controlling and manipulating them toward improved life outcomes. According to Lee, NLP mind control techniques, such as changing your physiology, can also affect how you think (2020) and feel. For example, if you want to exude confidence, start by controlling your body language to manifest that confidence outwardly. This will result in your mind eventually picking up on that display in reality. If I want to exude affection, I would physically hug my partner in the hopes that we can both feel that affection in reality. Controlling and manipulating your physiology can produce or elicit the desired state of mind. However, on the dark side of the coin, exuding an unfavorable state of mind does not usually produce the outcomes you want.

The second NLP mind control technique is vocally emphasizing **keywords** in a conversation (Lee, 2020). Doing this helps convince the other person to do something you want, given the point of emphasis. For example, if you stress the keyword, "do" in "do the dishes," the recipient of your command will be more likely to abide by and follow the directive. Emphasizing keywords is also an effective advertising tool. For example, the Nike slogan, "Just do it" emphasizes the keyword "do" to get you to take action. NLP mind control techniques run rampant in society, given their presence in nearly everything, from advertising to politics.

The third NLP mind control technique is **visualization** (Lee, 2020). Visualization is powerful because, when you imagine yourself achieving something, you are more likely to adhere to that path of success than if you hadn't. For example, if I visualize myself succeeding in my career aspirations, I will more than likely triumph in my field. Visualization helps the client picture the goal more clearly, especially if visual cues are the client's preferred form of communication. It is important to note, however, that since some societies are more visual than others, they tend to judge success based on appearances, which is not accurate nor representative.

Clearly, control and manipulation can take many prevalent forms that we don't even recognize, for good or bad. This is when one must actively take control of the situation and manipulate the outcome for the better; otherwise, we can become passive victims to mind control on a massive scale. Nevertheless, the real power comes from the individual controlling and manipulating their past and present to ensure the future is better for everyone.

> *"Those who control the present, control the past and those who control the past control the future."*

George Orwell

Chapter Summary

In this chapter, you have learned about the fundamentals of control and manipulation. In addition, you have also learned about being in control compared to being controlled. It is important to remember to take control of the past, present, and future to achieve success in life. Still, control and manipulation wouldn't be possible without effective NLP techniques to trigger people's subconscious. Lastly, people's subconscious can be controlled and manipulated by NLP mind control. To refresh your memory, here are the key points of this chapter:

- The main difference between control and manipulation is that having the power to direct something (control) is not the same as knowing how to do it skillfully (manipulation).
- Control is an active state compared to being controlled, which is passive.
- Being in control suggests agency, whereas being controlled does not.
- To avoid being controlled by a manipulative person, the individual can:
    - Have a strong sense of identity.
    - Have confidence in oneself.
    - Avoid being overly dependent.
    - Live in the present.
- Being in control allows the individual to exercise authority over their own autonomy and self-govern their choices.

- The rules of the game change when the person no longer wants the same thing. Their behavior would change to accommodate a different goal, making them less likely to be controlled.
- To take control of the past, present, and future, a person must be willing to change by refusing to:
  - Repeat past, nonadaptive behaviors.
  - React more than act.
  - Recreate past relationships and dynamics in the present.
- The skilled NLP Practitioner can trigger the subconscious of strangers by practicing control and manipulation type NLP techniques. Some of those techniques include (Beale, 2020):
  - Affirmation.
  - Amplifying good feelings.
  - NLP belief change.
  - NLP hypnosis and meditation.
  - Modeling.
- Some NLP mind control techniques include:
  - Changing your physiology to affect how you think.
  - Emphasizing keywords in a conversation.
  - Visualization.

In the next chapter, you will learn how to read and control people.

CHAPTER FOUR:

Reading and Controlling People

NLP Mind Reading

Reading a person's mind is about more than going to a psychic medium. It is a science containing methods that NLP Practitioners can use to understand *how* a person is thinking, not necessarily *what* they are thinking. For example, an NLP Practitioner can read a person's body language to determine their state of mind. Reading people through body positions and movements can be helpful in personal, friend, and business relationships, because it helps us not only communicate better, but also estimate the next move in that relationship. For example, if I am frustrated with my partner for whatever reason, furrowing my brows can express to them my frustrations. As a result, my partner's next move would usually be to ask me what's wrong. This interaction would then, in turn, propel the relationship forward. The facts are that my partner and I can read each other at any time, resulting in a healthy, interdependent relationship full of life. Clearly, reading people can produce positive outcomes!

NLP Mind Reading Through Body Language and Eye Accessing Cues

NLP mind reading through **body language** and **eye accessing cues** is helpful for both the NLP Practitioner and the client during sessions because either party can benefit the other. For example, the NLP Practitioner can use the client's body language to determine the latter's best course of action much easier than if they were merely using other traditional methods. In addition, the client would also benefit from the reading because they would learn healthier coping methods by following the NLP Practitioner's lead. Actually, it could even appear that the NLP Practitioner is following the *client's* lead in terms of the latter's subjective state of mind, body language, and eye accessing cues expressed. Both references for mind reading would help indicate the client's reality.

In addition, NLP mind reading is a combination of not only the science behind reading and interpreting body language and eye accessing cues, but also the NLP Practitioner's intuition. The ability to understand something right away can lead to improved directions and guidance during NLP therapy, as the NLP Practitioner would be able to respond quickly and appropriately to the client's body language and eye accessing cues. If the NLP Practitioner can accurately interpret the client's state of mind by the means of NLP mind reading, then there is a higher chance of success for all parties involved within this evolving practice.

Understanding Body Language in NLP

NLP mind reading through body language and eye accessing cues is done across various fields, in addition to NLP itself. For example, police detectives may employ the skill of reading body language to determine whether a criminal is lying, or if the former is making progress during interrogation. Beyond that, body language can still give people an impressive amount of information in terms of their current thoughts and feelings. The majority of that information is non-verbal; according to Bradberry, 55% of communication comes from body language, whereas 38% comes from vocal tone and only 7% comes from the actual words used during an interaction (2017). It is obvious that 55% is a big deal because it can give insight into the nature of human beings themselves. This is useful for many people in positions of influence. Some the body language that is easier to understand includes (Bradberry, 2017):

- Crossed arms and legs.
- Smiles that crinkle the eyes.
- Copying other people's body language.
- Posture.
- Eyes.
- Raised eyebrows.
- Clenched jaw.

Body language, like crossed arms and legs, suggests the individual is opposing your thoughts and viewpoints actively, while also refusing to be receptive to them. Important to note is that, even if their facial expression suggests happiness through a big smile, they may actually be isolated or disconnected from the other person's ideas, a situation in which they would be physically, emotionally, and mentally closed off. Crossed arms and legs may also signal the need for protection from the other individual's expressed ideas and/or feelings.

One form of body language that can be read easily through NLP practice and has been mentioned briefly is a person's smile. If a person smiles genuinely during a situation, you would see eyes crinkling to follow suit. In fact, the individual would not be seen smiling genuinely if their smile "doesn't reach their eyes," as the saying goes. A person's smile often infers approval, pleasure, or amusement, except in the case when a person is trying to hide something, like emotional or mental pain—in those cases, you might see a smile without eye crinkling. If crow's feet can't be seen around the corners of the eyes, that individual is not really *smiling*.

If someone is copying your body language, it suggests that person can feel a connection with you; therefore, they demonstrate a mirror effect. For example, if my friend smiles in a certain way, I may smile in the same manner. The action of doing so suggests the relationship is going well, and that I am happy to spend time with my friend. In addition, copying body language can entice the other person to open up to you, depending on the body language you use at that moment. An understanding of this concept can be helpful in NLP practice.

An individual's posture can also tell us a multitude of things, such as whether the person is feeling confident or tired; someone with a puffed out chest would impart that they have, or believe they have, power, whereas a slouch would suggest the individual feels less powerful. Having a decent posture is valuable because such a stance can also communicate respect from others. For example, when I was in army basic training, I had to copy or mirror the drill sergeants' body posture to show respect for them, myself, and the uniform.

Another form of body language that is easy to understand include the movement of a person's eyes. If a person purposely holds eye contact with you for a long period of time, then that person could very well be deceiving or outright lying to you. When this is the case, the person's eyes may not blink or move, which suggests that something is amiss. Always pay attention to the eyes. Make note that the average time for holding eye contact is about seven to ten seconds (Bradberry, 2017), so if someone holds eye contact for a longer length of time and starts making you feel uncomfortable, that person could be lying or trying to intimidate you. Recognizing this fact can be quite useful to NLP practice because the NLP Practitioner can figure out if the client is lying to them. Eye movements or lack thereof can communicate various subjective states of mind, among other things.

Raised eyebrows are also a form of body language to pay attention to because they can communicate emotions such as fear, worry, or surprise. For instance, if my friends throw me a surprise birthday party, my initial reaction of surprise when I enter the room may become obvious when my eyebrows elevate to a higher position on my face. Still, raised eyebrows can also suggest something behind the scenes, especially when the topic of discussion should not be eliciting surprise, worry, or fear from the reacting individual. In short, be cautious of raised eyebrows.

Last but not least, a clenched jaw can communicate tension, stress, and discomfort to the other individual during an interaction. For example, I usually clench my jaw when I have to get my blood drawn because the thought of a needle pricking my arm stresses me out. The phlebotomist doing the deed would usually have to distract me by talking to me during a blood draw, so I can relax a bit more and unclench my jaw. Body language communicates a lot of information about the individual, which makes the NLP Practitioner's job easier.

Understanding Eye Accessing Cues in NLP

Also making the NLP Practitioner's job less difficult is reading eye accessing cues from the client during a session. Eye accessing cues, similar to body language, can indicate the client's thoughts, or at least lead the NLP Practitioner in the right direction. In addition, eye accessing cues help the NLP Practitioner determine which representational system the client is accessing. To explain, a **representational system** would include sensory modalities like visual, auditory, or kinesthetic, which are then represented by methods and models that relate how the mind stores and processes information. When an individual uses their mind to think, the NLP Practitioner can determine which representational system they are using to communicate their preferred thinking modality—the NLP Practitioner would then notice these based on eye movements and cues. However, this method does not indicate exactly what the individual is thinking, merely *how* they are thinking. In short, the NLP Practitioner can track the individual's preferred thinking style through those eye movements, which is helpful to NLP processes.

As stated, eye accessing cues assist the NLP Practitioner by communicating whether the client processes information with visuals such as pictures, sounds, and feelings. Pictures are generally anything we can see in reality; sounds can include trickling of running water; and feelings may include happy or upset emotions. Thinking in different ways initiates noticeable changes in the body, and the body would also exert influence on how an individual thinks. For example, how an individual thinks would determine their eye movements, and their eye movements could stimulate various parts of the brain. More precisely, looking up, in terms of NLP movements, is associated with visual thinking, whereas keeping one's eyes level suggests auditory thinking. In addition, looking down is associated with kinesthetic thinking. Looking right or left during these NLP eye movements can determine if the individual is constructing or recalling visuals, sounds, or feelings. Eyes that move to the left indicate the construction of sensory modalities, whereas eyes that look to the right indicate a recall of sensory modalities. NLP eye movements can help the NLP Practitioner understand more about the person and their preferred thinking style.

NLP Accessing Cues: Visual, Auditory, and Kinesthetic

Each representational system has plenty of accessing cues in addition to eye movements and positions. Some other accessing cues include the position of the head and gestures; breathing; and tone, tempo, and pitch of the individual's voice. For example, accessing cues for a visual representation system would include: head up, gestures above the shoulders, breathing in the lungs, and a high-pitched voice with a high tempo of speech. Accessing cues for an auditory representational system would include: head leaning to one side, ear-level gestures, breathing in the diaphragm, and a varied speech tempo and tones. Lastly, accessing cues for a kinesthetic representational system would include: head down, gestures around the body, abdominal breathing, and slower speech with a deeper voice. Given these details about accessing cues and representational systems, people can determine their own preferred representational systems, along with preferred systems in others.

Behavior Indicators of Preferred Representational Systems

In addition, there are behavior indicators that can determine if a person's preferred representational system is visual, auditive, or kinesthetic. For example, there is evidence that I prefer the visual representational system because I tend to be organized, quiet, a decent speller, and I can be very detailed. Some other behavior indicators for visual people include:

- Neat and orderly.
- Observant.
- Appearance-oriented.
- More deliberate.
- Are better at memorizing by picture.

Behavior indicators can determine if an individual prefers the auditory representational system as well; for instance, if the person likes to talk to themselves, says words when reading, speaks in rhythmic patterns, and likes music, then they are probably an auditory person. Some other behavior indicators for auditory people include:

- Learn by listening.
- Talkative.
- Uses a phonetic approach when spelling.
- Enjoys reading out loud.
- Talk better than they write.

Beyond that, behavior indicators for a kinesthetic individual are that the person is generally physically oriented, learns by doing, gestures a lot, and also responds physically to the situation. Other behavior indicators for kinesthetic people include:

- Touch people and stand close.
- Move a lot.
- Larger physical reaction.
- Early large muscle development.
- Learn through manipulation.

Each representational system can help the NLP Practitioner ascertain not only how the individual thinks, but also how they learn, converse, spell, read, write, and imagine. If the NLP Practitioner is keenly aware of how the client thinks, then they will be better able to influence, persuade, or manipulate the client—and the subjective reality experienced—for an improved outcome. Otherwise, it would be much more challenging to help the client with their personal and professional goals.

Controlling People Through Their Preferred Representational System

Controlling people through their preferred representational system is accomplished through the application and practice of NLP techniques and tools that can improve the client's state of mind and change their subjective reality for more practical purposes and functionality. More specifically, the NLP Practitioner can match or mirror the behaviors, movements, and speech of the client, while basing the mirrored actions on the client's preferred representational system. This matching of the client's preferred representational system and the resulting manifestation of it will allow the NLP Practitioner to accommodate, direct, or control the client better. This is because, when the NLP Practitioner assimilates to their client and the latter's preferred representational system, the professional can then improve or change it, with the goal of improved outcomes and success.

Chapter Summary

In this chapter, you have learned about reading and controlling people. You learned that NLP mind reading through body language and eye accessing cues is useful to the application of NLP. It is also important to remember the various representation systems, as they will help both the individual and the NLP Practitioner communicate and understand each other. To refresh your memory, here are the key points of this chapter:

- Reading a person's mind enables the NLP Practitioner to understand how that person is thinking and feeling.
- Reading people allows us to communicate more efficiently.
- NLP mind reading through body language and eye accessing cues is useful because it determines the next course of action in therapy.
- Body language gives people an impressive quantity of information about what they are thinking and feeling.
- Body language can include (Bradberry, 2017):
  o Crossed arms and legs.
  o Smiles that crinkle the eyes.
  o Copying your body language.
  o Posture.
  o Eyes.
  o Raised eyebrows.
  o Exaggerated nodding.
  o Clenched jaw.
- Eye accessing cues can help determine which representational system is being accessed by the client.
- Types of preferred representational systems include visual, auditory, and kinesthetic.
- Behavior indicators of preferred representational systems include
  o Visual behavioral indicators:
- Neat and orderly.

- Observant.
- Appearance-oriented.
- More deliberate.
- Memorizes by picture.
  o Auditory behavioral indicators:
- Learns by listening.
- Very talkative.
- Uses a phonetic approach when spelling.
- Enjoys reading out loud.
- Talks better than they write.
  o Kinesthetic behavioral indicators.
- Touches people and stands close.
- Moves a lot.
- Larger physical reaction.
- Early large muscle development.
- Learns through manipulation.
- Controlling people through a preferred representational system can be accomplished through applying NLP techniques and tools.

In the next chapter, you will learn about getting inside people's heads through the use of body language.

CHAPTER FIVE:

Getting Inside People's Heads Through Body Language

Reasons for Learning and Mastering Body Language Reading and Application

Since body language is a more accurate indicator of an individual's state of mind due to how thoughts and feelings communicate and express themselves more naturally through it, learning and mastering body language is a valuable skill for discerning other people's intentions and motivations. In other words, people's intentions and motivations become clearer when you understand the reasons behind their body language. Whether it is to leave an impression on your coworkers or communicate the need for affection, learning and mastering body language will help you get what you want out of life as you master the manifestations and forms of expression.

People also use body language to give other people their opinions and judgments, and learning and mastering body language could also be useful for this reason. Some career fields may require learning and mastering body language for judgment or assessment include psychology, law, and even education. The impression an individual leaves through their body language can have consequences, depending on the context. For instance, a psychological assessment can affect the medicine prescribed to a patient. Case in point, according to Radwan,

93% of the impressions people establish about you is surmised by body language, whereas only 7% of that impression is based on the words you use (2017). Even so, remember that how you communicate through words is always just as valuable as body language.

Gaining Advantage Through Body Language

Using body language advantageously can benefit yourself in many ways. One of those benefits comes with using it for attraction. An individual can attract a potential partner through using their body language; if done right and with the right amount of communication, the arrangement can eventually lead to love and affection. Some people may use body language to lead people on, making the other person assume that the former likes them, when in fact, they don't. This may be advantageous to the individual because that person can conceal their true feelings, intentions, and motivations better from any frenemies they have, as necessary and to keep personal boundaries.

Another advantage of using body language to your advantage is being able to induce specific states of mind. This is called the **reverse effect** because, when an individual moves their body or poses in a certain way, specific states of mind can materialize in them. For example, if you stand with your back straight and elevate your head a little, you may start to gain feelings of confidence, giving you stronger beliefs in your abilities. Another example of the reverse effect is when an individual smiles. Someone else's smile can trick your brain into happiness by initiating a chemical reaction that improves your mood, decreases stress and blood pressure, and may even increase your lifespan (Spector, 2018). As we've seen through these examples, it can be advantageous to use body language, as it can enhance both your subjective state of mind and wellbeing.

Most Useful Body Language to Interpret and Take Control

There are various types of body language of which we can interpret and take control to optimize our individual situations, depending on the context and reason. For example, if the reason is to garner more sales, then the salesperson's body language should reflect confidence when persuading the customer to buy. However, if their body language does not reflect this emotion, then they can take a class or go to a professional about body language, so they can learn how to appear and feel more confident and relaxed on the job.

The interpretation of body language is not an exact science, however, partially because various cultures may have assigned different meanings to body language. According to Zhi-Peng, gestures can be challenging to interpret because any slight variations can convey any number of completely different meanings (2014). For instance, American culture has assigned the OK sign (pressing thumb and forefinger together, other three fingers spread out) as approval, whereas in France, the same sign would suggest that the other person is "worthless" or "zero" (as indicated by the circle created between the two principal fingers). Another example of body language meaning different things is eye contact—in the United States and Canada, direct eye contact shows sincerity or interest, whereas the same eye cue in Japan is considered disrespectful (Zhi-Peng, 2014). Be that as it may, the same body language can also convey common meanings in terms of body movements, gestures, facial expressions, and eye movements.

Someone is Offended, Uneasy, Shy, or Defensive

A person's state of mind can also be revealed when they are offended, uneasy, shy, or defensive. More indicatively, the person feeling any of these emotions will usually cross their arms and possibly their legs too, if the situation is intense enough. If you notice

313

another person is uncomfortable as a result of being in an unfamiliar environment, perhaps at a big gathering for work, that person will probably be folding the arms as a form of protection against that unfamiliar situation. This is why the posture is called the **defensive body language posture**, signaling one's uneasiness to those around them. It's almost as if the individual believes that by folding or crossing their arms and/or legs, they will supposedly be safer or protected from that environmental influence.

In addition, the defensive body language posture is also usually accompanied by additional facial expressions and specific body movements. Some of those facial expressions and body movements expressed during this time include recoil, a microaggression of anger, a clenched jaw, and pursed lips. For example, when an individual dislikes an uncomfortable situation or person, that individual will pull back or recoil. On the other hand, micro expressions of anger are also common when a person reacts defensively, in part because that individual's eyebrows will come down and their nose and top lip will come up, portraying disgust. As mentioned, another way to tell if a person is offended is when the person clenches their jaw tightly. In this defensive body movement, the person would have their jaw come forward and be possibly gritting their teeth, though you may not see it. Pursed lips are another indicator that an individual is uneasy and tense, usually done so the person can stop themselves from expressing vocally what they feel and believe.

However, the situation can be rectified or controlled when the individual takes responsibility for the offense. You can help them do this by asking them how they feel—this question can be accompanied by asking if they feel offended and how the situation can be rectified. This is useful to NLP because, if the NLP Practitioner can sense the other person's state of mind, that professional will have an easier time guiding that situation toward improvement. Once that is done and both parties feel comfortable, they can then continue the NLP session.

Someone is Evaluating or Thinking

When someone holds their chin in their hand, as if holding the weight of their thoughts and ideas, they are indicating that they are thinking or evaluating a situation. For example, I would often find myself doing this gesture when I write. In addition, someone using this body language to communicate is suggesting that they are listening to your ideas and thoughts while not only evaluating them, but also considering whether they are convincing enough. You would know if you have succeeded in getting through to someone if they nod their head while cupping their chin.

A thinker/evaluator's body language can also display whether their evaluation is positive or negative based on their use of gestures, such as smiling or clapping. However, there are other, less obvious positive cues that the other person may use, such as rubbing their eyebrow or adjusting their glasses—with the former, it's almost as if they were hoping to see the positive picture more clearly by moving their eyebrow hair out of the way (Parvez, 2015). I know I have adjusted my glasses plenty of times while evaluating something I view more positively than negatively.

There are also negative evaluation gestures that a person can use to signify a weak opinion of something. Some of the more obvious gestures pertaining to negative evaluation include closing eyes or looking away. These gestures will definitely let the other person know you are not quite in favor of the ideas they are presenting to you. Another gesture someone may employ is a little subtler: rubbing their nose. People may usually use this when they are angry, anxious, or self-conscious. It is also interesting to note that some people may be rubbing their nose to satisfy inflammation in that area brought upon by an increase in blood pressure when they lie—this phenomenon is known as the **Pinocchio Effect** (Parvez, 2015). This biological mechanism is efficient in lie detection, which is then useful in a variety of situations and careers associated with NLP practice.

Someone is Frustrated

Frustration can manifest outwardly in many ways through body language. It is easy to understand and interpret when the person does specific gestures, such as shaking their foot, tapping their hands in their lap, rubbing their face with their fingers, or even scratching themselves vigorously (Radwan, 2017). These frustrated movements can, in effect, release pent up energy within that person, especially when there is a situation that they cannot act upon. Still, the most obvious and widely accepted forms of frustration are when the person rubs the back of their neck or scratches the back of their head. Rubbing the back of one's neck while dealing with frustrating circumstances can help the person calm down because they are expanding that energy from its source.

We can also detect frustration through subtler body language, such as through someone's facial muscles, eyebrows, or lips. Slight movements in these areas are called **micro gestures**. For example, when I am feeling stressed or frustrated, my facial muscles may sometimes twitch. Other people may barely notice it; however, a professional trained in recognizing body language and cues may pick up on it. If someone is watching their friend—someone they probably know relatively intimately—they should be able to pick up those micro gestures much easier than if someone else were to because they can recognize their friend's behavior better. It is important to be able to detect micro gestures in your body language too, before trying to judge them in someone else's body language; for instance, a psychologist would be more effective if they are more aware of their own micro gestures prior to judging those of a client.

Someone is Anxious

Another form of body language that we can interpret easily is anxiety. When someone is anxious, they are usually expressing that feeling by fidgeting, usually in a number of different ways. Some of these fidgeting cues include sweating, fingernail biting, or constantly tapping one's fingers or heels on a table or on the ground. A personal example of mine would be that, whenever I have to wait at the doctor's office for an exam, I may fidget in my seat out of nerves. I may also move my left leg up and down quickly in an attempt to expend this nervous energy as I wait for the doctor to call my name.

In addition, expressing anxiety can affect various motor functions, such as walking or running, because that energy is causing one's body to become more rigid rather than relaxed. Originally, our ancestors would conceal themselves from predators by standing rigid and still, so they can avoid danger. It was as if their subconscious mind tightened up their bodies to avoid being recognized. Such instinct still appears similarly today. Oddly enough, it could be considered a form of ghosting, as the person tries to withdraw from observation. This anxious body language can be directed by an NLP Practitioner, with the professional trying to entice the person to calm down and perhaps even engage in some deep breathing exercises.

Someone is Bored

As we have seen, a person's body language can signal various states of mind, and this includes boredom. Boredom can be signaled by a person having droopy eyes, seeming inattentive, yawning, or fidgeting. As a personal example, when I get bored, I tend to feel tired, especially when I get stuck in a daily routine. The reasons for expressing boredom through body language include both a lack of interest and/or a readiness to take action. For example, when people drone on about subjects such as politics, it can put me to sleep because I have no interest in the topic. There are many reasons for boredom to occur.

The language of boredom is expressed in many ways, including tiredness, repetition, and distraction. For example, when an individual is bored, that person will distract themselves by engaging in other activities, such as looking at their cell phone. In addition, the individual trying to distract themselves as a result of boredom will usually avoid looking at the source of boredom, that being possibly a person or homework. Some distracting activities are repetitive, such as constantly tapping one's fingers. Last but not least, a person expressing boredom will sometimes look on blankly, in addition to having a slouched body. This posture could signal to a therapist or NLP Practitioner to switch it up or change the course of therapy.

Someone is Ready for the Next Step

Body language that indicates a person is ready to act can include pointing, tension, hooking, and movement. For instance, if one's body is pointed toward a person of interest—possibly the NLP Practitioner—then it is usually a sign that the former wants to take the next step in a sequence of events. In terms of tension, if a person is tense because they are doing something out of their comfort zone, their arms may grip onto something; for example, if you were at the dentist, you may be gripping the armrests on the chair while the dentist works on your teeth, completely ready to get out of that situation.

Hooking is another form of body language to indicate that the person is ready to take action. For this form, the person's hands hook slightly into their clothing, usually a waistband, and they would do this to show they are ready to move quickly if they need. Continuing with the subject of movement to demonstrate readiness, note that the beginning or first movement always lays the groundwork for further, successive movement. For example, I have a tendency to straighten the clothing under my coat before I go somewhere, like to a restaurant. The next movement I may do would usually be grabbing my purse on my way out the door.

Beyond the readiness language mentioned, there are also various reasons for why someone would be wanting to take action at that time. Some of these reasons include the person is leaving, ready to buy, continuing a conversation, or is ready to fight. If I am pointing in the direction of the door, my reason for doing so is because I want to leave or exit the situation. A person may be using readiness language when they are ready to buy a particular product, displaying the language to the salesperson when they point to that product. If my partner and I have an animated discussion, either one or both of us will be sending readiness signals to each other as we talk or continue the conversation. The final reason we will be mentioning here is during a fight when a person is readying their body to defend or attack. As a stubborn sibling, I would sometimes get into physical fights with my other siblings.

Using readiness language could be beneficial in many relationships, whether professional or personal, because such indicates to the other party that action needs to happen for that relationship to proceed in a positive direction. It would, therefore, be time to engage the individual with action if that person is ready.

Someone is Lying

Body language that reveals when somebody is lying usually involves shifts from that person's usual behavior. For example, if your friend usually meets your gaze when having a conversation, but that friend starts avoiding eye contact one day, then it could be an indicator that they are lying to you. When someone tells a lie, their amygdala— the part of the brain that processes emotions— becomes less responsive. This circumstance could escalate to the person becoming better at lying, so they may do it again successively. However, shifts in body language can still give them away. According to Jalili, movements of the body, expressions on their face, speech content, and tone of voice can all reveal a liar (2019).

One example of body language or behavior that implies a person is lying is movement involving hands. Hands that gesture after a conversation are telltale signs of a liar because, as the conversation is taking place, the liar's brain is too busy making up the lie and checking to see if you believe it. As a result, the hands may not gesture properly as they should during a conversation.

Another example of body language that a liar may use is squirming or fidgeting, as the person becomes increasingly nervous about getting caught. Nerves or nervous system changes can cause people to feel itchy or tingly, which provokes more fidgeting. This excessive body movement is not the norm for somebody telling the truth unless that person normally fidgets a lot.

A person may use facial expressions involving their eyes, mouth, or expressions when they lie. If the person lying during a conversation looks away a lot, it is because they are trying to think of what to make up next regarding the lie being told. On the other hand, if someone stares directly at you for way too long during a conversation, that could also suggest something is amiss. It is important to remember that the baseline behavior for the individual is usually different from when the person tells a lie. Mouth or lip movements also impart a lie when the person's lips roll back, which is a suggestion that they are holding back facts (Jalili, 2019). The individual's complexion may also change if they are telling a lie. It could go one of two ways—they become as white as a ghost, or flushed. Body language can be quite telling, especially during interrogations.

Speech content may also change when a person lies. For example, when someone says "I want to be honest with you," implies they felt the need to add an emphasis on their honesty to make up for a potential lie. Another example of speech changing during a lie is when the liar is looking for the words to make up the lie. In this case, while the person is thinking of the next word to use, they may use filler words such as "um" or "uh" numerous times during their lie. In addition, the person's tone of voice may become higher pitched, indicating they are stressed or nervous when telling the lie. This stress causes the vocal cords to become rigid as they tighten. As we've seen here, the act of lying clearly has its own body language, which is helpful in psychology as well as law.

Micro Expressions

Micro expressions are also a form of body language that can indicate various states of mind within an individual and whether that person is lying. Some universal micro expressions include that of fear, happiness, disgust, surprise, sadness, anger, and contempt. A micro expression is hard to fake because they are involuntary expressions on the face that occur when a particular emotion is felt (Markowitz, 2013). For instance, when a person is genuinely surprised, they may raise their eyebrows with their skin stretching under the eyebrow, have wrinkles on their forehead appear, open their eyes wide, and drop their jaw.

Such micro expressions on the face during an emotional experience do not last a very long time: about 1/15 to 1/25 of a second (Babich, 2016). Truth speakers and liars will display different forms of micro expressions because those expressions are involuntary, making them more accurate indicators of genuine thought. An NLP Practitioner can use their analysis of their client's micro expressions to gauge the latter's true state of mind and determine the next course of action pertaining to the client's life and the NLP session. In addition, the NLP Practitioner can reprogram the individual to go in the direction of a more beneficial outcome, given the authenticity of micro expressions, even when the client is lying about how they truly feel.

Talk to the Hand: Telltale Handshakes and Gestures

Another form of body language that can be interpreted and even controlled are handshakes and gestures. This form of hand-body language can be very telling about a person because the positions of their hands can display their intentions. For example, if a person is sociable, their handshake will probably be firmer than someone who is more introverted, whose handshake would probably be looser. In addition, a handshake can also be employed to impart dominance, shown if the person initiates the handshake, then uses their hand to guide or otherwise control yours (Muoio, 2014). Other forms of handshakes include the finger-crushing shake, the two-hander shake, the sweaty shake, the finger shake, and the no cup shake. The two-hander is arguably the most interesting handshake because it is usually used to reveal sincerity, honesty, and even intimacy, especially when the handshake is higher up than usual. However, this handshake can still be misleading, for example, when political leaders want to front friendship to outsiders, they may cup the other person's hand in a desire to take control!

Hand-body language also includes hand gestures, like showing open palms, pointing at somebody, steeping their fingers in front of one's face, standing with hands behind one's back, and clenching hands (Muoio, 2014). When someone shows open palms, this can suggest openness—unless the palms are down, instead suggesting authority. Pointing can suggest aggressiveness, whereas steeping your fingers in front of your face imparts confidence. You would often see people standing with their hands behind their back in the military when standing "at ease;" it would generally be used to show the opposite of superiority and power, along with respect to those who are in power. Be that as it may, clenching one's hands indicates frustration.

Handshakes become more memorable when they are done properly, depending on the context. The context could be a business meeting or a social gathering, and handshakes can leave quite a lasting impression during these events. In terms of neuroscience, a handshake can promote a positive atmosphere, full of good intentions and motivations. A confident handshake can suggest communication on a deeper level, reduced negative associations, and increased personal interest (Lee, 2020). It is evident that a good handshake can set the stage for further positive communications and interactions.

It's important to note that hand gestures can also convey meaning. For instance, shoving your hands in your pockets will project a reluctance to talk, whereas open palms can suggest sincerity. In addition, a downward-facing palm can suggest authority and power, whereas a closed hand with the finger pointed can signal an attempt to get someone to submit. For example, when your parents give you a directive, they may use a closed hand with a pointed finger to convince you effectively to submit to their authority. Other hand gestures include the precision thumbs, gripping fingertips, fist thrusting, and hand chopping. As we've discovered, hand gestures can tell you a lot about a person and their intentions.

Persuasive Body Language

Persuasive body language can project confidence in all sorts of situations, from professional to personal. Some body language gestures that reflect self-confidence include hands in front of stomach, fingertips touching, and using a power pose. For example, I notice the meteorologist I watch on television in the mornings always places his hands with the fingertips touching in front of his stomach, as he gives the weather report for the day. He appears to be very confident, even when he slips on his words. Other body language confidence gestures include (Radwan, 2017):

- Upright posture.
- Walking with wide steps.
- Doesn't panic.
- No fidgeting.
- Fewer speech mistakes.
- Proper eye contact.
- No closed gestures.
- Not looking to others for what to do regarding future actions.

It is important to be able to be able to read these body language signals in yourself and others because you will not only feel more confident and attractive, but the signals themselves will also convince people to like you more. For example, if my partner walks with wide steps, it may imply that they have no fear when encountering unfamiliar situations. In addition, many people find confidence to be sexy.

Body language signals are also valuable to professionals and businesses alike, especially when the salesperson is trying to persuade a prospect into buying their product and/or service. Some of these readable body signals come from the eyes, face, hands, arms, and feet. For example, when a potential customer is staring at the product you're trying to sell, it may be a good time to ask if they have any questions about it. If the customer smiles and nods at the same time, your presentation of the product was likely successful and you are probably good to go.

In addition, hands and arms can also communicate impatience, generally when the person drums their fingers (Wood, n.d.). Feet are also good to analyze, as they can signal whether the prospect is open or closed off to the salesperson, depending on the direction in which they are pointed. If the feet are pointed toward the salesperson, then they are open to the salesperson's ideas, whereas when the opposite occurs, they are probably unappreciative of the salesperson's advice. Body language signals such as these can tell the salesperson a lot about the customer's reaction to themselves and their product, so it is critical to learn as much about the various body signals as soon as possible.

Persuasion and Influence in NLP

Body language becomes more influential and persuasive when a person can mirror or match that of another person. For example, during an NLP session between a client and the NLP Practitioner, reading the other's body language and signals can become like a game.

If the client smiles, so would the NLP Practitioner because doing so creates rapport and trust when people see you are similar to them. This NLP rapport can then be guided and manipulated in the direction the NLP Practitioner wants it to go as they lead the client with their intentional body signals.

Persuasion and influence in NLP practice by means of NLP techniques and tools becomes possible when using one NLP technique in particular—**framing**. Framing is when the NLP Practitioner sets up the context of the situation by repeating back to the individual their original context. They would usually do this by restating it to indicate their own similarity to the person, thus building rapport. After all, the best words to hear are ones you just said! NLP framing is just one of the many NLP techniques and tools that can be quite influential and persuasive when done correctly.

If it is done correctly, it is possible to change a person's subjective state of mind by NLP framing. The NLP Practitioner would frame by controlling the context through the use of one's own subjective state, mirror neurons, language, and intention (Snyder, 2019). All these variables help to convince the client to anchor to the NLP Practitioner, thus building rapport and trust. Once the client trusts the NLP Practitioner, the client will use language to amplify their original state with trigger words. These trigger words can then be used by the NLP Practitioner to lead the client into further discussion by opening up a memory with values, associations, and emotional **hot buttons**. The hot buttons animate the client emotionally and can produce more feelings that change the client's perceptual filters. This is when the client will start to perceive the NLP Practitioner by the picture that the former just created of themselves. As you can see, NLP framing can be a very powerful tool of control, manipulation, and persuasion.

Chapter Summary

In this chapter, you have learned why you should learn and master body language. In addition, you have learned how to gain an advantage through the use of body language, while also understanding its most important forms, so you can interpret and take control of them. It is also important to remember what we went over about micro expressions, handshakes, gestures because understanding them better can help you influence and persuade others much easier. Furthermore, mirroring is another influential and persuasive technique to build rapport, especially when framing. To refresh your memory, the following are some of the key points from this chapter:

- Non-verbal body language can be an accurate indicator of a person's communication.
- You can gain an advantage in any situation by using persuasive body language.
- Although the general use of body language is universal, various cultures may interpret forms of it in different ways.
- Body language can indicate strong feelings.
- Involuntary expression of micro expressions can be useful to the practice of NLP because the NLP Practitioner can then gauge the client's true state of mind.
- Handshakes and gestures can reveal the client's true state of mind.
- Persuasive body language projects confidence in all sorts of situations, from professional to personal.
- Some forms of persuasive body language include (Radwan, 2017):
  - Upright posture.
  - Walking with wide steps.
  - Doesn't panic.
  - No fidgeting.
  - Fewer speech mistakes.
  - Proper eye contact.

- o   No closed gestures.
- o   Not looking to others for what to do regarding actions.
- Body language becomes more influential and persuasive when it can be mirrored or matched to fit the other person's body language, thus possibly influencing them to take action.
- NLP framing is a powerful NLP tool that an NLP Practitioner can use to control, manipulate, and persuade a client.

In the next chapter, you will learn all about NLP frame control.

CHAPTER SIX:

Control the Frame, Control the Game

NLP Framing Interpreted

NLP framing can be defined as the boundaries encapsulating an event or experience. In other words, a **frame** in NLP terminology is a person's mental template that filters or colors their everyday perceptions, influencing their behaviors and interactions (Catherine, 2014). In NLP framing, the person's mental template can be changed, altering how they see and experience reality; reality would change as the person experiences it if an NLP Practitioner "framed" the person.

Brain's Response to NLP Framing

NLP framing affects the brain through the restructuring of limbic system links between the amygdala and the hippocampus. The **amygdala** is in charge of managing your emotions, while the **hippocampus** produces and stores your most relevant memories. More specifically, the **prefrontal cortex** and the **thalamus** interact with the hippocampus, amygdala, and the rest of the limbic system to fish out the memory that is most appropriate for the attempt at NLP framing.

NLP Framing Edits an Emotional Response

Thus, NLP framing edits the emotional response to that specific memory by increasing or decreasing the emotions associated with that memory. For example, negative framing can decrease the person's emotions by assisting them with detaching themselves from that memory. This negative framing would accomplish this task through subduing or inhibiting any links between the emotions and that memory. On the other hand, positive framing tries to amplify an otherwise normal memory into a more powerful one by using the person's imagination and senses, putting in extra focus toward increasing its emotional impact.

NLP Framing Based on Intentions

NLP framing is based on intentions. More specifically, NLP framing is based on the intentions of the NLP Practitioner and the client as they interact during an NLP session, based on the reasons for having the session in the first place. For example, if the client wished to have the session because they wanted to reframe an experience they had as more positive, then the intentions of the NLP Practitioner would probably be to increase any positive associations and feelings they have toward that event or memory. The reasons for improving the client's subjective state of mind in reference to the event or memory would be that the client benefits emotionally, psychologically, and maybe even physically.

Categories of Intentions in NLP Framing

There are also categories of intentions when it comes to NLP framing. Some of those categories include subconscious intentions, conscious intentions, preset intentions, evolving intentions, and conditional intentions. **Subconscious intentions** are hidden or suppressed from conscious awareness, whereas **conscious intentions** are intentions we pay close attention to, and would usually be the kind that occupy our daily thoughts. For example, you may be "in the zone" while working on a task and may not even be aware of it, given subconscious intentions; however, you are conscious about the *purpose* for the task. **Preset intentions** usually involve plans, whereas **evolving intentions** happen in the moment. **Conditional intentions**, interestingly enough, are useful if the conditions for it are met. As we've seen, there are various competing intentions in life and in NLP practice.

Setting Strong Frames in NLP

Setting strong frames in NLP is sometimes necessary to accomplish the overall objective. This is because there are many variables that can affect the strength of the frame's intentions, such as time, flexibility, and knowledge. For instance, a short-term time frame can be strong, like getting groceries from the store, whereas a long-term time frame, like paying down debt, can be weaker. In addition, flexibility plays a role because, if you can work within subframes to accomplish the objective of the main frame, then the chances of success become higher than if you remained inflexible. Knowledge also plays a key role because, the more knowledge the individual has, the more likely they can accomplish the overall objective. Strong frames require strong intentions as well, even if there are many frame strength variables along the way.

Knowing What NLP Frame to Adopt

Figuring out which NLP frame to adopt for the individual context is key because the frame can affect the client, direction, goals, and overall outcome of the NLP session. If the NLP Practitioner is aware of the individual they are trying to persuade, then it will be easier to choose the right frame. Such personal variables include who the individual's identity, their motivations, chosen form of expression, micro expressions, values, and what they really want (Snyder, 2019). Once this knowledge is obtained, then it becomes easier to convince the person to do what you want. Knowing what frame to adopt can also be determined by answering the following questions:

- What does this person need to be for them to take the actions I want?
- What subjective states of mind does the person have to be in to want to take those actions?
- What's in it for the person?
- What is the outcome?

If the correct frame is chosen for that individual, the person will become more than likely to open up, which will ultimately help both the NLP Practitioner and the client. More specifically, the correct frame will help the NLP Practitioner elicit the information the professional needs to move the NLP therapy session in the direction it needs to go, and the client will benefit from the outcome.

Reasons for Creating a Strong Frame in NLP

To create a strong frame, the NLP Practitioner will have to adhere to a few prerequisites. One such requirement is a strong intention, which is necessary to ascertain the will of the client and see the task through to its fulfillment. Another requirement for a strong frame is flexibility, due to there sometimes being various subframes within the main frame. If the NLP Practitioner isn't flexible, then it will become more challenging to accomplish the main objective of the NLP therapy session. The next requirement for a strong frame is that the client and NLP Practitioner would need to put it to the test to determine its tolerance and strength of survival. For instance, if my goal is to lose weight, then I have to take action repeatedly to make that happen, especially if I am tempted to fall off the horse by binging out at a buffet. Strong frames also require the individual not to shift and redefine the frame because doing so will only make them lose sight of the original goal. In short, a person has to hold firm to accomplish the objectives and goals of the frame.

NLP Frame Strengthening Exercises

Sometimes NLP frames need to be strengthened to become and remain strong. To do this task, the person can follow a few frame strengthening exercises. Some of those exercises include:

- Avoid cursing or using strong swear words.
- Adhere to a shopping list.
- Stick to a regular sleep schedule.
- Work out everyday.
- Have concrete life goals.
- Socialize, but keep score.
- Incline people to smile.
- Take an acting class.
- Engage in Tai Chi in public.
- Keep score of the intentions set before every conversation.

The reasons for some of these frame strengthening exercises include learning how to control oneself by sticking to something like a shopping list, a regular sleep schedule, and the like. In addition, having well-defined, concrete life goals can give the individual something to work toward. Socializing helps develop stronger frame control as the person interacts with more people, while inclining people to smile will pull others in emotionally. It is also suggested to take acting classes for stronger frame control because doing so will teach the person to "act" well while employing strong frame control. Engaging in exercises such as Tai Chi in a public space can also help the individual learn to no longer care about what others are thinking and the fact that others are watching them. Lastly, keeping score on conversational intentions will improve frame control because the person would be practicing following through on those intentions.

7 NLP Frames and How to Apply Them

There is a variety of NLP Frames in NLP practice, and some of those NLP frames are the Outcome Frame, the Ecology Frame, the As If Frame, the Backtrack Frame, the Relevancy Frame, the Contrast Frame, and the Open Frame. The **Outcome Frame**, more defined, is an exercise that will help you discover what people want, then learn the resources to acquire their wants. It is applied by simply asking the individual what they want. Another frame is the **Ecology Frame**, which is defined as the impact of an action or event on the bigger systems in which we take part, such as family, community, and even the entire planet. The Ecology Frame is applied by asking about the integrity of the desired action and how that affects the integrity of others and their respective systems.

On the other hand, the **As If Frame** implies that a person should fake it until they make it, allowing for the exploration of possibilities and innovative problem solving if the situation were different. Beyond that, the **Backtrack Frame** is defined as returning to a point of reference to clarify the information, so the person can move forward and realign the direction of the communication and interaction. It is applied by restating what was said by using the other individual's keywords, which checks if there is understanding and agreement.

Then there is the **Relevancy Frame**, which keeps the discussion pertinent by asking "how is that relevant to the outcome or agenda of this discussion?" The **Contrast Frame** is defined as comparing and contrasting options and alternatives to show that action needs to be taken now. This frame is applied by contrasting the present situation with the desired outcome, which helps highlight which action should be taken. Finally, the **Open Frame** is completely non-scripted, allowing the individual to discuss and express whatever it is they feel like talking about at that specific moment. As we can see, these frames can be quite useful and can be applied to a variety of contexts to help the recipient toward the desired outcome.

Reframing in NLP

Reframing the original NLP frame can be beneficial in certain circumstances—when the original NLP frame no longer applies to the current context, it must be restructured and adapted to be viable again to the individual and the situation. According to Hall, **reframing** is defined as shifting our thoughts with a different perspective resulting from reclassifying and redefining the frame-of-reference into a different classification or category (2010). In effect, reframing allows us to be more creative, as it supplies a new reference structure from which to view things. This, in turn, can change our experiences, thoughts, and interactions, among other things.

Reframing can be accomplished in a few different ways, including de-framing, pre-framing, post-framing, counter-framing, outframing, and metaphorical framing. **De-framing** is when we pull the meaning apart, whereas **pre-framing** is when the idea of action is reclassified. In addition, **post-framing** is when a point of view is established beforehand by structuring a frame ahead of time. Post-framing is creating new points of view from a future reference point, so that, when the person refers to a previous action, a different meaning would materialize. Furthermore, **counter-framing** requires counter examples to be provided to the person and/or context. **Outframing** is defined as creating a new frame about the idea by stepping aside from a meaning, thus allowing the other frame into existence. Last but not least, **metaphorical framing** is when a story or a metaphor is used to frame things in a similar situation. Reframing allows the individual to adapt creatively to change while the person's mental versatility frames and reframes their subjective experiences.

Using Frame Control to Influence People

Frame control can be used to persuade people by demonstrating behavior consistency through congruence in facial gestures, tone of voice, and body language, ultimately pulling people into going along with you (Your Charisma Coach, 2020). For example, if I listen consistently to what my partner has to say by leaning in and looking them directly in the eyes, they will be more likely to go along with my ideas or suggestions when I have something to say. In short, my consistent behavior is what will keep my partner's interest, and he will hopefully follow my lead. Frame control is influential because it sets social expectations that can make a powerful impression on the person, as long as you don't change your behavior toward them. Frame control sets the stage for further actions and reactions once you have defined it.

The Russell Brand Method and Exploiting Other People's Words and Weaknesses

One interesting frame control strategy is the Russell Brand Method. The **Russell Brand Method** of frame control includes a strong belief system, confident body language, clear state of mind in which emotions don't overwhelm, and capability to exploit another individual's words. More explicitly, a strong belief system with a powerful vision will support the arguments of the individual, given continual practice of that belief system. Secondly, confident body language also influences frame control, displayed by baring one's chest, practicing a commanding tone of voice, walking like a CEO, and being aware of one's gestures and body language postures (Iliopoulos, 2015). In addition, a clear state of mind in which emotions don't overwhelm is also important because it allows the individual to control the frame in comparison to losing it.

Still, the capacity to exploit others' individual words is also a powerful aid in the Russell Brand Method because doing so allows the person to turn it back around onto the messenger. For example, if the person is unaffected by other peoples' attempts to harass them, it is suggesting a calmer presence, thus giving the individual time to assess the words used against them. The Russell Brand Method of frame control is effective in exploiting people's words and weaknesses because most people react to the situation instead of taking action themselves.

Taking Back Control of Your Own Mind in Frame Wars

Taking back control of your own mind in frame wars is necessary to be able to manipulate the situation back in your favor. This can be done by challenging the unobserved and by creating a new discussion (Basu, 2016). Challenging the unobserved will allow the individual to make the other party talk about the bigger perspective, thus giving the former the chance to divert from the actual discussion. Furthermore, this act interrupts the other party and their thinking. In addition, asking questions can create another discussion in which the person can lead the other party away from their frame and mindset. In other words, the second part of taking back control of your own mind in frame wars is to create a new discussion, as doing so pulls the other party out of their own frame and gets them to consider and talk about other relevant frames. This method is useful for leading a conversation in their favor.

Chapter Summary

In this chapter, you have learned about various aspects of NLP frame control. You have learned about what framing is, as well as how to set a strong frame. You have also learned about the seven NLP frames and how to apply them, while considering the art of reframing itself. Also, critical to note is the use of frame control to influence people; for example, the Russell Brand Method. Last but not least, you have learned how to take back control of your own mind in frame wars. To refresh your memory, here are the key points of this chapter:

- A frame is a person's mental template that filters their everyday perceptions, which would then influence the person's behaviors and interactions (Catherine, 2014).

- NLP framing affects the brain through restructuring limbic system links between the amygdala and the hippocampus.
- NLP framing edits the emotional response to a specific memory by increasing or decreasing the emotions associated with the memory.
- NLP framing is based on intentions.
- NLP framing has the following categories of intentions:
  o Subconscious intentions.
  o Conscious intentions.
  o Preset intentions.
  o Evolving intentions.
  o Conditional intentions.
- Setting strong frames is sometimes necessary to accomplish the overall objective.
- Knowing which frame to adopt for the individual context is key, and can be determined by asking:
  o What does this person need to be for them to take the actions I want?
  o What subjective states of mind does the person have to be in to want to take those actions?
  o What's in it for the person?
  o What is the outcome?
- Frame strengthening exercises are sometimes necessary to strengthen the frame. Some exercises include the following:
  o Avoid cursing or using strong swear words.
  o Adhere to a shopping list.
  o Stick to a regular sleep schedule.
  o Work out everyday.
  o Have concrete life goals.
  o Socialize but keep score.
  o Incline people to smile.
  o Take an acting class.
  o Engage in Tai Chi in public.
  o Keep score of the intentions set before every conversation.

- There is a variety of NLP frames, some of which include:
  - Outcome Frame.
  - Ecology Frame.
  - As If Frame.
  - Backtrack Frame.
  - Relevancy Frame.
  - Contrast Frame.
  - Open Frame.
- Reframing is shifting our thoughts to a different perspective resulting from reclassifying and redefining the frame-of-reference into a different classification or category (Hall, 2010).
- Frame control can persuade people by demonstrating behavior consistency through congruence in facial gestures, tone of voice, and body language, ultimately pulling people into going along with you (Your Charisma Coach, 2020).
- The Russell Brand Method of frame control includes a strong belief system, confident body language, clear state of mind in which emotions don't overwhelm, and the capability to exploit another individual's words.
- Taking back control of your own mind is done by challenging the unobserved and creating a new discussion.

In the next chapter, you will learn all about hypnosis and NLP Duo.

CHAPTER SEVEN:

Hypnosis and NLP's Potency

How Hypnosis and NLP Work Together

Hypnosis and NLP work together by influencing the mind and behaviors of an individual through their subconscious and conscience in similar ways. Since the subconscious can influence our thoughts, behaviors, actions, and vice versa, programming or restructuring the mind through hypnosis and NLP becomes quite effective. Both NLP and hypnosis use body language and tone of voice to influence the individual's subconscious, with the goal to put the individual in a more suggestive state. Within this state, the hypnotist or NLP Practitioner will have an easier time getting the person to follow the former's wishes. In addition, the effectiveness of NLP increases if the individual is hypnotized, as they become more open to influence, suggestion, and guidance. Similarly, if the individual is being reprogrammed through NLP, then their subconscious also acquires new ways of thinking and feeling about everyday experiences. Interesting to note is that while NLP programs the mind to discipline the subconscious to respond more efficiently to daily events, hypnotism uses the person's subconscious to influence their mind with a similar effect. In short, NLP influences the conscious mind to control the subconscious, whereas hypnotism influences the subconscious to then affect the conscious part of our brains. Combining these two practices is an effective method for improving an individual's life.

Rules of Hypnosis

Although NLP and hypnosis are very similar in their respective methods and outcomes, hypnosis has more free reign to influence the mind, given it is less scripted in its application and practice. Hypnosis has fewer presuppositions characterizing its practice, which allows it to have more leeway for free play. Even so, hypnosis has some important rules to help with its effectiveness. According to Casale, those rules are (2012):

- Don't hypnotize an individual who has epilepsy, a mental condition, or is otherwise disturbed.
- Don't try to construct subconscious changes.
- Leave out the theatrics and do not trick the individual.
- Avoid unexpected responses that can cause the individual to panic due to unexpected environmental changes. It is important to watch for this because there will be an increased environmental sensitivity on the individual's part.
- Ensure the individual is free from any induced beliefs when taking the person out of the trance.
- Be sure to take your time in a safe and controlled environment.
- Treat hypnotism as a relaxation tool, not an entertainment gimmick.

These rules for hypnosis practice are necessary for various reasons. One of those reasons is to treat the inductee ethically and with the utmost respect and consideration; treat them the same as you would hope another hypnotist or NLP Practitioner would to you. Another reason for the rules of hypnosis is to ensure that all parties involved are safe and sound before, during, and after the session. This assurance is necessary to prevent any mistreatment toward the individual, as well as any potential abuse of practice; otherwise, less desirable outcomes may occur. The rules of hypnosis help structure and guide its application into more ethically sound outcomes and benefits.

Setting, Priming, and Inducing Hypnosis

In addition to the rules of hypnosis, hypnosis is also distinguished by the setting, priming, and inducing of the inductee by the hypnotist. This is necessary to get the individual in the right frame of mind to undergo hypnosis. To initiate the hypnosis session, the **setting** itself must be ripe for relaxation, which is done by ensuring the inductee is in a comfortable, relaxed, and usually inclined position, so they can become more calm and peaceful. Hypnotists will often make use of a comfortable couch, for example. In addition, it is critical that the hypnotist make sure there are no unexpected interruptions, like a sudden knock on the door, because this could interfere with the hypnosis and even bring the inductee out of their state too quickly, thus affecting the person subconsciously. Most importantly, the inductee needs to trust their hypnotist because, otherwise, the attempt will be less successful, given the inductee will be less confident that their hypnotist can effectively do the deed.

Also important to the practice of hypnosis is priming the person before the start of the session. More specifically, **priming** is the act of making something ready for action. In hypnosis, this is done by confusing the person, making them more suggestible while their prefrontal cortex becomes too busy trying to understand the confusion (Casale, 2012). It is akin to confusing a telemarketer purposefully to distract them from trying to sell you something you don't really need. For example, I could use bad grammar to throw off a person or even ask them a nonsensical question. Doing so will shock the person to the point where they may become even more suggestible, given the brain won't be as able to filter out the confusing message or suggestion with proper reason.

Once the stage has been set and the individual primed, it is time to induce hypnosis. This is done by instructing the inductee to relax progressively, deeper and deeper until their entire body is in a state of total relaxation. For example, the hypnotist could count backwards from ten to zero, with the goal to increase the sense of calm and tranquility within the individual. More specifically, the hypnotist will employ visualization and imagery by asking the client to imagine relaxing in a specific setting, as the hypnotist calmly counts backwards.

Inducing hypnosis requires the hypnotist to use a calm voice while expressing positive words and sentence structure because, otherwise, the intended meaning of the message may get muddled. It is all about the individual and their subjective state of mind and experience, so if they become uncomfortable for any reason, it becomes time to end the session by waking the person up carefully from the hypnosis.

Using Hypnosis and Magic Suggestive Language

Using hypnosis requires the power of suggestion through language. As we've seen, language can be influential, and we will learn that it is not only in *what* is said, but in *how* it is said. In other words, how the intended meaning is framed and characterized can influence how the recipient receives that message. For example, if I use directives instead of suggestions to convince someone to act, there will be less freedom of interpretation because the directive is more specific. Directing someone to clean their room is more specific than if I indirectly suggested it through ambiguous language that left room for interpretation, such as saying "Just do it." On the other hand, suggesting a course of action through non-specific language can be more influential and powerful because it leaves room for personalizing the intended meaning, given there is more room for that interpretation.

As was just mentioned, the magic of suggestive language is that it leaves plenty of room for interpretation with its purposeful vagueness. For example, Nike's slogan "Just Do It" allows the individual to take those words at face value and consciously. Along with this, the slogan also allows the person to develop a meaning unconsciously and specific to their current situation and context at that time (Evolution Development, n.d.). Similarly, television advertisements are known for being influential and suggestive with their vague language used to convince a person to buy their product or service.

In conclusion, vague language can be more suggestive and influential because it targets a person's subconscious, which is helpful in hypnosis because it allows the hypnotist to plant suggestions in the inductee's mind. With hypnosis, language is specifically vague but purposefully influential, with action verbs and other words used suggestively.

Milton Model Overview

Also using suggestive language is the **Milton Model**, which originated from the hypnotherapist Milton H. Erickson. Erickson utilized language effectively in his practice to achieve results faster than that used in traditional therapy. By requiring ambiguous yet influential language patterns in its practice, the Milton Model helps the client deduce their own meaning from the communication, then apply it to their experience of reality. This personalized interpretation can then be useful to the client's goals because it guides the action needed by the client to accomplish therapeutic results and outcomes. In short, the use of the Milton Model in therapy, hypnosis, or NLP is an effective tool to elicit action from the individual.

Dangers of Hypnosis

Speaking of manipulation and control, the dangers of hypnosis are very real. This is because some hypnotists do not have positive intentions, while others simply lack knowledge, which ends up causing unintended harm to the recipient. According to Tyrrell, the dark side to hypnosis that ethical hypnotists need to be aware of includes the following (2015):

- Taking away the inductee's volition.
- Questionable intentions of the hypnotist.
- Constructing false memories.
- Causing hallucinations.
- Unwanted telepathy.
- Hurting the individual's "essence" or character.

The risks and dangers associated with hypnosis warrant that the highest ethics and moral standards would have to be applied to avoid harming the individual psychologically, emotionally, and even physically as a result. Such harm may not only distress the individual, but also leave a lasting mark on their subconscious, affecting their everyday life detrimentally. If the hypnotist or hypnotherapist doesn't possess integrity and compassion, then the inductee might suffer from direct effects toward their own life, such as loss of family, work, or mental health. Therefore, it is important to practice hypnosis ethically, so you can avoid negative consequences for everyone involved.

Resisting Hypnosis

On that note, sometimes it is necessary to build resistance to hypnosis when it is used covertly on you and without your permission. For example, consumerism involves the use of pervasive hypnotic advertisements layered with subliminal messaging—without your permission—to get you to spend your hard-earned money on a specific product or service. Knowing how to defend yourself before such a situation occurs is the best defense you have that can help you resist hypnosis temptation. Some of the best defenses to help you counteract and resist the powerful effects of hypnosis include (David, 2010):

- Knowledge and awareness of the self and psychology manipulation.
- Restating the hypnotist's thoughts for clarity.
- Refusing to give out any information about yourself.
- Putting off decisions until the experience is over.
- Not abandoning outside interests or contacts.
- Avoiding being around people who amplify guilt.
- Having at least one critical friend who is not afraid to doubt the veracity of any facts presented to you or them.
- Seeking information before joining a group.

It is also important to safeguard and protect your personal boundaries; otherwise, the hypnotists unethically engaging in covert hypnotism could be able to manipulate your feelings, thoughts, and behaviors once they get past your defenses. To avoid this, enforce your personal boundaries like a protective shield around your person in any way you can. That way, nothing sketchy or questionable can affect your integrity as an individual. Important to note is that some of these resistance techniques take practice to be effective against the more covert hypnotists.

Ways Hypnotists Break Resistance

On the other hand, there are ways hypnotists can break the recipient's resistance to their hypnotizing attempts. For example, the hypnotist can isolate the individual from familiar surroundings, such as family and friends. Doing so helps break that individual's resistance, as they get placed in unfamiliar territory, which then makes them more susceptible to external influences. Some other ways hypnotists break resistance include (David, 2010):

- Giving the person unconditional acceptance from a deceivingly friendly group of people.
- Isolating the individual from conflicting ideas.
- A false authority figure, seemingly having special knowledge that others look to for advice.
- A false philosophy that appears to have all the answers to your questions.
- Overwhelming the person with activities that result in less autonomy of thought or action.
- Providing a false sense of "Us" versus "Them."
- Using covert hypnotic techniques.

However, resisting the hypnotists' attempts to brainwash the individual is possible if the latter is knowledgeable about the practice beforehand. Knowledge is *key!* Otherwise, if you don't know what can hurt you, you might end up becoming a tool or pawn for the hypnotists' benefits and goals. In this instance, ignorance does not equate to bliss and, unfortunately, there is a lot more information known for breaking down resistance than there is to build it up. More research is needed to protect the common individual from undue influence, control, and manipulative forces.

Covert Hypnosis Trance Signs

Speaking of manipulative forces, covert hypnosis includes many signs that the unknowing individual is either going, or already is, in a trance. For example, dilation of the pupils suggests the trance is beginning to take effect, as it displays relaxation in the individual's gaze. It is important to know these signs because otherwise the individual can get pulled something they might regret later via hypnosis. Some more trance signs of covert hypnosis include (Mask, 2020):

- Changes in pulse.
- Changes in breathing patterns.

- Facial features relaxing.
- Absorbed attention.
- Changes in the blink reflex.
- Eyelids get heavier.
- Person becomes motionless.
- Involuntary twitches of muscles.

Knowing the trance signs of covert hypnosis can help protect you and help you recognize if and when you are entering into a trance. Any individual who knows and can recognize these physical trance signs will be better equipped to resist unethical hypnosis practices. In addition, the individual will gain more control over their own reactions to the hypnosis attempt and respond appropriately by snapping out of it in time before something potentially detrimental happens. It is important to remember that the goals and outcomes of hypnosis and NLP should be constructive and beneficial to the individual, and not destructive.

Chapter Summary

In this chapter, you have learned about how hypnosis and NLP can work together to influence the mind, while also studying how hypnosis can use suggestive language to influence a person's subconscious. We have gone over the dangers of hypnosis and why it is sometimes vital to resist the attempt of the hypnotist if they are practicing an unethical covert hypnosis. Beyond that, you have also been educated about various ways hypnotists can break a person's resistance. It is also important to be aware of the trance signs of covert hypnosis to protect ourselves from undue influence. To refresh your memory, here are the key points of this chapter:

- Hypnosis and NLP work together by influencing the mind and behaviors of the individual through the subconscious and the conscience.

- The rules of hypnosis are to treat and influence the individual into the desired outcome ethically.
- Setting, priming, and inducing hypnosis is critical to the goals and outcome(s) of hypnosis.
- Vague language can be more suggestive and influential because it targets the individual's subconscious.
- The Milton Model was created to manufacture agreement in the individual by employing ambiguous yet influential language patterns.
- The risks and dangers associated with hypnosis warrant the highest ethics and moral standards to avoid harming the individual psychologically, emotionally, and even physically as a result.
- Building resistance to hypnosis is necessary when it is used covertly and without your permission.
- Some ways to counteract and resist hypnosis include (David, 2010):
  - Knowledge and awareness of self and psychological manipulation.
  - Restating the hypnotist's thoughts for clarity.
  - Refusing to give out any information about yourself.
  - Putting off decisions until the experience is over.
  - Not abandoning outside interests or contacts.
  - Avoiding being around people who amplify guilt.
  - Having at least one critical friend who is not afraid to doubt the veracity of the facts presented to either you or them.
  - Seeking information before joining the group.
- Equally important is knowing how hypnotists can break resistance, as it can help the individual avoid becoming a tool for any unstated agendas.
- Ways hypnotists break resistance include (David, 2010):
  - Giving the person unconditional acceptance from a deceivingly friendly group of people.
  - Isolating the individual from conflicting ideas.

- A false authority figure who seems to have special knowledge that others look to for advice.
- A false philosophy that appears to have all the answers to your questions.
- Overwhelming the person with activities, which results in less autonomy of thought or action.
- Providing a false sense of "Us" versus "Them."
- Using covert hypnotic techniques.
- Knowing the trance signs of covert hypnosis can help the individual from becoming influenced unethically into doing or participating in something shady.
- Trance signs of covert hypnosis include (Mask, 2020):
  - Dilation of pupils.
  - Changes in pulse.
  - Changes in breathing patterns.
  - Facial features relaxing.
  - Absorbed attention.
  - Changes in the blink reflex.
  - Eyelids getting heavier.
  - Person becoming motionless.
  - Involuntary twitches of muscle.

In the next chapter, you will learn about powerful language patterns based on the Milton Model.

CHAPTER EIGHT:

The Milton Model's Powerful Influence

Milton Model Interpreted

The Milton Model is the prototype for suggestive hypnotic communication based on Milton Erickson's purposefully vague and ambiguous use of language that activates the client's subconscious and extracts its own interpretation of the message received. More specifically, the Milton Model is the medium of communication that can influence the client and their subconscious to act by deducing their own individual meaning of words that came up during a hypnosis or hypnotherapy session. The use of the Milton Model during hypnosis creates a state of focused attention in the client, with the client being preoccupied by their attempts at interpreting a meaning of non-specific language. This, in turn, creates a heightened state of suggestibility in the client, thanks to the Milton Model's use of "metaphors for artfully vague suggestions" (Excellence Assured, n.d.).

The Milton Model can be broken down further into three respective components that help the individual to understand its process. These three components are rapport, overloading conscious attention, and indirect communication ("Methods of Neuro-Linguistic Programming," 2019). These all work together to induce a trance by getting in touch with the subconscious of the individual. For example, the first component of **rapport** aids receptivity between the client and the hypnotist through certain NLP techniques, such as mirroring. This rapport is then what allows the hypnotist to lead the client in transforming their subjective state of mind, which then moves us toward the second component of the Milton Model: overloading the client's conscious attention.

Overloading the client's conscious attention is done by employing purposefully vague and ambiguous language that has the conscious mind trying to figure out the meaning of what was just said. This action then effectively diverts the attention of the person's conscious mind. It is this diversion that allows the subconscious mind to thrive, leading into the third component of the Milton Model, which is indirect communication.

Indirect communication, in this sense, not only accesses the subconscious mind, but also directs it into full awareness with the power of suggestion embedded in the language used during the hypnosis session. This is because the non-specific language allows the client to elicit their own meaning from it, which is why the Milton Model works like a charm. In the Milton Model, each respective component helps the other achieve success, specifically for changes and results that the client wants.

As mentioned, the Milton Model was influenced by Milton Erickson, who is considered the father of hypnotherapy. Erickson was a leading practitioner in his time, and involved himself in many professional endeavors related to his practice. Some of these professional endeavors include founding the American Society of Clinical Hypnosis, doing lectures and seminars, and running a private practice. Erickson kept himself engaged in his line of work as he was becoming renowned for his success.

In addition, the Milton Model mirrors Erickson's use of ambiguous language to make the client extract a meaning most appropriate for that individual and their current situation. This permitted Erickson to induce and make use of a person's trance and subsequently helping people conquer their problems and achieve practical results. Because of this success, Erickson was studied by Richard Bandler and John Grinder, who ultimately created The Milton Model in The Patterns of the Hypnotic Techniques by Milton Erickson.

Although the Milton Model is based on Erickson's work, Erickson himself had to learn from his colleagues in the field at the time as well. For example, Erickson learned to think highly of the client's subconscious mind and treat it with respect from having followed his colleagues' examples. Erickson also believed that there is a positive intention behind every action, and he based this belief on how people make the most beneficial choice they can time given the resources available to them. Another important thing to note is that Erickson held his client's reality in high esteem. Erickson clearly respected his clients, which may have influenced the general presupposition that there are no inflexible clients—only inflexible practitioners.

In short, the Milton Model was influenced by the man himself and is practiced in hypnotherapy. Since Erickson used vague and ambiguous language with his clients to achieve the desired results, so does his famous model. Erickson was the master at "providing the context with as little content as possible, so his clients could then paint the picture" (NLP World, n.d.). Similarly, the Milton Model ensures the most pertinent meaning is elicited from the language that frames the context.

Lastly, the Milton Model and its nonspecific but suggestive language is used so widely today in fields like psychology, law, business, and advertising that it is sometimes difficult to notice it in society, in part because we have been conditioned to accept it as commonplace. Therefore, the next time you go to the movies and watch the advertisements beforehand, take note of the vague and suggestive language used and how you react to them. Try your best to remain uninfluenced by them.

Milton Model's Powerful Language Patterns

Powerful language patterns in the Milton Model can structure, influence, and manipulate thoughts and behaviors just by their very existence. When we use and apply these powerful Milton Model language patterns to our daily lives or during a hypnosis session, our thinking begins to change. For instance, according to Elston, the receiver of that patterned message will begin to move into higher levels of thinking rather than simply detailing the content of their thinking (n.d.). In addition, inducing relaxation can occur when certain language patterns lead into it, and other Milton Model language patterns can help the client contemplate possibilities with a more extensive interpretation of the world. In other words, sometimes perspective can make all the difference.

Milton Model language patterns not only provide that perspective, but they are also a language of change that influences the client to take action. For example, the language pattern **cause-and-effect** suggests that one thing will lead to another via "If...then." This is helpful to know when the client needs to act or think about the effect something may cause if the hypnotist links the two ideas together in this pattern. Some other helpful Milton Model language patterns include (Elston, n.d.):

- **Mind Read**—Alleging to have knowledge of another's thoughts without detailing how you came to that knowledge.
  - "I know you're thinking…"
- **Ambiguity**—Lack of specificity.
  - Phonological: "you're" and "your"—same sound, different meaning.
- **Lost Performative**—Conveying value judgments without identifying the source of the judgment.
  - "Walking is good."
- **Double Bind**—Invites choice, despite there really being no choice.

- o "Do you want to talk now or later?"
- **Presupposition**—The linguistic equivalent of assumptions.
  - o "Will you be changing your perspective now or later today?"
- **Unspecified Verb**—Suggests action by alluding to how the action will take place.
  - o "She caused the issue."
- **Universal Quantifier**—Universal generalizations without referential index.
  - o "Every; No One; All; Everyone"
- **Utilization**—Takes account of the entire listener's experience to support the speaker's intention.
  - o Perhaps during a session, a colleague accidentally opens the door, the practitioner can say, "The opening door is an opportunity to invite new ideas into your life."
- **Embedded Commands**—A command forming a larger part of the sentence marked by body language changes that the listener's subconscious will pick up on.
  - o "I will not imply that change is easy."
- **Comparative Deletion**—A comparison made without specific reference to what is being compared.
  - o "You will like it more."

This list is by no means exhaustive, as there are many other powerful Milton Model language patterns to help guide the hypnotherapy session. It is important to note that although these powerful language patterns can be learned consciously, they are practiced and take place subconsciously, as language itself is a spontaneous and organic activity. In addition, using the Milton Model's language patterns would take at least a few years of practice for the user to become comfortable and fluent in applying them. Case in point, Erickson practiced for years to become adept at communicating to hundreds of clients and refining these powerful language patterns and techniques. In short, it is clearly important to practice as much as possible.

Just like learning a new language takes practice through written and oral communication and expression, so does learning to "speak hypnosis." It takes months of writing the language patterns down more than a few times a day, in addition to conversing fluently with the Milton Model language patterns. You will be most successful only when you can articulate these powerful language patterns with ease.

The language patterns in the Milton Model are applicable to just about any situation due to their use of non-specific language. Some of this non-specific language includes unspecified nouns and verbs, unspecified referential indices, and unspecified verbs and adverbs. Unspecified nouns and verbs compel the client to employ the imagination to fill in details such as the *who's* and *how's*. This is useful when the speaker becomes too detailed or specific, which could potentially decrease influence and break rapport. Secondly, the use of unspecified referential indices, like the word "this," compels us to guesstimate the specifics, in addition to making an internal decision about the sentence topic (Elston). Finally, the use of unspecified verbs and adverbs within the Milton Model of powerful language lets us fill in the context with our own experiences and knowledge. Unspecified language is leading and suggestive because it allows the client to deduce their own meaning and intentions from it, which then influences and guides the client even further.

It is clear that the powerful use of language within the Milton Model can shape and influence the direction, goals, and outcome of a hypnotherapy session, in addition to the client being influenced as a direct result. This is why it is critical to practice learning how to appropriately use the powerful language within the Milton Model. It is also important not to underestimate the potency of language, even if verbal language accounts for only a small part of communication. The verbal language used in therapy per the Milton Model makes the words count just as much as the non-verbal language that the client and the practitioner use during their interaction.

Chapter Summary

In this chapter, you learned all about the powerful language patterns the Milton Model uses to direct, guide, and influence therapy and the client. In addition, you learned about the Milton Model itself, plus its originator, Milton Erickson. To refresh your memory, here are the key points of this chapter:

- The Milton Model is the prototype for suggestive hypnotic communication, based on Milton Erickson's purposefully vague and ambiguous use of language that activated the client's subconscious and had it extract its own meaning and interpretation of the message received.
- The Milton Model's three components are rapport, overloading conscious attention, and indirect communication.
- The Milton Model was influenced by Milton Erickson, who is considered the father of hypnotherapy.
- The powerful language patterns within the Milton Model move our thinking toward higher levels, rather than simply detailing the content of our thinking.
- Some powerful language patterns of the Milton Model include:
  o Mind Read.
  o Ambiguity.
  o Lost Performative.
  o Double Blind.
  o Presupposition.
  o Unspecified Verbs.
  o Universal Quantifier.
  o Utilization.
  o Embedded Commands.
  o Comparative Deletion.
- One must practice learning to speak hypnosis through written and oral communication.

- Unspecified language can be leading and suggestive because it allows the client to deduce their own meaning and intentions from it, which then influences and guides them.

In the next chapter, you will learn about hypnotic conversations.

CHAPTER NINE:

Hypnotic Conversations

Power of Words

Words can be very powerful because they have the capacity to affect our subjective state of mind and everyday experiences by influencing our thoughts, behaviors, reactions, and actions. Words can even elicit emotions and evoke memories with their connotations and contextual interpretations. Words have the power to help us communicate and understand each other. In addition, words not only influence *what* we think, but also *how* we think, given they can structure one's mind through repeated conditioning. Without words, our world and experiences would be much different. In short, words are one of mankind's greatest achievements.

Words are so powerful that they can also trigger us consciously or subconsciously through the use of trigger words. **Trigger words**, loosely defined, are words that can incline an individual to take action. For example, certain verbs can be considered trigger words because they allude to an action, like the word "remember." When someone asks you to remember something, the action of being able to recall the past experience or event will trigger a memory. This can then evoke emotions that are associated with the memory. Trigger words are important to hypnosis because the individual's subjective state of mind can be influenced and manipulated with their use.

When someone uses words in a conversation to move you to react, respond, or act in a specific way, conversational hypnosis occurs. **Conversational hypnosis** is the use of trigger words in a conversation that can induce reactions, responses, and actions. The trigger words in a conversation are known to (NLP Training Dubai, n.d.):

- Activate our senses.
- Stimulate the imagination.
- Create associations and friendships.
- Help us visualize a specific picture in our minds, related to the words.
- Close deals.
- Bring relationships closer.
- Have the power to distract.
- Help us correlate ideas we otherwise may miss.

Conversational hypnosis allows us to communicate on a profound level, which helps us become more influential and persuasive by targeting the unconscious mind using body language, thoughts, and words. The use of **hot words** can bypass the critical factor and permeate the individual's subconscious because they are emotionally powerful enough to induce a strong response or reaction in the listener. For example, politicians, motivational speakers, and even your parents may use hot words to influence you to take action. Some hot words might include (Mcleod, 2009):

- Expletives.
- Value judgments about self.
- Sensory words.
- A named emotion.
- Precision words.
- Action words referring to the self.
- Extreme value judgments about others.

The power of words in my own experience has been one of transformation because, in learning about how to use and employ specific words in various situations, I can bring about positive changes to my life. Positive changes such as education, marriage, and even a career, as a result of the influential power of words has enriched my experience of life itself. It all comes down to how you use words that can change your life for the better. Especially in careers that make it their business to influence people, the power of words can determine whether a professional achieves success.

Hypnotic Power Words to Remember

Hypnotic power words are the kind we use every day. Whether you're talking to your partner, instant messaging your mom on Facebook, or writing a letter to your pen pal in another country, **hypnotic power words** are ordinary words woven into commonly used language. There is really nothing extraordinary about them. You don't have to have a degree or certification to use them, nor do you have to be a linguist to apply them. In fact, power words are simply run-of-the-mill, yet this is what makes them so special. This is because their frequent use in language and communication means they are more widely accepted and less challenged by people, meaning less resistance to their use. Therefore, what makes everyday words power words is not necessarily what you say, but how you say them.

As I mentioned in the previous chapter, power words or hypnotic power words are capable of inducing action. Some of those actions may include: activating our senses, stimulating our imagination, or correlating ideas. It is amazing how so much can happen based on everyday power words like the word "because;" for instance, *because I drank a lot of coffee, I am able to work more efficiently*. More specifically, the word "because" can help ideas correlate and flow more smoothly. This can be very useful in conversational hypnosis because it also aids the client in understanding cause-and-effect, in addition to creating useful associations.

Another hypnotic power word is the word "and." The word "and" can help ideas and thoughts build upon each other, painting a more detailed picture for the client. As you read this chapter, you'll gain more knowledge *and* skills. The word "and" is a useful conjunction that joins ideas and phrases, which can help the client to coordinate things into a relationship, establishing harmony and efficiency (Lexico, 2020). This is helpful to conversational hypnosis and everyday life because the word helps bring about agreement and concord from the individual.

In addition, the hypnotic power word "as" is another conjunction that is used to connect ideas. For example, *I will take breaks as I work*. This is helpful to conversational hypnosis because the word helps induce action, which can influence appropriate responses. For example, as you listen to the sound of rain falling on the ground, you can relax more deeply.

The word "imagine" is another powerful hypnotic word because it stimulates the individual's mind to visualize a scenario. For example, imagine yourself achieving success after you read this book. Even the rock and roll music group The Beatles wrote a masterpiece entitled, "Imagine." The word also allows the individual to experience the feelings or thoughts they want to have.

"Which means" is an effective power phrase to use in conversational hypnosis because it is used to explain or define something in more detail to the client. For example, *I will buy some more beads, which means I will make a bracelet with them*. The phrase "which means" determines the character of the noun preceding it and demonstrates the quantity, possession, or nearness to the speaker (Your Dictionary, n.d.). This is clearly helpful in conversational hypnosis because the individual will be able to understand more of what the hypnotist means by the latter being more specific in the second clause.

Conversational hypnosis has plenty more words to induce reaction, action, thoughts, and behaviors. Some other hypnotic power words to use include (Ledochowski, 2019):

- Just pretend.
- The more.
- Every time.
- What's it like when
- Supposed.
- Remember.
- What would it be like if.
- Find yourself.
- Realize.
- Sooner or later.

Hypnotic power words stimulate the unconscious mind and induce action of some kind, given their powerful influence through not only in what is said, but also in how it is said. In addition, hypnotic power words can frame the context for the individual, which can help guide and direct their thoughts, feelings, actions, and behaviors. This is useful to the hypnotist, who can then manipulate and control the client and the outcome of the hypnosis session.

Are You a Conversational Hypnotist?

Conversational hypnotists are experts at influencing everyone they meet. They know how to get you to do what they want because they are persuasive with their controlling and manipulative techniques. Their skills can work well on your unconscious mind, thoughts, feelings, and even behaviors. In short, conversational hypnotists know how to convince you to acquiesce to the will and agenda of others because they make use of their natural gifts as influencers. However, even the most skilled conversational hypnotist had to learn to master specific skills to win you over. For example, one of the crucial elements of persuasion is having the right mindset, which can make all the difference in determining if the situation is conducive to influence to begin with.

Another crucial aspect of successful conversational hypnotists is their ability to make use of influential power words, as they can give your presentation the power and energy it needs to make an impact. The right words can determine if and how your listener will respond to the message received. For example, words such as imagine, realize, and remember can initiate a sequence of events that trigger the subconscious into action. These words would do this by penetrating the region of the mind that is most likely to react to these words and their connotations.

The third crucial element of a conversational hypnotist is showing congruence between your body language, words, and thoughts. This is important because the listener will find you more believable and credible if your verbal and non-verbal body language matches each other. In other words, your words and actions have to be in sync; otherwise, the receiver of your message will be less likely to buy into whatever it is you're trying to convince them of. You can't be doing one thing while saying another.

A conversational hypnotist has many tools and techniques in their arsenal that can make or break the deal. Some more of those techniques include:

- Working on your attitude.
- Being consistent in what you say and do.
- Building rapport with the individual.
- Following the ABS Formula.
  - o Absorb attention.
  - o Bypass the critical factor.
  - o Stimulate the unconscious mind.
- Captivating the individual with interesting stories.
- Making use of linguistic bridges (like and) and power words.
- Making use of hypnotic themes to set the mood.

- Inflaming things with the use of hot words (or emotive words).
- Learning how to recognize trance signals (Ledochowski, 2019):
  o Relaxed face.
  o Pupil dilation.
  o Breathing changes.
  o Heavy eyelids.
  o Lack of movement.

In order for these tools and techniques to work, it is important to establish a connection with the individual; otherwise, hypnosis may not be as effective, given the lack of association with the recipient. When this connection is established, then the conversational hypnotist can employ even more tools of the trade to influence and persuade the other person in the conversation. Such tools include (Radwan, 2017):

- **Pattern interrupt**—Interrupting regular patterns to program the mind of the person.
- **The Zeigarnik effect**—Telling someone an incomplete story to engage the conscious mind with hypnotic commands until the rest of the story is told.
- **Negative words**—The use of negative words to initiate the opposite action.
- **Ambiguity**—The use of ambiguous words to propel the subconscious mind into action.
- **Hypnotic keywords**—Programs the subconscious mind.

A conversational hypnotist definitely has many tools in their arsenal that they can use to influence and persuade; however, the most important tool is the words used to convey the message. Words can add depth, meaning, and context to the message, as well as define context and how it comes across to the listener. Since words have so much power and influence, it is important to use them with care because they can affect the individual on so many levels. In short, words do more than influence; they color the language with which we live our lives.

Chapter Summary

In this chapter, you have learned all about the power of words, their influence, and their use in conversational hypnosis. You have also learned that how something expressed through words is as important and valuable to what is expressed by those words. In addition, you have learned about hypnotic power words that can influence and direct a person's thoughts, feelings, actions, and behaviors. Remember that conversational hypnosis can control and manipulate your unconscious mind into action, suiting the will and agenda of the conversational hypnotist. The conversational hypnotist is a major factor for why we must use words with care. To refresh your memory, here are the key points of this chapter:

- Words have the power to affect our subjective state of mind and everyday experiences by influencing our thoughts, behaviors, reactions, and actions.
- Trigger words can stimulate the subconscious into action by inducing reactions and responses to what is said.
- Hypnotic power words can frame the context for the individual, which can then guide and direct their thoughts, feelings, actions, and behaviors.
- A conversational hypnotist's most important tool is the words used to convey their message because they add depth, meaning, and context to what is said.

In the next chapter, you will learn about NLP anchoring techniques.

CHAPTER TEN

Persuasive NLP Anchoring Techniques

Anchoring Interpreted

Anchoring is a useful NLP technique that the NLP Practitioner can use during a session to induce a specific state of mind, emotion, or feeling in the client. With anchoring, they would be making use of a particular touch, word, or movement to allow the client to recall that desired feeling now and later. Another way to view NLP anchoring is that it is similar to bookmarking a specific website or a place in a book to return to it later. The only difference is that, instead of using the web browser or page to identify the desired destination, the NLP Practitioner would employ words and touch to signify the desired outcome, whether it be a feeling or state of mind. In short, NLP anchoring is similar to grounding oneself in a desired feeling or state of mind by associating it with something in the external environment, such as touch, object, or spoken word, so the person can experience it again.

Defining Anchoring

NLP anchoring is more distinctly defined by Mind Tools as "the process of linking an internal response with some external or internal trigger, so the response can be expeditiously summoned [again later]" (2019). It's almost as if a magician can conjure up a desired state of mind by snapping their fingers. In reality, anchoring is useful to the practice of NLP because it can put the individual in the right frame of mind to undergo even more therapeutic NLP techniques. Therefore, anchoring would help the person achieve their initial goals and the desired outcomes. NLP anchoring is conducive to setting the context during an NLP session and persuading the individual into taking a particular action. If I were to use the technique on myself, I could anchor the feeling of calm to the action of taking a deep breath, thus making myself more likely to recall that feeling after taking a deep breath when I am tense. As you can see, NLP anchoring can be very useful in many situations and contexts.

Background and History of NLP Anchoring

NLP anchoring has an interesting background and history. The development of NLP anchoring is likened to Ivan Pavlov's famous experiment on classical conditioning, in which he had dogs conditioned to salivate when they heard a bell chime. More specifically, if one constantly induces a behavioral response with a conditioned stimulus while another (neutral/unconditioned) stimulus is present, the response and the unconditioned stimulus will eventually correlate, creating a conditioned stimulus. After a while, the behavioral response will no longer require the original conditioned stimulus for the new one to cause that behavioral response. Back to the origin's main experiment, Pavlov's dogs were classically conditioned to expect food after hearing the ringing of a bell, and they eventually began to salivate whenever they heard the bell. Similarly, an individual undergoing NLP therapy can be classically conditioned to give a behavioral reaction once a stimulus materializes, such as a touch, word, or movement. After a while, the individual would associate that touch, word, or movement with the desired state of mind without the NLP Practitioner's assistance. NLP anchoring is a subtle form of classical conditioning, in which reactions or responses become automatic and reflexive after some time.

This conditioned automatic response via anchoring was first noted in Bandler and Grinder's book entitled, *Frogs into Princes* (1979). Their book is essentially a how-to describing the techniques for setting anchors and how they can affect positive change in our lives. The book is based off of Milton Erickson's masterful use of anchoring, especially with the auditory system, to change his clients' lives for the better. Erickson would use his vocal tone to induce trances in his clients and create human change innovatively. We could say that Erickson is the father of anchoring as well, although Pavlov may have influenced it to some degree.

Anchoring's Relevance in Daily Life and Marketing

The relevance of NLP anchoring today is that it constantly appears in our daily lives and across all aspects, like in marketing career fields. One way NLP anchoring is useful is in how it can condition us to respond more appropriately to a situation, event, or stimulus in our lives. For example, if you usually respond to hunger by grabbing the most convenient junk food you can find, try anchoring yourself to respond to hunger more appropriately by already having healthier snacks within reach. At first, it may be challenging to train or condition yourself to respond in healthier ways to stimulating situations or events, but with enough time and practice, anchoring can improve your life by giving you healthier ways to cope and manage any situation.

NLP anchoring is also useful within the field of marketing because products and services can be marketed through stimuli to recall a behavior and their product or service. For example, McDonald's golden arches might incline you to eat one of their cheeseburgers, due to the presence of the golden arches reminding you of their products and the behavior of eating. McDonald's has sold their products many times over with this logo. Another example would be the use of the Mayhem character from the Allstate commercials advertised on television. To explain, Mayhem's reckless behavior in Allstate commercials is the stimulus that makes you want to buy Allstate insurance, "so you can be better protected like me." The anchoring of reckless behavior to a character like Mayhem reminds us of the need for insurance, given Mayhem's association to Allstate and human behavior. As a result, Allstate insurance has become even more successful in selling their products to consumers. In conclusion, anchoring can be used in a variety of contexts and for a variety of reasons.

Brain's Reaction to Anchoring

According to a study done at Rutgers University, the anchoring process in our brains can be described as:

Engagement of cortical regions previously linked to emotional regulatory functions may be significant for enhancing or sustaining pleasant feelings during positive reminiscence, thus dampening the physiological stress response, therefore recalling happy memories elicits positive feelings and enhances one's well-being, suggesting a potential adaptive function in using this strategy for coping with stress.

(James, 2017)

In other words, what happens in the brain during anchoring is a process in which the brain bypasses stress by using positive thoughts and memories to elicit positive feelings. This may also be due to the emotion and memory parts of the brain being in close proximity to each other via the hippocampus and amygdala. The neuroscience of anchoring is quite informative, and allows NLP Practitioners and everyday people to render stress effectively into more positive associations and outcomes.

NLP Anchoring Techniques Steps

Positive outcomes can be achieved with NLP anchoring techniques because they induce a positive state of mind in the individual. In addition, the classic NLP anchoring technique is not really that difficult, and anybody from the common person, to a salesperson, to a trained NLP Practitioner should be able to pull it off. Still, NLP anchoring must be done with the utmost care, consideration, and respect for the individual, similar to hypnosis in that regard. The person can be anchored by following some simple steps:

- **Step One**—Observe the state of mind built up in the individual.
- **Step Two**—Set the anchor by applying touch to a part of the individual's body, like the arm.
- **Step Three**—Practitioner holds the anchor for as long as the state is peaking, usually about 20-30 seconds.
- **Step Four**—Practitioner tests the anchor by applying the same touch to the same part of the body, in the same manner as before.
- **Step Six**—Observe the client to see if the same state originates when the touch is applied.

The practice of NLP anchoring can be very effective to elicit change in the individual because doing so allows that person to develop improved coping mechanisms and the internal resources. sp they can then deal with external events and situations. For example, a gentle pat on the back could elicit a positive state of mind to help me cope with challenging situations more efficiently. Now I've learned to associate a pat on the back with a positive state of mind and coping mechanisms via NLP anchoring.

When to Use NLP Anchoring

Anchoring is often used when the individual wants to attract, entice, tempt, or otherwise seduce a person into a specific state of mind or action that would suit the former's agenda. For example, if I wanted to entice you into buying one of my beaded bracelets, I would ask you about a happy memory. While you are recalling that memory, I would use a particular gesture or touch to anchor or ground you to that happy memory and the emotions associated with it. That way, you would be more likely to purchase my beaded jewelry because happy feelings are associated with the gesture and my person. As a result, you will associate the happy feelings with being around me now, due to the transfer of it from your person to mine. It is a trick that can swindle the individual of those happy feelings associated with the memory, unless they associate it with the individual doing the anchoring.

NLP Anchoring Process

The anchoring process might seem pretty simple, but there is a science to doing it correctly. For example, the individual must completely access the state of mind with clarity; otherwise, anchoring becomes less effective. In addition, the NLP Practitioner has to observe their client keenly to notice when that state of mind peaks at its strongest, or else the anchor won't work. A failed anchor can occur if there is less emotion or lack of state of mind to associate it to. The third step in the anchoring process requires the NLP Practitioner to break the state by disengaging the touch or word. This has to be done carefully because the individual coming out of that specific state might be a bit disoriented. Last but not least is the fourth step to the anchoring process, which is to fire the anchor to test it. This means the NLP Practitioner has to use the same touch or word to initiate the state of mind again to see if it works. The NLP Practitioner has to be spot-on when testing the anchor; otherwise, it won't seem as natural to the individual. Remember the four steps to the anchoring process are:

- Coax the individual into accessing the state of mind.
- Provide an anchor as the state peaks.
- Break that state by disengaging.
- Test the anchor again to see if it works.

The anchoring process is a delicate operation because nuances in body language, tone of voice, and even behavior can throw off the attempt to anchor. This is why the anchoring process requires congruence in body language from the NLP Practitioner. The associations and connections made from anchoring depend on it because then the NLP Practitioner can appear more credible to the individual.

The Different Forms of Anchoring in NLP

The different forms of anchoring are unique and specific to each individual situation. For example, **stacking an anchor** is when the NLP Practitioner has the individual access many different experiences that elicit the same state of mind, so the NLP Coach can anchor the experiences in the same place (Carroll, 2013). This strategy is useful because it helps the client learn to deal with those experiences effectively by tying them all together. This technique could work well for dealing with negative experiences, too.

Another form of anchoring is collapsing anchors. **Collapsing anchors** involves the NLP Coach helping the client acquire a resourceful state when there previously wasn't one, due to a context in which the client lacked choices. This is achieved by anchoring the unresourceful state of mind to a particular place, whereas the resourceful state becomes anchored to a different place. It is helpful to have two different anchors representing various states on different sides of the body because it will be easier to collapse the unresourceful state into the resourceful state. This is done by firing the two independent anchors at the same time, then releasing the unresourceful anchor before the resourceful one. The NLP Coach can then test the strength of the resourceful anchor by firing it. If the response is the same as before when the resourceful anchor was initiated, then the NLP Coach has succeeded in creating a resourceful state for the client.

The third form of anchoring is chaining anchors. **Chaining anchors** happens when the unresourceful state is too big in size to collapse, making it necessary to create an intermediate state akin to a bridge between the beginning state and the end state. If the anchors are chained properly, one will lead to the next when fired, allowing the client to build a bridge or link between various states. This is helpful to the client because it can lead the individual to the desired state, especially when the states are very different from one another.

Another form of anchoring is sliding anchors. **Sliding anchors** are necessary when the NLP Practitioner or Coach must calibrate the intensity of the individual's state without stacking them; the method which was described previously. For example, a sliding anchor will depend on the NLP Practitioner's touch point, matching the intensity of the individual's state of mind. This is useful to the individual because overwhelming or strong feelings can be controlled or manipulated to the desired strength the client wants.

Last but not least are spatial anchors. **Spatial anchors** can be manipulated or controlled without touch; instead, it is done spatially by the NLP Practitioner or Coach. For example, to imitate or represent stacking anchors, the NLP Practitioner would access the resource state repeatedly by physically stepping into the appointed anchoring space. Sometimes, it can help the client to see a physical representation to understand the process of anchoring itself.

NLP Anchoring Techniques in Sales

Anchoring techniques in sales evoke specific responses, which then lead to the closing of the sale by the means of an anchor or trigger, producing a response in the individual. That anchor or trigger could be a specific word or a touch that persuades the individual to purchase your product or service. For example, if I use shaking your hands to introduce myself when selling Girl Scout cookies, I could trigger you into buying them with a persuasive smile and conversation. In addition, some more specific anchoring techniques in sales include the use of spatial anchors, anchoring state elicitation, anchor chain, and price anchoring.

The first anchoring sales technique uses physical actions and gestures to evoke emotional responses and overcome objections. For example, I could step into your personal space and smile as I try to sell you my product. In fact, using **spatial anchors** to overcome objections to the sale reminds me of salespeople at the mall trying to invade your personal space and sell you a product. This is because, as you try to walk by them, they would sometimes invade your personal space first to give you a sample of what they are trying to sell; they may try to spray some perfume or cologne on you to get you to overcome any objections you may have of buying it, for example.

The second anchoring sales technique, **state elicitation**, connects a physical object to an emotional state. For example, I could connect the remote control to my interest in watching my favorite shows on television. By connecting the remote control with excitement in watching Star Trek, I can evoke this emotional state by simply presenting the remote control. Another example is the use of my coffee cup at work because I can connect it to feeling productive (given the caffeine). By simply seeing the coffee cup, a feeling or productivity resonates in me and I work more efficiently.

The third anchoring sales technique is using an **anchor chain**, which involves moving an audience from one state to another by use of spatial anchors. For example, I could link emotional states to spatial anchors and shift between them when I want my audience to shift their state of mind. Stepping to the right could indicate understanding, whereas stepping to the left could indicate agreement.

The fourth anchoring sales technique is **price anchoring**, which is when the price of one product is compared to another, more expensive one to convince you to buy the more expensive product. For example, "Similar laptops sell for $300, $400, or even $500! But you can get this laptop for only $199.99!" Consumers will think they are getting a deal because the price is anchored higher than what it is selling for. In conclusion, anchoring sales techniques can be very effective to trick you into purchasing a product or service being sold.

The Art of Anchoring and Mind Control

Anchoring and mind control requires the use of language patterns to act as triggers or anchors that influence and control our responses, which then also influences us to do things without our knowledge, consent, or awareness. This is partly because these linguistic anchors have been conditioned into our minds from birth, making it challenging for the average individual to discern them and the reactions they cause. For example, the word "no" can act as an anchor or trigger for negative experiences, associations, and states of mind. Be that as it may, mind control through the anchoring of language patterns can also influence our lives beneficially.

Anchoring Used to Attract Women

The skill of attracting a woman through anchoring can be a nuanced endeavor, depending on certain variables such as personality, mindset, context, compatibility, and whether she likes you to begin with. In fact, using anchoring to attract a woman will not work if none of these variables are in place. If there is a mutual attraction, then anchoring will have a higher chance of being successful in this field. The two kinds of anchoring most widely used to attract and keep a woman are emotional anchoring and expectation anchoring. We will talk about these more in detail in the next sections.

Emotional anchoring is when a woman is conditioned to feel specific emotions relating to you, an object, or a situation. In other words, emotional anchoring is when the woman connects the emotions she feels to you whenever she is in your presence (Amante, 2020). For example, if a woman meets you at a festival, then she will probably start associating with you the feelings of excitement she had when she met you in that specific context. On the other hand, if a woman met you at the library during the day, she might associate calmer feelings with you. Knowing this can be useful for setting up a date with her because she may be more likely to want to see you again if the anchor fits.

As mentioned, the second kind of anchoring used to attract a woman is expectation anchoring. **Expectation anchoring** is when you anchor to yourself an expectation, so the woman can expect or associate it with you. For example, if you tell her, "We should get coffee sometime," she will probably expect a date with you in the near future. In addition, it is okay to raise or lower expectations depending on the situation. Expectation anchoring can determine the course of a relationship because "whatever expectation you anchor to her is what she is going to expect from you" (Amante, 2020). In conclusion, you can use the art of anchoring to attract a woman, given the right conditions.

Anchoring Used in Sales

To use anchoring in sales, the salesperson must undertake a few actions to seal the deal. Those actions can make the chosen anchors work for the salesperson by (Woodley, n.d.):

- Convincing the individual to experience the appropriate emotion.
- Assisting the individual into that emotion, perhaps by amplifying it.
- Attaching an anchor—like a location, tone of voice, or movement—to the emotion.
- Directing the conversation away from the main topic into other topics.
- Employing the anchor at the right time to recreate the emotional experience you desire your client to have.

Anchoring used in sales can be effective because it ties emotions to the specific anchor, which then persuades and leads the individual into closing the deal. This is obviously good for business. It is the practice of anchoring in sales that determines whether a business thrives or simply survives.

Chapter Summary

In this chapter, you have learned all about anchoring. You have learned about its definition, history, and relevance in both daily life and marketing. In addition, you have learned how and when to use NLP anchoring. It is also important to note the anchoring process itself, along with its various formats. Lastly, you have learned about the art of anchoring and mind control via its applications in attracting women and increasing sales. To refresh your memory, here are the key points of this chapter:

- NLP anchoring is similar to grounding yourself in a desired feeling or state of mind by associating it with something in the external environment, like a touch, object, or spoken word, so you can experience it again.
- NLP anchoring is similar to classical conditioning.

- NLP anchoring is useful to marketing because products can be marketed by the use of a stimulus to recall a behavior associated with that stimulus and the product or service.
- NLP anchoring can be effective in eliciting change in an individual because it allows the person to develop improved coping mechanisms and the internal resources to deal with external events and situations.
- Anchoring is often used when the individual wants to attract, entice, tempt, or seduce someone into a specific state of mind or action that suits their agenda.
- The four steps to the anchoring process are:
  o Coax the individual into accessing that state of mind.
  o Provide an anchor as the state peaks.
  o Disengage to break that state.
  o Test the anchor again to see if it works.
- Different forms of anchoring include:
  o Stacking anchors.
  o Collapsing anchors.
  o Chaining anchors.
  o Sliding anchors.
  o Spatial anchors.
- Using emotional and expectation anchoring can help with attracting women.
- Anchoring used in sales is effective because it ties emotions to the specific anchor, which then persuades and leads the individual into closing the deal.
- Anchoring techniques in sales evoke specific responses, which then lead to closing the sale by the means of an anchor or trigger, producing a response in the individual.
- The four anchoring sales techniques are:
  o Spatial anchors.
  o Anchoring state elicitation.
  o Chain anchors.
  o Price anchoring.
- Anchoring in sales involves:

- o Convincing the individual into experiencing the appropriate emotion.
- o Assisting the individual into that emotion, perhaps by amplifying it.
- o Attaching an anchor, like a location, tone of voice, or movement, to the emotion.
- o Directing the conversation away from the main topic into other topics.
- o Employing the anchor at the right time to recreate the emotional experience you desire your client to have.

In the bonus chapter, you will learn about some more NLP techniques that anyone can use.

CHAPTER ELEVEN:

Bonus Chapter — More Suggestive NLP Techniques

NLP for Business

The inception of NLP in many businesses has created a higher degree of success because it teaches business people to become better communicators, thus bringing in more clients, sales, and profit. The NLP practice in business allows the business itself to thrive because productivity increases as a result when people can communicate more effectively within. In addition, being able to communicate more effectively will allow the brand message to be conveyed with more emphasis to potential prospects.

According to Lenka Lutonska, NLP is like an "SOP for the mind, allowing for progressive communication, that provides applications in leadership, marketing, and sales" (Barratt, 2019). This progressive communication can then lead to successful companies experiencing more returns than most. In other words, it pays to learn how to become a more effective communicator, which is necessary in today's business market, due to increased competition, informativeness of the Internet, online communication, and advertising.

Top Three Easy-to-Incorporate NLP Tips

Effective communication begins with learning some simple communication solutions that can transform your business into a more successful one in time. These solutions and skills involve learning to articulate in the same manner as your client, viewing things from a different point of view, and reviewing your beliefs to examine their relevance to the situation. The first skill of learning to adopt the same language as your client is very useful because the client will not only feel more understood but also more willing to acquiesce to your business requests. Once the client's preferred representational system is known, speak and articulate in the same manner. For example, if your client expresses themselves in more a visual manner, perhaps try using diagrams to get your point across.

The second skill of viewing things from a different point of view is helpful to business because doing so allows the professional to detach from the situation, due to there being more objectivity from seeing the situation for what it is. For example, once the professional giving a presentation can view things from the audience's point of view, the business person becomes more likely to place themselves in an objective observer's mindset. This can then set in motion improved product launches, sales conversations, and even presentations.

The third skill of reviewing your beliefs and examining their relevance is also important because doing so allows the business person to overcome their limited assumptions by first identifying the belief to deconstruct it. Otherwise, limiting beliefs and assumptions can affect our wellbeing negatively and, consequently, our performance in business and other areas of life. This calls for even more NLP techniques to help change those beliefs into something more constructive and beneficial. It is clear that effective communication with these three solutions will help your business in becoming more successful.

Language Pattern to Bypass Objection

The use of specific language patterns to bypass resistance, especially in sales, is incredibly useful to garner success in any business. The trick is to understand the motivation behind the objection, choice, or action; more specifically, if you can understand the individual's beliefs that make them think, talk, or act in a specific way, then you can understand what they are saying in a conversation, and even switch it around on them if necessary. For example, if April the salesperson was trying to sell her product, and she heard an objection from the prospective buyer, she would simply try to discover the motivation behind the objection by asking herself about the prospective buyer's beliefs that make them think, talk, or act that way. It is clearly helpful to learn the underlying motive or truth for the comment, behavior, or belief.

Beyond that, recognizing this aspect can then allow you to present the information differently by rephrasing it to suit the motivation behind the objection. For example, instead of sounding confrontational by jumping straight into the issue, try rewording the question or sentence non-threateningly and rechecking your understanding. You can ask yourself, "Can I check if I understand this properly?" then go into the issue, perhaps by making a comparison suggesting that changing the situation, instead of letting it stay the same, would be less difficult, given the consequences. This also helps the business person check their solution against what they think the prospective client is or isn't doing.

NLP in Building Relationships

The use of NLP in building and maintaining relationships is valuable and beneficial to the people involved because it can help them communicate and understand each other better. When the people in a relationship communicate and understand each other better, then the relationship itself will improve because the quality of the connection and interactions will increase many times over. This is where NLP comes into the picture because it will give you insight and knowledge into how the human mind and the resulting behavior works to affect each other. In other words, NLP techniques can facilitate how we think, feel, react, respond, and act in relationships, which can then help improve communication within them while also aiding them to run more smoothly.

Some helpful ways in which NLP techniques can build and maintain relationships include choosing the right partner, listening to your partner, building rapport, and releasing your passion or emotions. For example, choosing the right partner for yourself becomes easier when you have an awareness of your own internal map and preferred representational system because self-knowledge can help you decide if another person's internal map and preferred representational system are compatible with yours.

There is great value in listening to your partner and hearing what they have to say. If you listen openly to your partner without judgment, they can feel more understood and validated, simply because you gave them your attention and time. Taking the time to listen can help the relationship in a variety of ways because you will be better able to discern the intended meaning of the message, which would then facilitate the relationship.

The NLP technique of building rapport with the client is also useful in building and maintaining other relationships as well. This is because it can garner trust, support, and confidence in the people within the relationship, whether that relationship be romantic, platonic, or familial. In addition, building rapport with your partner can show you have interest in them, which can then lead into a deeper relationship. Also important to note is that, since building rapport elicits trust between the people in a relationship, personal walls or boundaries can disappear, allowing people to be themselves in the relationship.

Finally, the use of NLP techniques in personal relationships can help build and maintain them by teaching the people in the relationship to release their emotions and passions in safe and healthy ways. For example, the NLP technique of releasing a kinesthetic anchor can keep the relationship exciting and remind the people in the relationship how much they are cared for, valued, and loved.

Attracting a Man with NLP

Attracting a man through the use of NLP is similar to training him to respond to you appropriately. This period of training could involve improving communication and seduction skills by using NLP techniques, such as mirroring, to increase rapport with him. Another NLP technique that can attract and seduce a man is speaking to him purposely slow and rhythmically, which would pull him in to listen to what you have to say. This strategy works because using your tone of voice can set the mood for the interaction to occur. Some more subtle NLP techniques to attract a man also include matching/mirroring your feelings to his when he expresses them in a conversation or otherwise. For example, if he says he is feeling happy because it is Friday, you can smile and say something like, "The end of the work week makes me happy, too." Especially valuable to attracting a man is anchoring because with the technique, you can get him to associate whatever positive feelings he has to being around you, be it a touch, look, or word. In conclusion, attracting a man with the use of NLP techniques can be very effective in winning his heart.

NLP VAKOG Brain Code in a Relationship

NLP can help relationships flourish and thrive because its practice is effective in bringing people closer to understanding each other on a deeper level, which then promotes the feelings, reactions, responses, and actions within it. NLP can also help facilitate relationships by understanding your own and your partner's preferred representational system or sensory modality whenever they communicate with you. For example, if your partner uses a visual system primarily, then the person will need to *see* your expression of love. If you are a kinesthetic-minded individual, you will need to *feel* the love to believe it. These various sensory modalities can be described in NLP as "**The Brain Code, V-A-K-O-G (Visual-Auditory-Kinesthetic-Olfactory-Gustatory**)" (Moghazy, 2018). This code is relevant to know because knowing these sensory modalities can help you match up with an individual who has the same preferred sensory modality, or at least one that is complementary. Similarly the **NLP VAK model** represents the three interpersonal communication modalities in which we communicate the language of love (Bundrant, n.d.). Knowing which interpersonal communication modality you and your partner each prefer can help the relationship blossom.

Unleashing the Power of the Subconscious in NLP Techniques

Using the power of the subconscious mind in tangent with NLP techniques is critical because our subconscious influences, manipulates, and controls every aspect of our lives, from emotions, to thoughts, to behaviors. In addition, the subconscious acts as a locus of control that guides your conscious mind, the latter of which then communicates back to the subconscious. Although communication is bidirectional, we need the conscious part of the mind to influence the subconscious part because it will help you influence your life to operate in the direction of your goals.

One way to influence the subconscious mind into enhancing life is to purge negative-self talk and fear; you can accomplish this task by using the countering or delete button techniques. According to Mayer, **countering** a negative thought is possible by replacing it with a positive thought, which will help your mind to make positive associations instead of negative ones (2018). In addition, the **delete button technique** is when you visualize pushing a delete button in your mind to destroy the negative thought. Both of these techniques are effective in influencing the subconscious.

Another way to spur the subconscious mind into more activity is to learn how to harness and foster your desire so you can use it to achieve your dreams. This is accomplished by using the bridge-burning, small wins or progress bar, and motivational techniques. The **bridge-burning technique** is immensely helpful because, by figuratively burning the bridges in your mind, you dismantle the safe, predictable harbors at either end of the bridge, thereby leading yourself into one direction only: forward. The **small wins** or **progress bar technique** allows the individual to keep track of smaller wins in light of bigger goals, which can make your process appear motivational for you, especially if you can see the bigger picture. Last but not least is the **motivational technique**, which has you discover what motivates you and can give you the energy to work toward your goal (Mayer, 2018).

Unlocking the subconscious mind is easier when you can visualize or picture the outcome of the goal ahead of time. This is because doing so will put you in the mindset of already having achieved it, which can then be effective for cultivating the desire of doing it in real time. Imagine yourself succeeding, then ask yourself the following questions:

- What am I doing?
- What am I wearing?
- What am I saying and feeling?
- How do I act?

Imagining this reality will guide you toward the desired outcome.

Some additional techniques for unlocking the subconscious to fulfill your dreams are **autosuggestions**, which are a way of "introducing thoughts to the subconscious mind" (Mayer, 2018). For example, take the mantra technique and the reading out loud technique. The powerful **mantra technique** of vocalizing or thinking repeatedly about a positive mantra like, "I can do more than I think," is helpful in achieving your goals because the more you repeat it, the more you will believe it. Restating your goals is the power of mantras, which is great for convincing your mind. Similarly, by stating and vocalizing your goals several times a day via reading them out loud, it reinforces your desire to accomplish the goal and desired outcome. The more techniques there are for unleashing the power of the subconscious, the better!

The Power of Autosuggestion in NLP

Autosuggestion is a powerful NLP technique that unlocks the subconscious by having the person present the thoughts they need to accomplish their goals to themselves. We do this all the time; for instance, I may say to myself that I need to focus more on the task at hand and, in turn, my focus will increase. Another autosuggestion could be to smile more by instructing yourself to smile at everyone you meet. Autosuggestions are effective in eliciting the desired state of mind, so you can eventually accomplish the objective.

Some more autosuggestion techniques are ones I have already mentioned, including the use of repetition and visualization to tap into your self-administered subconscious mind programming. Another technique is the use of affirmations. Affirmations or positive self-talk uses the present tense stated in the first person to allow the individual to reprogram their mind to think more positively, which can then guide their behavior in more positive directions. This form of self-suggestion is obviously beneficial because the individual's state of mind will determine their behavior and thoughts, thus influencing their life.

Autosuggestion can be a powerful form of self-hypnosis if done correctly. To engage in this technique, it is important at first to identify what you want to change, which will motivate you and give you a goal to work toward. The second step for engaging in autosuggestion is to relax yourself because it will let you become more open to suggestion, especially autosuggestion. The third step is to believe in yourself, as doing so will guide you toward positive thoughts and outcomes, as compared to the opposite. The fourth step is to simply feel your emotions, since their strength will influence your subconscious beneficially. The fifth step for engaging in autosuggestion is to think positively because doing so will get your subconscious to respond by the means of self-administering positive commands. In other words, you think; therefore, you are. The sixth and final step is to constantly practice the autosuggestion anytime you can, until you are one with it. In conclusion, autosuggestion is a great technique for reprogramming your mind through self-hypnosis and creating positive change.

Some other forms of autosuggestion include (Wise Goals, n.d.):

- Creating your own catchy statements to encourage yourself toward change.
- Changing one word in the autosuggestion to make it kinder.
- Playing the detective can help differentiate between opinion and fact.
- Using memorabilia to relish the past, creating positive emotions and affecting change.

Autosuggestion can help you implement a goal-setting mindset because it can reframe your thinking by creating a different state of mind or context from which to work from. This will ultimately help the individual to support themselves and the effort to create positive change. Another important tip to remember is that positive self-talk will improve your performance as you work toward achieving the desired goal and outcomes. In other words, you will feel motivated to do your best in working toward your goals. The third tip to remember regarding autosuggestion is that visualizing the goal will help you picture it, which attracts the reality of it into your life (Sukhia, n.d.). If you can see it, you can believe it! Also, important to note is that powerful people possess the power to effect positive change.

Re-aligning a Sense of True Power in NLP for Real Success

Re-aligning a sense of true power in NLP for real success involves priming the mind to consider the best that life has to offer by using pure motives such as love, compassion, and empathy. On the other hand, the use of selfish, self-promoting motives, like material gain, as the rationalization for practicing NLP can ultimately disrupt the natural laws of the universe by creating an imbalance of resources and power. This will only serve to affect the same intentions and motives you put out; therefore, to create true change, we must embody and personify positive values, such as integrity, to make a real difference.

Chapter Summary

In this chapter, you have learned all about other NLP techniques that can be applied and practiced in a variety of situations and contexts. For example, the practice and application of NLP techniques can be useful in business, personal relationships, and even yourself. To refresh your memory, here are the key points of this chapter:

- NLP in businesses can create success because it teaches people how to be better communicators, thus bringing in more clients, sales, and profit.
- The top three communication hacks in business via NLP are:
  o Speaking the same language as your client.
  o Viewing things from a different perspective.
  o Examining your beliefs.
- Some language patterns to bypass objections when marketing or selling a product are:
  o Learn and understand the underlying motive or truth for the comment, behavior, or belief.
  o Present the information differently by rephrasing it to suit the motivation behind the objection, choice, or action.

- o Check your understanding by re-wording the sentence, phrase, or issue non-threateningly.
- o Make a comparison suggesting that changing the situation, instead of staying the same, would be less difficult, given the consequences of staying the same per the objection.
- NLP techniques facilitate how we think, feel, and act in relationships, which can help them run more smoothly and improve communications.
- Some helpful ways that NLP techniques help build and maintain relationships include:
  - o Choosing the right partner.
  - o Listening to your partner.
  - o Building rapport.
  - o Releasing your passion or emotions.
- Attracting a man through NLP is similar to training him to respond to you appropriately via techniques like mirroring.
- NLP helps facilitate relationships by understanding yours and your partner's preferred representational system or sensory modality when they communicate with you.
- Understanding VAKOG (Visual-Auditory-Kinesthetic-Olfactory-Gustatory) can help your love life by helping you understand which sensory modality you and your partner prefer.
- Unleashing the power of the subconscious mind with NLP techniques is critical because the subconscious influences, manipulates, and controls every aspect of your life, from emotions, to thoughts, to behaviors.
- NLP techniques to unlock the power of the subconscious mind include:
  - o Purging negative-self talk and fear by using the countering or delete button techniques.
  - o Harnessing and fostering your desire to achieve your dreams is done by using the bridge-burning, small wins or progress bar, and the motivational techniques.

- o Visualizing or picturing the outcome of your goal ahead of time can help it become a reality.
- o Autosuggestions introduce thoughts to the subconscious mind by:
  - Repetition.
  - Visualization.
  - Creating your own catchy statements.
  - Changing a word in the autosuggestion to make it kinder.
  - Playing the detective to differentiate between opinion and fact.
  - Using memorabilia to create positive emotions that can affect positive change.
- Autosuggestion helps to implement a goal-setting mindset because it can reframe your thinking by creating a different state of mind or context from which to work toward your goals and dreams.
- Re-aligning a sense of true power in NLP for real success involves priming the mind to consider the best that life has to offer; it does this by using pure motives such as love, compassion, and empathy.

FINAL WORDS

Although the use of NLP is controversial, it is also beneficial to anyone who decides to apply it to their situation. NLP, or neuro-linguistic programming, can be helpful for relationships, business, and the people because its practice and application can create successful outcomes, no matter the context. There are environmental influences that can affect the practice of NLP, such as rationalizing its use for personal gain and power. Even so, NLP can help us to effectively adapt to the many environments or contexts we find ourselves in by reprogramming the mind to develop, progress, and evolve into a more functional instrument, thanks to the power of suggestion, influence, and persuasion. In short, NLP is useful because it can change how we think, perceive, react, and respond to life's challenges.

The mindful use and practice of NLP can put power back into your own hands by helping you control your mind and achieve favorable outcomes. In addition, NLP can help you to align your programming and beliefs with your own success, and not against it. For example, the practice of self-hypnosis enables people to introduce constructive thoughts into the unconscious by using specific NLP techniques, such as autosuggestion and anchoring. Other NLP techniques, like hypnotic power words, can stimulate the subconscious into action by inducing reactions that can directly influence our thoughts, behaviors, and feelings. Also important to note is NLP framing because of its ability to transform a person's mind by restructuring the limbic system links between the amygdala and the hippocampus, thus also changing the person's reality.

The evolving science of NLP is proving to be useful in fields such as psychology because it produces tangible results with how it can influence, manipulate, and control people. For instance, according to Zaharia, Reiner, and Schutz, in a study that "measured the level of anxiety in fifty participants with claustrophobia, anxiety scores significantly reduced after NLP sessions during the MRI examination" (2015). It is clear that NLP produces efficient and valuable results in a variety of contexts and situations.

The real power of NLP is evident in the topics and knowledge presented throughout this book. We have looked at how it can be applied in real world applications and examples. By shedding light upon the subject and practice of NLP, you are now more informed and ready to take action yourself to improve your life, and the lives of those you care for. It is up to you to decide how you use and apply this information, but I would err on the side of caution because mind programming is serious business that can also potentially hurt, beyond its healing properties. For example, the many cults that take advantage of the individual by manipulation and subterfuge.

Studying and practicing the NLP techniques present in this book will allow you to take control of your own life while you learn how to harness the power of your subconscious. You do this to influence and guide your thoughts, feelings, and behaviors more constructively and successfully. By taking control of your own mind, others with more malicious intentions will be less likely to manipulate and control you as well.

The potential of NLP to improve lives is unlimited and boundless. This is in part because NLP is versatile and adaptive to a variety of situations, contexts, and people. In addition, NLP itself is more open-ended and less structured, allowing for more self-directed opportunities like teaching yourself to think more positively. It is these self-directed opportunities that allow you to take control of your destiny by choosing to manipulate your mind and the outward manifestations of it. Once you make that choice, NLP is no longer a manipulative tool, but a helpful medium to change the course of your life.

Your life will change once you are more open to its opportunities via NLP because you now understand that what you do affects your mind, and your mind affects what you do. This relationship's bidirectional and interrelated nature allows you to focus mindfully on the present and learn to make better decisions later on.

NLP is a powerful tool of change that can create positive realities by inducing newer, more efficient ways for you to adapt and acclimate to your surroundings and events. By changing the context via reprogramming your mind, you can change the picture. A different perspective allows our thoughts, behaviors, and feelings to shift toward a more positive direction, serving to benefit our goals and fulfill our dreams. It is this shift that helps NLP guide its reception by reprogramming the mind to respond more appropriately to the picture itself.

If you want to be an agent of change, then NLP is the catalyst to make it happen. All it takes is a little bit of integrity, compassion, and empathy for you and everyone around you. Yet, to deal with change effectively, you must be open to it to begin with, which is where NLP can offer you tools to make that happen. Being open to suggestion, change, and influence can greatly improve your life trajectory; a trajectory in which you are no longer a victim of circumstance, but an empowered agent of change.

RESOURCES

Amante, C. (n.d.). How to use anchoring to mesmerize women. *Girls Chase*. Retrieved February 19, 2020 from https://www.girlschase.com/content/how-use-anchoring-mesmerize-women

Anchoring. (2019). *NLP World*. Retrieved February 19, 2020 from https://www.nlpworld.co.uk/nlp-glossary/a/anchoring/

Anchoring: NLP technique (n.d.). *NLP Secrets*. Retrieved February 19, 2020 from https://www.nlp-secrets.com/nlp-technique-anchoring.php

Andriessen, E. (2010). The philosophy and ethics of neuro linguistic programming. *The Princeton Tri-State Center for NLP*. Retrieved February 7, 2020 from https://nlpprinceton.com/the-philosophy-and-ethics-of-neuro-linguistic-programming-nlp/

Babich, N. (2016). How to detect lies: Micro expressions. *Medium*. Retrieved February 12, 2020 from https://medium.com/@101/how-to-detect-lies-microexpressions-b17ae1b1181e

Bandler, R. (2009). Messing with your head: Does the man behind neuro-linguistic programming want to change your life - Or control your mind? *Independent*. Retrieved February 7, 2020 from https://www.independent.co.uk/life-style/health-and-families/healthy-living/messing-with-your-head-does-the-man-behind-neuro-linguistic-programming-want-to-change-your-life-1774383.html

Barratt, B. (2019). 3 basic NLP techniques to bring more success to your business. *Forbes*. Retrieved February 20, 2020 from https://www.forbes.com/sites/biancabarratt/2019/07/11/3-basic-nlp-techniques-to-bring-more-success-to-your-business/#17fd0b063078

Bass, M. (n.d.). 5 powerful auto suggestion techniques to take control of your life. *Mind to Succeed*. Retrieved February 20, 2020 from https://www.mindtosucceed.com/auto-suggestion-techniques.html

Basu, R. (2016). Frame control, stealing your mind back. *The NLP company*. Retrieved February 14, 2020 from http://www.thenlpcompany.com/case-study/stealing-your-mind-back/

Beale, M. (2020). NLP techniques: 85+ essential neuro linguistic programming techniques. *NLP Techniques: Neuro-Linguistic Programming Techniques*. Retrieved February 8, 2020 from https://www.nlp-techniques.org

Body language secret: How to spot a bored person. (n.d.). *Mentalizer Education*. Retrieved February 11, 2020 from https://mentalizer.com/body-language-secret-how-to-spot-a-bored-person.html

Bored body language. (n.d.) *Changing Minds*. Retrieved February 11, 2020 from http://changingminds.org/techniques/body/bored_body.htm

Bradberry, T. (2017). 8 ways to read someone's body language. *Inc.* Retrieved February 9, 2020 from https://www.inc.com/travis-bradberry/8-great-tricks-for-reading-peoples-body-language.html

Bundrant, H. (n.d.). What is neuro-linguistic programming - NLP - And why learn it? *iNLP*. Retrieved February 6, 2020 from https://inlpcenter.org/what-is-neuro-linguistic-programming-nlp

Bundrant, M. (n.d.). Controlling people: Nine subtle ways you give others too much power. *iNLP*. Retrieved February 9, 2020 from https://inlpcenter.org/everyone-tries-to-control-me/

Bundrant, M. (n.d.). Love languages of NLP - Using VAK to increase awareness. *iNLP*. Retrieved February 20, 2020 from https://inlpcenter.org/love-languages/

Bundrant, M. (n.d.). NLP eye movements: Can you tell when someone is lying? *iNLP*. Retrieved February 9, 2020 from https://inlpcenter.org/chunk/coaching-exercise-eye-accessing-cues-business-making-decisions-solving-problems-2/

Campbell, S. (2017). How to use autosuggestion effectively, the definitive guide. *Unstoppable Rise*. Retrieved February 20, 2020 from https://www.unstoppablerise.com/autosuggestion-guide/

Carey, D. (2017). Anchoring sales techniques. Retrieved February 19, 2020 from https://smallbusiness.chron.com/anchoring-sales-techniques-21435.html

Carey, T. (2015, August 23). The secret to controlling other people.. Retrieved February 8, 2020 from https://www.psychologytoday.com/us/blog/in-control/201508/the-secret-controlling-other-people

Carroll, M. (2013). NLP anchoring. Retrieved February 19, 2020 from https://www.nlpacademy.co.uk/articles/view/nlp_anchoring/.

Casale, P. (2012). NLP secrets. Retrieved February 14, 2020 from https://www.nlp-secrets.com/nlp-secrets-downloads/NLP Secrets.pdf

catherine. (2014, October 9). Introducing frames. *Mind Training Systems*. Retrieved February 12, 2020 from https://www.mindtrainingsystems.com/content/introducing-frames

Coordinate. (n.d.). In *Lexico*. Retrieved February 18, 2020 from https://www.lexico.com/en/definition/coordinate

Ellerton, R. (2008). Meta-model of Milton-model. Retrieved February 16, 2020 from http://asbi.weebly.com/uploads/4/4/7/7/4477114/ebook-milton-model-summary.pdf.

Ellerton, R. W. (2012). *Win-win influence: How to enhance your personal and business relationships*. Renewal Technologies Inc.

Elston, T. (2018). NLP training – The Milton model – Language for change. Retrieved February 16, 2020 from https://www.nlpworld.co.uk/nlp-training-the-milton-model-language-for-change/

Eng, D. (Ed.). (n.d.). Use NLP to attract a man. Retrieved February 20, 2020 from https://visihow.com/Use_NLP_to_Attract_a_Man

Eye accessing cues. (2019). *NLP World*. Retrieved February 9, 2020 from https://www.nlpworld.co.uk/nlp-glossary/e/eye-accessing-cues/

Firestone, L. (2016). Is your past controlling your life? *Psychology Today*. Retrieved February 8, 2020 from https://www.psychologytoday.com/intl/blog/compassion-matters/201611/is-your-past-controlling-your-life

Frame control: The big secret to starting fun conversations. (n.d.). *Your Charisma Coach*. Retrieved February 14, 2020 from http://www.yourcharismacoach.com/vault/frame-control-the-big-secret-to-starting-fun-conversations/

Frank, M. (2019). 25 secrets of influence and persuasion. *Life Lessons*. Retrieved February 12, 2020 from https://lifelessons.co/personal-development/nlpinfluencepersuasion/

Goldrick, L. (2013). Are covert manipulation techniques ethical? *Common Sense Ethics*. Retrieved February 7, 2020 from https://www.commonsenseethics.com/blog/immorality-of-covert-manipulation-techniques

Golden, B. (2017). Being controlled provokes anger. So does feeling controlled. *Psychology Today*. Retrieved February 8, 2020 from https://www.psychologytoday.com/intl/blog/overcoming-destructive-anger/201706/being-controlled-provokes-anger-so-does-feeling-controlled

Goodman, M. (2018). NLP practitioner notes. Retrieved February 7, 2020 from https://vadea.viaafrika.com/wp-content/uploads/2017/10/NLP-Practitioner-Training-Notes-MD-Goodman.pdf

Grinder, J. & St. Clair, C. B. (n.d.). Is the NLP "Eye Accessing Cues" model really valid? *Bradbury AC*. Retrieved February 9, 2020 from http://www.bradburyac.mistral.co.uk/nlpfax09.htm

Hall, M. (2010). The magic you can perform with reframing. *Neuro-Semantics: International Society of Neuro-Semantics*. Retrieved February 13, 2020 from https://www.neurosemantics.com/the-magic-you-can-perform-with-reframing/

Hartmann, T. (2018). NLP and the power of persuasion - Neuro-linguistic programming [Video file]. *YouTube*. Retrieved February 6, 2020 from https://www.youtube.com/watch?v=sPC2DKswfs0

Henger, K., & Byrne, L. (2019). How to tell if you've offended someone and what you can do to win them over again. *Now to Love*. Retrieved February 10, 2020 from https://www.nowtolove.co.nz/lifestyle/sex-relationships/body-language-how-to-tell-if-youve-offended-someone-win-them-over-again-suzanne-masefield-39815

Home. (n.d.). *Psychoheresy Aware*. Retrieved February 8, 2020 from https://www.psychoheresy-aware.org/nlp-ph.html

How the conscious and subconscious mind work together. (2015). *Mercury*. Retrieved February 14, 2020 from http://www.ilanelanzen.com/mind/how-the-conscious-and-subconscious-mind-work-together/

How you can read people's minds (But not in the way you think). (2017). *Daily NLP*. Retrieved February 9, 2020 from https://dailynlp.com/how-you-can-read-peoples-minds-but-not-in-the-way-you-think/

Hutton, G. (2017). Frame control exercises. *Mind Persuasion*. Retrieved February 13, 2020 from https://mindpersuasion.com/frame-control-exercises/

Hutton, G. (2018, June 6). Milton model. *Mind Persuasion*. Retrieved February 16, 2020 from https://mindpersuasion.com/milton-model/

Iliopoulos, A. (2015). The Russell Brand method - An impressive frame control strategy. *The Quintessential Mind*. Retrieved February 14, 2020 from https://thequintessentialmind.com/the-russel-brand-method/

InspiritiveNLP. (2008). John Grinder discusses what's ethical in NLP [Video file]. Retrieved February 7, 2020 from https://www.youtube.com/watch?v=3pFTMdq0v6Y

Jalili, C. (2019, August 21). How to tell if someone is lying to you, according to experts. *Time*. Retrieved February 11, 2020 from https://time.com/5443204/signs-lying-body-language-experts/

James, G. (2017, May 23). How to instantly reduce stress, according to brain scans. *Inc.* Retrieved February 19, 2020 from https://www.inc.com/geoffrey-james/how-to-instantly-reduce-stress-according-to-science.html

Laborde, G. (2008). Resist hypnosis and hypnotic conversations. *Influence Integrity*. Retrieved February 15, 2020 from https://influence-integrity.blogspot.com/2008/04/resist-hypnosis-and-hypnotic.html

Lawson, C. (2019, January 8). How to seamlessly break down someone's resistance during hypnosis with the non-awareness set. *Hypnosis Training Academy*. Retrieved February 15, 2020 from https://hypnosistrainingacademy.com/break-down-resistance-during-hypnosis/

Ledochowski, I. (2019, October 10). 15 incredibly effective hypnotic power words to ethically influence others - 2nd edition *Hypnosis Training Academy*. Retrieved February 18, 2020 from https://hypnosistrainingacademy.com/3-surefire-power-words-to-gain-power-and-influence-people-fast/

Ledochowski, I. (2019, January 8). 9 essential skills you must master before becoming a seriously skilled conversational hypnotist - 2nd edition. *Hypnosis Training Academy*. Retrieved February 18, 2020 from https://hypnosistrainingacademy.com/becoming-a-great-conversational-hypnotis

Lee, B. (2017, August 15). A weak handshake is worse than no handshake. *Lifehack*. Retrieved February 12, 2020 from https://www.lifehack.org/620939/body-language-deliver-memorable-handshake

Lips body language. (n.d.). *Changing Minds*. Retrieved February 10, 2010 from http://changingminds.org/techniques/body/parts_body_language/lips_body_language.htm

Louv, J. (2017). 10 ways to protect yourself from NLP mind control. *Ultra Culture*. Retrieved February 7, 2020 from https://ultraculture.org/blog/2014/01/16/nlp-10-ways-protect-mind-control

Martin. (2018). Using specifically vague language in your advertising. *Evolution*. Retrieved February 7, 2020 from https://www.evolution-development.com/specifically-vague-language-and-marketing/

Mask, T. (2019). 10 trance signals in covert hypnosis. *Hypnosis Unlocked*. Retrieved February 15, 2020 from https://www.hypnosisunlocked.com/10-trance-signals-in-covert-hypnosis/

Matsumoto, D., & Hwang, H. C. (2018). Microexpressions differentiate truths from liees about future malicious intent. *Frontiers in Psychology*. Retrieved February 12, 2020 from https://www.frontiersin.org/articles/10.3389/fpsyg.2018.02545/full

Mayer, G. (2018). Subconscious mind - How to unlock and use its power. *Thrive Global*. Retrieved February 20, 2020 from https://thriveglobal.com/stories/subconscious-mind-how-to-unlock-and-use-its-power/

Mcleod, A. (2015). Hot words & hot language. *Angus Mcleod*. Retrieved February 18, 2020 from https://angusmcleod.com/hot-words-hot-language

Methods of neuro-linguistic programming. (2019). In *Wikipedia*. Retrieved February 16, 2020 from https://en.wikipedia.org/wiki/Methods_of_neuro-linguistic_programming#Milton_model

Milton Model. (2018). *NLP World*. Retrieved February 15, 2020 from https://www.nlpworld.co.uk/nlp-glossary/m/milton-model/

Mind Tools Co. (2019). NLP eye accessing cues. *Mind Tools*. Retrieved February 9, 2020 from https://www.mindtools.co.th/personal-development/neuro-linguistic-programming/nlp-eye-accessing-cues/

Mind Tools Co. (2019, September 24). NLP anchoring - Feeling good for no reason. *Mind Tools*. Retrieved February 19, 2020 from https://www.mindtools.co.th/personal-development/neuro-linguistic-programming/nlp-anchoring/

MindVale. (2016). NLP hypnosis: how do NLP and hypnosis work together? *Medium*. Retrieved February 14, 2020 from https://medium.com/@mindvale/nlp-hypnosis-how-do-nlp-and-hypnosis-work-together-36e399aa5897

Moghazy, E. (2018). Understanding NLP for healthy relationships. *Marriage.com*. Retrieved February 20, 2020 from https://www.marriage.com/advice/mental-health/understanding-nlp-for-healthy-relationships/

Morris, M. (2017). What is NLP and how do I use it to create success? *Matt Morris*. Retrieved February 6, 2020 from https://www.mattmorris.com/what-is-nlp/

Muoio, D. (n.d.). Body talk: Talk to the hand – The body language of handshakes and hand gestures. *Arch Profile*. Retrieved February 12, 2020 from http://blog.archprofile.com/archinsights/body_language_handshakes_gestures

Newman, S. (2018). Why anyone would want to control you. *Psych Central*. Retrieved February 8, 2020 from https://psychcentral.com/blog/why-anyone-would-want-to-control-you/

NLP Dynamics. (n.d.). Eye accessing cues exercise. *NLP Dynamics*. Retrieved February 9, 2020 from http://www.distancelearning.academy/wp-content/uploads/2015/02/Eye-Accessing-Cues-Exercises.pdf

NLP Milton Model. (2019, May 17). *Excellence Assured*. Retrieved February 16, 2020 from https://excellenceassured.com/nlp-training/nlp-certification/milton-model

NLP skills: Reading eye accessing cues. (2019). *Daily NLP*. Retrieved February 9, 2020 from https://dailynlp.com/eye-accessing-cues/

NLP technique: Framing. (n.d.). *NLP Secrets*. Retrieved February 13, 2020 from https://www.nlp-secrets.com/nlp-technique-framing.php

NLP technique - Positive framing. (n.d.). *NLP Secrets*. Retrieved February 13, 2020 from https://www.nlp-secrets.com/nlp-technique-positive-framing.php

NLP technique: The history of NLP. (n.d.). Retrieved February 9, 2020 from http://www2.vobs.at/ludescher/Grammar/nlp_techniques.htm

NLP today. (n.d.). *NLP School*. Retrieved February 6, 2020 from https://www.nlpschool.com/what-is-nlp/nlp-today/

NLP values, trance words and politics (2015). *The NLP Company*. Retrieved January 7, 2020 from https://www.thenlpcompany.com/mind-control/nlp-values-and-politics/

Non verbal communication. (n.d.). *Maximum Advantage*. Retrieved February 11, 2020 from http://www.maximumadvantage.com/nonverbal-communication/non-verbal-communication-how-to-know-if-someone-is-bored.html

Palokaj, M. (2018). 23 body language tricks that make you instantly likeable. *Lifehack*. Retrieved February 12, 2020 from https://www.lifehack.org/316057/23-body-language-tricks-that-make-you-instantly-likeable

Parvez, H. (2015, May 14). Body language: Positive and negative evaluation gestures. *Psych Mechanics*. Retrieved February 11, 2020 from https://www.psychmechanics.com/positive-and-negative-evaluation/

Quantum-linguistics. (n.d.). *Neurochromatics*. Retrieved February 6, 2020 from https://www.neurochromatics.com/quantum-linguistics/

Radwan, F. (n.d.). Body language: In state of anxiousness. *2 Know Myself*. Retrieved February 11, 2020 from https://www.2knowmyself.com/body_language/body_language_anxious

Radwan, F. (n.d.). Body language: In state of unease, shyness, and defensiveness. *2 Know Myself*. Retrieved February 10, 2020 from

https://www.2knowmyself.com/body_language/body_language_defensive_posi
tion

Radwan, F. (n.d.). Body language and micro gestures. *2 Know Myself.* Retrieved February 11, 2020 from https://www.2knowmyself.com/Body_language/body_language/micro_gesture s

Radwan, F. (n.d.). Body Language & thinking. *2 Know Myself.* Retrieved February 10, 2020 from https://www.2knowmyself.com/body_language/body_language_evaluation

Radwan, F. (n.d.). 5 ways to hypnotize someone during a conversation. *2 Know Myself.* Retrieved February 18, 2020 from https://www.2knowmyself.com/5_ways_to_hypnotize_someone_during_a_con versation

Radwan, F. (n.d.). Reading body language. *2 Know Myself.* Retrieved February 10, 2020 from https://www.2knowmyself.com/body_language/body_language_main

Radwan, F. A. R. O. (n.d.). Using body language to your advantage. *2 Know Myself.* Retrieved February 10, 2020 from https://www.2knowmyself.com/body_language/body_language_reverse

Radwan, M. F. (n.d.). How to convince someone to believe in anything. *2 Know Myself.* Retrieved February 12, 2020 from https://www.2knowmyself.com/Psychology_convincing_someone/Convincing _someone_to_Believe_in_anything

Radwan, F. (n.d.). How to read people's minds (Learn how to read people). *2 Know Myself.* Retrieved February 8, 2020 from https://www.2knowmyself.com/body_language/Mind_Reading/knowing_what _other_people_are_thinking_of

Ready body language. (n.d.). *Changing Minds.* Retrieved February 11, 2020 from http://changingminds.org/techniques/body/ready_body.htm

Self-hypnosis and hypnotherapy. (n.d.). *SkillsYouNeed.com.* Retrieved February 20, 2020 from https://www.skillsyouneed.com/ps/self-hypnosis.html

7 most effective mind control techniques tips in NLP. (n.d.). Retrieved February 7, 2020 from https://www.mindorbs.com/article/7-most-effective-mind-control-techniques-tips-nlp

Sewdayal, Y. (2019). Controlling behavior: Signs, causes, and what to do about it. *Supportiv.* Behavior: Signs, Causes, and What To Do About It. Retrieved February 7, 2020 from https://www.supportiv.com/relationships/controlling-behavior-signs-causes-what-to-do

Smith, A. (2018). Introduction to NLP anchoring 8: Chaining anchors. Retrieved February 19, 2020 from https://nlppod.com/nlp-anchoring-chaining-anchors/

Smith, A. (2016). Framing and some commonly used frames in NLP. *Practical NLP Podcast.* Retrieved February 13, 2020 from https://nlppod.com/framing-commonly-used-frames-nlp/

Snyder, D. (2010). Anti-mind control - Building resistance to unethical persuasion and black hypnosis. *NLP Power*. Retrieved February 15, 2020 from https://www.nlppower.com/2010/07/04/anti-mind-control-building-resistance-to-unethical-persuasion-2/

Spector, N. (2018). Smiling can trick your brain into happiness - And boost your health. *NBC News*. Retrieved February 10, 2020 from https://www.nbcnews.com/better/health/smiling-can-trick-your-brain-happiness-boost-your-health-ncna822591

Steber, C. (2017). 11 subtle signs someone may be uncomfortable around you. *Bustle*. Retrieved February 10, 2020 from https://www.bustle.com/p/11-subtle-signs-someone-may-be-uncomfortable-around-you-7662695

Sukhia, R. (2019). Goal setting mindset: The power of autosuggestion and visualization. *Build Business Results*. Retrieved February 20, 2020 from https://buildbusinessresults.com/goal-setting-mindset-the-power-of-autosuggestion-and-visualization/

Sum, Y. (2004). The magic of suggestive language. *Dr. Yvonne Sum*. Retrieved February 15, 2020 from http://www.dryvonnesum.com/pdf/The_Magic_of_Suggestive_Language-NLP.pdf

Sweet, M. (2017). 015 - Learning frames of NLP - And how to apply them. *Mike Sweet*. Retrieved February 13, 2020 from https://www.mikesweet.co.uk/015-learning-frames-nlp/

The body language of confidence. (n.d.). *2 Know Myself*. Retrieved February 12, 2020 from https://www.2knowmyself.com/body_language/body_language_self_confidence

The definitive guide to reading microexpressions (facial expressions). (n.d.). *Science of People*. Retrieved February 12, 2020 from https://www.scienceofpeople.com/microexpressions/

The hypnotic power of words. (2019). *NLP Training Dubai*. Retrieved February 17, 2020 from https://www.nlptrainingdubai.com/the-hypnotic-power-of-words/

The power of NLP. (2018). *Glomacs*. Retrieved February 6, 2020 from https://glomacs.com/articles/the-power-of-nlp

Thomas, A. (2019). NLP in Relationships. *Anil Thomas*. Retrieved February 20, 2020 from https://www.ttgls.in/nlp-relationships/

Tippet, G. (1994). Inside the cults of mind control. *Cult Education*. Retrieved February 7, 2020 from https://culteducation.com/information/8530-inside-the-cults-of-mind-control.html

Tosey, P., & Mathison, J. (1970). NLP and ethics - Outcome, ecology and integrity. *Neuro-Linguistic Programming*, 144-160. https://doi.org/10.1057/9780230248311_12

Tyrrell, I. (2018). The uses and abuses of hypnosis. *Human Givens Institute*. Retrieved February 15, 2020 from https://www.hgi.org.uk/resources/delve-our-extensive-library/ethics/uses-and-abuses-hypnosis

Use autosuggestion techniques to create changes faster. (n.d.). *Wise Goals*. Retrieved February 20, 2020 from https://www.wisegoals.com/autosuggestion-techniques.html

Waude, A. (2016). Emotion and memory: How do your emotions affect your ability to remember information and recall past memories? *Psychologist World*. Retrieved February 19, 2020 from https://www.psychologistworld.com/emotion/emotion-memory-psychology

Westside Toastmasters. (n.d.). The social leverage in active hand gestures. *Westside Toastmasters*. Retrieved February 12, 2020 from https://westsidetoastmasters.com/resources/book_of_body_language/chap2.html

What is covert hypnosis? Discover the 4 stage covert hypnosis formula. (n.d.). *Rebel Magic*. Retrieved February 15, 2020 from https://rebelmagic.com/covert-hypnosis/

Wilcox, D. G. (2011). NLP, mind control, and the arrogance and downfall of power. *Ezine Articles*. Retrieved February 20, 2020 from https://ezinearticles.com/?id=6036132&NLP,-Mind-Control,-and-the-Arrogance-and-Downfall-of-Power=

Woodley, G. (n.d.). Anchoring in sales. *Selling and Persuasion Techniques*. Retrieved February 19, 2020 from https://www.sellingandpersuasiontechniques.com/anchoring-in-sales.html

Wright, S., & Basu, R. (2014). Hypnotic language patterns to bypass resistance. *The NLP Company*. Retrieved February 20, 2020 from https://www.thenlpcompany.com/case-study/hypnotic-language-patterns-to-bypass-resistance/

Your definitive guide to neuro linguistic programming. (2017). *Inner High Living*. Retrieved February 14, 2020 from https://innerhighliving.com/neurolinguistic-programming-guide/

Teaching determiners in articles. (2017, August 11). *Your Dictionary*. Retrieved February 18, 2020 from https://education.yourdictionary.com/for-teachers/teaching-articles-and-determiners.html

Zaharia, C., Reiner, M., & Schütz, P. (2015). Evidence-based neuro linguistic psychotherapy: A meta-analysis. *Psychiatria Danubina, 27*(4), 355-363. https://www.ncbi.nlm.nih.gov/pubmed/26609647

Zhi-peng, R. (2014). Body language in different cultures. *David Publisher*. Retrieved February 10, 2020 from http://www.davidpublisher.com/Public/uploads/Contribute/550928be54286.pdf

Dark Seduction and Persuasion Tactics

The Simplified Playbook of Charismatic Masters of Deception. Leveraging IQ, Influence, and Irresistible Charm in the Art of Covert Persuasion and Mind Games

Emory Green

TABLE OF CONTENTS

INTRODUCTION

What is seduction? There are so many different examples of it: the politician who draws crowds and followers who sometimes act like they're under a spell. The one who isn't conventionally attractive yet is constantly accompanied by beautiful partners. A speaker who holds the entire room enthralled. The woman you know with several kids who's always been able to find a man to take care of her. The man you and your friends talk about who seems to have a different lover every night of the week. Maybe you've been enticed by someone who's incredibly alluring, although you can't quite figure out why. Or you have friends who can't seem to resist these temptations in the flesh.

The power of seduction is undeniable. And yet, it doesn't seem entirely acceptable in a polite society. When the topic is discussed, it's morally ambiguous. Good? Bad? Somewhere in between? But seduction is a science and doesn't have to rely on opinions. The ability to fascinate others isn't just an art, but a science. Understanding human nature and psychology is key to learning seduction. Everyone can learn the tips and tricks, as long as they have a handle on the basics. Anyone reading this book can use the tools I describe to enchant and influence other people. Perhaps even more importantly, they can learn to recognize when someone is trying to seduce them, so whether you welcome the ploy or not, you'll understand what's going on.

Seduction comes with its own set of risks and rewards. The rewards from successfully seducing others can be incredibly gratifying! But there are risks, too. Be aware that there is a cost to playing this game. The book you're holding in your hands uncovers the secrets of both the advantages and the disadvantages of seduction.

You'll understand what is going on behind the scenes of current seduction controversies, that is in addition to techniques you'll learn to attract others or to defend yourself. I'll also discuss the art and the science that drives this force inside us.

Let me be upfront: I'm not a "pick-up artist"! I'm a man of science who puts scientific findings into action. I've studied the research and I've also studied the powerful people - the "alphas" - who rule the world. These people run multi-million dollar companies and are looked up to by millions of people who want to know their secrets. One of their hidden advantages is the way they're able to wield the power of seduction. They're incredibly magnetic and people are strongly drawn to them. This is not an accident. It's the result of their knowledge of how to enchant people.

I wanted to spread this knowledge beyond these few alphas and make more of them if you are willing! Note that alphas are not exclusively male. There are plenty of women with this ability, too. The people with whom I've already shared this knowledge have been incredibly grateful for the experience. They've told me how many opportunities opened up for them once they began to implement these tools and how many opportunists they dodged once they understood what was going on! They've also been thankful for the blissful world that blossomed before them after I explained the techniques of seduction. No longer are they ignorant about the art and science behind the magic of the seducer. I'm excited that people are starting to realize how far they can go to achieve their dreams and desires once they start to use the information in this book.

I also realize as I spread this knowledge that it is helping people understand human nature so much better, once they understand that there is no magic spell, only the leverage of human desires. This is the kind of information people want to know, but no one wants to talk about it. By reading this book, you are setting the foundation for getting what you want.

Readers are often curious about how psychology and seduction work together. You might have read an article about the "art of seduction". But without the scientific background, it may sometimes seem TOO powerful and too potent of a force to be left in your untrained hands! Or maybe you have doubts about whether it works without any research behind it. This book shows you how potent a force seduction is, but one that relies on human nature and psychology, backed by data. Others who've absorbed this information found the power within themselves, understanding their nature and their ability to attract what they want from life and a partner.

Once you've read this book, you'll be in control of your power. You'll be more aware of your ability to entice others into doing as you would like them to do. Understanding the desires, strengths, and vulnerabilities of both your power and that of others will be yours. When you begin to use the techniques I describe in this book, you'll discover that you have an edge on success and happiness. More opportunities will begin to present themselves to you, not just in your career or in seeking romantic love, but in all aspects of your life.

Right now, successful people are using these tools. They're the ones with an edge. Do you want someone else to scoop up your dream life or your dream partner? They might not even know they're waiting for you. Someone else might be charming them while you're still trying to figure out what you want to do. Let's face it, there are plenty of others with this information who are treating you as prey because you don't have the tools yet. Become the seducer instead. Unlock the power in your nature to use it for good. As you'll discover later in this book, influencing others doesn't have to be predatory or manipulative. You can use it for the greater good, in addition to using it to your advantage.

Discover the secrets behind the art of seduction. Learn the science that underlies human nature and human psychology. Be empowered to choose your best life. This book doesn't judge you and your desires.

At this point, the only person who can stop you from unlocking this power is you.

Enjoying this book so far? Remember to head to the last page of this book bundle for a bonus bite-sized yet valuable free resource on Conversational Hypnosis. This mini e-book is the easiest way to learn how to be a successful conversational hypnotist. Curious about the benefits it can do to your normal day to day conversations? Get your copy now! This free resource is available for a limited time only

CHAPTER ONE

True Seduction

What's the meaning of the word "seduction"? People often think of this power in relation to sex. A man who seduces women may be a "pick-up artist" or a Romeo. A woman who seduces men is a seductress (as is a woman who seduces other women). Think of the other ways in which you've heard the word "seduce" or "seduction". Some politicians are known for their charisma and their ability to make the person they're speaking with feel like the only one in the room. You may have heard popular or famous speakers "seduce" their audience with their magnetism. Excellent sales reps are sometimes also known to "seduce" their prospects into buying.

What do they all have in common?

Seduction: A simple definition

When looking at the dictionary, the ambiguous nature of the word is clear. Some of the meanings are negative, but others are positive.

1. To lead astray...corrupt.
2. To persuade or induce sexual intercourse.
3. To lead or draw away, as from principles…
4. To win over; attract; entice[1].

---

[1] https://www.dictionary.com/browse/seduce

Interestingly, the Latin root of the word is much more neutral. It comes from the Latin "*se ducere*", which means "they lead". This is really what seduction is about: leading. Naturally, some leadership is bad, some is good, and some is neutral. You can think of seduction as leading someone. If you want the other person to have sex or fall in love with you, you're leading them to see you as an attractive person. When you're up on stage, you're leading the audience to listen to you and find you credible. If someone else is trying to seduce you, they're trying to lead you to what they want you to do.

The paradox of seduction

This type of power is inherently manipulative. However, seduction is not forceful. It's not rape, when looking at it in the context of love or sex. It's about the process and, more importantly, persuasion, not physical violence or threats. It's also not one-sided, so there is consent on both sides, at least at the end. It may not start this way. The seducer wants to get their way. When the other person succumbs, it's not because they've been forced to, either physically or mentally. They've succumbed because the seducer has made the prospect of conceding so alluring and so enticing. For example, consider a female virgin who's been enticed to have sex with a man for the first time. Because seduction is aimed at the sensual side of human nature and not the logical, rational side, she may very well come to view the encounter negatively. This could happen if she sees her capitulation to the seduction as being weak, or if she feels "used" and not cared for afterward.

On the other hand, someone who's been a virgin, possibly for longer than she would have liked, may feel liberated by having been "taken". A woman whose culture treats sex as dirty or wrong may subsequently feel relieved that she'd been taken. Or she may awaken to her own feminine power, which she may have been unaware of, or even told that she didn't possess.

"The desire of the man is for the woman, but the desire of the woman is for the desire of the man." - Madame de Stael

Seduction can wear many faces, so it's too simplistic to suggest that the results are always negative for the one seduced. Seduction can be pleasurable and also paradoxical: the effects may be positive and/or negative. The truth is that many people want to be seduced. They want to feel special, to fall under a spell, if even for a short time, and to be appreciated and be viewed as worthy of seduction. When it comes to sex, arousal is one of the most potent human experiences - most of us want more of it! The thrill of seduction is the anticipation of it. Not the culmination of desire, or the achievement of the goal. The excitement comes in savoring the process and stretching out the length of the game in order to fully enjoy it. Anticipation is key to the enjoyment of many experiences - even vacations. The pleasure of thinking about an upcoming vacation can sometimes even outweigh the happiness you feel on the trip itself![2] Many people find a happier life when they spend more time enjoying the lead-up to big, fun events and slow down and savor the moment.

The difference between seduction, persuasion, and manipulation

These three ways of communicating in order to influence other people are closely linked, but they don't all mean the same thing. The word with a more positive connotation is "persuasion", which is simply communication intended to alter another person's behavior. There's no stress on the person being persuaded and they are aware of the intent. No one is hiding anything and the facts are known to both sides. Persuaders often use logical arguments to make their case. The other person is free to question the assumptions. If they find the

---

[2] https://www.psychologytoday.com/us/blog/shameless-woman/201207/the-power-seduction

argument holds, they may well accept the case that's made and change their behavior, as the persuader hoped.

Ads often use well-known techniques to persuade their audience to purchase something. Emotional appeal, the bandwagon effect, and other methods are common. Design and color are also used to create campaigns that will bring in buyers. Although some of these approaches are known to and understood by the wider audience, some of them are not. This brings us into the other two above-mentioned arenas, where both sides are not equally equipped to handle the attempted influence.

While manipulation is intentional, just as persuasion is, part of this intent is to deceive the one being manipulated. Facts or knowledge is hidden in order to bring about the results that the manipulator wants. You might sometimes see this in person, but it's also common in marketing and political campaigns, where the manipulator tries to give only a little to receive a lot. One well-known manipulative device is reciprocity[3], in which the one doing the manipulating gives a little something which makes the receiver feel obligated to do what they want.

A political campaign might send out buttons or stickers, so the receivers feel obligated to donate to the campaign and perhaps volunteer on the ground. Many nonprofit groups send out all kinds of items - bags, calendars, umbrellas, and t-shirts - to get donations. They're relying on a characteristic of human nature which tells us that if someone gives you something, whether or not you asked for it, you're obliged to reciprocate.

Sellers often manipulate buyers. They assess the buyer's purchasing power and then use one technique or another to sell something more expensive. Ever feel manipulated in a car dealership? There's a reason for that! Manipulation is temporary because the

---

[3] http://opinionsandperspectives.blogspot.com/2010/11/persuasion-manipulation-seduction-and.html

person being manipulated will no longer trust the other. Relationships are based on trust and communication. Once that's breached, the two sides cannot maintain a relationship. Persuasion and seduction are normally longer processes because manipulation works only over a short period of time. Unlike the logical use of persuasion, manipulation is based on emotions.

Seduction lies somewhere between manipulation and persuasion. Like manipulation, the seducer plays on their target's emotions. They're not as open as if they were simply trying to persuade the other to do something. They may hide their true intentions. For example, a Romeo may entice a woman into believing that a romantic relationship is on offer, when really they just want to have sex. But the deceit is more subtle and less coercive than with manipulation. There's a promise made to the other, just as in persuasion - but the promise is more likely to go unfulfilled in a seduction.

Ads and movies are particularly susceptible to making empty promises. How often have you seen an ad for a food that made you so hungry you had to buy it, only to realize that the product looks nothing like what was shown on TV (this is especially true for fast-food restaurants) and it didn't even taste very good. Or maybe you saw a trailer for a movie that looked terrific, but the movie itself was only ho-hum? These ads and trailers were seductive, not truthful.

Modern seduction techniques

Successful businesses focus on pleasing the customer. Companies known for terrific customer service, or excellent conversion turning them into clients, have always been able to create the idea of an ideal world - one where there are fewer problems, less pain, and more pleasure. Humans tend to be averse to loss, so the avoidance of pain actually is more important than the creation of more pleasure. Humans also tend to be attracted to uncertainty. A man who makes his attraction obvious to a woman is less desirable than a man who sends conflicting signals. In turn, men are enticed by a "coquette": a woman who teases, flirts, and denies.[4] This type of seduction stands out in a world where people are often aggressive when trying to sell you on what they want. This "scarcity effect" also provides good results for marketers. "Act now or the bonus will be gone" will often prod customers into action. As mass media and advertising work together to seduce consumers into spending their money, it's important to remember that consumers respond to these messages. We are all contributing to the society in which we live, not just as consumers, but also as human beings searching for romantic partners.

Now that women have their own ways of making a living, they're not as dependent on men as they were generations ago. Men have to provide an emotional reason for a woman to go out with and have sex with them. They need to seduce in a way that might not have been necessary centuries ago. For a long time, it was assumed that women only "put up" with sex. This may have had something to do with the fact that she had to marry quickly if she wanted to be taken care of. We, in the modern world, know that women like sex, but they can't be seen to enjoy it too much, lest they are called a slut, or worse. Women want to be seduced and romanced and feel attractive and alluring. Teasing, flirting, and seducing a woman are all modern ways for a man to have the relationship he wants. Drawing out the anticipation for both of them makes it even more pleasurable. The key here is that logic has nothing to do with it! It's all about playing with emotional appeal and it's a social game, not a rational one.

Chapter Summary

- Seduction comes from the Latin "they lead" and, depending on the context, may be seen as positive or negative. Sometimes both.

---

[4] https://coolcommunicator.com/social-seduction-creating-space-anticipation/

- People want to be seduced, whether it's by a potential lover or something else.
- Seduction as an influencing technique is less open and more emotional than persuasion, yet less deceitful than manipulation.
- Modern seduction techniques recognize that we know more about human nature than ever before.
- Since women can live independently in a way they couldn't before, men seeking a woman need to use seductive techniques if they want a romantic/sexual relationship with a woman.

In the next chapter, you will learn about the history and psychological background of sexual seducers, including famous ones.

CHAPTER TWO:

The Names and Faces of Seduction

When talking about romantic and sexual seduction, there are plenty who have gone before us. Men and women throughout the ages have understood how to use human nature to influence others to get what they want. There are different types of seducers and they have similar traits. You'll probably find it helpful to learn from those who have mastered the techniques of seduction.

Famous seducers in history

You've probably heard of Giacomo Casanova since many male seducers are commonly called "Casanovas". He was a Venetian who loved to love ladies in trouble. He'd solve her problem and give her little gifts before enticing her into his bed. Then, he'd get bored and leave. Sounds familiar, right? Notice how he started the seduction, though, once he selected his target: he got her out of whatever difficulty she was in. In other words, he was the "white knight" who came to her rescue.

Another well-known male seducer was the Englishman, Lord Byron. A poet and a soldier, he was a man of action who could write and he was catnip to the ladies (and to men as well). The movie star Errol Flynn swashed and buckled with the best of them. Even accusations of statutory rape didn't hurt his reputation, though that might be different if he were swashing today.

Famous basketball player Wilt Chamberlain claimed to have slept with over 20,000 women. The numbers seem mathematically suspicious; given that he would have had to have eight different women every week after he turned 16. The women he hit on noticed that, although he was confident in himself (being a 7-foot-tall rich man probably didn't hurt), he was still respectful of them. More recently, Jack Nicholson and Russell Brand, both performers, are known to have mastered the techniques of seduction. Nicholson is famous for his bad-boy attitude and the up-to-no-good gleam in his eye. Brand is better known for his wit and charm…plus his hair!

The club to which famous seducers belong is by no means a male-only institution. Cleopatra, the last Pharaoh of Egypt, played the coquette. She used both Mark Antony and Julius Caesar to work her "magic". Catherine the Great of Russia used her affairs differently. After she tired of her lovers, she gave them good jobs in her government. And in the case of former lover Potemkin, they helped her procure new lovers that met her standards for intelligence, as well as performance in bed.

The rise of seduction communities

In the game of seduction, when thinking about men seducing women, men have always needed to stand out in the crowd and make the woman feel special, then to win her trust and ultimately a place in her bed. Many men might dream about leaping from standing out in the crowd to going to bed, without all that work in the middle.

In Scotland in the 1600s, it was believed there was a secret word a man could whisper in a woman's ear to get her into bed without all the work of winning her over. This word was protected by a secret order of men who trained horses. The society, known as the "Horseman's Word", also guarded agrarian rituals that involved the magical word, thought to have been provided by Old Scratch himself.[5] The word caused horses to halt until the horseman released them from their spell and it also rendered women powerless against a seducer. In fact, unmarried girls who were impregnated by horsemen weren't looked down upon, because the devil's power in the word made them helpless. In other words, it wasn't her fault that the word had been used against her.

The society was like a trade union protecting horsemen. The best of these horse trainers were granted special benefits: the word that dominated horses and women and higher pay. It also behaved like the Masons, with secret handshakes and the like. Once landowners used tractors instead of horses, the Horseman's Word was absorbed into Masonic temples. It turns out, at least according to more modern members of the society, that the power didn't come so much from a word as it did a potent blend of oils and herbs that attracted both women and horses.

In the 20th and 21st centuries, seducers began to form communities, particularly through the internet. In the early days, young men mostly had to rely on their peers (who generally knew as little as they did) or, if they were lucky, older male mentors for information about dating and finding a desirable woman. More information became available with the rise of magazines like Playboy, which advertised books such as the 1970s classic "How to Pick Up Women" by Eric Weber.[6] This may be where the term "pick-up artist" originated.

However, when the AIDS crisis hit in the 1980s, advice veered back toward staying safe during sex. The 1990s and Oprah brought women's sexual needs into the mainstream. By the turn of the century, with the rise of the internet, communities for men to learn the art of seduction began to flourish. From the mysteries of neurolinguistic

---

[5] https://www.ancient-origins.net/history/enchanted-sex-word-scotland-s-secret-seduction-society-008114
[6] https://historycooperative.org/the-history-of-the-seduction-community/

programming (NLP), which is essentially the same as hypnosis, to "negging", men taught other men about more modern, or at least updated techniques. To neg a woman is to give her a backhanded compliment, like telling her she's "cute - like my bratty little sister."[7] This method was intended for use on beautiful, glamorous, and secure women, to pique their interest instead of fawning over them as so many men did. Unfortunately, in the wrong hands, the technique could develop backlash. Men used it on insecure women or those who weren't conventionally attractive, causing heartache and damage, instead of the space for the game of seduction.

Internet message boards became a place for men to congregate anonymously and share their seduction theories. They were able to share stories of what worked and what didn't, from a strictly male point of view and without worrying about family values. One of these men was known as "Mystery", famous for wearing a top hat and a feather boa. He referred to this as "peacocking", or spreading a magnificent display to attract a female of the species. He also did magic tricks to entice young women. Young men imitated him in his "pick-up artist" image. So many men were members of "The Community" online, that eventually, a man named Neil Strauss wrote a book on the movement, entitled, "The Game: Penetrating the Secret Society of Pick-Up Artists". The book and a TV show on VH1 made pick up artistry even more popular, to the point that most young men had heard of it. Some dismissed it, but others studied it closely to find the secrets of seducing women.

Feeding on its popularity, men who called themselves gurus of the game could just walk in off the street and claim to be experts. Books, CDs, seminars, and boot camps flooded the market. Groups of men began to go out and hit on women to try out the techniques. To beat the competition, some in the community began to focus on the psychology of the game and how young men were getting in their own way due to inner hang-ups and roadblocks. Currently, the community

---

[7] https://historycooperative.org/the-history-of-the-seduction-community/

is concerned more about physical and mental fitness in order to make themselves an alluring target for women, rather than trying to hit up women in packs.

There are now plenty of communities on the internet that provide dating advice. They seem to be less concentrated on gurus and what experts have to say and more about crowdsourcing advice. Tactics in many cases are more about seduction and less about outright manipulation, which is a trap that pick-up artists often fall into.

The Dark Triad of seducers

As mentioned in the introduction, there is a science behind the art of seduction. In the examples above, men have relied mostly on the art. Gossip, what was passed down from other men, the examples other seducers set, and the like. Science has identified three psychological traits that are often found in successful seducers, known as the Dark Triad. The three are narcissism, psychopathy, and Machiavellianism.

What exactly are these traits? Narcissism is demonstrated by dominance, a grandiose view of oneself, and a sense of entitlement. It's been shown that this trait is primarily male and it exists in all kinds of cultures.[8] A narcissist finds it easy to lure someone into bed and then kick them out a short time after sex. It works well for casual sex, which has greater negative consequences for women (pregnancy, slut-shaming), so men are also more likely to be interested in casual sex than women. Since narcissists tend to parade their resources more than other men, they are sometimes more attractive to women.

Men also tend to score higher on having Machiavellian impulses than women do. This trait involves being deceitful, manipulative, and insincere. They're known to pretend to be in love to get the casual sex

---

[8] https://scottbarrykaufman.com/wp-content/uploads/2013/09/The-Dark-Triad-Personality.pdf

they want - this trait is also conducive to casual sex, as is psychopathy, where people are callous, lack empathy, and can be hostile to others. Overlaid with this is a superficial charm and people with this characteristic tend to have many sexual partners and also be rated more attractive, not only by themselves, but also by women. Yet again, this trait is more common in men than it is in women. The Dark Triad appears to favor what the scientists call "short-term mating". The rest of us refer to this as casual sex. The question then is, why do women go for men with the Dark Triad or even one of these personality characteristics? Evolutionary psychological theory claims that women, who must be more sexually selective than men due to the higher cost of sex for them, have certain traits they look for in a man. It's to their benefit to choose a dominant man because these men can typically obtain more resources for the family. Dominant men are usually confident and assertive. Dark Triad attributes create the illusion for women that the man is socially dominant, whether or not he actually is. A man who's anti-social appears strong and masculine, a psychopath appears to be confident, and aggressive men tend to come off as dominant. A man with a grandiose sense of himself comes off as ambitious and driven, which are also features of dominant men. Someone who's high on the Machiavellian scale tends to accumulate power and understands it almost intuitively, which may suggest to the female observer that he himself is powerful.

Earlier, I talked about leaving some uncertainty as catnip for a potential sexual partner. Men who rate high in Dark Triad traits tend not to care what others think of them, which is a technique that stands out to people-pleasers. That little frisson of danger makes the game of seduction all the more exciting for the one being seduced.

Can you think of anyone you know who's a great example of the Dark Triad? I'll give you one: James Bond. He's always seducing a new lover and he doesn't stick around afterward. The women in the movie fall for it every time, but this is not so far from real life!

Narcissism has been shown to rate higher in dating than the other features of the Triad.[9] The charm and attentiveness that goes along with this trait tends to be more attractive to women, compared to Machiavellianism or psychopathy. These characteristics can help men get ahead at work, not just in the mating game. The characteristics of the Dark Triad are also linked with openness to new experience, high self-esteem, and curiosity, which are also attractive features in the boardroom. In addition, the Triad tends to enhance competitiveness. Ranking high in characteristics surrounding psychopathy and Machiavellianism frightens off would-be competitors and is attractive to superiors.[10]

However, although these behaviors are to an individual's advantage, it causes harm to the organization. Dark Triad employees freeride on other employee's coattails. They're more likely to steal from the company, sabotage it, and not bother to show up when they don't feel like it. Although they may have personal success, their actual work performance is poor. The superiors they have seduced along the way ignore their lack of productivity.

If you're not psychotic about it, some aspects of Dark Triad attributes can actually be used for the greater good. Leaders have to make unpopular decisions, so it's best if you're a leader not to care too much about what other people think. Special Forces and other elite squads have to move on from pulling the trigger and killing someone else, lest they are killed themselves. Surgeons have to emotionally detach from the fact that they're cutting into another person's body in order to perform it successfully. Moderate Dark Triad traits can also benefit an organization. Those who are intermediate in Machiavellianism are often good employees because they're good with networking and managing. Military leaders who can key in on the bright side of narcissism with egoism and high self-esteem, but moderate their manipulativeness, are often very effective. In other

---

[9] https://www.sciencedirect.com/science/article/abs/pii/S0191886913006582

[10] https://hbr.org/2015/11/why-bad-guys-win-at-work

words, lower doses of Dark Triad attributes can be beneficial! Too much and we see the dark side of them.

Alpha males and alpha females

Where did the concept of "alpha males" come from in the first place? The origin of this term comes from animal studies, where an alpha male is literally the leader of the pack. Alphas in these types of hierarchical animal groups are high-status and have access to more resources than other males. Typically, determining which member of an animal group is the alpha can be made by observing the males as they fight each other. The winner becomes the alpha and gets to choose whichever mate he wants. He is in a position of power.

Human males in a position of power are known to exploit women for their benefit. They do it because they can and they're in a position to do so. However, not all alphas are men. Some are women. They're talented, ambitious, and driven. An alpha female is confident and believes (like her male counterparts) that her potential for achievement has no limits. They're able to regulate their emotions because they have EQ or emotional intelligence. This allows them to smooth over social and business interactions. As part of their EQ, they can set the tone for other women to have good discussions without falling prey to backbiting and gossip. They have a deep drive to learn more and become experts in their chosen subjects. Known for both their mental and physical strength, an alpha female is not only asked for help, but is comfortable asking for help when she needs it. She tends to come from solid family foundations, which makes it easier for her to venture out into new experiences. There can be only one alpha female, but for an organization to run well, there should be one (instead of none).

However, men can't be divided into alphas and betas, as pop culture and earlier alpha male studies would have it! In the absence of context, women don't find domineering men or submissive men attractive, which suggests that there's more than one way to attract women.[11] When dominance becomes aggressive, it's a turnoff. But when dominant means confident and assertive, women are attracted. Women don't mind so much if dominant men want to compete with each other, but they don't find men who might become aggressive with them a turn-on. In fact, women like dominant men best when they are agreeable and not narcissistic.

In humans, it's not always about physical strength. Men can become sexually desirable when they acquire prestige, which can come through social channels. Actual performance is a factor in genuine self-esteem, which is an attractive characteristic. Being alpha is also context-specific: a CEO of a large multinational corporation will no longer be the alpha in the general population of a prison.

While dominance may be desirable in a harsh or extreme environment, prestige provides men with more resources in more situations, which is more attractive than someone who uses coercion and force in "polite" society. An alpha with prestige is not only considered stronger, but also more moral and socially skilled. An alpha who is "merely" dominant may be rated as strong, but not thought of as ethical or skilled.[12]

The nine types of seducers

Now that you have a background in the psychology and history of seducers, both male and female, you may want to understand the different ways in which seducers operate. Maybe one of them will resonate with you. Or, maybe you'll understand the seducer in your life a little bit better.

---

[11] https://greatergood.berkeley.edu/article/item/the_myth_of_the_alpha_male
[12] https://greatergood.berkeley.edu/article/item/the_myth_of_the_alpha_male

Rake

This seducer is driven by his libido. Women are charmed by his intense desire. They don't get defensive around him because he doesn't seem to be holding anything back. The Rake's attention and passion seem all-consuming. Many women ignore the red flags because he doesn't come across as calculating. Words are his weapon. Women find men good at wordplay alluring, and the Rake milks it for all he's worth when he's in pursuit. He won't stick around for very long and marriage is definitely not what he sees in the cards for himself. Lord Byron and Errol Flynn were both Rakes.

Ideal Lover

An Ideal Lover may be male or female. Either way, they reflect the fantasy of whoever they're trying to seduce. Casanova became the white knight that the women he chased wanted. He'd study a woman as he pursued her, discovering what it was she wanted, and then gave it to her, unless, of course, she wanted marriage.

Madame de Pompadour started in life as a middle-class woman, but she seduced King Louis XV of France by being what he wanted in a mistress. She never allowed him to be bored, which was exactly what he wanted.

Interestingly, being an Ideal Lover doesn't just work in romance: politicians benefit when they mirror what the electorate wants, as in the case of President John F. Kennedy.

Dandy

Many of us feel it necessary to obey gender roles - masculine and short-haired for men, feminine with long hair for women. We tend to be intrigued with those that are more fluid, or who present differently from their gender. A feminine Dandy is a man who often pays more attention to his clothes, hair, and figure than most men do, but still has something about him that seems dangerous - this is very enticing for women!

Rudolph Valentino dressed in flowing robes and wore a lot of makeup for his role in the movie "The Sheik", yet since he still came off with a little danger, women loved him. Being a Dandy is not just being effeminate because, without a touch of menace, this isn't seductive to women. Similarly, a masculine Dandy creates excitement and confusion for her potential lovers. George Sand was a well-known woman who wore men's clothing in an exaggerated way.

Whether male or female, the Dandy is all about the pleasure of living, including eating wonderful food and living with beautiful objects.

Charmer

To be a Charmer, all you need to do is deflect attention away from yourself and onto your target. Make the person you're with feel better about themselves because you don't argue or hassle them. The more you do so, the more power you have over them. Unfortunately for some of you, this type is the seducer without sex! There's always sexual tension, but it goes unresolved. Charmers flatter the self-esteem and vanity of others. If there's any unpleasantness, the Charmer remains unruffled.

Catherine the Great, arriving in Russia as a young German princess, bided her time. She charmed the court by acting as if she had no interest in power at all. Pamela Churchill (who was married to Winston Churchill's son at the time) wooed the wealthy widower Averell Harriman. Though at first, the hostesses in Washington D.C. were suspicious of her, she charmed them, too. She later became a noted hostess and philanthropist.

Benjamin Disraeli charmed Queen Victoria when he was Prime Minister. He sent her copies of reports and made other concessions to her. In response, she made him an earl. He understood that her sober exterior hid the heart of a woman who wanted some seduction in her life.

Charmers seduce by not talking much about themselves. They know where to focus: on their target, and they do so subtly. It's not the harsh, glaring light of attention but more of a pleasant glow that makes the other person feel warm and special.

Charismatic

This seducer has an inner quality that creates an intense presence. It's often an intense self-confidence, but might also be boldness or an inner serenity. They leave the source of it a mystery, but people are drawn to the way the quality displays itself. They're leaders, often mass leaders, and their targets want to be led. Charismatics play with repressed sexuality, but their appeal is actually quasi-religious. Their victims see their extraordinary quality, whatever it is, as a sign from God. How else could they have it and be so different from everyone else?

A Charismatic tends to be theatrical and play with language. They don't seem entirely safe, but call for adventure and excitement. Joan of Arc's intense visions made her a Charismatic. Rasputin seduced early-1900s Russia, particularly Tsar Alexander and his wife the Tsarina. He never tried to downplay his contradictions, which the (highly artificial) court found entirely alluring. Elvis Presley had some demons and when they came out in his music, they exhibited a sexual power. He had a stutter that only went away when he performed.

A good example of a political Charismatic was the Russian Communist, Lenin. He was not only incredibly confident, but determined and organized in his work. He excited workers into revolution. The Argentine radio star Eva Duarte married Juan Peron, who was then elected President. Though she went from soap operas to more serious speeches, she touched everyone who listened to her. Another Charismatic who was a master of language was Malcolm X.

He helped a long-oppressed portion of society release their emotions with his speeches and actions.

Being a successful Charismatic depends on being successful. Once the audience believes that you're losing, they'll turn against you.

Natural

Some people are easily seduced by a lover with the playfulness of a child. Adulthood can be extremely artificial, never saying what you want to say to your boss or friends. Naturalness in an adult is enticing. A Natural seducer retains the spirit of childhood, but when calculating who and how to seduce, they're very adult.

Charlie Chaplin found that he was alluring to any number of women by playing up his weakness. He made people at once feel sympathy for him and also superior to him, which is an incredibly seductive place to be. Josephine Baker took Paris by storm. She refused to be loyal to any club, creating space for the managers to chase her. Because she played her roles so lightly, the Parisians never tired of her.

Star

Although our lives are no longer nasty, brutish, and short, they can still be quite harsh! The Star makes people want to watch them, though no one is allowed up close. They allow us to use our imaginations for what a fantastic life they must lead, while keeping their distance at the same time.

JFK kept America guessing what was behind his eyes and smile. His effect was deliberate, not accidental. Marlene Dietrich was famous for the coldness which overlay her beauty and her face was a blank mask onto which directors could project anything they wanted.

A Star appears like a myth or dream come to life. They avoid direct answers and appearing too real. They allow their fans to know something about them, which paradoxically makes them want to know more. But a true Star doesn't let anyone know everything about them because part of their allure is the fantasy that others project onto them.

Siren

This type is normally a woman - a siren is a seductress. She takes her name from the goddesses whose song was so sweet they caused sailors to crash upon rocky shores. She's a woman who loves sex and uses it to get what she wants.

Cleopatra is a famous example of this type. Sirens provide theatrics and drama that enthrall men. They embody a man's fantasy and there's no need to be conventionally attractive to put a man under a Siren's spell. Marilyn Monroe is another example. She taught herself how to be more enticing to men and she was successful. Her breathy voice made them want to get closer to her to listen. Her touch of vulnerability, which for her was a need for affection, drew men to her.

A siren offers a little bit of danger with her pleasure, which is extremely alluring.

Coquette

This seducer is the master (or mistress) of teasing - of promising yet never delivering total satisfaction. They make their lovers wait until they're ready and delay satisfaction as long as they like.

"...[W]e are only really excited by what is denied us, by what we cannot possess in full." - Robert Greene

Josephine alternately coaxed Napoleon Bonaparte to her and sent him away without seeing him, which both enraged and excited him. Warhol became famous when he stopped begging for people to notice him and instead withdrew from others. Coquettes are not jealous themselves, but incite jealousy by paying attention to a third party, which drives their intended target wild with desire. It's incredibly effective on a group as well, as dictators Mao Zedong and Josef Tito demonstrated.

To seduce, you have to have some measure of self-esteem and self-confidence. If you're insecure and too vulnerable, it's a turn-off. There's a bit of sexual tension underlying every type of seduction, more pronounced in some and less in others. Being able to entice another human being means observing them closely enough to play on others' emotions and weaknesses.

Chapter Summary

- There have been all kinds of seducers throughout history and studying how they were able to attract others can help those who seek to become seducers themselves.
- Seduction communities come and go with the zeitgeist and currently focus on the seducer becoming more appealing to their potential lovers.
- The Dark Triad of seduction includes narcissism, Machiavellianism, and psychopathy. Moderate expressions of these traits are more beneficial than strong expressions.
- Though we commonly discuss alpha males, there are alpha females as well, though their characteristics are often different from their male counterparts.
- Anyone looking to improve their seduction game can examine the nine archetypes of seducers and take their cues from them.

In the next chapter, we'll discuss the elements necessary for successful seduction.

441

CHAPTER THREE:

Elements of Seduction

Let's break down the art of seduction a little more. You probably aren't enthralled by every person you meet because not everyone has that certain something that's necessary to be alluring. If you are enthralled by every person you meet, that's a different matter! When you're easily seduced, people have more power over you than they should. Recognizing what a Rake is doing, for example, will help you avoid being so quickly placed under another person's spell.

What do seducers have that others don't?

We can actually define that "certain something". There is a range of behaviors seen in the various types of seducers, as we discussed in chapter two, however, they do tend to have some qualities in common. Because people tend to be attracted to those who are confident and personable, a seducer will at least appear to have these attributes too, otherwise, their ploys can't get off the ground! They're charismatic and passionate, believing very deeply in themselves and also in being positive. No matter what happens, they are not easily ruffled or thrown off their game.

You know by now that one of the quirks of human nature is that we like a bit of a challenge and prefer that the prize is not given up too fast. Someone who is at least a little bit distant, or alternately repels and coaxes us toward them, is highly desirable. Seducers maintain this aura of mystery. We find elusiveness intriguing. Interested? Not interested? People keep coming back for more. These seducers also may appear to be in tune with their targets. They seem to be more sensitive to others' needs, sometimes presenting the solution before their audience has even mentioned the problem! They want to get to know their target, in order to push the right buttons. The target feels special because the seducer is investing so much time and attention in them. The seducer may also reveal their carefully chosen vulnerabilities, knowing that their target will feel it necessary to respond in kind.

Knowing that people enjoy being led, a seducer's voice is always calm and controlled. They like wordplay, especially of the suggestive kind! They're also in control of their body movements. Their gestures may not be easy to read or overt since they're carefully cultivating that air of ambiguity that human beings are so intrigued by. They will make a lot of eye contact, being very attentive when they're drawing in their targets.

Who is easily seduced?

When it comes to romantic entanglement, there are women with certain qualities and in situations who are more prone to being seduced, which ends in heartbreak for them when the seducer gets bored and takes off, as they inevitably do. If you resonate with any of these characteristics, be wary when someone magnetic and charming crosses your path!

Constantly dissatisfied

Someone who is always complaining and sad is easily swept off their feet. Seducers temporarily lift the sadness, as they act interested in the complainer and make them feel special. They're also great at concocting a fantasy of a better and more romantic world, compared to the reality of life.

If this is you, there are a number of ways to either change your reality or change the way you look at it. The first is to have an attitude of gratitude. What can you be grateful for in your life? What do you love about your life? Reality can't be all rainbows and puppies all the time, unfortunately. But the more you find things to like about your life and change the things you don't like, the less you'll need a fantasy. The seducer will be less attractive to you, simply because they can't really offer you anything that you want.

Active imagination

Seducers give off signals. Their actions wave red flags for those who are paying attention. But a target with an imagination doesn't see the obvious signs that they're dealing with a seducer who is planning to love them and leave them. Seducers induce fantasies that can be easily pictured by someone with a good imagination. The target can get so wound up in the beautiful future that the seducer promises that they miss the cues which would otherwise tell them that it is not going to happen. They're also very skilled with language and it's easy to be caught up in their words.

Make sure, if you know you possess a vivid imagination, that you are looking at your potential lover's actions, not just listening to their fantasies. That will help you see the red flags when they begin waving.

You typically ignore red flags and the opinions of family and friends

Similar to those with active imaginations, you're so immersed in the fantasy and the charm that you ignore the signs you should be heeding. You have arguments which suggest that you're incompatible because you don't share common values, or the other person doesn't seem to ever want to do what you want to do. Your friends and/or family warn you about the signs they see. Perhaps they know people who've been burned by your seducer, they've seen them around town in the company of attractive people, or they can see that the seducer is making you unhappy. Or maybe your behavior has changed for the worse. They love you and want the best for you.

It's true that sometimes other people won't be able to see what you see in someone and that's not always a bad thing. But if everyone around you is telling you the same thing, you should listen to what they have to say.

People-pleaser

The reality is that many people, women especially, are socialized to please others. They go through life believing that their value and worthiness depends on external approval. It's not entirely surprising that people-pleasers fall under a charming spell so easily. When the seducer pulls back, as they must, the people-pleaser will do anything to win back that approval and attention. Otherwise, they'll end up feeling worthless or that they're not good enough to be loved.

If this is you, working on your need for external approval will help you immensely, and not just to repel or ignore seducers! You are worthy of love, no matter what anyone says, and you need to love yourself first. Only once you've achieved this should you search for a romantic partner. Kick 'em to the curb if they start withdrawing and find another one!

Willing to use sex to try for love

Someone with low self-esteem is often willing to have sex too soon, in the hopes that it will lead to love. But with a seducer, it only leads to a broken heart because they are only in it for the sex.

Oxytocin is a neurochemical that promotes bonding and women release it when they have sex. They may end up feeling bonded to the man they just had sex with, who could not be feeling less willing to partner up with them! If this is you, be choosier about who you have sex with. Ask yourself what will happen if you have sex with a certain person and it doesn't become love. If you don't like the consequences, avoid going to bed with them.

You make bad compromises for the sake of the relationship

New people in your life bring new adventures and that's not a bad thing! When you find that you're compromising your values to be with someone, this is a bad thing.

Does your new partner make you spend too much money? Or rush you into sex too fast, before you're really comfortable with it? Are you partying so hard every night it's hard to get to work in the morning? Are you associating with people you wouldn't otherwise, due to their bad characters and/or habits? If so, being single is better than what you're doing.

You stay too long

Has the relationship become obviously dysfunctional? When all you do is argue or clash (or worse) with your partner, there's no reason to stay. Some people do, out of fear of being single. But is it really worse than staying with someone who damages your self-esteem and who doesn't support you in any way?

Here again, being single is actually better. Don't let your desire for love and affection blind you to your own reality.

Signs of seduction

You may or may not have recognized yourself in the list above. But even if you're not easily seduced, you might still fall under someone's spell. Here are some signals to watch out for:

To begin with, you consent to the seduction. (Otherwise, if there's no consent, its rape.) We're not victim-blaming here. The key to seducing another is that the pursuer uses deceit and manipulation to obtain that consent. You didn't freely give it because your seducer was hiding their intentions from you. Moreover, you likely would not have consented if your pursuer hadn't lied or deceived you.

For example, you might not consent to sex unless you believed that the other person was in love with you, or at least willing to explore being in a long-term relationship with you. Knowing this, and also knowing that they had no desire for anything other than sex, your seducer may have led you to believe that they wanted a relationship with you. Had you known all they wanted was sex, you wouldn't have agreed to go to bed with them in the first place.

The seducer doesn't really care about their target and all they want is a boost to their ego or some personal pleasure out of the chase. While they may appear interested in order to further their pursuit, they're not particularly interested in anyone but themselves. This one might be a little harder to suss out because most seducers are skilled at pretending interest! Or, they may genuinely be interested so they can figure out which of your buttons are best to push.

Look at their actions. Do they remember the little, unimportant details that make you who you are and aren't about sex? Or is their interest geared mainly toward finding out what charms and entices you? When they talk about other people, is it in the service of themselves or do they seem curious about others? Are there other narcissistic tendencies that you spot? It's unethical to deceive someone into getting what you want, but many seducers use this ploy, especially in the romantic arena, where it's commonly believed that men want one thing and women another! This is not necessarily true. In a perfectly ethical world, both sides have the same information and consent is mutual. This is not the world we're living in, however.

Three-step model: attraction, comfort, and seduction

The first thing the seducer needs to do is to attract their target. Because they tend to be magnetic and charismatic, this is usually not the hard part for them! They know how to stand out in a crowd and draw attention to themselves. This is where the seduction begins, before they even approach the person they're interested in. All eyes are on them, which also makes them look popular and confident. Once they make direct contact, they'll make their target feel empowered and interesting. Being direct in their approach makes them look courageous. People like risk-takers, as they're a novelty.

Or they might try the indirect approach, which consists of asking an (apparently) random question. This maneuver is designed to smoothly engage in conversation. Whether the indirect or direct opener is used, the seducer normally pivots to wordplay, charm, and humor - all of which are known to attract others. Sometimes seducers, especially men, will open up a conversation with a woman they're not interested in. Once a man is seen talking to a woman, especially an attractive one, other women may be interested in him, as well. Interestingly, other species are known to perform this "mate choice copying",[13] in which females of the species copy other females in choosing a specific male for mating. But the seducer can't give too much away, upfront. No one wants the prize handed over to them on a silver platter. Once the target is hooked, they'll start withdrawing. This is confusing and intriguing, which keeps their target's attention. The relationship continues over time, as normally seduction doesn't occur all in one go. In order to keep the interest levels high, the seducer has to sustain some emotional tension - keeping their audience off-balance and wanting more.

Next is the building of the relationship. Comfort and trust with the pursuer have to be established before the target can be enticed into the seduction. Increased eye contact makes the pursued feel that the seducer is interested in them. The pursuer may also lean toward their target, decreasing the personal space between them. In addition to using wit, the seducer also uses the power of touch - not in a sexual way, at least at first. But humans respond with trust even with a brief

---

[13] https://journals.sagepub.com/doi/full/10.1177/147470491201000511

touch of a hand. It promotes bonding between the two. The brain releases neurochemicals when the body is touched, including oxytocin, which is the bonding chemical.

Physical affection and rapport-building continues up to and during the seduction itself, to maintain the levels of trust necessary for the target to agree to have sex. The decision has to be made emotionally, not logically. The seducer will use words and body language for emotional appeal and emotional rapport. This is not trust built on similar experiences or values, but on a similar drive, both have (or the pursuer appears to have) to be in a physical and romantic relationship.

Chapter Summary

- Seducers have qualities that make them stand out from the ordinary, even if their charm and charisma are superficial.
- Some people are easily seduced because they're dissatisfied with their lives or have other unfulfilled needs that a seducer can exploit.
- Signs of seduction involve consent that appears mutual, but isn't, due to deceit on the part of the pursuer.
- The model of seduction encompasses three main stages: attraction, comfort and trust-building, and the seduction itself.

In the next chapter, you will learn the rules of the game of seduction.

CHAPTER FOUR:

The Rules of the Game

The art (and science) of seduction is really a game with two principal players. Others may be involved around the edges. When a man initiates a conversation with a woman he's not trying to entice, in order to attract another one that he does intend to seduce, minor players are involved. Typically, in a romantic seduction, it's played with two people.

Game types

There are three main types of game that can be played, at least when it comes to sexual seduction.

1. Direct

The direct conversation opener I talked about in the last chapter is most often used for this type of game. Here, the pursuer is up-front in their approach to the target. They're not using other women to draw their target in, but are coming to her directly and expressing their attraction. It doesn't mean being crude, necessarily, just expressing interest. For those who fear rejection, this might seem like a terrifying task! But, because it makes you look like a brave risk-taker, your target will probably find your confidence attractive.

This technique also means less manipulation and less knowledge about human nature because you're not trying to be sly about it or use some human characteristic to your advantage. At some point, you'll likely need to be direct in your approach anyway. Especially when you're "closing the deal" to have sex.

2. Indirect

By contrast, when you're playing an indirect game, you don't let your target know you're attracted until after they've already displayed some attraction to you. This skips over the potential of rejection that's always a possibility of the direct game. It's a strategy game in which you draw out your target to discover things about them and have them qualify themselves for sex with you. Once you've displayed a bit about yourself, to attract them, they then reveal more about themselves. You can test to see if they're actually interested in you before you let them know that you are sexually interested in them.

The problem with this type of game is that there's usually a sexual tension between the two sexes anyway. If you're going for the indirect technique, you have to maneuver yourself so they're not aware upfront of your sexual interest in them, yet keep the tension strong enough that you can attract them and then build the comfort level.

3. Social

When using the social game, you need to know about some human quirks in order to use them as leverage against your target. Here's where the "mate choice copy" technique might come in. Ideally, you want to enter the venue with a crowd of people and have your target wondering who you are. You don't have to be high-status to attract the one you want to seduce, but you do need to be confident and socialize.

Who are the players of the game?

In chapter two, I discussed the different types of seducers. There are various types of victims, as well. In general, they lack something that their seducer is able to exploit or use for leverage. The pursuer must be careful that they're reading their targets correctly, though. Most of us hide or at least try to hide our weaknesses and vulnerabilities. Someone who comes across as tough and strong might, in fact, be protecting a heart soft as a marshmallow!

Some victims are actually former seducers, who had to stop due to family or other pressures. They may be resentful or bitter about this change because they miss being able to seduce people. When you're pursuing them, though, remember that they need to think they're the ones seducing you, not the other way around. Other seducers have lived their life of pleasure and are feeling jaded. They can often be easily seduced by someone who appears young and innocent because it brings back memories of their own youth.

A target who fetishizes the exotic leads an empty inner life and wants to fill it up with exotic treats. An exotic pursuer fits the bill, especially if you exaggerate a bit. Those who are bored with their lives will fill it with drama, so don't chase a drama queen with the promise of safety and security. Other victims may be highly imaginative people who find that reality just doesn't match up to their fantasies. Spoiled children need novelty and the firm hand their parents never gave them. A target who doesn't want to grow up and take responsibility is also searching for a parent.

Someone who was once a star (athlete, student, actor, whatever), who now leads a drab existence, will absolutely perk up once someone lavishes some attention on them. Likewise, someone who's beautiful or especially handsome is always worried they're losing their looks. Seduce them by paying homage to their looks, but also to another characteristic (like brains, wit, or personality) that no one else has paid much attention to. You might find a target who acts like they're whiter than snow, but deep down, they're both terrified of and titillated by the thought of forbidden pleasures in the bedroom. Others are under no illusion about their actual purity, but they also want to taste these as-yet-untasted fruits.

People who are power-hungry need to release some energy, so being a tease works very well for them. Some leaders are genuinely powerful, but because they are leaders, they need someone to break down their walls for them and end their isolation. Others hide their need for power under the guise of being a rescuer. Other targets may have spent so much time in their heads and working on their (perceived) mental superiority that a physical pursuer comes as something of a relief to them. They also tend to be insecure underneath, so you can play on that, too. Some victim's inner voids are so huge that they try to fill it with worship: a cause, a religion, or an idol. Their minds are overactive and they're also physically understimulated. For someone whose senses are overstimulated, they actually need more sensual pleasures, as they tend to be shy.

If someone's gender is fluid or ambiguous, they're most likely looking for another gender fluid person to stir up some of their repressed desires.

Is seduction ethically responsible?

Some states in the US, at least at one time, made certain types of (sexual) seduction illegal.[14] If a man tricked a woman by promising marriage or used other trickery, and if the woman was under 25 or previously a virgin or the man was over a specific age, the seduction could be rendered a crime. In the modern world, however, women have more agency and so seduction isn't a crime. Although many people still view it as immoral, there's definitely a case to be made for ethical seduction!

---

[14] https://www.britannica.com/topic/seduction

Avoiding total lies and false impressions is important. If you have no intention of marrying your conquest, don't promise a wedding. And don't give off the impression that you're willing to consider a wedding, either. If you're trying to charm someone into having sex with you, make it clear that your end result is sex, not a trip down the aisle or a long-term relationship. Not only is this the ethical way to do it, it also shortens the process of getting into bed. In popular culture, the woman who is marriage material doesn't have sex until much later in the relationship. When she knows that marriage isn't in the cards, she doesn't need to act like marriage material and she doesn't need to keep putting up obstacles between you and sex. And if you don't know her very well, how would you know if she was someone you wanted to marry in the first place? Acting like she's marriage material right away is dishonest because you'd need to get to know her better in the first place.

An obviously immoral way to seduce someone is to use your power or status. The "casting couch" in Hollywood, though it's been used a lot, is unethical. If you're someone's boss and you require them to go to bed with you to keep their job, this is not seduction at all. It's a pure power play and there's nothing alluring or enticing about it.

However, what if you were to do things right? Treat your partner as a whole person that you're attracted to? Everyone finds that approach charming! Knowing what your target responds to isn't manipulative because everyone does it. The power relationship is equal - most people figure out this aspect of human nature pretty quickly if they don't already know it when they begin dating. With an ethical seduction, there's still plenty of flirting, teasing, and wordplay involved, if both partners enjoy it. But, the pursuer makes clear what they're after and the target picks up on these signals and responds in kind. When the response is positive, the seducer can then start making the moves to close the deal and end the journey with sex. If the response is negative, the pursuer may change targets and begin again.

Everyone involved in this type of seduction has realistic expectations about what is happening. No one gets hurt because they don't have false hopes that end up clashing with reality. Both parties are attracted to each other. There's no reason to ramp up one's attractiveness with artifice or game-playing. Consent is mutually given because both parties are clear about what's expected.

Drawing the line

In the online seduction community, some men have no desire to be "pick-up artists" who have sex with women and then discard them because they can. These men are just looking for dating advice, so they can have better dates and more sex. There's nothing necessarily immoral or unethical about this. But where should the line be drawn? Some of the seduction techniques come from NLP (neuro-linguistic programming), which is thought to enhance communication techniques. It's also often considered to be deceitful and manipulative because the people using it aren't open about it. Is it abuse if you have a lot of seductive power and you use it to your advantage? As noted above, seduction can be manipulative and have destructive consequences.

Sexual harassment happens with both male and female supervisors. If the employer is using their hiring and firing power to force an employee into sex, that's coercive and not seductive.

Chapter Summary

- There are three types of seductive games people play: direct, indirect, and social - each of which has its advantages, disadvantages, and techniques.
- There are many different types of targets that seducers will find easy to pursue, especially if they understand human

nature and the various ways in which people experience a lack of something in their lives.

- Seduction doesn't have to be manipulative and deceitful, as long as the seducer makes their intentions clear.
- Using one's power and status to coerce someone else into having sex is a clear line between seduction and lack of consent.

In the next chapter, you will learn about the art of seduction.

CHAPTER FIVE:

The Art of Seduction

Anyone who takes the time to learn this art can be a master (or mistress) of the seduction game. It combines a knowledge of human nature with historical experience obtained over centuries. You'll need to know the type of seducer that you most resemble and uncover the strategies that will work for you and your specific type. If you resonated with any of the victim types discussed in chapter three, stay away from them as your targets!

An introduction to the techniques of seduction

People like mystery and uncertainty. It keeps them drawn in, wanting to find out what happens next. If you've chosen your target correctly, they'll be doing their best to uncover your mystery and take you for themselves. Competition is also seductive. Develop the charisma that leaves your targets wanting more. You'll need to appear confident because that's another characteristic that hooks people easily. Hook them, but don't let them get too close to you. Distance gives you the mythic aura you want to cultivate.

Be the hero or heroine of a great drama, but remember, as with all heroes, you can't get too close to the common people. Stay up on that pedestal as long as you can. Act as if your power is innate and a gift of creation. Hard work and discipline is a boner-killer when it comes to seduction. Don't let on that you've been practicing and studying.

Whatever type of seducer you are, you want it to appear effortless. After all, anybody can put in hard work to achieve a goal, but a successful seducer is not just anyone! They're a rare being with a huge presence that others are attracted to, but can't necessarily get close to, at least not until the seducer lets their target in. There eventually should be a touch of vulnerability - just a touch - being needy turns most people right off. This allows the pursued to feel special because they're the ones allowed to touch the hem of the seducer's garment.

The keys to seduction lie in your ability to show charisma, even if you don't necessarily think of yourself as naturally charismatic. You must be confident and act like you have a plan. Be mysterious enough that you intrigue others. Pull them in, then push them back. Make your target work for the opportunity to be seduced by you because people don't trust gifts given too freely.

Phases of seduction and their techniques

We've discussed the overall journey of seduction: attraction, comfort and rapport-building, and the actual seduction. Let's go into the seduction phases in more detail and discuss the strategies that go along with each.

Cut the target out of the pack and incite desire and attraction

You'll need to select your target carefully to make sure they fit in with your type and that you can address the void they have within themselves. Ignore the ones who aren't attracted to you or who you can't appeal to because they're just a waste of your time. Show that you're the seducer by being choosy. There may be a number of people who seem open to your charms, but you don't need to take the first one on offer. This would be a move based on insecurity, not confidence, so it will eventually backfire. You might choose someone who seems shy because they often respond well to being approached and would like to be drawn out. Your target shouldn't seem to be too busy. Too much work on your part and they won't have the time to spend with you that you need to be successful in your seduction.

Once you've selected a good target who's ready for you, start making conversation. Get to know a little about them so you can use that information for later, especially little tidbits about their youth or childhood, or something about what makes them tick. Once they're comfortable talking to you, you can make an unusual or surprising suggestion - something they find intriguing. You don't want to pay them too much attention, at first. Remember how attractive distance is. Once you've made the approach and intrigued them, you want them to come to you. They want to feel like the seducer, not the seduced. Backing off also lets them use their imaginations a little bit. That's more alluring than spelling everything out for them. Send mixed or ambiguous signals. Most people are so obvious that you'll come across as more interesting. You must also let them know you have complexity that can't be addressed in one initial meeting. They'll need to get to know you better to uncover this intriguing and mysterious quality. If you present as innocent and cherubic, you'll need to let out a hint of cruelty or danger to keep them interested.

Playing on vanity can provide great rewards! If you're interested in a specific person, flirt with their friend. This is one way to create a "triangle of desire", which is an excellent way to lure in your target. Women especially are attracted to men with a "rakish reputation", so use that to your advantage. While you're in the first phase of seduction, you'll be planting seeds for later. One seed is to make them worried about the future. Bring up in them the doubts and securities you learned in your conversation. This prepares the ground for your second seed of insinuation, which is that you'll be able to address this void in their life. This is a good time to play along with them. What a coincidence that you enjoy what they enjoy! You adapt to their mood, which plays to their ego.

Unsettle them with confusion and pleasure

Creating suspense is key! Do things they don't expect from you, which keeps them coming back for more. They want to know what happens next and you don't want to make that too obvious. People love novelty, so attract them with it, but also use it to keep them off-balance. Remember to add in that little touch of vulnerability from time to time and strategically show a little weakness or vulnerability. Avoid doing it accidentally because you'll come off as insecure or confident. Decide what weakness you'll let them taste and when. Make it enough to make them feel superior or strong, at least for a brief time. It should be natural to your character, so even though you're using it in a calculated way, it won't appear calculating.

Don't be reliable. If you choose, for example, to send them a letter or flowers, don't do that on a regular basis. You want them panting after you, not the other way around. Use your words! Seduction is about emotional appeal. Flatter, use heavily loaded language, appeal to their vanity, ego, and self-esteem. Wrap them in fantasies and rich, imaginary worlds. They won't have the will to resist when you're using language as leverage. You'll need to pay attention to detail, so you know which buttons to push. Be poetic, be vulgar (if your target is OK with it), naughty, or sensuous, but don't be ordinary. Embody their fantasies. In your conversations, hopefully, you discovered what it is they're looking for. Now, you want to blur the lines between fantasy and reality by being that fantasy figure they've been dreaming of for so long. All this will help you isolate them from their natural environment: physical, mental, emotional, encouraging them to depend more on you than they have yet.

Deepen the effect and push them onto the ledge

Show your target that you are the embodiment of their dreams, according to the seed you planted. If you're playing the white knight, now is the time to manufacture a drama or crisis (if there isn't one already), so you can swoop in and fulfill their fantasies of being rescued, for example. Whatever type of seducer you are, don't worry about looking silly or making a mistake. Anything that looks like a sacrifice is going to impress your target and reinforce the idea that you're their dream lover in the flesh.

People love to feel like they're exploring their dark side. You might help them push past self-imposed limits, or maybe limits put in place by society. Either way, let them feel like you're leading them to transgress and explore something they have always wanted but never dared. Normally, this will be sexual in nature! You can engage in behavior that's forbidden to most, which makes you dangerously enticing. Allow your target to enjoy the lure of the forbidden.

Make sure, whether you're seducing someone who's vain about their appearance or not, that you express attraction beyond the physical. Many people have insecurities and worries about their bodies and you don't want those anxieties to scare them off. Make them so aware of their weakness that they can't concentrate on you. Express your appreciation for something that's not physical. Appeal to something sublime to redirect them, like religion or the occult, or even an amazing work of art. The key to this phase is not to focus exclusively on pleasure. You lure them in with your promise of being the hero, or heroine. Once you've paid attention to them, you want to back off abruptly. Interested, interested, interested…now bring the pain. Suddenly, you're no longer attracted to them. You can even drive yourselves into a breakup, so they feel the emptiness in their lives without you. Then you can bring back the pleasure, until you need to ratchet up some more tension and back off once more.

Don't avoid conflict. You'll need to maintain the sexual tension and that's not possible without some conflict. Pull them in and push them away and repeat. Vary the times you spend in pleasure and in pain, so it's not boring or predictable. Maybe this breakup is for real! You don't want them to figure out a pattern.

Push them off and move in

Introduce some jealousy into the equation. As usual, nothing too obvious. Drop some hints about your possible interest in another person, then let your target's imagination run wild. Willpower is linked to sexual libido in a way that you can easily exploit. If they're waiting for you to come to them - if they believe they're being pursued - the sexual temperature is low. Raise it up by inciting some new emotions, tension, and jealousy. Get them involved in the pursuit, instead of relaxing and waiting for you. While they're getting hotter and hotter, you're totally nonchalant. After all, everyone expects the hero or heroine to be cool, calm, and collected. Meanwhile, you're watching for signs of their libido warming up. They might start blushing, even crying. Keep an eye out for revealing slips of the tongue, too. These are all signs that they're ready for you to close the deal.

You are the pursuer, even if they mistakenly think that they're chasing you. This also means you're the one who has to make the bold move. It's up to you, but you still must maintain your aura of cool and mystery. You're making the move, but you can't be desperate for their response. Afterward, you might still need to stir the pot to maintain your elusiveness. But when you are done or disenchanted, make sure you end it. Don't continue out of pity or because you don't have anyone else. Make a clean break if you can. If you can't, get them to break up with you by deliberately using some anti-seductive behavior.

Seduction notes for beginners

There are a few things you need to know to get you up to speed. They'll also help you master the art of seduction.

Turn off your phone

In order to maintain your focus on learning and seduction, you need to avoid distractions. Being too immersed in your phone means that you will be too easily turned away from your goals by an ill-timed notification or text message. Plus, your potential targets will be insulted, not attracted, when you start looking at your phone as you're speaking to them. Staying away from your phone helps you get into a flow state, in which you're focused on what you're doing. Flow states are key for creativity, too.

Study

Watch what successful seducers are doing. Watch how they play the game. Reading about them in this book gives you a good background, but you'll help your game leap forward by watching what works out in the world and copying it. Find a mentor if you can. They also can help you make the most of your seducer personality and give you some tips and tricks on how they do what they do. You can also YouTube or search well-known charmers and watch them online.

Visualize

You can do this "in the field", as well as at other times. Visualization is a mindset trick that successful athletes and business people all use. What does a successful night in the field look like? Why are you trying to improve your seduction game and what is your goal? Whatever it is, play it as it lays. When you're about to set out for the night, imagine in your mind how you want the night to go. Picture how you will find an appropriate target and how you'll slide into conversation with them.

Consistent practice

Like so many other journeys in life, seduction and improving your game are endurance contests. They are marathons, not sprints. So don't wear yourself out practicing too much in a short period of time and then needing too much time to recover. Instead, practice a bit each day. Some days you might only take 10 minutes, other times you might be able to work on it for an hour. Don't overwhelm yourself with too much too soon. Take it easy enough that you actually have time to improve, as well as time to reflect and learn from each practice session.

System of learning from your practice

For most people, this practice will be in the form of "field notes". Once you return home from a practice session, relive the night. Write it down because leaving it in your head means you won't get the full power of reflection. When you're writing, take special note of what went well. Did you say something that piqued your target's interest, or did you try a casual touch to increase bonding? Also, take note of what didn't go well. Maybe your indirect game was a little too indirect and didn't let the target understand your attraction.

What was going on in the outside world where you practiced? What was going on internally? Did anything trigger your insecurities and were you able to handle them or do you need a game plan in case it happens again? What do you want to try again? Is there something new you might want to test out? Or something that in your opinion failed so badly you never want to use it again? Most mentors will want to hear your notes.

Balance between too easy and too hard

If you're only practicing the easy stuff, like approaching targets who appear desperate for some interaction, you won't improve. You'll stay mediocre and won't be able to master your game. On the other hand, if you're constantly aiming too high beyond your current abilities, you won't really know what went well and what didn't. You just don't know enough to make that determination and you won't be able to improve by constantly going too hard, either. Plus, it's very easy to get discouraged when you're aiming at the impossible because you'll be failing.

Limit what you want to focus on in each session and that way you'll be able to learn more quickly.

Sleep

Brains need rest! Cell repair and other processes can only take place when you're asleep, so you need to make sure you're taking time for sleep. Learning happens during sleep too, as memories and experiences get encoded. Nap if you need to, so you can stay up late and practice your game later at night.

Chapter Summary

- Seduction involves art and techniques that have been acquired over centuries.
- Each phase of the seduction contains techniques applicable to that phase, no matter what type of seducer you are.
- You can improve your game faster with a few hacks, including consistent practice and taking notes on your practice sessions.

In the next chapter, you will learn seduction techniques in more detail.

CHAPTER SIX:

Seduction Techniques 101

Here, I'll discuss the techniques that men use to sexually seduce women. Just a reminder that these are based on centuries of knowledge and experience, including what men have discovered about how women work and how to leverage that information into seduction.

Introduction to the best techniques men use to seduce women

There are a couple of common maneuvers that men have used successfully to entice women into bed. One is acting like a Player or Casanova, meaning that you're known for your amorous pursuits and you're very smooth and debonair about it. You ardently love 'em, and then you leave 'em. If you're a Player, you know you have skills that other men don't have. Generally, you have your pick of the women you want because you use these smooth maneuvers and strategies. The media makes the single life, at least for men, fun and glamorous. Settling down is perceived to be boring and sometimes even the death of sex. Who wouldn't want to be out there flirting with a different woman every night?

Players usually don't bring their women into their lives. They have so many they don't want to keep introducing new people to their friends and family. They're confident and allow the ball to fall into their target's court, so the target can pursue them instead. Their ultimate goal is sex, as quickly as possible.

There are several different types of Players. They might be the only decent-looking and/or single guy in their office or town, so women flock to them! Others are known for how much attention they pay to the opposite sex, plying them with drinks, compliments, and teddy bears. Or a man might play the mystery card, where he lets drop little hints about his life and the complexities of being him…but no one gets all the information, even though all the women are trying to find out! And, of course, there's the bad boy who's hard to predict and never dull. When people talk about him being the bad boy, women line up at the door to try to prove them wrong. They won't. He really won't find a long-term relationship that he wants to be in.

No matter what kind of Player appeals to you, it means being super cool and playing by your own rules. You can't be like all the other guys, or else you'll blend into the crowd. Women want someone who dares to be different. Show them that you're different. In being cool, you do need to be above it all. No one responds well to desperation, so get them curious about you. Intrigue them, but don't give them what they want right away. Keep them hooked. Playing hard to get works for you in this situation. People always want what they can't have, so let your target know they can't have you and watch them try!

Women like a man who's witty. If a man speaks quickly enough and in monotone, he can induce a near-trance in his target. This is one of the advantages of neuro-linguistic programming or NLP. A Player works with all their senses, not just words, but scent, sight, and touch. He'll appeal to her brains, too, and ask her what she thinks. He can be playful and definitely unpredictable. He might surprise her with gifts or take her somewhere spontaneously. A good seducer has several language tricks up his sleeve, in addition to being smart and charming. He can act like the hero that will wipe her tears away. If the woman is having problems in her current relationship, the seducer can talk about how sad she looks and seems.

The converse of this is acting like you need her protection, her shoulder to cry on. You're having problems in a current relationship, which may or may not be a romantic one. But it could be a problem at work or with friends, too. You're showing some vulnerability and making her feel like the strong one. Acting like a romantic man is also a great way to lure in the target. Citing classical quotes or reading her poetry is a trick most women fall for. Paying attention to what the target wants will help you determine whether she's a "bad girl" or a good one. But, whichever one she is…play to the opposite. If she's a good girl, she wants to be bad, or at least taste some forbidden fruit. If she's a bad girl, she wants romance. When you're attuned to the details, you'll be able to do something special for her that she appreciates and she'll begin letting down her guard.

You might even try starting a rumor about yourself! Something calculated to appeal, or something that a woman will be inclined to defend you on. As with all seduction techniques, be deliberate about it. Don't accidentally let go of some information about yourself, or allow someone else to start rumors. Calculate your approach and your maneuvers.

You can be an asshole and seduce plenty of women, but you have to be genuine about it - uncaring. You're an asshole because you don't care about the results, or about society or rules. But if you're spiteful because you're reacting to something you care about, you won't be able to attract women. Aloofness works well, especially with women.

Right now you might be wondering why being a Player and an indifferent asshole works so well when luring women to your bed. It's called the "sexy sons" hypothesis.[15] Women want to have sons who will be attractive to the opposite sex, so they will have sex with men

---

[15] https://www.psychologytoday.com/intl/blog/slightly-blighty/201508/the-sexy-sons-theory-what-women-are-attracted-in-men

who are attractive to other women. It's thought that female orgasm is a way to make fertilizing the egg more likely. Evolution directs orgasm to occur with more desirable mates. In this context, "desirable" means possessing the genes that women want to pass on to their potential sons in order for them to attract desirable women. Research has found that women have more orgasms with men who other women also find attractive, which helps validate the sexy sons' hypothesis.

Mind games and covert seduction

The previous suggestions were a little obvious, but now we're going to delve into more of the activities that may not be as clear to both participants of the game. These types of games use the target's mind against her a bit more than the others you've read about so far.

Cold reading

One way to start messing with a woman's mind is to try "cold reading", which is the same tactic that many so-called mediums and mind readers use. You'll need to be able to read female body language pretty well to make this tactic work. In it, you make suggestions that apply to many women and let her mind and imagination do the rest. It's especially effective if you read her palm because you then get to let the sense of touch work its magic, too. Whether or not you're doing the cold reading, make sure you stay playful and interesting.

What are the basics of a cold read? Whether you're playing the seduction game or setting yourself out as a medium or tarot card reader, you're operating on the same basic set of assumptions - that people are more alike than they are different and major life events are the same for all: birth, puberty, work, marriage, having a child, aging, and dying. People don't visit cold readers because they're happy, but because they're trying to solve a problem. Most of the time, these problems are due to love, money, health, or the lack thereof. A good cold reader, one that can make a living at it, has a keen eye for detail. They notice jewelry, skin, clothing, and other accessories that tell them what the problem is likely to be. You may not have this eye for detail or even care very much about it. But most people, even if we have different goals and aspirations, share the same outlook on life. A lot of beliefs are driven by culture, so if you know the woman's culture, you probably already know a lot about her beliefs and outlook.

As it turns out, you can do pretty well even with a "stock spiel", as long as it's vague enough that it covers a large number of women. The best ones are about three-quarters positive, with about a quarter of the reading negative.[16] As long as you're confident and act like you know what you're doing, your target will probably be convinced that you have accurately read her and she'll be amazed at what you know. This works because when someone hears potentially contradictory statements, their brains immediately start trying to make sense of things. Put them together in some sort of coherent fashion. Good vague tactics to use include talking about different parts of her. You can contrast two parts: "Your smile is so innocent, but I can see something darker in your eyes." Or sometimes they're one way - say, adventurous and bold - and other times they're timid and don't want to take risks. Since this applies to most people, it's pretty safe to say! If you know some basic body language tidbits, you can use those, too. "I know you're emotionally closed off because you're standing there with your arms crossed over your chest."

Start your cold reading playfully. You might even tell her you're psychic, to get her intrigued. Or, you can start with a general statement that's probably true and go from there. You want to bring in her emotions, so you might start with a "negative" emotion, like anxiety, and then tell her something positive about it. Once you've done some generic cold reads, use a touchier one, like the "closed-off" example above. The women you cold-read will be surprised by how much you know, which lets their defenses down, so you can learn quite a bit

---

[16] https://heartiste.net/cold-reading-is-a-potent-seduction-tactic/

about them at a deeper level than with some other techniques. Since you already know so much about them, it's not a big deal for them to confess deeper vulnerabilities. This allows you to connect with your target, especially if she's conventionally attractive and only used to men commenting on her looks. You can add in some statements about sex or repression to get her thinking about your ultimate goal, even if unconsciously.

The more cold reading you do, the easier it will become. With a glance, you'll be able to read your targets and show them your amazing power. It's a great way to build rapport while you're making her feel comfortable with you because you'll "discover" things that the two of you have in common. Cold reading is probably not going to get a woman to go all the way to bed with you, so you'll need to use some other methods, too. But it's a quick way to get a woman's attention and show her some unusual powers, unless she identifies as a skeptic, in which case she'll mess with you as you attempt your reading! You may also find as you discover more about her that you don't really want to spend more time with her and can gracefully make an exit!

Hover and disqualify

Another tactic is known as "hover and disqualify". You can probably guess what it means! The benefit is that it can work no matter your level of game, or what type of seducer personality is closest to yours.

First, you get near your target physically, so she has to see you. Best not to do this in a creepy way, but find a (plausible) reason to be in her vicinity. If she's standing at the bar, you have the built-in excuse of buying a drink. If she's standing off somewhere else, you might pull out your phone and pretend to check it. Don't get so lost in your notifications that you forget why you picked that particular spot! Don't face her, but it's best to be in a position so that you can see what she's doing, in case you see a good time to approach. This is the "hover" part.

Next, you want to appear to disqualify her as a potential partner by overtly checking out another woman while you're standing near your target. This will incite some jealousy and heat her up a bit. You'll need to ensure that she sees you checking out the other women, so you may need to be more overt instead of subtle here. If another woman has a terrific butt, make an obvious show of checking out that butt.

The "hover and disqualify" technique does a few things for you. First, because you're not looking directly at your target, you don't seem to be too interested in her, or too needy. Standing near her but looking at other women sends mixed signals. People find these signals confusing and enticing, so the more you send the better! Jealousy is a sexy emotion and your target may see your attention to another woman as a challenge to her. Women love challenges! Once you've executed the technique, you can approach your intended target. You can do it right away, if the opportunity presents itself, and you can do it smoothly. Otherwise, you may have to walk away for a short period and then return.

There are a few things to be careful of with this technique, or it might not work. Don't look at the "disqualifier" for too long, or you'll seem creepy. Notice her, check out an obviously attractive feature, but then look away after you're sure your target has noticed. It's also possible that your target will be so self-conscious that she doesn't rise to the occasion: she allows herself to be DQ'd without putting up a fight or resistance against it. You can try showing her a bit more attention if this happens, but you may just need to move on.

Negging

The technique you've most likely heard of in relation to being a pick-up artist is "negging". You aim a mild insult (too mild to cause much offense) at a woman, which is surprising because men don't typically do that to women they want to have sex with! The element of surprise is a novelty that the human brain craves. Women, particularly very attractive ones, aren't used to anything but praise. You'll stand out in a crowd using this tactic. Negging expresses a mild disinterest in the woman, which again is unusual and attention-getting. It puts you in control of the situation. Now she's trying to earn your approval, as the result of the back-handed compliment you gave her, rather than the other way around. Even if you don't consider yourself a pick-up artist, you might use negging to spice up your interactions a little bit.

Negging should be used carefully. It's intended for women who are physically very attractive because, for them, a backhanded compliment is unusual. For women who are not conventionally attractive, it may not be so much of a novelty. When done in a matter-of-fact way, it doesn't work very well because women find it so creepy. It's best used after a little flirtation and back-and-forth with the woman and said in a flirty or playful tone, as well.

Social proof

The tactic of social proof is also a good one to use, no matter how much you've practiced seduction. It's based on the assumption most people make that if many people are making a certain choice, it has to be the correct option. For example, which restaurant do you go to? The one that has no customers, or the one that's bustling with diners? You go to the busy one because you assume there must be something wrong with the other one if no one's eating there.

This even works with things like choosing to go to college. If you live in a place where no one goes to college after they've finished high school, you probably won't go either. On the other hand, if everyone you know goes to college, you're likely to attend, as well. When are you going to buy an online course: when you see an ad that looks good and tells you how good the course is, or when your friends told you what a difference the course made in their lives? Naturally, you'll go with your friends' recommendations.

How does this work in the seduction scene? Social proof is when you're surrounded by other women or known to have had sex with other women. They want to be with you, so your target will recognize that she needs to choose you because you're the socially correct option.

There are three main ways that you can build social proof, relatively quickly. One is to be seen in the company of other women. This works best if your crowd is attractive, young women. It still works if you have a cool friend and you're hanging out with him and his squad. You'll get some spillover effect. You can also approach another woman or group of women and start talking to them in an animated way and, at some point, excuse yourself to have a conversation with your target. This is a little bit like disqualifying, but not quite the same.

The second way is to be a social butterfly and work the room. The more people you meet, the more people want to meet you. That's just how the social animal goes. When people want to talk to you, you'll come off as high-status. You must really be "somebody" if everyone wants to meet you! You'll be intriguing and women will want to get to know you. The downside to this type of social proof is that it's too easy to slide into entertainer mode and forget the reason you're here. Or you'll be on such a manic high energy that you won't be able to pull it back to be cool and indifferent when you need to approach a woman.

Keep moving in the crowd until you find a woman that you do want to get to know better. Don't get stuck talking to someone who isn't interesting (male or female) for too long. But, once you do find that intriguing woman, you need to have the wherewithal to stop your flitting around and work on her.

Finally, find a place where you're known. If you don't have one already, you can find one for yourself. You'll want a bar or nightclub where you can get to know the staff and regulars. It should also be a place where there's plenty of turnover, meaning new women appear consistently. You don't want to pick a place where you'll only be seeing the same faces every time you go because your game will wear very thin, very quickly. It should also be a place where women are looking to meet new partners, not a coffee shop or tearoom where they go to hang out with friends. They should be coming to this place with the idea that they'll find a man to have some sexual or romantic time with. The venue ideally has little nooks or tables where you can bring a woman to get away from the high energy and focus on your seduction. Best of all is a place that has different floors and distinct spaces, so you can change venues without leaving.

To build up your cred once you've found such a place, go to it consistently. Just as with your practice sessions, you don't have to spend a long time while you're here, but you need to make regular appearances. To get to know the staff, it's best to get here a little early or at off times, so they're not too busy to spend some time with you. Get comfortable with it and explore all it has to offer. You want to know where you can take a woman for some seductive one-on-one time. Study it, so you know when the women typically arrive and can be there for the newbies.

Kino-escalation

Ever heard of kino-escalation? It relies on the erotic power of touch to help you connect with the woman you want to have sex with. Recall that touch helps release the bonding neurotransmitter oxytocin. Touching a woman says a lot about you, all of which is good. It shows that you're confident and not worried about whether you'll scare her off. It demonstrates that you're a physical type of guy. Women find confident men who aren't afraid to use touch very sexy. Just as with your speech, you need to touch a woman with self-assurance and make it deliberate. Otherwise, you'll seem unsure, which is a definite turnoff.

When you start off at night, you'll often need to lean in close and touch, in order for her to be able to hear what you're saying. But, if you're starting with touch during the day, you can't whisper in her ear when you first meet, it's too creepy. Adjust accordingly.

It's much harder to seduce a woman when you don't use kino-escalation. Touch is very powerful! If she gives you positive signals, you can keep going. These are demonstrated by her leaning into you and maybe even reciprocating the touch. If she's neutral, she won't move or touch you back. If the response is negative, she'll pull away from you. If you receive a neutral or negative signal, it doesn't necessarily mean that you should give up. She's not comfortable with you right now, so back off and give it some time before you try again. If she sends you a signal that you went too far, you can calmly and deliberately back off. Don't yank your hand back like you touched something hot because that also reads as not being confident. Even with touch, you shouldn't be consistent or predictable. If she's demonstrating that she likes a certain way you're touching her, stop for a bit. You'll begin again later.

When you're touching, don't be ham-handed about it. Light touches are the way to go - her arm briefly when you want to make a point, your knee against hers when you're crowded together. Don't leave your hand on her like a dead weight. You can break into the kino by touching her on the shoulder as a sign of approval. It's not sexual, but it is touch, and it leads the way for more to follow. When you lead her from one place to another, hold her hand. Recall earlier that a good place for you to be known is one that has separate spaces. It's a great idea to move her from one venue to another and you can hold her hand while you do it.

Once you've started more of a conversation, your touching can be a bit longer: hugging, stroking. Hold her by the waist, especially at a nightclub when you're struggling to talk over the music. The bonus to holding her waist is that you can gauge whether it's OK to go in for a kiss. Even a kiss is kino. Kiss the same way you're doing the rest of your touching: deliberately and with no hesitation. If she pulls back, let her go, and try again a bit later if she's signaling you to go for it.

Nightclubs are great for dancing. Many women love to dance and you can hold her hand as you lead her out to the floor. Dancing also allows you to be physically much closer to her and to touch her more intimately.

As long as it's okay at your venue, you can escalate to groping and making out eventually, as she becomes more comfortable with you. But if you can't close the deal, it's a bad idea. She'll cool off and recognize what you're trying to do, rather than staying caught up in the moment. If you can get her to the location, making out is an excellent way to escalate in terms of touch. You want her just dying to get into your pants, so turn her on with touch. Kiss her neck, play with her thighs, and use your fingers to great effect.

The key with kino is to escalate. Start small, with light brushes of her shoulder or arms. If you go too heavy too fast, you'll turn her off. Watch for her responses: if she wants you to back off, do it smoothly and deliberately. Give it a few moments before you go in again and you may want to start off with light touches (minor kino) first. Make sure she's comfortable with the light touches before you move to the medium (medium kino). And, again before you have sex (major kino). All phases must be respected or you'll be rejected for going too fast too soon.

Female psychology and the Shogun method: An overview

The next chapter delves more deeply into the Shogun method, but you should know that you can use female psychology to get her to be interested in you. It involves making her happy, but she also has to go through extremely negative experiences with you.

If you're a guy who doesn't mind sleeping around, you don't mind using mind control techniques, and you're OK with making a woman suffer a little bit in order for her to be yours, you should consider the

Shogun method. It's a bit controversial and may be considered manipulative, but if that's OK with you, it could work. If you're either a psychopath who likes hurting women or your goal is to sleep with as many women as you possibly can until the day you die, you should move on to another technique.

Chapter Summary

- There are common tricks that work for men to seduce women, among them, being a Player or Casanova.
- More covert operations include mind games, like negging, cold reading, and "hover and disqualify".
- A more potent seduction technique is the Shogun method of making women suffer mentally in order to be yours.

In the next chapter, you will learn all about the Shogun method and other more devious seduction tactics.

CHAPTER SEVEN:

Devious Tactics of Seduction

So far, the techniques we've discussed have been a bit more innocuous. Yes, they're mind games, but the woman still has the choice of backing off or not being compliant. There are some more devious ways to seduce a woman, that involve more manipulation and deceit. In these techniques, consent isn't necessarily entirely mutual, because she may not be aware of what you're doing. But they will last longer and be more permanent, compared to some of the pick-up artist strategies that are designed for the short term.

Shogun method

When you use this tactic, you've crossed over the line and moved from seduction into enslavement. The trick here is to isolate the woman and separate her from her family and friends, so she ends up depending on you. (Remember you don't want to use this if all you really want to do is love 'em and leave 'em!)

There's a step-by-step roadmap that must be followed in order for the Shogun method to work, known as the IRAE roadmap. These letters stand for Intrigue, Rapport, Attract, and finally, Enslave. First, intrigue her and next, build rapport. Once you do this successfully, she'll then be attracted to you. Then, and only then can you mentally enslave her, which is a total emotional addiction to you, for life. If you try to do these steps out of order, it doesn't work. If you try to build rapport without intriguing her, you won't have a deep enough foundation with her. And there can't be a deep enough attraction without rapport-building and so on.

The PUA community puts the emphasis on men's inner game, but the Shogun method exploits weaknesses in women's psychology. Shogun sequences are designed to command her attention and lure her to make the choices you want her to make. This is all based on science - not movie-style mind control, but principles based on what we know about the brain, including NLP and applied psychology. Studies show that women can be polygamous and also hypergamous: they'll "mate-switch" if a better male than the one they currently have comes along. This is an opportunity for a willing Shogun practitioner, though also a risk.

This method can help men move out of the friend zone, recover after heartbreak and start over, and even bring back an ex they don't want to let go. Followers of the method say that you don't necessarily need to know a lot about women, as long as you take the steps as directed and have a basic understanding of the science, it will work.

Each of the stages in IRAE has its own sequences, or patterns, to help you draw the woman in:

During the Intrigue stage, you want her to be enticed by you. One sequence is to anchor the feelings she has for some object to you, as well. Identify her passion and have her transfer it to you. If she has a higher power or believes in such things, you can use it to create intrigue in her mind. Ask her about love and relationships. If she's a beautiful woman, let her know that you're interested in something more about her than just her looks.

Rapport-building is similar to techniques used in the pick-up artist scene. But you'll go a bit deeper than they do. You'll find her hidden weakness and show that you're the solution to her emptiness. All human beings have a need to belong to a group and so you'll create a shared group that consists only of the two of you.

Once you've built this deep rapport, it's time to move on to the Attraction stage. Building on your shared world, you'll show her how similar the two of you are. Invoke her dream guy, showing his similarities to you…and her current boyfriend's vast difference compared to the dream guy (if she currently has a BF that you need to be rid of). Then you'll show her that you're the perfect boyfriend.

The Enslavement stage has two phases. The first is where you isolate your target from her current environment, so she becomes dependent on you. Then, you use the Black Rose sequence, explained below, to erase her current identity and replace it with one that's subservient to you. This stage is not possible if you haven't gone through the previous three.

Implanted commands

As you're probably well aware, no one, including women, responds well to direct commands. But what if you planted a seed in the subconscious? This is the technique behind implanted commands. Instead of commanding her to do something directly, you camouflage it in such a way that she'll be charmed into it. You do have a direct command in your statement, which is what gets implanted, but you're not giving an actual order.

Here's an example: "I could tell you to commit to me, but someone like you needs to consider everything carefully before you make the right choice." "Commit to me" is the direct command, but that's not what she hears. And yet, that's what her subconscious absorbs.

Fractionation

Freud initially discovered this psychological tactic.[17] It uses hypnosis, persuasion, and psychology to uncover the secrets of a particular brain. It can be used during any of the IRAE stages.

---

[17] https://sibg.com/using-fractionation-in-seduction/

Typically in the seduction community, fractionation is a combination of hypnosis and the effective use of body language to make an emotional connection with the woman. You put her into a trance and remove her from it, repeatedly, leading to her emotional addiction to you.

If you're concerned about ethics, salespeople and Hollywood do this, too! They put you into the trance, snap you back into reality, and put you under again. In this technique, you tell a story where emotions conflict rapidly, from happy to sad and back. Her emotions should be on a rollercoaster: up, down, sideways! A little confusion is good. Intensify the feelings as you go. You can even do this in one sentence, in which you express approval of the woman's perceived weakness or your disapproval of her positive attributes.

Instead of the story, you can also ask her questions, moving back and forth from present to future - even better if you anchor her positive thoughts to you. You can also do this physically, by having her follow you. Move further away each time. Can you fractionate over text? As part of face-to-face enslavement, yes, but it doesn't work on its own. It is good when you don't know her that well and are still in the intrigue/rapport stages. If you're already with her - for example, you're looking to enslave your wife, then you want to deepen the attraction using implanted commands.

You'll need to send two texts to make sure that the command slips by and that she focuses on the second part of the message, which is the part that entices her. The command is implanted into her subconscious through the first one. As always, especially when you're expressing disapproval, you must do it confidently. She needs to chase you, not the other way around.

Black Rose sequence

This is the final step in the IRAE process and the enslavement here is complete. Your target's identity is erased, to be replaced by one that submits to you emotionally. Remember, we're not talking about physical enslavement! This is a form of fractionation, where the rollercoaster ride goes very high and very low. You're using hypnosis to get her so absorbed by the character you've created that her experience with you is emotionally intense. You'll have her feel these highs and lows in her body and she'll be shifting back and forth from pleasure to pain. This induces a trance, during which you can introduce a more submissive identity.

It's easier to get her in the right frame of mind if you tell her to pretend to be hypnotized. The mind has a hard time role-playing, so this will help her slip into the trance you're looking to induce. Giver her positive affirmations (not about her body, but about some other characteristics, so self-doubt doesn't rise up). Then, create a vivid future world with her, making sure you hit all of the senses. If you want to implant sex, for example, you could vividly create a future projection of the two of you in a romantic entanglement. You don't want to be crude or vulgar at this stage. Give her a little twist at the end - "Of course that wouldn't happen!" You can use this to get rid of a boyfriend too - imagine the dream lover whose traits are similar to yours and her current lover will fall well short.

The future projection is key for her to develop that emotional attachment to you and your imagined future together.

Chapter Summary

- Other covert tactics use the power of mind control to have and dominate the woman you want.
- The Shogun method uses a four-step process and sequences within those steps to control the woman you desire.

In the next chapter, we will focus on the secrets of successful female seductresses.

CHAPTER EIGHT:

Seductress Secrets of Seduction

Although men and women want similar things from life, the tricks a seductress uses are a bit different from her male counterparts. As I discussed earlier in the paradox of seduction, both men and women want to be seduced. They want to feel the thrill of attention and experience the charm and enticement used in seduction.

The ambiguities of seduction

Men have long used their physical power and status to dominate women and other men. Yet, it's not only men who take power from others and use it to their advantage. As male seducers tend to be calm and confident, women dress and use make-up seductively to attract a potential mate. Both women and men are at the mercy of their "lizard" brains - the parts that we inherited from our reptilian ancestors. This part of the brain is quite different from our rational, thinking human brains. Seduction appeals to the lizard brain and logic and reason are thrown by the wayside when we're being seduced. This is true for men as well as women. Society is designed to appeal to the rational, human parts of the brain. But, underneath we're animals that yearn to return to the wild!

Introduction to men's psychology

One simple seduction trick that works on almost everyone: find the emotion that most entices your target and provide plenty of it! If you're dating a shrink, they like to feel insightful. So, make them feel that their insights are both welcome and amazing. Men say they value honesty in their partners. If you've had cosmetic procedures, like a boob job or facelift, men wonder if you're being dishonest about other issues, too.

Here's a trick you might not have thought of if you desire an intelligent man: look at his body hair. High intelligence in men is correlated with an abundance of body hair.[18] Not exactly an expected insight!

Although men and women are more alike than they are different, some specific differences relate to how you should approach men you intend to seduce. The part of the brain that makes people territorial is larger in men than in women. That's why they can become violent when they perceive a threat in either their physical or relationship territory. So is the amygdala, which is a part of the lizard brain that is intimately involved in the fight-or-flight response, but also sexual desire.

Finally, the area of the brain that's devoted to sexual pursuit is also much larger in men than it is in women. Boys begin manufacturing gobs of testosterone once they hit their teens - 20 times the amount of their female peers - which means they're hormonally and mentally very interested in sex. It's also why they glaze over at the sight of female breasts - the visual circuits in their brains are constantly searching for fertile partners.[19] This doesn't mean that he's constantly thinking about the pair he just got a good look at. The attention comes and then dissipates. Then, he'll start thinking about

---

[18] https://www.dailymail.co.uk/femail/article-426320/The-psychology-seduction.html

[19] http://edition.cnn.com/2010/OPINION/03/23/brizendine.male.brain/index.html

other things, like what's for dinner. Don't misunderstand his poker face, though. His emotional reactions are as strong and sometimes even stronger than a woman's - he just hides his better.

Maybe because his visual circuits are stronger, men don't need to have a lot of context or relationship in order to be aroused. Mainly, they just need to see the body parts they want to see and they're good to go.[20] That's why dressing seductively and putting on suggestive make-up works so well - men are visual creatures in a way that women are not. Men don't do well with ambiguity in a hierarchy. Their brains prefer a clear chain of command and the military can actually help curb aggressive behavior, simply by reducing this anxiety.[21]

Men are also often happy with a number of sexual partners - novelty is attractive to all brains and men don't have the same social pressure about being slut-shamed. Some of them are very attuned to women who are lonely or lacking something in their lives. They may be upfront about their intentions and will assume that women are looking for sex, too. Having sex can be a transcendent experience.

"It is the ecstasy of wanting and being wanted." - Anonymous

If you're a woman interested in older men, know that they go through a time of life called andropause. If his wife has had kids, his testosterone level dropped while she was pregnant. During andropause, he actually starts manufacturing more estrogen. If his testosterone gets too low, he'll be grouchy and irritable and may need to supplement and get more exercise. He might be a great grandfather if he's got a lot of the bonding hormone oxytocin sloshing around. He could be more affectionate with his grandkids than he ever was with his own. Older men get very lonely after widowhood or divorce and you might just be the right person to get him socializing again.

---

[20] https://www.psychologytoday.com/us/blog/love-and-sex-in-the-digital-age/201506/what-turns-guys-understanding-male-sexual-desire
[21] https://www.livescience.com/14422-10-facts-male-brains.html

Women have more mirror neurons, which are the nerves that fire when they reflect on what someone else is doing. They're key to empathy, which is why women are often more emotionally attuned to their partners than men. When men spot an attractive potential partner, their brains release dopamine. This occurs whether they're partnered or not. The decision to make a move or not can be disastrous, depending on the circumstances, and yet men continue to do it. Why? Much of it comes down to higher testosterone levels. A man with lower testosterone is more suited to having a family and sticking to it. Research shows that men with higher amounts of testosterone tend to get married less often and when they do marry, they're more likely to cheat and/or get divorced.[22]

Beautiful women cause the man's larger amygdala to fire at approximately the same time that his decision-making center in the prefrontal cortex (part of the rational brain) checks out - not a good time for good decision-making! Strong visual circuits mean that gorgeous girls and porn activate dopamine much more for men than they do for women. Women have better access to the right hemisphere of the brain, which is good and bad for relationships. It tends to be more negative, which is partially why women get depressed more often than men. But they're also good at seeing the overall, big picture, which leads to women dumping men more often than the other way around. They're more negative but can also see when something's not working out faster.

Body language and nonverbal cues

Communication isn't expressed mostly in words, as many of us often think. Over half the message is delivered nonverbally, including gestures, posture, and facial movements. In fact, words are less than 10 percent of communication![23] Many aspects of body language are the

---

[22] https://www.menshealth.com/sex-women/a19516672/understanding-sex-and-the-brain/

[23] https://sexyconfidence.com/how-to-seduce-men-with-body-language/

same for men as they are for women. Standing up straight with shoulders thrown back exudes confidence - standing with arms crossed denotes defensiveness.

Signs of seduction include prolonged eye contact. Making eye contact shows interest in the other person. Looking a hint too long and then slowly looking away can be quite erotic. You might also slowly and obviously drop your gaze to his lips. Lick your lips, smile slyly, or use other similar facial expressions. Touching is also very suggestive when done right! And a positive, pleasant tone makes a big difference when you're seducing, compared to a harsh one.

Earlier, you learned about some of the tactics that men use to seduce women. These same cues can work for women trying to seduce men. For example, familiarity breeds interest. They have to notice you before they can be attracted to you. Walking back and forth near your target helps them get used to seeing you. Even bumping into them, especially if you're in a crowded scene, will achieve this goal as well. In addition, movement catches the eye. You might choose to drop something - maybe not your phone, which could break, but your keys or a napkin. This will also attract interest.

Another way to exploit the human brain's desire for novelty is to appear exotic. If you're a different culture or ethnicity, play it up. Emphasize your differences from the standard look. This will help you get noticed in the crowd and also appeal to those who like the exotic. You'll promise adventure just from your looks when you're not boring and/or the norm. Brains also love symmetry, so do your best to look symmetrical. The right clothing can really help with this.

Let them know that you welcome their approach. Particularly if you're shorter than he is, it can be very effective to duck your head a bit and then look up through your eyelashes. It's a bit like a little girl and makes you look innocent. He'll know you won't bite his head off if he starts talking to you!

When you're talking to your target, make a cute move, like lifting one shoulder and cocking your head. It works! Show a little vulnerability, which will particularly appeal to men who have rescuer fantasies. Touch your neck, which is a sign of weakness. Or your wrist, which is another point of weakness. Hold your right wrist with your left hand and you'll look approachable.

Reflect the movements he's making. Do you mirror someone you have no interest in? Of course not. He'll get the message. Use your posture to seduce him, too. When you hold your shoulders back and stand tall, it pushes out the breasts that (many) men love to look at. Give him a genuine smile that reaches your eyes, not the smile of a flight attendant or other service worker. Face him, especially (this is going to sound weird) with your belly button. Even if your head's turned away, most of your body is aimed in his direction, which tells him you're interested. Recall that movement draws attention and play with your hair. Twirl it, toss it back, and slowly put it up while you're in front of him and let his imagination run wild!

Toying with clothes can also be very sensual. Slipping your foot slowly and deliberately in and out of your shoe. Slowly and deliberately cross and recross your legs, playing with the pendant that dangles just above your breasts. Swing your hips. Lean toward him, which signals interest. You also want to stand or sit closer than strangers normally position themselves. Not too close, in the friends and family zone, but not so far that he can't tell you're drawing him in. You can turn your shoulder toward him, put the opposite hand on that shoulder, and lean your cheek on your hand - especially when you're making eye contact the whole time.

Maybe even more importantly, make sure you're wearing clothes and accessories that make YOU feel good! They'll help you feel more confident. Rather than worrying about tugging at your hem or that stupid button that keeps wanting to slide out of the buttonhole, you can focus on when you want to flash your brilliant smile or lick your lips suggestively. You can also stay in the moment of the seduction, doing what comes naturally and feels right that very second. This is the most enjoyable way to be with a man. You can read his reactions and ramp up what gets a positive reaction to lure him in.

Temptress mind games

Now you've mastered the art of using physical cues to mess with your target, it's time to start playing some mind games. Men are supposed to be the calm, rational, logical ones. Being unpredictable and irrational creates a powerful attraction for some men who like to be swept up in an emotional game. You can also stir him up by using mixed feelings, where you alternate between heat and distance. It's confusing, unpredictable, and probably novel for him, too.

Similarly, try mixed signals when you want to, well, mix it up. Push-pull is a good example of this game, but try some variations, too. Assume an angelic appearance but be naughty underneath. If you've got a baby face, wear serious clothes, like a business suit. Or, you can try wearing a white dress to pump up the innocent look, but make the dress and accessories VERY revealing. If you're wearing a business suit and look like you're no-nonsense, act submissive or have very innocent lingerie underneath.

Just as triangulation works with women, a woman can play this game with men. Incite jealousy by drawing him in, then flirting with another man. Get him emotionally hot and bothered.

Women are supposed to be either a Madonna or a whore, so…play both! He'll appreciate the confusion and not knowing which way is up and he'll love the tumble into bed. While you're making out, enjoy the lust and the pleasure sensations. Then stop and resist for a bit. This also plays into the unpredictability that men enjoy. You'll probably find that you enjoy it, too! You're lost in the urge…but then you have to fight your desire…which you'll eventually succumb to anyway. But he doesn't know that and you'll create some real suspense for him. Short bursts of extreme sexual action combined with withdrawal will leave him both dazed and dying for more. Whirlwind sexual passion is exactly what he wants and he wants more of it. So, of course, you can't give it to him again right away - that's just too boring and predictable. Egg him on in weird places, like waiting in line at the store, where you can brush his crotch. When you're dining with parents, give him a little footsie action.

Be dangerous - remember he's supposed to be logical, so a touch of craziness might just be what the seduction doctor ordered. Not full-on crazy, though! Enough that it's novel and unpredictable. Conversely, some men really dig a maternal act, so let a little regression creep in. Tuck him under the covers, kiss him on the forehead. This is a great way to hook a Player. Or, invert the regression so you're acting more youthful. Men love to revisit their youth, particularly older men who can be fatherly and still get sex, for them, this is a potent combo. Sugar daddies in particular fall for this one pretty easily. Don't be too much of a baby though, that's off-putting.

Use your words. It's true body language is more important in communication, but why not let your words really count? Don't be too vulgar or crude or swear: you still want to demonstrate that you're a high-quality woman. But you can be incredibly suggestive with your words, while using some of the body language techniques described in the last section. Touching and poking below the belt also works very well. You might "accidentally" brush against his chest or crotch, or brush him *with* your breasts or crotch. You can be more obvious about his crotch too, which deliberately asks him if he's man enough to come for you. He is. And if not, you're not interested anyway, are you?

If he's cheated or otherwise hurt you, guilt-trip him. Let him know how much he hurt you. This won't work with a narcissist, who doesn't care if he hurt you, or a sociopath, where the cruelty is the point.

Speaking of cruelty, you need to be careful with this last mind game. Violence and emotional abuse are not something you want to inflict on people. Having said that, sexual aggressiveness, violence, and attraction can be incredibly powerful when combined. Sex during a fight can be absolutely amazing and aggressiveness plus sex, dominating your man, will appeal to any latent masochistic tendencies he might have.

Triggering emotional attraction in men

In earlier chapters, I mentioned that seduction is a game of emotions. Although men believe themselves to be logical and rational, they can be swept away with emotions just as women can. In fact, you need him to set aside his thinking brain in order for him to be seduced. The human brain loves patterns and it loves recognizing patterns. The trick is to know which patterns unlock the emotions in men because some are different from the ones that work on women.

People feel good when they're making progress toward a goal. Often, the little gains end up being more pleasurable than the goal itself! That's why standard goal-setting suggests you should identify your big goals, but then make smaller ones so you can see progress as you go. With men, playing hard to get taps into this instinct for the chase and tiny achievements toward the ultimate goal of sex.

Imagine one little girl fleeing from a war-torn country - there's a point to this, I promise - with her little backpack, not knowing where she's going. You feel empathy for her plight, don't you? You want to help her. But when you imagine millions of people fleeing this country, not knowing where they're going, with only the worldly possessions they can carry, it's harder to empathize. In research, this is called compassion collapse and it happens because the human ability to empathize decreases when there's no meaningful way to help. This is why nonprofits will often feature one specific child or family in their calls for donations[24]. Men are naturally less empathetic than women in the first place. They want to make their woman happy,

---

[24] https://commitmentconnection.com/the-secret-to-understanding-what-triggers-attraction-in-men/

but that goal is too vague and they don't really know how to go about it. Unless you give them particular ways to make you happy and trigger his empathy, they'll drift off into not caring about you. Men like missions, so give him one. It doesn't have to be finding the Holy Grail, but something he can easily picture in his mind.

People's natural instinct is to do favors for others. We've been socialized to give and that's often what women do when trying to lure a particular man to them. But that's not the right way to truly develop a bond. Instead, ask him for a favor. Research shows that the human brain is more activated when giving a gift than when receiving it.[25] So ask him to give you something. It doesn't have to be an actual present - advice is better. Ask him for his help on a problem you're having at work, or maybe he can find out what new tires you should put on your car!

Men want relationships that fit who they are, in the way that they want to see themselves. If a man wants to see himself as a hero, he'll bond to the woman who allows him to be that hero. He needs to enjoy who he is when he's with you. Most men want to be the hero. That's how they've been socialized. Bond with him by telling him a story that reveals some needs of your own and helps him meet those needs. Now it feels right for him to be with you because you're feeding that need he has.

In addition to helping him be the version of himself that he's always wanted, there are ways to be emotionally attractive to men.

Be patient

We all fumble through this life having lost the instruction manual! Men like women who don't demand everything be done the right way the first time all the time. They also like someone who asks what they meant first before taking offense because they didn't phrase it correctly.

---

[25] https://www.huffpost.com/entry/how-to-scientifically-trigger-his-emotional-desire_b_59bab8b4e4b06b71800c3781

Remember, women have the upper hand in the language aspects of the brain.

Be a good listener

Contrary to popular opinion, men do like to talk. But it can be hard for them to have serious discussions. Let them express their full thought before jumping to conclusions.

Be self-confident

Don't spend too much time talking about your flaws, especially the physical ones. Let him see you as self-assured. That takes the burden off him to fulfill this need.

Be in the moment

Leave the past in the past. No one really enjoys listening to memories dredged up about bad ex-boyfriends...or even good ones! Enjoy the relationship you have in front of you. This tactic also helps him feel less insecure compared to your previous relationships.

Focus on the positive

Who likes a Debbie Downer? Not men, anyway. Give their ideas some time to ripen before you start criticizing or pointing out flaws.

Communicate honestly and openly

If there's a problem, let him know so he can fix it. Recall that men have less empathy than women, so they're going to be even worse at reading minds. He can't do it, so don't make him. Ask him about things to make sure that you understand his intentions, instead of assuming that you know what's going on in his head.

Be a secret-keeper

In a strong relationship, you'll be opening up to each other and revealing secrets that many other people don't know about you. Keep the secrets he tells you like you're a lockbox. No one in your family needs to know his vulnerabilities and weaknesses and don't throw them back in his face during an argument.

Appreciate the effort made

None of us are perfect. Building on patience, men like it when you also see that they've made a genuine effort (when they've made one, of course). They probably didn't get it right on the first try, but they tried, and they love it when you acknowledge that.

Hot buttons for the hero instinct

Now you know how important it is to make a man feel like a hero when you want some kind of relationship with him. If you're genuinely in distress, this might be pretty easy. But what if you're not? Fortunately, there are some methods to use to trigger it without a crisis in your own life. Even if you're a strong, independent woman, use his hero instinct to bond him with you.

We already discussed asking him for help or advice. Even little everyday things will trigger his desire to be a hero. You might already be an expert on fixing cars and toilets. So what? Let him lift a finger to help you. If you're having difficulty opening up a jar, ask him to do it. It's a tiny thing, but when you show you appreciate it, he will feel like the hero he wants to be.

Letting him be a man, with male hobbies and male decor, is also greatly appreciated. Men like the fact that you're feminine, but they don't necessarily want to be feminine themselves. If his place is messy, well, who cares. You're just enjoying spending time with him.

If you don't like the sports he watches, don't make him watch the Hallmark Mysteries & Movies channel with you instead.

Just like women, men don't like it when things come too easily. They like a bit of a challenge, which is another reason playing hard to get works so well with them. You can find other challenges for him and ways to earn your respect. Don't give it automatically - let him work for it. Have your man win you over by succeeding in the challenge you set for him.

The language of male desire

Emotional triggers are different for men and women and so is the language that gets you all hot and bothered. Make sure he's hearing the words that work for him, too. Some of them may seem a little silly to you, but you're triggering his affection for you so that you can bond more deeply - in language that works with the male brain. Tell him that you're his. This offers the loyalty he craves. You might also say you want only him, which will ease his anxiety about coming on too strong. Assure him that you're in it together, which will soothe any financial worries he might have.

As we've discussed, men are visual creatures and appealing to some of his physical characteristics in a way that makes him more secure will provide great rewards. You might ask him if it's getting bigger, which helps him put to rest all his insecurities about size. (And most men have this insecurity, even if they don't show it right away.) Or the perennial, "Have you been working out?" Women go to the gym, but men workout, so you're flattering his masculinity while soothing any physical appearance issues he might have. When you want to trigger that hero instinct, let him know he makes you feel safe.

Appreciate the things he does for you while showing your vulnerability. "When I met you I wasn't sure I deserved you, but you always know the right thing to say when I'm feeling down." Let him know that he excites you even when doing more mundane things, like hugging. This gives him the idea that underneath, you are always thinking and fantasizing about him.

And don't forget to tell him you love him!

Chapter Summary

- Men's brains are more visually oriented and bathed in testosterone, so they have different triggers, including the thrill of the chase and the visual pleasure of lingerie.
- Body language and nonverbal cues work very well on visually-oriented men to draw attention to yourself and deepen the attraction.
- Different mind games and emotional triggers, as well as different language, will bond men to you for as long as you wish.
- This is especially true when you trigger his hero instinct and allow him to be your hero, even in little ways.

In the next chapter, you will learn how to use seduction techniques outside a romantic or sexual relationship.

CHAPTER NINE:

Applied Seduction

So far, most of our discussion has been about romantic or sexual seduction. But seducing others at work, or even in your everyday life, can bring you great rewards. Obviously, you're going to approach your supervisor or other colleagues in a completely different way! But you can use some of the same techniques in a different way, with the same ultimate goal: to get what you want from other people.

Seduce your (nonsexual) way to a career boost

Let what you've learned about romantic seduction unlock the potential for more career opportunities.

Use a creative approach to get past the gatekeepers

You know you could get the business - or the job - if you could just get in to see the right people. But they're usually very busy and they've hired people to keep them from being bothered by every vendor or every job applicant. The gatekeepers could be the receptionist, the personal assistant, or even HR. They've heard the same opening lines a million times and they're tired of it. They'll shoot you down before you even have a chance.

If you hit them with something they weren't expecting, you can slide right past them before they even know what hit them. Even an interesting or creative story could work.

On LinkedIn, a social platform mostly for the business-to-business (B2B) crowd, I saw a post that talked about how a job applicant entered an office acting like a delivery guy and delivered a box of doughnuts along with their resume. They got right through the gatekeepers!

Don't be boring

The human brain's love for novelty isn't just for sexual partners. Our brains love anything new. Just as you can't bore a potential lover to death because they'll just take off, you can't bore a potential business partner to death either. Talk about something different. Do something different in the interview to get them to engage with you. Be fun and interesting, just as you would with a new seduction target.

Show social proof

Just as I recommended that you hit the club with tons of attractive people to show your magnetism, companies love to see that you've worked with other well-known companies. If you could make it there, you could make it anywhere: the Sinatra test.[26] For freelancers and consultants, social proof often shows up as testimonials or case studies.

You're the prize, so use some swagger

People like to see confidence and that doesn't change just because you're in the boardroom instead of the bedroom. Being needy and desperate turns off members of both sexes, whether you're trying to sell a product or yourself as the company's new hire. When you

---

[26] https://www.news.com.au/finance/work/seduction-tactics-to-boost-your-career/news-story/6fce129b118a03dfde4b68c4169ababf

interview, have the attitude that you're also interviewing them to make sure it's the right fit for you. Act like you've got so many companies chasing you, you can choose who you work with.

Just as when finding a new romantic partner, being chased by plenty of others may or may not be true. But it's good practice to act as if it is. Bring on that swagger. Don't tell them only what they want to hear or try too hard. That's a major turn-off!

Don't fall for their tests

Similarly, prospects, clients, and interviewers may push you to see how far they can go. They may lowball you on price or fees. If what they're offering doesn't work for you, make sure they know it. Don't be so desperate for the business that you're willing to incur a loss to work with them.

Be attractive so they come to you

You're cool, calm, and collected, luring them in rather than chasing them. Sound familiar? You also don't want to lower your price (see above) because the cost isn't what drives people to buy. If you drop your price, you're not more attractive, you're just less profitable.

"Be the flame, not the moth." - Casanova

Don't chase your customers or sales. Be so attractive that you're the flame and customers (or hiring managers) come to you instead.

Keep flirting after you close the deal

Continue to nurture your clients even after they've made the purchase. This will help you increase follow-on sales, as well as referrals. Keep the relationship going and you'll be a sales all-star instead of having to chase after the sale. Word of warning, however:

acting distant is not going to lure in your clients the way it lures in romantic partners!

Seduction in business, marketing, and sales

Give your (business) targets enough information about you and/or your business or product to tantalize them. Awaken their curiosity and playfulness, just as you would do for a romantic target. Use whatever kind of social charm you've got. For example, some people are witty, others are cute. Some play on their intelligence. Whatever comes naturally to you, use it.

People don't like to be sold to, so the trick is to sell them without selling them! This sounds hard, but the tactics of seduction help you do this. You can create events that don't seem like marketing tactics, though of course, they are. Even though men are more visually-oriented than women, pretty much all humans are visual. Make sure your marketing contains enough pictures to get your point across. I discussed in earlier chapters the fact that seduction is about filling a need, or a lack, that someone has. It works exactly the same way in sales. You develop a connection with your prospects and clients so that you understand what their needs are.

Most clients don't really need the widget or gadget or whatever service you're selling. What they need is validation from their supervisor. A way to get their jobs done faster, not for the sake of the job, but so they can go home earlier and spend time with their families. They're looking for a way to save money so they can allocate more budget to other projects, or look good in front of their superiors.

Another way to look at it is that customers like something to aspire to. Your product helps them be a better version of themselves. You just have to figure out what version they're looking for and target that. If you're a writer, your prospects don't need your words so much. They need someone else to take care of something that bewilders them or frees up time for them to work on their business. Selling vacuums?

Your prospect doesn't need a robot vacuum that has a 3-liter capacity. They need to find more time they can spend with their families. As you develop your relationship, you uncover these needs and then you position yourself as the perfect person with the perfect product or service to take care of this need. People don't buy based on logic and reason. They buy based on emotion, which is the basis of seduction, too.

Build emotional connections with your targets. You can ask them questions that skew them towards you and your product, as long as you ask in the right away. You can also prep the environment with music, scent, and visual appeal in order to sway them.

Remember that it takes time to build these relationships. When you go to the club, most of the time you can't jump directly from approaching a potential lover to having sex with them in a brief period of time. You need to let the attraction and comfort develop before you start closing the deal. Likewise, if you jump right from introducing yourself to a hard sell, your prospect will be turned off. Take the time to build the connection first instead of scaring them off. Sometimes it's just not going to work. The sale isn't going to happen. As long as you detach yourself from the results, you'll be fine. You're freed up to go attract the next prospect. If you are too attached to the outcome, every rejection is crushing.

When you're selling with seduction, you end up doing less work. You're not chasing down as many leads, but working with well-qualified ones who want to do business with you. Seducing your prospects can be more fun because it's about skill instead of brute-force numbers. Digital content is the bait you drop. Once you've created it you can dunk in lots of different pools to see which ones rise to it more often, without much more work on your part. Let the prospects qualify themselves and come to you. You can help them qualify themselves by letting them feel like they're a member of some elite club. Your product is not for everyone. In fact, it might be too powerful for some!

Shut off the phone when you're with your self-qualified prospects. Or any prospects, for that matter. Watching someone get distracted by their phone is a business boner-killer, too. Listen to what they have to say. Everyone likes undivided attention! Make it about them, not you (or your quota). Enjoy the journey. If you're using the seductive methods correctly, you'll probably find the seduction is better than the close! This works best if you genuinely believe in the product or service that you're selling. If you don't, it's very hard to get into the mindset that you're doing your prospects and clients a favor by giving them the opportunity to purchase. Visualize your success as part of having the right mindset.

See yourself overcoming objections, without coming across as desperate. Picture yourself in conversation and getting the information that you need to know to solve their problem. The mind can't tell the difference between a real scene and an imaginary one, so give it successful scenes. Make sure your visualization includes emotions and other senses too, so that you're having a complete experience. You can also visualize what life is like for your prospects, by stepping into their shoes and seeing the world from their perspective instead of yours. When you're selling, provide a rich fantasy for your clients as to what their life looks like when you've solved their problem. Shift their focus on to you with grabby headlines, or some drama. Confuse them and use plenty of humor, as long as you're not acting goofy.

Your clients and prospects need to have the right frame of mind and be ready to buy when you actually start selling. You can help this process along by taking them on a mental journey, usually with a story, that makes them think they do have a need for whatever you're selling.

You're in charge and you display that with your self-assurance, without being a bully or ordering people around. As noted before, people like to be led. Be the leader that gets them to believe it's their idea to buy, not yours! You can also use the "guru phenomenon" to increase sales. Sometimes a product doesn't take off until a guru, influencer, or expert has signed off on it. If you don't have a guru handy, you can just quote an authority figure in the field. Let the prospect's imagination take off from there. Want to improve even more on that idea? You, too, can become a guru, or expert on the subject. Position yourself that you have the edge on whatever your clients are looking for. Help them shift their perception of you. You can add in tips and advice to your sales copy.

When you're negotiating, you want to appear a little mysterious. Like you have a card you haven't played...because you don't need to. You're not desperate for a good outcome, because you're too confident for that. Your negotiation partner has to come to you and impress upon you how good their solution is for you. Again, this should sound pretty familiar to you by now!

To be clear, you're not trying to use or manipulate the other side. You're just confident and empowered, which makes you seductive in business. Don't make yourself too available, or rush to let prospects know everything about you. Maintaining a little bit of an air of exclusivity is attractive. Do you want to pitch someone in the media? Maybe you're looking for more eyes on your product or service. Here's another good place to practice your seduction techniques. Journalists are people, too! Nail your intro and don't make it too long. Be concise enough that your message is clear. Would you send out a mass email to all the people you know when you're searching for a date? That would never work, and it doesn't work on media contacts either. Send personalized messages, tailored to your target. Make sure that you're aiming at the right target. If your message is about consumer products, don't send it to the reporter who covers the foreign news beat.

Follow up and not in a creepy way. Sometimes emails get buried or the journalists themselves are buried under mountains of work. If you don't hear back, try them again. But don't stand outside their (online) door with your finger on the doorbell either.

Once your target has succumbed...keep flirting! Nurture the relationship, just as you do with other business contacts.

All this can be broken down into three major categories. When you're using seductive selling and marketing, you:

1. Entice them

Your creativity, humor, and confidence are all designed to make prospects and clients come to you. To chase you and your product. To feel that it's designed just for them and their needs.

2. Enrich them

Create a lasting bond with them by connecting, listening, and discovering what their needs are.

3. Enable them

Let them imagine what a comfortable and less costly life they'll lead with you guiding them! Painting the rich fantasy future seduces them into believing that you're the answer.

Everyday seduction

By being able to charm people, you can entice them into giving you what you want. As long as it's in their power to do so! There are plenty of arenas outside business and bed where a little seduction goes a long way.

Desire

First, you have to be clear about what it is you want. When you don't know, you can't figure out the steps to get there, much less entice anyone into giving something to you! They must understand what you're asking for in order to provide it. Suppose you go out to the club, but you're not entirely sure why you're there. Is it to have fun with your friends? Find a man to have sex with? Find a woman to start a relationship with? Depending on your goal for the evening, you'll do things very differently. You don't approach friends the same way you open up to a potential lover.

Once you've figured out what you want, you'll know what language to use and what you need to ask for or allow people to give you. You'll go into a situation knowing what you need to do in order to get what you desire.

Self-confidence

By now you've recognized that seduction has a lot to do with leading other people. You may not always want to make it clear that you're the one in charge because some people need to believe that they're the ones in charge. This doesn't bother you…because you know they're wrong! In order to be led, however, people need to believe in the leader. If they don't, they will simply refuse to follow. Which means you need to act and speak like the leader you are. This is much easier when you radiate self-assurance. It's an invitation to the people who want to follow because it signals to them that here's someone who knows what they're doing! This is especially true for men, who need clear social hierarchies to feel comfortable.

Non-verbal communication

The body tells most of the story, so make sure that you know how to use it. Even when you're not feeling particularly confident, you can stand in confident poses. When it comes to confidence, "fake it 'til you make it" actually works. Stand up straight with shoulders back, this is a confident pose, as is standing with your legs spread wide, taking up the room that you deserve. Hold your head high and make direct eye contact. It's people without self-confidence that look at their feet, the door, anywhere but the face of the person they're speaking with.

You can also express what you want and don't want without using words. Using your arms crossed in front of you as a shield, leaning away from someone who's in your space, and other similar poses let people know they're not welcome. By the same token, making eye contact, smiling, and putting your phone away, all signal positive intentions toward your target.

Arousal

In order to do as you'd like, your target needs to feel an emotional pull towards you, strong enough to push past any kind of inertia. Once you've discovered their need and lured it out of them, they'll want to do as you wish. Seduction is a way to understand what the other person wants. It's only after you've satisfied their emotional need, whatever it is, that you can entice them to do what you want them to do.

Chapter Summary

- Seduction isn't just for sex.
- Similar seductive methods taught earlier can help you boost your career without sex.
- Business, marketing, and sales are all more effective when you use seductive techniques, such as discovering their emotional needs and filling them.
- There are many times in daily life when seducing other people gets you what you want.

In the next chapter, you will learn about using seduction to find your way through life.

CHAPTER TEN:

Using Principles of Seduction to Navigate Through Life

Now you have a good understanding of seduction and how to use it to find business and romantic partners. But you can also use it to forge a path through life. You don't have to be manipulative or deceitful, but you can be seductive. You can think of seduction as basically communication, leadership, or leveraging your knowledge of human nature.

The lost art of seduction

Another way to look at seduction is that it's based on surprise. The novelty our brains crave is sated by someone who keeps surprising us. This is how you hook a romantic partner for life: you continually surprise them. It's when people get bored or feel that they're in a rut that the thought of cheating is likely to rear its ugly head. But if your partner doesn't know what's going to happen next? They'll stick around just to find out!

You can't use the element of surprise all the time, but often enough to spice things up. It works very well too when you're starting to lure in your target. They'll love the fact that you're spontaneous and unpredictable. Boring is not attractive, or enticing, or alluring. The more you can spice things up and change them around, the more they'll be thinking about you. It's also the habit of getting into someone's head. We've lost that ability, as we spend more and more time in front of screens and passively accepting the entertainment that some company's algorithm provides. In order to seduce someone, you must observe them closely. Notice the details that give them away. Find the soft spot underneath your target's exterior.

Whether you're looking for a customer or a lover, you'll see the best rewards when you're able to uncover their emotional needs. Remember that seduction is about emotion and that doesn't change whether you're selling a vacuum or yourself as a sexual partner. What needs does your target have that are unmet? You'll need to pay attention to what they say (and don't say) and ask them questions. See how they respond to different stories. Your phone isn't going to tell you that and neither is your video game or social media feed or laptop screen. The only person who can tell you about your target is your target themselves. They might spill it out all upfront, or you might need to tease and entice it out of them.

Power in seduction

In civilized society, we don't usually demonstrate (or take) power by physical force. We have to do it indirectly, which often involves deception. People are pretty gullible when it comes to appearances. This is why acting as if you're confident works so well. You seem like you're confident and so people believe you are.

Mastery

To master something, there are a couple of major requirements. One is that you practice the thing consistently over time. You're always working on it and always trying to improve. The second requirement is that you love it! There's no way you're going to be able to put in the hours over time if you don't love it. There's a lot of repetition, especially of the basics when you're first beginning. You have to learn all the rules and processes. Usually, you're starting on the bottom floor, working your way up as you go. None of this is sustainable or even bearable if you don't love it. You may already have a pretty good idea of what you love. But what if you don't? You have to try lots of things, in that case, to find something. Don't get discouraged if it doesn't happen right away. You might need to expand your search parameters if you keep trying things with no results.

Once you find it, you'll need to make sure you're learning and acquiring skills to go with it. Centuries ago, in Europe (and still today in some European countries), you'd apprentice yourself to an existing master and have them teach you the ropes. These days, the apprenticeship could be in the form of a job. When you're trying to master something, you may not want to take the job with the highest salary on offer. Apprenticeships were usually pretty menial, at least to start. You want to find the job that will promote the most learning for you. Back then, they also didn't have the distractions of the internet, as we do. You'll never master anything if you spend your time on the internet. Just as you need to put the phone down to focus on your target in seduction, put it down when you're trying to master a skill. You need to practice it yourself, not watch endless videos about it or fall down the rabbit hole with tangential topics.

Learning mastery is also learning to avoid or tune out distractions. Once you have the basics down or finished your apprenticeship, you've got to test and experiment. What techniques work for you and which don't? Can you bring any other life experience to shed light on the problem? In other words, you've got to challenge yourself to stay in mastery. If you allow yourself to stop learning and stagnate, you'll lose your grip. Learn the rules so you can break them and find out which ones should stay broken.

Benefits of learning how to seduce

One major advantage of learning how to seduce is that those who do can also learn how to detach from the outcome. The game doesn't work every time. More importantly, when you're so attached to the results, you'll often come across as desperate and needy. But when you can let go of the outcome and focus on the process, you'll be calm and cool without even having to think about it. If you don't get the result you wanted, you'll just try again at another time. You've learned to deal with rejection. Some people never get it and they're crushed every time! But you know it happens and you know that you can bounce right back up. You don't spend a lot of time anticipating it because you know you'll get rejected some of the time. Big deal. Just move on to the next target and don't take it personally. When you know it's just part of the game, it's easier to handle.

Most people who have mastered seduction also end up with fewer regrets because at least they tried! They don't subject themselves to a lot of "if only" and "I wish I'd approached that person" because they went ahead and gave it a shot.

"You miss 100% of the shots you don't take." - Wayne Gretzky

Recent research has shown that when people are on their deathbeds, they don't tend to regret what they actually did. Their regrets are for what they didn't do: like spend more time with other people. If you're out there on a regular basis talking to other people, you won't regret it later. Will you have bad days? Yes. Will there be days full of rejection? Yes. But that doesn't mean that overall you'll do worse than if you'd never been out there. You've learned about how important a positive mindset is. When the negative thoughts come, you just shake them off. Otherwise, you'll be spending too much time in your head instead of out there approaching and opening.

When you come across someone you want to seduce, or even just make them feel important for whatever reason, you know how to listen actively. By now, you're observing details and trying to understand what's going on in the other person's head. You're not listening just to find out when the person will stop speaking so you can jump in with your opinion! Engaging in a conversation can bring you unexpected dividends. There are some days when you just don't want to go out.

Maybe a rejection really did sting or you're kind of tired or whatever. You also know that you need to get out there and practice consistently, so you make sure you go out, even when you're not feeling it. Showing up is half the battle! You've now trained yourself to get out there, whether or not you particularly want to. You can say that you're disciplined and consistent as a result of this practice. Rather than feeling sorry for yourself, you get up and go. It's hard to stay depressed and blue when you're out having an exciting time!

Get what you want in life with these key principles of seduction

You may not call yourself a pick-up artist, but you've got some serious seduction techniques under your belt at this point. Seduction isn't a hobby, though. It's not just about learning how to have sex with someone you really want to have sex with or to get the job you want. It's a fundamental life skill that you need to have in your toolbox. Seduction helps you find happiness because you're able to go out into the world and choose your romantic partner, friends, and other people to be around who support you. Choosing who you spend time with means that you don't settle for whoever happens to be around you, but someone who is truly compatible with you. Don't let doubts and self-limiting beliefs hold you back from getting what you want, or putting these principles and techniques into daily practice in your life. Social seduction skills are learned; just as other skills are. And just like other skills, the more you practice, the more you improve!

The key to navigating your way through the world is that you're much more likely to get what you want when people like you. Being likable is crucial, or else you'll find life very difficult. Fortunately, you can use the principles of seduction to get people to like you, even if you don't necessarily want to lure them to bed or sell them something. Just going out to a restaurant can be better when the wait staff likes you! It's still about finding that unmet need in the other person and filling it in a way they've never experienced before. Are you unhappy because you feel like the world isn't giving you what you want? Perhaps a pay raise, a date, love, companionship? Turns out you need to give to the world before it gives to you.

"Life is a seduction." - Raj Persaud

Instead of being focused on your own unmet needs, find out about someone else's, especially their key frustrations. Use small talk in a specific way to find out what drives the other person and what they need. Once you've given to the world in the form of meeting the needs of one person, you'll find that the world starts giving back - the partner you want, the friends you want. It's also important to remember that there isn't one way to be seductive. Whatever your natural strengths might be - wit, humor, intelligence - use them to charm others into getting what you want. It's not necessarily about being gorgeous. You can be, sure, but you don't have to be to seduce other people. Have you ever seen someone who seems to have eager admirers at their feet wherever they go, but they're not even good looking? They've learned the skills of seduction, so they don't need to be good-looking. One interesting experiment showed how seduction works. Groups of students were sent on dates. One group was told to agree with everything the date said. One was told to disagree with everything. The third group was told to disagree with everything during the first half of the date and then agree with everything in the second half. Afterward, the dates rated how attractive they found the students.

As you might expect, the first group was moderately attractive and the second group was rated as hideous! But the third group was found most attractive of all. Having read the previous parts of this book, this might not surprise you at all. The dates thought the third-group students needed a little time to warm up to them and that they had warmed the students up. In other words, that they had done the seducing. Casanova (reportedly) found an attractive actress in a bar who had a lisp and couldn't pronounce her Rs properly. Did he offer to send her to elocution lessons? Did he tell her to go see someone he knew who had experience with the problem and could work with her? No. He went home and wrote a play that had no Rs in it. Once complete, he returned to the bar and presented it to her. Seduction complete! This was probably the first time anyone had actually written a play for her, much less one that was tailored to the issue that she had. He didn't tell her that she needed fixing or that he was interested in her. She had to get her problem fixed first. So, he wrote the play.

How many times do we inadvertently indicate that the other person needs fixing? We'd probably think we were helping the actress if we offered her elocution lessons. But the play was sexy. Its message of, "Don't change a thing! You are perfect the way you are!" is incredibly sexy. And, of course, she was seduced by it. She didn't really need elocution lessons. She needed a play that wouldn't feature her speech impediment. That's the need that Casanova met, in a way no one ever had before.

You can think of relationships as having three phases: attraction, interest, and maintenance. In a long-term relationship, you'll continue that cycle many times, or else interest can fall off a cliff or people get bored. This is true for romantic or sexual relationships. But it's also true for many other relationships you have in your life: with customers, with friends, and many others. Take these principles and psychological techniques and use them to improve your life. Is it a game? Maybe. But others are certainly playing it, so you're going to have a hard time if you refuse. Give before you expect to receive - that's the way it works best for you to ultimately achieve your goals and get what you want in life.

Chapter Summary

- Seduction is almost a lost art because not enough people pay attention to the human being in front of them, being distracted with their own needs and electronic gadgets.
- You need to be able to seduce people to get what you want, including power.

- Mastery of seduction requires time and persistent practice and there are side benefits to this practice, as well.
- Seduction is a life skill you need to learn to survive, not just a hobby or way to have more sex.

CONCLUSION

Seduction is both an art and a science. It builds on fundamental knowledge that we have about how the human brain works, including the differences between male and female brains. This is important when we talk about sexual seduction! But it's also an art, in regards to how you use verbal and nonverbal communication to attract your targets and lure them in. Although in recent years, "pick-up artist" (PUA) groups have become known for their attempts to teach men how to pick up women, in reality, seduction communities have been around for a long time. Some are fortunate enough to be mentored by someone who knows how to play the game, but not all are.

Seduction has been popularly thought of to be the province of people who are strong in one or more characteristics of what's known as the Dark Triad: narcissism, Machiavellianism, and psychopathy. Research actually shows that people who are moderate in one or more of these traits can actually be very successful in business and other aspects of life. There's a lot of debate about whether seduction is moral. Certainly, to those who think of seduction as a game for men to have sex with women and then leave them, it looks immoral, or unethical, at the least. But popular stereotypes don't tell the whole story. A seducer gets to know their target so that they can identify their unmet need. This may mean that their target is showered with attention, which they might not be getting enough of elsewhere. A key technique in seduction is getting into another person's head and seeing the world as they do - stepping into their shoes. Granted, this is with the ultimate goal of getting what the seducer wants. But, it still doesn't sound very narcissistic, does it? Learning what makes the other person tick and surprising them with little gifts (not necessarily monetary) is another seduction technique that benefits the other person, too.

For those who may still think seduction is immoral, consider that it's an important skill for everyone to learn. To get what you want from the world, first, you need to give. Find the other person's unmet need and then fulfill it in a way they've never seen before. You also need to be likable to attract the right people to you. You can learn to seduce others into liking you.

Knowing what you want from the world helps you to choose partners: romantic, business, or even just friends who bring out the best in you and support you. When you don't learn the skills of seduction, you'll end up with whoever's near you and they may or may not be the most compatible. It's not about having a hobby, it's about survival. To lead the life you want to lead, you'll need to seduce other people in one way or another. Seduction is different from manipulation, where your intentions are concealed from the target. For example, men sometimes manipulate women into bed by having them believe they're interested in a romantic relationship when all they want is sex. Both sexes can seduce, however - it's not limited to just one gender.

Some seduction techniques are different depending on whether you're seducing a man or a woman. Men place more emphasis on the visual and they can reliably be enticed to do a woman's bidding if she triggers his hero instinct. Women often respond well to fantasies that are rich in detail, as well as witty wordplay.

There are plenty of seducer archetypes - the Rake, the Siren, the Coquette. There are also plenty of victims out there! These are sometimes those who have an unmet need, whose reality is so dull that anyone even slightly interesting is like a breath of fresh air. Anyone feeling like they're in a rut, in any kind of way, is a target for seducing. Many seduction techniques are universal, not restricted to one gender or one type of target. They may not only be used to entice a sexual prospect, but business and sales, as well. Human beings love novelty, so surprises or doing something different will usually get the attention you want. We also have unmet needs and a person who promises to fulfill those needs will be very well received. Most people want to be led, so it's crucial for the seducer to be confident and self-assured, not thrown by any tests or disagreements their targets might try to raise as an obstacle.

Humans tend to like a bit of a challenge. We don't necessarily want everything handed to us on a silver platter. A very effective technique, whether you're seducing a sexual target or a prospective client, is to let them come to you. Naturally, you'll need them to be attracted and interested in you and/or your product for this to work, but you don't want to chase them down. Needy and desperate is a turn-off, so create a little distance. You know how great you are (or at least you're projecting it to them), so eventually, they'll come to you. Seduction is not logical and it also may not have anything to do with how physically attractive you are. Most people have a strength that they can use to charm others. For some, it is being beautiful or handsome, but for others, it might be wit or humor. If you've ever seen someone with tons of rabid fans who isn't conventionally attractive, they're using some other strength that comes naturally to them.

You don't have to sleep your way to the top, though you can certainly seduce your way there! If you're a salesperson, you want your prospect hungry for your product. When they believe that they need it and that it's the answer to all their problems, you don't even have to sell them. Remember not to be too available! You'll stir up that need, show them that you're the one who can meet that need, and let them rush to you instead of the other way around.

When you're in business, no matter how you feel about the PUA community, one thing that they teach is very important. Seduction is a process: attraction - comfort - seduction, and trying to adopt these phases out of order results in failure. You won't get customers dying to work with you (or women to sleep with you) if you don't attract them first. You can't seduce them until they've built a comfort level with you. You can end up doing less work because you're making fewer cold calls and allowing the prospects to qualify themselves.

There are a number of ways to do this, but it's important that the phases be respected, in business and in bed. If you're trying to sell the instant you meet people, it's not going to work and will lead only to frustration. You need to put in some time with them first before you start trying to close the deal. Time is important in seduction. Not just taking what's needed for the process, but also recognizing that it will take time for you to master these skills. You need to practice them on a consistent basis in order to reach mastery. If you're working on seducing women, you need to talk to one a day or work on your game every day. If you're working on seducing someone in business, you need to be in contact on a regular basis so you can figure out that need and keep flirting after you close it.

I promised to teach you what you need to know about seduction - what it is, how it's been used, and how people currently use it. I've also given you techniques that you can learn and use in real life to get what you want and that's really what seduction is all about. If there's only one thing you take away from this book, it should be this: seduction is a necessary skill that you can learn if you practice consistently. Some people are born knowing how to entice and allure, but many of us aren't. Fortunately, it's something you can learn. If you work on it on a regular basis, you'll improve. It doesn't matter what you look like or how much money you have, as long as you learn and use these methods of seduction.

RESOURCES

About-Secrets. (2013, June 30). Seduction marketing. Retrieved February 19, 2020, from https://www.slideshare.net/mfr786/seduction-marketing

Acton, F. (2020, January 6). Fractionation Texting. Retrieved February 17, 2020, from https://fractionation.net/fractionation-texting/

A-hole Game: Day 1. (2009, January 12). Retrieved February 16, 2020, from https://web.archive.org/web/20140711073602/http:/heartiste.wordpress.com/2009/01/12/a-hole-game-day-1/

Amante, C. (n.d.-a). How to Use Social Proof to Get Girls | Girls Chase. Retrieved February 17, 2020, from https://www.girlschase.com/content/how-use-social-proof-get-girls

Amante, C. (n.d.-b). Tactics Tuesdays: Deconstructing the PUA Neg | Girls Chase. Retrieved February 17, 2020, from https://www.girlschase.com/content/tactics-tuesdays-deconstructing-pua-neg

Anonymous. (2004, June 27). Some of my best friends are women. Retrieved February 18, 2020, from https://www.theguardian.com/world/2004/jun/27/gender.menshealth3

Avery. (2018, September 7). Kino Escalation: How To Attract Women With Physical Touch -. Retrieved February 17, 2020, from https://redpilltheory.com/2018/09/06/kino-escalation-how-to-attract-women-with-physical-touch/

Barbe, O. (2004, November 5). Sex on the Brain. Retrieved February 18, 2020, from https://www.menshealth.com/sex-women/a19516672/understanding-sex-and-the-brain/

Barking Up the Wrong Tree. (n.d.). Seduction, Power and Mastery: 3 Lessons From History's Greatest Minds. Retrieved February 20, 2020, from https://www.bakadesuyo.com/2014/02/seduction-power-mastery/

BBC. (n.d.). Unpacking the Psychology of Seduction. Retrieved February 20, 2020, from https://www.bbc.com/reel/video/p07l3r3q/unpacking-the-psychology-of-seduction

Bergreen, L. (2017, July 26). 10 Seduction Tips and Tricks from Casanova Himself. Retrieved February 16, 2020, from https://www.tipsonlifeandlove.com/love-and-relationships/10-seduction-tips-and-tricks-from-casanova

Best PUA Training. (2018, May 3). Kino Escalation - Early, Mid Set Kino and Kiss Closing. Retrieved February 17, 2020, from http://www.bestpuatraining.com/kino-escalation

Bey, B. A. (2018, October 29). Here's Why Pitching is a Lot Like Seduction. Retrieved February 19, 2020, from https://www.mediabistro.com/climb-the-ladder/skills-expertise/heres-why-pitching-is-a-lot-like-seduction/

BigEyeUg3. (2017, June 6). 4 Signs you are too easily seduced. Retrieved February 10, 2020, from https://bigeye.ug/4-signs-you-are-too-easily-seduced/

Black Rose - Free Download PDF. (n.d.). Retrieved February 17, 2020, from https://kupdf.net/download/black-rose_58e52d47dc0d609438da97f1_pdf

Brandstory. (2016, September 3). The art of seduction – how to get customers to want you. Retrieved February 19, 2020, from http://www.brandstoryonline.com/seduction/

Britannica. (n.d.). Seduction. Retrieved February 15, 2020, from https://www.britannica.com/topic/seductio

Brizendine, L. (2010, March 25). Love, sex and the male brain - CNN.com. Retrieved February 18, 2020, from http://edition.cnn.com/2010/OPINION/03/23/brizendine.male.brain/index.html

Broucaret, F. (2014, December 23). Seduction: 10 Gestures and What They Reveal. Retrieved February 18, 2020, from https://www.mariefranceasia.com/lifelove/decoding/les-10-gestes-seduction-du-desir-59008.html#item=1

Buffalmano, L. (2019, November 2). How to Mind Fuck a Guy: The Ultimate Guide (With Examples). Retrieved February 18, 2020, from https://thepowermoves.com/make-him-crazy-about-you/

Burras, J. (n.d.). Power: Domination or Seduction. Retrieved February 18, 2020, from http://www.jonburras.com/pdfs/Power-Domination-or-Seduction.pdf

Calo, C. (n.d.). Switching From Logical to Social: The Art of Seduction. Retrieved February 7, 2020, from https://www.waytoosocial.com/the-art-of-seduction-blog/

Carter, G. L., Campbell, A., & Muncer, S. (2013, June 12). The Dark Triad Personality: Attractiveness to Women. Retrieved February 7, 2020, from https://scottbarrykaufman.com/wp-content/uploads/2013/09/The-Dark-Triad-Personality.pdf

Chamorro-Premuzic, T. (2015, November 4). Why Bad Guys Win at Work. Retrieved February 8, 2020, from https://hbr.org/2015/11/why-bad-guys-win-at-work

Coast, M. (2019a, November 4). 3 Ways to Trigger The Hero Instinct in Your Man. Retrieved February 18, 2020, from https://commitmentconnection.com/3-ways-to-trigger-the-hero-instinct-in-your-man/

Coast, M. (2019b, November 4). The Secret to Understanding What Triggers Emotional Attraction in Men. Retrieved February 18, 2020, from https://commitmentconnection.com/the-secret-to-understanding-what-triggers-attraction-in-men/

Cool Communicator. (2019, November 12). Social Seduction, Creating Space and Anticipation. Retrieved February 7, 2020, from https://coolcommunicator.com/social-seduction-creating-space-anticipation/

Cowie, A. (2017, May 22). The Enchanted Sex-Word of Scotland's Secret Seduction Society. Retrieved February 8, 2020, from https://www.ancient-origins.net/history/enchanted-sex-word-scotland-s-secret-seduction-society-008114

Cross, E. (2020, January 15). Obsession Phrases Review: What Makes Him Truly Obsessed With You? Retrieved February 18, 2020, from https://www.lovemakingexperts.com/obsession-phrases-review/

Definitions.net. (n.d.). What Does Seduction Mean? Retrieved from https://www.definitions.net/definition/seduction

Dictionary.com. (n.d.). Seduce. Retrieved from https://www.dictionary.com/browse/seduce

Drapkin, J. (2005, May 1). Hpw to Seduce a Lover. Retrieved February 18, 2020, from https://www.psychologytoday.com/us/articles/200505/how-seduce-lover

Edwards, D. (n.d.). Seduction or abuse? Is seducing someone ethical or is it manipulation? Retrieved February 15, 2020, from https://steemit.com/ethics/@dana-edwards/seduction-or-abuse-is-seducing-someone-ethical-or-is-it-manipulation

Eliason, N. (n.d.). The Art of Seduction by Robert Greene: Summary, Notes, and Lessons. Retrieved February 15, 2020, from https://www.nateliason.com/notes/art-seduction-robert-greene

Emory University. (2004, March 16). Study Finds Male And Female Brains Respond Differently To Visual Stimuli. Retrieved February 18, 2020, from https://www.sciencedaily.com/releases/2004/03/040316072953.htm

Essays Writers. (n.d.). Persuasion, Manipulation and Seduction. Retrieved February 7, 2020, from https://essayswriters.com/essays/Analysis/persuasion-manipulation-and-seduction.html

Farouk Radwan, M. (n.d.). Why women like men with dark triad traits | 2KnowMySelf. Retrieved February 8, 2020, from https://www.2knowmyself.com/Why_women_like_men_with_dark_triad_traits

Farquhar, S. (2017, September 3). Shogun Method *. Retrieved February 17, 2020, from https://seductionfaq.com/blog/shogun-method/

Female Psychology. (n.d.). Retrieved February 17, 2020, from http://www.the-alpha-lounge.com/female-psychology.html

Finkelstein, K. (n.d.). The Influence of the Dark Triad and Gender on Sexual Coercion Strategies of a Subclinical Sample. Retrieved February 7, 2020, from https://bir.brandeis.edu/bitstream/handle/10192/28572/FinkelsteinThesis2014.pdf?sequence=1

Fisher, D. (n.d.). 7 Quick Tips to Help You Learn Seduction Faster | Girls Chase. Retrieved February 16, 2020, from https://www.girlschase.com/content/7-quick-tips-help-you-learn-seduction-faster

Francis, M. (2007, January 3). The psychology of seduction. Retrieved February 18, 2020, from https://www.dailymail.co.uk/femail/article-426320/The-psychology-seduction.html

Ganz, M. (2013, October 31). Covert Seduction – How to Mess with Women's Minds. Retrieved February 17, 2020, from https://sibg.com/covert-seduction-mess-with-womens-minds/

Ganz, M. (2016, August 4). Black Rose Sequence – How You Can Seduce Women Using Mind Control Enslavement. Retrieved February 17, 2020, from https://sibg.com/black-rose-sequence-how-you-can-seduce-women-using-mind-control-enslavement/

Ganz, M. (2020, February 4). Fractionation Seduction Technique: All You Need To Know! Retrieved February 17, 2020, from https://sibg.com/using-fractionation-in-seduction/

Get the Guy. (2010, December 21). The Player: Why Men Long To Be Casanovas And How To Spot If He Is One – Men's Personalities Part 3. Retrieved February 16, 2020, from https://www.howtogettheguy.com/blog/player-mens-personalities-part-3/

Greene, R. (n.d.). The Art of Seduction. Retrieved February 8, 2020, from http://radio.shabanali.com/the-art-of-seduction-robert-greene

Hardy, J. (2020, January 30). The History of the Seduction Community. Retrieved February 8, 2020, from https://historycooperative.org/the-history-of-the-seduction-community/

Her Way. (2020, February 13). The Best Thing That Is Going To Happen To You This Year Is You. Retrieved February 18, 2020, from https://herway.net/relationship/3-simple-ways-to-unlock-the-hero-instinct-in-your-man/

His Secret Passion. (2019, March 30). Best 8 His Secret Obsession Phrases That Make A Man Fall In Love. Retrieved February 18, 2020, from https://hissecretpassion.com/secret-obsession-phrases/

Honan, D. (2019, January 30). James Bond's guide to seduction. Retrieved February 8, 2020, from https://bigthink.com/think-tank/james-bonds-guide-to-seduction

Hyman, R. (n.d.). Cold Reading: How to Convince Strangers That You Know All About Them. Retrieved February 17, 2020, from https://web.archive.org/web/20140716020736/http://www.skepdic.com/Hyman_cold_reading.htm

kartjoe. (2017, April 4). A modern man living guide to seduction PDF EBook Download-FREE. Retrieved February 7, 2020, from https://www.slideshare.net/kartjoe/a-modern-man-living-guide-to-seduction-pdf-ebook-downloadfree

Kaufman, S. (2015, December 10). The Myth of the Alpha Male. Retrieved February 8, 2020, from https://greatergood.berkeley.edu/article/item/the_myth_of_the_alpha_male

Kings of the Web. (2020, February 6). Cold Reading Is A Potent Seduction Tactic. Retrieved February 17, 2020, from https://heartiste.net/cold-reading-is-a-potent-seduction-tactic/

Kozmala, M. (2019, February 2). The Body language of seduction. Retrieved February 18, 2020, from https://businessandprestige.pl/the-body-language-of-seduction/

Lizra, C. (2017, December 10). Seduction in Business. Retrieved February 19, 2020, from https://www.powerofsomaticintelligence.com/blog/seduction-in-business

LoDolce, A. (2019, October 24). How to Seduce Men With Body Language: 12 Perfect Seduction Tips. Retrieved February 18, 2020, from https://sexyconfidence.com/how-to-seduce-men-with-body-language/

LoDolce, A. (2017, September 14). How To Scientifically Trigger His Emotional Desire for You using This Technique. Retrieved February 18, 2020, from https://www.huffpost.com/entry/how-to-scientifically-trigger-his-emotional-desire_b_59bab8b4e4b06b71800c3781

M., S. (2020, January 4). Shogun Method Review (Is Derek Rake The Real Deal?). Retrieved February 17, 2020, from https://www.calpont.com/shogun-method/

Madsen, P. (20212, July 7). The Power of Seduction. Retrieved February 7, 2020, from https://www.psychologytoday.com/us/blog/shameless-woman/201207/the-power-seduction

Magical Apparatus. (2019, December 1). The phases of a seduction - Alpha Male. Retrieved February 13, 2020, from https://www.magicalapparatus.com/alpha-male/the-phases-of-a-seduction.html

Magical Apparatus. (2019, December 26). Using Cold Reading - Seduction. Retrieved February 17, 2020, from https://www.magicalapparatus.com/seduction-2/chapter-ix-using-cold-reading.html

Mallens, T. (2015, September 4). 3 rules the art of seduction can teach you to boost your sales & marketing. Retrieved February 19, 2020, from https://www.linkedin.com/pulse/3-rules-art-seduction-can-teach-you-boost-your-sales-mallens-bsc-mba

Martin, C. (2010, November 11). Persuasion, Manipulation, Seduction, and Human Communication. Retrieved February 7, 2020, from http://opinionsandperspectives.blogspot.com/2010/11/persuasion-manipulation-seduction-and.html

Martin, T. (n.d.). Creating A More Effective B to B Sales Prospecting Program. Retrieved February 19, 2020, from https://conversedigital.com/social-selling-sales-training-posts/b-to-b-sales-prospecting

MensXP.com. (n.d.). MensXP.com - India's largest Online lifestyle magazine for Men. Offering tips & advice on relationships, fashion, office, health & grooming. Retrieved February 17, 2020, from https://www.mensxp.com/dating/seduction-science-/600-cold-reading-her-mind.html

Merriam-Webster. (n.d.). "Negging" Moves Beyond the Bar. Retrieved February 16, 2020, from https://www.merriam-webster.com/words-at-play/negging-pick-up-artist-meaning

Nguyen, V. (2013, August 17). 7 Life Lessons to Learn from Pickup Artists.

Retrieved February 20, 2020, from https://www.selfstairway.com/pickup-artists/

Nicky Woolf. (n.d.). "Negging": the anatomy of a dating trend. Retrieved February 17, 2020, from https://www.newstatesman.com/blogs/voices/2012/05/negging-latest-dating-trend

Nixon, R. (2016, March 23). 10 Things Every Woman Should Know About a Man's Brain. Retrieved February 18, 2020, from https://www.livescience.com/14422-10-facts-male-brains.html

Oesch, N., & Miklousic, I. (2012). The Dating Mind: Evolutionary Psychology and the Emerging Science of Human Courtship. *Evolutionary Psychology, 10*(5), 147470491201000. https://doi.org/10.1177/147470491201000511

Presaud, R., & Bruggen, P. (2015, August 15). The Sexy Sons Theory of What Women Are Attracted to in Men. Retrieved February 15, 2020, from https://www.psychologytoday.com/intl/blog/slightly-blighty/201508/the-sexy-sons-theory-what-women-are-attracted-in-men

Rake, D. (n.d.). How to Hook Up With Beautiful Women - Using "Player" Seduction Tactics. Retrieved February 16, 2020, from https://ezinearticles.com/?How-to-Hook-Up-With-Beautiful-Women---Using-Player-Seduction-Tactics&id=2481207

Rake, D. (2020, January 17). Shogun Method - A Critical (Self) Review *. Retrieved February 17, 2020, from https://derekrake.com/blog/#Four-Steps-To-Eternal-Enslavement-8211-The-IRAE-Model

Rauthmann, J. (2014, April 1). Mate attraction in the Dark Triad: Narcissists are hot, Machiavellians and psychopaths not. Retrieved February 8, 2020, from https://www.sciencedirect.com/science/article/abs/pii/S0191886913006582

Razzputin. (n.d.). Knowing How to Use Kino Effectively on Women. Retrieved Winter 160, 2020, from https://www.waytoosocial.com/how-to-use-kino-effectively/

Riggio, R. (2016, February 10). 6 Seductive Body Language Channels. Retrieved February 18, 2020, from https://www.psychologytoday.com/intl/blog/cutting-edge-leadership/201602/6-seductive-body-language-channels

Roberts, M. (2016, August 4). Black Rose Sequence®. Retrieved February 17, 2020, from https://sonicseduction.net/black-rose-sequence/

Rogell, B. E. (2013, August 26). Seduction tactics to boost your career. Retrieved February 19, 2020, from https://www.news.com.au/finance/work/seduction-tactics-to-boost-your-career/news-story/6fce129b118a03dfde4b68c4169ababf

Rogell, E. (2013, August 22). Seduction Tactics For Your Career. Retrieved February 19, 2020, from https://sea.askmen.com/entertainment/216/topten/seduction-tactics-for-your-career

Rolstad, A. (n.d.). The "Hover and Disqualify" Pickup Technique | Girls Chase. Retrieved February 17, 2020, from https://www.girlschase.com/content/hover-and-disqualify-pickup-technique

S, P. (2017, April 5). Raj Persaud: The Psychology of Seduction at TEDX U. of Bristol (transcript). Retrieved February 20, 2020, from https://singjupost.com/raj-persaud-the-psychology-of-seduction-at-tedxuniversityofbristol-transcript/

Seltzer, L. (2013, September 17). The Paradox of Seduction. Retrieved February 7, 2020, from https://www.psychologytoday.com/us/blog/evolution-the-self/201309/the-paradox-seduction

Shogun Method Fractionation - Free Download PDF. (n.d.). Retrieved February 17, 2020, from https://kupdf.net/download/shogun-method-fractionation_5913cf2adc0d60bf4c959eb0_pdf

Sicinski, A. (2018, December 8). Breaking Down the Intoxicating Art of Romantic Seduction. Retrieved February 10, 2020, from https://blog.iqmatrix.com/art-seduction

Simon, C. (2012, February 16). Don't be Seduced! 6 Crucial Warning Signs. Retrieved February 10, 2020, from https://www.psychologytoday.com/us/blog/bringing-sex-focus/201202/dont-be-seduced-six-crucial-warning-signs

Sinn, J. (n.d.). 3 Ways to Use Cold Reading to Attract Women. Retrieved February 17, 2020, from https://ezinearticles.com/?3-Ways-to-Use-Cold-Reading-to-Attract-Women&id=6169379

Skills Converged Ltd. (n.d.). Skills Converged > Body Language of Seduction. Retrieved February 18, 2020, from https://www.skillsconverged.com/FreeTrainingMaterials/BodyLanguage/BodyLanguageofSeduction.aspx

Snowden, J. (2020, February 7). Shogun Method: My Confession (A Review). Retrieved February 17, 2020, from https://sibg.com/shogun-method/

T, S. (2015a, November 5). The Three Types Of Game Pickup Artists Use To Attract Women: Part 2. Retrieved February 13, 2020, from http://seductioncommunity.com/attraction/the-three-types-of-game-pickup-artists-use-to-attract-women-part-2/

T, S. (2015b, November 5). The Three Types Of Game To Attract Women: Part 1. Retrieved February 13, 2020, from http://seductioncommunity.com/attraction/the-three-types-of-game-to-attract-women-part-1/

Tan, J. (2020, January 10). Customer Seduction: How to make customers LOVE your brand... Retrieved February 19, 2020, from https://www.referralcandy.com/blog/customer-seduction-make-customers-love-brand-infographic/

TED Talks: The power of Seduction in our Everyday Lives. (2013, July 30). Retrieved February 19, 2020, from https://www.payscale.com/career-news/2013/07/ted-talks-the-power-of-seduction-in-our-everyday-lives

The Doctor. (2019, August 27). The ethics of Seduction. Retrieved February 15, 2020, from https://thedoctorsdiary.com/women/ethics-of-seduction/

The Natural Lifestyles. (2015, February 11). Why Learning Seduction Is Not

Optional. Retrieved February 20, 2020, from
https://www.youtube.com/watch?v=onqLFdYY5Rw

Vandeweert, W. (2015, July 22). Use Cold Reading to Pick Up Girls. Retrieved
February 17, 2020, from https://willemvandeweert.wixsite.com/cold-
reading/single-post/2015/06/08/USE-COLD-READING-TO-PICK-UP-GIRLS

Van Edwards, V. (n.d.). The Alpha Female: 9 Ways You Can Tell Who Is an Alpha
Woman. Retrieved February 8, 2020, from
https://www.scienceofpeople.com/alpha-female/

Way, H. (2020, February 13). The Best Thing That Is Going To Happen To You
This Year Is You. Retrieved February 17, 2020, from https://herway.net/love/8-
ways-men-use-fractionation-seduction-make-fall-love/

Weiss, R. (2015, June 20). What Turns Guys On? Understanding Sexual Desire.
Retrieved February 18, 2020, from
https://www.psychologytoday.com/us/blog/love-and-sex-in-the-digital-
age/201506/what-turns-guys-understanding-male-sexual-desire

Wendell, R. (n.d.). Cold Reading Your Way to Great Conversations | Girls Chase.
Retrieved February 17, 2020, from https://www.girlschase.com/content/cold-
reading-your-way-great-conversations

Williams, S. (2012, March 14). Are You Easily Seduced? Retrieved February 10,
2020, from https://www.yourtango.com/experts/shay-your-date-diva-
williams/are-you-easy-be-seduced

Wilson, B. M. (2011, October 23). The great seducers. Retrieved February 8, 2020,
from https://www.independent.co.uk/life-style/love-sex/seduction/the-great-
seducers-928178.html

Wilson, J. (n.d.). Social Psychology: The Seduction of Consumers. Retrieved
February 7, 2020, from
https://pdfs.semanticscholar.org/be16/b695b47eee8f82e5af8ac3da2589d76b27
99.pdf

Woman Knows: 12 Tricks That Men Use to Seduce Women. (n.d.). Retrieved
February 16, 2020, from http://www.womanknows.com/understanding-
men/news/71/

Woman Knows: Playboys: Uncovering the Mystery. (n.d.). Retrieved February 16,
2020, from http://www.womanknows.com/understanding-men/news/316/

Yohn, D. L. (2016, March 9). To Win Customers, Stop Selling And Start Seducing.
Retrieved February 19, 2020, from
https://www.forbes.com/sites/deniselyohn/2016/03/09/to-win-customers-stop-
selling-and-start-seducing/#443e2ed451c1

Gaslighting Games

*The Manipulative Power to Play with
People's Minds and Control Them for Life*

Emory Green

TABLE OF CONTENTS

INTRODUCTION

We are all driven by desires and wants and we all have an innate need to control certain aspects of our lives and those of the people around us. We want people to love us a certain way, talk to us in a particular manner, and treat us with respect. And there is absolutely nothing wrong with that. But what if, hypothetically speaking, you or the other person in the relationship is always controlling the outcome of your interactions by being manipulative and using words and actions that push the other party to respond in a manner that is only beneficial to them? Does that make them just selfish or are they gaslighters?

In this book, I will expose the difference between the selfish, naturally manipulative tendencies of narcissism and gaslighting. Gaslighting is a very specific form of manipulation that any one of us can fall into, either as the perpetrator or the victim. Not only will I define what gaslighting is, I will also give real-life examples of gaslighting and how it occurs in various aspects of our lives. Reading this book will help you be able to identify the different techniques and tactics used by gaslighters or begin to notice them in your behavior if you are one. Our love for others and our opinion of ourselves can shade the truth about gaslighting behavior, but this book lays intentions bare.

As an author and a person who works with people of great ambition and drive, I have found that every one of us has the capacity to gaslight, but to varying degrees. The difference between all of us is that some people will welcome this manipulative and controlling streak, as long as it benefits them, while the rest of us will pull ourselves back from being manipulative in consideration of the other person. The unfortunate truth is that gaslighting has become a way of life and its effects can be felt throughout society, from politics and work relationships to, of course, personal relationships, as well. It is a learned behavior that can be acquired from childhood, especially if you were gaslit or saw it happening to a member of the household, like a parent or sibling.

Manipulation can change the way we parent, work, play, and socialize. It can and will affect our relationships with members of the opposite sex and take away the power that enables us to make informed and beneficial decisions about our lives. Imagine, for a minute, a mother experiencing gaslighting. She will not only question her reality but her decisions because of the gaslighting and this will affect her children and spouse directly, creating an unhealthy home environment. Now replace that mother with yourself and you will see that gaslighting has an effect on everyone around the affected individual because it is such an insidious form of abuse. It can take place gradually over a prolonged period of time without anyone noticing it, causing irreparable damage in some cases.

Your life can be drastically changed by the things you don't know and gaslighting in your life may be apparent or it may be hidden under the guise of love and looking out for your interests. You may not be a victim of gaslighting in your relationships, but perhaps you know someone who is. Or perhaps you have heard of someone who is. Or maybe you have interacted with a gaslighter. With gaslighting, there is often the feeling that something is wrong or the feeling you are being pushed to accept something that is not in line with your perception. Oftentimes, gaslighters are people we trust, so you don't believe they could be manipulating you. But, if you understand what gaslighting is, how it is done, and what it is meant to accomplish, you have a better chance of questioning the manipulation before it gets too far. It is safe to say that shutting down any form of gaslighting in your life or the lives of those around you can save a life.

Learning about gaslighting is an excellent place to start to help you nip such relationships in the bud before they become toxic and destructive. All the aspects of gaslighting that you need to know about are in this book and you can use it as your guide to maneuver this minefield of emotional abuse that has become an insidious part of our culture and society. But what do you do when you identify gaslighting in yourself or in others around you? Working on change is the hardest part that a gaslighter has to embrace. If this is you, let this book help you to become a leader, friend, companion, or partner who looks beyond your own intention to the good of all others around you. This book will help you understand the real impact of having power over people. You ought to get this book if you have no more intentions of being led on.

This quote by Albert Camus says it best with regards to gaslighting, "Nothing is more despicable than respect based on fear." And may I add to this, manipulation.

Enjoying this book so far? Remember to head to the last page of this book bundle for a bonus bite-sized yet valuable free resource on Conversational Hypnosis. This mini e-book is the easiest way to learn how to be a successful conversational hypnotist. Curious about the benefits it can do to your normal day to day conversations? Get your copy now! This free resource is available for a limited time only

CHAPTER ONE:

Gaslighting 101

What is gaslighting?

Gaslighting is a nefarious type of psychological manipulation of an individual that makes them doubt their sanity, truth, beliefs, judgment, perception, values, and even memories. The main aim of gaslighting is to cause the person to have low esteem and/or to gain power over the person. Gaslighting happens gradually in a relationship and the actions may seem harmless in the beginning.

Gaslighters use certain very specific terms to cause confusion and muddy the waters, so the victim's perception of events seems unreliable or even fictional. They may say something like, "I don't know what you are talking about" or, "That didn't happen like that, you are just making stuff up" or, "You are just being emotional." Used frequently enough over a long period of time, the victim starts to doubt their memory, get confused about even the most obvious happenings in their lives, and more and more rely on the abuser to corroborate their reality.

Gaslighting has been a weapon used by many abusers who prefer to use emotional abuse on their victims so their actions are not easily noticeable by others. This allows them to maintain power over their victims for a longer period of time. The typical result of gaslighting is living with cognitive dissonance, which means the victim holds two different points of view at the same time that are in contradiction with each other. For example, they may recognize that the abuser is not being honest or is intentionally misleading them. But they have so much love for them that they are willing to tell themselves they must be wrong about the other person. As a result, they continue to enable the other person's abuse, which eventually whittles away their cognitive abilities.

History of gaslighting

The terminology "gaslighting" came from the 1938 play, Gaslight, also known as Angel Street, in the United States. The play, which was later adapted into movies in 1940 and 1944, was about a woman, Bella Manningham, whose husband, Jack Manningham, manipulated her into thinking she was mad. The husband literally dimmed and brightened the lights in their home and pretended that nothing happened in a bid to make the wife doubt her sanity. This play is a perfect depiction of a desolate relationship in which one party tries to undermine the other's sense of reality and, in the process, causes them mental harm. If this play is anything to go by, gaslighting has been a technique used by abusers for a long time.

Looking past this play as just another pastiche melodrama, its re-enactment by various playwrights over the years has shown that the subject matter is still relevant in modern times, especially as the techniques and tactics used in gaslighting have become more advanced. In the play, Jack Manningham also isolates his wife from her support system in order to make himself the sole interpreter of her reality. Unfortunately, in the play, his ploy works and she becomes dependent on him to discern and translate the situations in her life while, at the same time, falling more into hopelessness and despair.

Examples of gaslighting today

The gaslighting effect has appeared in decades of studies about psychoanalysis and it has also manifested itself in different TV shows over the years. One of the personalities that is considered the most prolific gaslighter of modern times is, unfortunately, the president of the United States, Donald Trump. The term gaslighting can be attached to anything that is made to sound surreal enough to cause you to question your perception of reality. There have been quite a number of gaslighting instances associated with the President of the United States, where he has tried to make his opponents seem unhinged for questioning his actions and those of his close consorts. Here are a few examples:

Brett Kavanaugh and Dr. Christine Blasey Ford

During the confirmation hearing of Brett Kavanaugh, President Donald Trump called Dr. Christine Blasey Ford's accusations that Kavanaugh had sexually assaulted her in high school fabricated and a hoax. The following remarks by the president created an atmosphere where the victim's reality was questioned and her memory challenged, just because time had passed after the fact.

The president remarked: "The American public has seen this charade, has seen this dishonesty by the Democrats. And when you mention impeach [sic] a justice of the United States Supreme Court who is a top scholar, top student, top intellect, and who did nothing wrong and there is no corroboration of any kind. It was all made up, it was fabricated. And it is a disgrace. And I think it's really going to show you something come November 6."

Somehow Brett Kavanaugh's perceived intelligence was enough to falsify everything that Dr. Ford said and it called into question the validity of her version of the events.

Donald Trump and Hilary Clinton

As a woman in a presidential race, Hilary Clinton faced quite a number of questions and a lot of scrutiny about her stand on women's issues. But when the presidential candidate tackled issues about women or stood up for women's rights, then-candidate Donald Trump accused her of playing the "woman card".

On the campaign trail, Trump kept insinuating that Clinton had no chance of winning if she wasn't playing the woman card. This argument was meant to not only invalidate the issues that Clinton focused on when it came to women, but it was also supposed to make her look like a weaker candidate who had nothing to offer the American people except her gender. This is despite the fact that Clinton served in the previous administration and was even voted as the most popular public servant of her ilk in front of President Obama and vice president Joe Biden.

In one of his rallies in Spokane Washington, Trump claimed that Clinton accused him of raising his voice while speaking to women. "She's going - did you hear that Donald Trump is raising his voice while speaking to women. Oh, I'm sorry, I'm sorry. I mean all men - we're terrified to speak to women any more - we may raise our voices."

This statement portrays Clinton as an opponent who is looking to curtail the freedoms of men and policemen in how they conduct themselves around women. It is meant to put the fear in men that women are going to gang up against them with the help of Hilary Clinton. Gaslighting Clinton worked very well with some voters, who bought into his portrayal of her as the beginning of the end of the natural order of things as they knew it. It played to their gender resentment and gender bias, especially in homes where the woman made more money than the man.

Donald Trump's incivility when he talked about Clinton and his constant accusing her of playing the woman card was meant to diminish her worth as a leader to the voters and, unfortunately, many voters bought into this argument. In this case, Donald Trump succeeded in gaslighting the American people and Hilary Clinton. He effectively changed the perception of reality for voters, making them feel like he was the only solution to keep things in their "natural order". He also managed to gaslight Clinton by making her look like an unworthy candidate because she cared about matters like childcare and pay equality for women. This tactic was actually meant to keep Clinton silent about women's issues because Trump didn't feel like he had a handle on them and he couldn't try and become an advocate for women so late in the game after his Access Hollywood tape.

As a gaslighter, in this case, Donald Trump was trying to silence Clinton's arguments by painting her standards and opinions as oppressive and unreasonable.

Kellie Sutton and Steven Gane

Kellie Sutton was not a famous person, but a 30-year-old mother of three who lived with a bully of a boyfriend, Steven Gane. But in a landmark case that punished the gaslighters, Steven Gane received a sentence of four years and three months. He was also slapped with a criminal behavior order that will last for 10 years from 2018. This order requires Gane to notify the police of any sexual relationship that he has that lasts more than 14 days. The notification must be done within 21 days of the beginning of any relationship.

In this case, Steven Gane was found guilty of using coercive and controlling behavior within an intimate relationship, assaulting the victim by beating and assault occasioning actual bodily harm. According to the judge in the case, Phillip Grey, the abuser wormed his way into her affections and home and then sought to control and dominate her. The judge said that Gane treated her like a meal ticket that was his to control, treated her as a possession, beat her, ground her down and broke her spirit. He further said, "Her (Kellie) texts and Facebook messages show the contempt and hostility with which you treated her. You regard women as objects you wish to use. You even referred to Miss Sutton in abusive and crude terms after her death. Your behavior drove Miss Sutton to take her own life. She threatened to kill herself and you told her to do everyone a favor and go ahead and do it."

Gane admitted he was a jealous man and his gaslighting actions were meant to exert control over his lover. According to Kellie Sutton's mother, Pamela Taylor, she was a bubbly, happy person who was funny, affectionate, and caring. However, she changed after getting into a relationship with Gane and became withdrawn and anxious.

This is the first time a conviction has been made for a gaslighting offense following the death of a victim. In the United Kingdom, the coercive and controlling legislation came into effect in 2015 and police have hailed this move as a milestone. This legislation is a section of the Serious Crime Act of 2015.

Gane and Sutton were together for only five months. In typical gaslighter behavior, he ingratiated himself to his victim by moving into her house and doing the things she needed to be done around the house, as well as buying stuff for her. This was a ploy to get her to become reliant on him. As time went by, he pulled her away from her family and friends, became more controlling even beating her when she went out without telling him where she was going. The victim hid the reality from her family and even when she eventually took her own life, they were unaware of the gaslighting going on in her life.

Steven Gane exhibited typical gaslighting behavior in controlling and coercing his partner. But in his case, it was a lethal combination of emotional and physical abuse. According to her friends, he saw the vulnerability in the single mother of three and capitalized on it. Gaslighters will always look for a weakness and exploit it to their advantage.

Russia gaslighting Americans

Since the 2016 election, Americans have been gaslit by the Russian propaganda machine that seeks to dismiss the perception that Russia manipulated the American electorate and changed the course of American politics, as if it was a figment of their imagination. Russian agents hacked into the Clinton campaign, as well as the Democratic National Committee and Democratic Congressional Campaign Committee with the aim of releasing sensitive information from the campaign. They also spread propaganda about Clinton on Twitter, Facebook, and Instagram and even staged campaign rallies in Pennsylvania and Florida. All of this information is corroborated by the United States Intelligence Community.

However, when asked about their interference in the American elections, Russian President Vladimir Putin denied everything and instead pointed a confusing finger at their neighbor, Ukraine. In the typical deflecting behavior of a gaslighter, Russia's president pretended not to know or understand that his agents, using cyber tactics, introduced false narratives into the 2016 U.S. election which favored Donald Trump and caused damage to the Clinton campaign.

The main reason for this manipulation was to ensure the election of a candidate they could manipulate into the highest office and wield power over him. Clinton was tough on Russia and supported the sanctions in place against the country for their actions in Ukraine. When found out, Russia pointed a finger elsewhere and also began a campaign of discrediting the U.S. Intelligence Community, using their own president, no less.

U.S. Special Counsel Robert Muller uncovered evidence of a Kremlin-led operation to interfere with the elections. He also found out that 12 Russian intelligence officers infiltrated democratic emails and used phony social media accounts in order to spread divisive narratives. By 2017, 56 percent of American's believed that Russia interfered in the election, but this also means that 44 percent didn't. This is a huge percentage and it represents a large number of people who have had their perception of reality interfered with by statements like these from Putin and Donald Trump.

Putin said, "We don't have and never had any plans to interfere in U.S. domestic politics." But, according to Putin, their government can't stop private citizens from expressing their views online about U.S. politics and its developments. "How can we ban them from doing that? Do you have such a ban with regard to Russia?"

Trump: "I don't believe they interfered." In another instance, he said "Knowing something about hacking, if you don't catch the hacker in the act, it's a very hard thing to say who did the hacking. With that being said, I have to go with Russia. Could've been China, could've been a lot of different groups."

By casting aspersions on the validity of the claims, as both presidents did, and as people in high authority holding a lot of sway, the two leaders gaslit the American people into thinking that their perception of reality was not accurate. Notice that not only did they deny the action, they also pointed at other potential perpetrators. This helped them advance an alternative narrative for those who believed the hacking took place. They both understood that the facts pointed to hacking. However, deflecting the blame from Russia is just as important as denying the claim. This tactic of muddying the waters works very well for gaslighters because their victims can often barely find the grounds to make accusations stick.

Charles Manson and the Manson family

Charles Manson was a prolific gaslighter that took gaslighting tactics to the next level by influencing well-educated people to leave their lives behind. He then unleashed them onto the world to commit murder for him. Like most gaslighters, Manson portrayed himself as the next savior of the world and the rest of the world as misfits and sycophants. Most people thought that Manson was going around recruiting teenage serial killers. In fact, he was meeting the needs of vulnerable young women and, depending on their vulnerability, he exploited their specific need.

For example, if a young woman was looking for spiritual guidance, he would offer that in his warped form. If she needed a father figure, he would act in such a manner that she would find fatherly comfort from him. Not only did this make them exceedingly reliant on him, but by making them a part of each other's lives, he gave them a family and a connection that most were missing. He even called his cult the "Manson family".

Manson made them a part of his life and, for the first year in 1968, there was a deep sense of family, affection, and fulfillment between them all. Unfortunately, the years spent with Manson were in a haze of drugs, so different people in the cult remember the events differently. The timeline of the Manson story spanned two years and, by mid-1969, Manson had started ordering members of his family to kill people for him. The first victim was a friend of the Manson family by the name of Gary Hinman, who was killed by members of the family because he failed to give Manson money. The next person on his hit list was Roman Polanski, a famous film director, and his wife was the unfortunate victim. Polanski's home was targeted because a music producer who had rejected Manson lived there previously.

Having manipulated the members of his family into regarding him as their messiah, he advanced what is known as his Helter-Skelter Theory. This theory advanced the notion that African-Americans and whites would have a race war that would see thousands perish. Manson planned for the family to disappear into caves to emerge when the war was over, in order to rule the world. But when his music career flopped, he told his members that they would have to start helter-skelter themselves by committing crimes in upscale neighborhoods. This was to demonstrate to the African American community how to carry out the violence. However, clearly the murders were revenge killings for Manson against people who didn't help advance his music career.

The men and women used by Manson all completely relied on him for their understanding of reality as translated by him. In their eyes, he was not an abuser. Instead, they saw a charismatic and inspiring leader with the vision and purpose to transform their lives and humanity for the better. This trait is known as optimism bias, in which victims look on the bright side of things, even when there are clear discrepancies in the behavior of the abuser. Optimism bias exists in all of us, but it becomes more pronounced in victims of gaslighting.

Love Island's Adam and Rosie

In 2018, participants in the show Love Island, Adam and Rosie, showed how gaslighting can become a part of dating life. Viewers were concerned about how Adam used very typical gaslighting tactics on his then partner, Rosie, making her feel like she was the reason for his pursuing the new girl on the show. Adam told Rosie that he was dumping her because she was acting like a child. The failure to take responsibility for his actions and, instead, putting it on Rosie, made her feel like she was responsible for his bad behavior.

By trivializing the reaction of his partner based on his actions, Adam showed gaslighting behavior. And, apparently, when he was in a relationship with another participant by the name of Kendall, he also used gaslighting tactics on her. For example, he would say to her, "I've done nothing to make you think that I would pick someone else." This, despite the fact that he was carrying on with Rosie at the time. And the fact that he exhibited gaslighting behavior with Kendall and with Rosie every time he was interested in someone new, showed a pattern in his behavior.

Gaslighting has been seen on the show with other participants, like Joe Garratt. Garratt famously made his partner Lucie Donlan feel there was something wrong with her for being friendly with the male participants on the show, in particular Joe's rival. In his words to her, "I'm not happy with it. It's strange. I think it is time for you to get close to the girls." Joe received a lot of backlash for his gaslighting of

Lucie and was voted off the show. But more importantly, he had to be whisked off to a safe house as a result.

When intimate feelings are involved, gaslighting can be a gateway to an abusive relationship and it can quickly morph into physical abuse. The victim is likely to stay in an unhealthy relationship because they have become comfortable with the nature of the relationship. With time, the abusive pattern continues and escalates.

CHAPTER TWO:

The Gaslighter's Tale

Narcissism is at the core of gaslighting behavior. In each of the examples I gave in the previous chapter, the gaslighters feel superior to the victim and believe the victim should look up to only them. Because they can't achieve this naturally, they resort to coercive and manipulative behavior to erode the confidence of the victim and make them question their perception and judgment calls. This effectively puts the victim in a vulnerable position, which the gaslighter can then exploit by making themselves seem like the be-all, end-all to the victim.

Inside the mind of a gaslighter

When dealing with a gaslighter, you will find out there are those who understand what they are doing and those who aren't even aware of their actions. Famous gaslighters, like Charles Manson, did not just embark on a journey to recruit and manipulate young women out of the blue. Manson took a class that was based on Dale Carnegie's book "How to Win Friends and Influence People". The manipulation tactics he used on his followers were learned from this book. This book wasn't written with nefarious manipulation in mind. In fact, some of the world's greatest minds, like Warren Buffet, have also benefited from the teachings in this book. But Manson applied the techniques in an evil manner to suit his own needs.

This is a classic example of a gaslighter who intentionally learned how to manipulate people, applied the tactics they learned, and used them for their own means. Some gaslighters are aware of their behavior and willfully target vulnerable people whom they can easily control.

The opposite of this is a gaslighter who is not truly aware of their actions. This is especially true of authoritarian personalities who tend to think in absolutes. To them, things are black or white, so the other person either does what they say or does not. These are the hardest types of gaslighters to help because they do not identify themselves as having a problem. The result is, however, the same for both the aware and unaware gaslighter - they get a payoff when their victim becomes completely reliant on them. They both want to have control over their victim's thoughts, whether they feel like they are doing it for their good or for their own benefit.

The gaslighter personality

The gaslighter personality is typically found in people who have two contradictory issues at play within themselves. They have self-esteem and self-worth issues and the only way for them to feel in control is by manipulating people and the situations around them to favor them. But they also have an inflated sense of importance. This makes them feel in charge of their own lives and also very entitled. The gaslighter can be either a schemer and a master at distorting the facts, or they can be an overbearing authority figure who doesn't like to be questioned and sees things only through their personal prism.

Narcissism plays a huge role in gaslighting behavior because it helps the gaslighter to mask their insecurity. Narcissism is a personality disorder in which a person has an inflated sense of their own worth and importance. They also have an insatiable and deeply entrenched need for admiration and attention, plus a complete lack of empathy for others. At the slightest criticism, a narcissistic person will lose their mask of self-confidence, sometimes resulting in violence because their insecure side is suddenly exposed. For such people, any actions by the victim, like questioning a decision or even asking for clarification, can be considered a criticism, making them lash out at the victim.

For example, if a wife asks a gaslighter husband about his spending of the family income, the man may feel like she is questioning his ability to make good decisions. As a narcissist, he will take this as an insult and may become abusive in that instant. It is very easy for a person with a narcissist personality disorder to become a gaslighter because of their sense of entitlement and preoccupation with being admired. On the flip side, a person with a gaslighter personality also exhibits behaviors like being withdrawn and moody when things don't go their way. In addition, they experience difficulty adapting to any changes in their environment. They also secretly have feelings of shame and insecurity over certain aspects of their lives. Some gaslighters can also suffer from depression, which makes them more likely to abuse alcohol and drugs.

Ultimately, the gaslighter personality has a persistent urge as part of their behavior to control others around them by any means necessary.

Why they do it

The main reason why gaslighters go to the lengths they do to control people is because of the power it gives them. The need for dominance helps them feel good about themselves because they are already dealing with feelings of insecurity and low self-esteem in themselves. The gaslighter may try to frame their actions as being of benefit to the victim, but they are, in fact, for their own benefit.

There are cases when people will gaslight someone close to them in order to cover up a misdeed, like an affair or drug use. In such a situation, the gaslighter is not your typical narcissist. Instead, because they are afraid of the repercussions of their behavior, they will make the other person question their reality to protect themselves. The one thing to recognize is that no matter the reason why one is gaslighting, their sole intention is to benefit themselves at the expense of the other person.

Gaslighters also like to use these techniques to feel a sense of security, especially if they have grown up with some level of insecurity in their environment. Because gaslighting is a learned behavior, the abuser uses it as reflex protective behavior to protect their feelings and help them feel in control of their life. This learned behavior is picked up from their environment and, when they see that it works, they will try it on their first victim. If they successfully manipulate people around them, it becomes a cognitive strategy for survival.

Gaslighter confessions

It is crucial to understand that gaslighters are human beings too, despite their behavior. They crave self-preservation and acceptance, which they honestly believe their actions bring to them. It is because of this need for acceptance and belonging that gaslighters may continue to gaslight their loved ones, despite seeing their suffering. They may be afraid of being alone or looking like a loser. As a result, their self-preservation takes precedence over any feelings of guilt or empathy.

As an author who has listened to many stories about gaslighting from both victims and abusers, I have heard gut-wrenching stories that leave fully functional men and women with debilitating fears and anxieties for a long time and, in some cases, even for the rest of their lives. One such story that I came across was in BBC Stories and it involves a Canadian lawyer by the name of Greg and several women he gaslit in during their relationships.

During therapy, Greg realized that he was a gaslighter and, on further probing, connected the beginning of his behavior to a relationship he had at the age of 21. Greg is a self-confessed serial gaslighter with 11 relationships under his belt and he used gaslighting techniques on each of the women. By the age of 28, he recognized the gaslighting pattern in his relationships and he spoke out in order to help women identify the telltale signs of a gaslighter.

His first relationship as a law undergrad was with a master's degree student by the name of Paula. He was unfaithful, carrying on several affairs behind her back, but she was intelligent enough to know what he was up to. Greg didn't want to break up with her, but neither did he want to give up his other lovers, so he resorted to gaslighting her to create uncertainty in her mind about what he was up to.

One of the ways he created an alternative reality is by making her question her relationship with social media. He started to pretend she had an obsession with social media. To make his statements more palatable to Paula's intelligence, he started off by making it a joke about how crazy she was about social media. Greg was leaving a footprint of his infidelity on social media. With time, he started using demeaning language when she raised issues about his social media use, making her feel like she was just being dramatic and paranoid about what she saw. He would act like it was a joke, whenever she confronted him.

The constant gaslighting made Paula start to doubt what she was seeing, believing she was overreacting and not confronting compromising situations for the fear of being too dramatic. So she apologized for doubting him and promised to spend less time on social media. This gave Greg the freedom to continue with his lifestyle. He was at the beginning of the gaslighting behavior pattern, in which one uses lies and exaggeration to offer an alternative narrative. The more extreme end of the spectrum involves using controlling, coercive, manipulative, and sometimes even physical means to dominate the other person.

According to Greg, despite Paula being a feminist and well-educated, she believed the narrative he fed her about the other women being the liars and people who couldn't be trusted. As a result, she resented the other women and even when she met them and found out they were good people, Greg's version still won the day. With this gaslighting tactic, Greg was effectively isolating her from others who could tell her the truth, all while feeding her anxiety about what she saw on social media.

Greg chose the type of woman that most people would assume would not be affected by emotional abuse. He said he targeted highly successful and intelligent women who are actually even more receptive to being gaslit compared to their less successful counterparts. Such women tend to be conscientious and generally do the right thing, making them trustworthy and willing to trust others more easily. They are also agreeable and empathetic to a fault. These are typically the qualities that have made them successful in their careers, but they can be exploited, making them vulnerable to gaslighting.

According to Greg, many abusers approach relationships with a checklist or a blueprint of what they can target to make that person more vulnerable. He said that his victims all came with an idea of what they thought a successful relationship should look like, often depictions from movies and fairytale love stories. He further explains that, as a gaslighter, you look at this narrative the victim wants the relationship to follow and you set about laying it out, but to fit your own needs. You then begin to do things over a period of time that supports the narrative you want the victim to fall for.

Greg claims that, although he wasn't physically abusive or aggressive with any of the women, looking back he understands the damage he did was psychological. His advice to women who are seeing signs of gaslighting in their relationship is to talk to male friends. He explains that male friends are likely to notice gaslighting behavior in other men and are likely to be brutally honest with their female friends. Female friends, on the other hand, can be intimidated easily and are likely to tell the victim what she wants to hear. In fact, he was wary of his ex-girlfriend's male friends because he knew they could see right through his tactics.

As a man, talking about getting gaslit is almost taboo, as most people feel a man can't be abused by his partner, especially if it's a woman. Many men suffer gaslighting at the hands of their wives and girlfriends for years before they can even bring themselves to accept what is going on. This shows that gaslighting is not confined to women as the victims, alone.

In the same BBC series, I came across the story of an American man whose wife gaslit him, traumatizing him for many years. If he made plans with his friends, she would bring up an argument, preventing him from going out and later feign not recalling he was supposed to meet his friends. She would call his work and act like something was wrong at home and, when he came home, she would accuse him of overreacting, acting like she didn't make it sound serious. In the end, he lost his job because of these incidences.

She would hang up a picture and when he complimented it, she would claim it had been hanging up for over two weeks and she couldn't believe his stupidity at not noticing it. He began to doubt his memories because of such things since he couldn't remember seeing it before.

Unfortunately, help for men in abusive relationships is far less, compared to resources for women. Men are expected to put their foot down to stop the abuse. But the truth is that gaslighting happens to all genders and the effects are equally devastating.

Are you a gaslighter?

If you have doubts about whether you are a gaslighter, this simple question may be the first place to start:

Do you put down your partner or child or any other person close to you, wait for their response, and then attack their response, making them feel incapable of making a sound judgment call? You may believe that their judgment was flawed concerning a particular subject. However, if you make this a constant habit, where you make the other person doubt their ability to make sound decisions, you are a gaslighter. The unaware gaslighter may think they are just being reasonable or being honest. Such people believe in being brutally honest, only they are just being brutal in their control of the other person. They may tell you that they are rational and cool-headed and don't like expressions of anxiety. You can expect them to say things like, "You are being too sensitive" because they feel justified to say whatever they want to say in their abrasive manner.

The aware gaslighter, on the other hand, is very methodical in how they set up their victims for the fall. They will begin by being extra nice or helpful and gain the other person's trust. Their jabs will at first come as jokes or a guilt trip. The gradual escalation into full-blown domination and gaslighting takes months or even years.

Another question to ask yourself is, "Do you ever use phrases that make the person question themselves? For example, do you call them crazy? Or call their friends or family crazy? By making them feel like they are irrational in their thoughts, opinions, choice of friends, or even hobbies, you are gaslighting the person.

For a gaslighter, every act of control, coercion, and domination over their victim is a power trip and this can become addictive. This is why they will use the victim's smallest actions to make them feel like they are not acting rationally.

The final question to ask yourself is, "Do you feel insecure about yourself and derive comfort from making the other person question themselves?" With this question, it is important to investigate whether you are just an emotional abuser who likes to have control over how your partner feels or a gaslighter who wants to go the extra mile and discredit them by making the person question their sanity.

Three types of gaslighters

Psychoanalysts have, over the years, identified three types of gaslighters based on their behavior patterns. Respected voices in this field, like the Associate Director of the Yale Center for Emotional Intelligence, Dr. Robin Stern, have taken over two and a half decades to learn about the effects of these gaslighters and their specific tactics on their victims. Here is what you need to know about these three types:

The Glamour Gaslighter

The Glamour Gaslighter always starts out as a gentleman, which is meant to sweep his victim off their feet. If it is a woman, they will be elegant and charming, sometimes even delicate and dainty in her actions. She may act like a damsel in distress, needing her victim's manly attributes to come to her rescue. The male Glamour Gaslighter will buy expensive gifts and take the victim to the best restaurants, making her feel like she is the center of his world

Not only does he target her but also her loved ones, from friends to family, making her the envy of everyone in her circle. But in small ways, he begins to control her. In the beginning, it may be scheduling activities together that coincide with plans she has made with family or friends. This forces her to choose him over them. He will drop subtle remarks like, "Well, I guess spending time with me is not as important to you as it is to me." Some may try to instill the fear of a break up by saying, "It's okay. Go hang out with your friends. I will take so and so...full disclosure though...we had a thing before I met you and she still holds a candle for me." This is meant to make the victim feel insecure and jealous enough to make the victim abandon her plans for his.

In the same scenario, the female Glamour Gaslighter may dress provocatively to go out after finding out that the man has made plans to hang out with his friends. She will let him know that she is going out with an ex-boyfriend or a colleague from work, making it clear that her date has feelings for her. The aim of her actions is to make him jealous enough to abandon his plans. Suddenly, she is furious at him for overreacting and causing her to feel guilty about wanting to go out to have a good time. She blames him for being manipulative and he is forced to placate her and assure her that this wasn't his intention, all the while he is wondering if he overreacted and whether he caused her to change her plans for him.

The male Glamour Gaslighter will abruptly become furious at his partner for the smallest of things, like laughing at a joke with his friend, wanting to pay for something when they are together or even giving a male friend a hug. The accusations will range from trying to show him up in public to not behaving like a good girlfriend. Of course, the woman is unsure of what she has done wrong and the more she tries to argue her case, the more she seems to upset him. To bring back the peace in the relationship, she will immediately try to make things right between them by apologizing and promising to be more considerate. After all, he is a good man and she just made him angry with her actions.

This pattern continues where the original love comes back intermittently, but most of the time the gaslighter is controlling their partner with their actions and words.

The Intimidator Gaslighter

This type of gaslighter is a bully, who uses aggression and even physical dominance to get his way. The Intimidator Gaslighter is typically male because he has the physical strength to make his victim do his bidding or resort to violence. With the Intimidator, there are no subtle references to what they want. Rather, he is abusive and will show aggression in public,

Such gaslighters are prone to sulking, silent treatment, threats, and playing on their partner's deepest fears to get their way. For example, they will threaten to take the kids away because their partner took the kids out of the house without his permission. If the partner's deepest fear is being a failure as a parent, they will use this fear by saying something like, "You act just like your mom and you know how she was. I don't think you are a good mother to my kids and I will take them away from you." The victim, out of desperation, promises to ask his permission to take the kids out. She will start to believe that her parenting skills are not up to par, which causes her anxiety.

The Intimidator Gaslighter will continually bully the victim, even in the presence of other people, often putting her down in public.

The Good Guy Gaslighter

This gaslighter is loved by the victim's family and friends tell her that she is lucky and will not find someone like him again. They act like an amazing guy or woman in public, treating their partners with respect and affection, but behind closed doors, the façade drops and they become vicious. The problem with this kind of gaslighter is that their actions in public discredit any attempts by the victim to paint a different picture. The Good Guy Gaslighter relies on public perception to keep their actions hidden. The victims are usually afraid or ashamed to tell on the gaslighter and, because of this, the abuser can get away with years of abuse without anyone knowing what is happening.

For example, a Good Guy Gaslighter may be having a meal with his girlfriend and she sees a male friend. He comes over to their table, where she stands up to give him a hug. Unlike the Intimidator Gaslighter, who may storm off at this gesture and show aggression to his partner in public, the Good Guy Gaslighter will reach out for a handshake, introduce himself, invite the friend to join them and proceed to be charming and even friendly. However, inside he or she is seething and neither the girlfriend nor the friend can tell. At the earliest opportunity, behind closed doors, he will accuse her of flirting with the man, having an affair, and making a fool of him. Why? Because of the way they hugged or how they looked at each other. He makes her promise not to see her friend again.

The victim starts to believe that maybe she lingered on the hug or maybe she was too attentive when her friend was speaking. She will apologize and promise to not have any interaction with the friend. And she may even stop hugging male friends altogether because of this.

CHAPTER THREE

Dancing With the Devil

See the signs

Being in love can be great but the important thing is not to lose yourself in the process of loving another. The signs of gaslighting can be seen clearly if one knows what to look for. You can look for these signs in all types of relationships, from intimate, family, business, and even friendships.

Subtle signs of gaslighting you won't even notice

Like I mentioned previously, gaslighting is gradual and, in most cases, a subtle form of emotional abuse that can take place over years, leaving the victim completely disoriented because of the erosion of their sense of reality. These are some of the techniques gaslighters use:

Blatant lies

Gaslighting is based on blatant lies told by the abuser to the victim to throw them off-kilter. By introducing a huge deliberate lie, the abuser lays the groundwork for tearing down the victim's perception of reality. Usually, the victim can tell she or he is being lied to, but because the lie is being told with a straight face and the abuser is sticking to their alternative facts, the victim's sense of reality is thrown off and they begin to doubt their own version of events. One lie after another will soon erode the victim's sense of reality, keeping them reliant on the abuser for the "correct" reality.

Lying is one of the key behaviors in gaslighting. We can even say with certainty that for gaslighting to occur, the abuser must use blatant lies.

Countering

This technique involves the abuser telling the victim that they remember something incorrectly. This usually happens when both the victim and the abuser have experienced the same event or the victim has seen something the abuser has done that is not in line with their expectations of their partner. Usually whatever has transpired is not a pleasant event.

The abuser will typically try to undermine the credibility of the victim's memory of the event. To do this, they will counter their version of events by providing an alternative narrative. With this technique, there is a semblance of subtlety, meaning the general description of the experience will be similar to a large extent, but the areas that portray the abuser in a bad light will be omitted or tweaked to be favorable. For example, a woman sees her husband having dinner with another woman after he told her he would be at a business meeting that evening. Upon confronting him, he concurs he was having dinner with a woman, but she was the client he was meeting and what seemed like an intimate conversation was just him being attentive because the business deal is crucial for the company.

Trivializing

Gaslighters like to trivialize the issues that matter to the victim. This is effective in making the victim feel like their opinion or perception is inconsequential. It works extremely well, leaving the victim with low self-esteem and self-worth. Isolating someone who feels unworthy is easier because they already believe that they don't matter and no one will miss them.

When they are not trivializing matters, they are usually pretending not to understand why the issue matters to the victim. For example, if one person is gaslighting another about finances, every time the other person asks about their finances, the abuser will say something along the lines of "I don't know why you are worried about my spending when I have told you we are financially stable." Or, "Why are you questioning me about money when you know how bad you are with finances."

Discrediting

Discrediting the victim is a ploy right out of the gaslighter's playbook. This tactic entails convincing the people around you that you are unstable and insane. Good Guy Gaslighters and Glamour Gaslighters are quite good at convincing the victim's loved ones that they are a good fit for their partner. This is one of the reasons why gaslighting victims may not want to talk to their loved ones about what goes on behind closed doors.

Sometimes, even parents and siblings are so blinded by the charm of the abuser that they fail to notice the pain and suffering of their own loved ones. In some cases, the victim's support system is so completely overtaken by the abuser that people in the support system begin to gaslight the victim, as well.

Stonewalling

This involves the abuser completely shutting out the victim by not engaging them in conversation or refusing to listen to them entirely. They may also change the subject so they don't have to address the issue their partner is trying to raise. Usually, this tactic lays the ground for the abuser to play the victim and place the fault for the disagreement on the victim.

For example, if a man asks his gaslighting wife where she was and why she didn't come back home last night, the wife can refuse to answer or refuse to listen to him and walk out of the room. When she comes back into the room, she will talk to him about dinner plans she is arranging for him and their friends. Now, if the man tries to steer the conversation back to the issue of her staying out all night, she will make him feel guilty for not appreciating the effort she is putting in order to create a fun time with him and their friends. She will probably say something like, "I can't believe how selfish you are, not even appreciating my efforts towards this dinner. Instead, you want to make me feel guilty about going out to have a little fun with my friends. I am sure I told you about last night a couple of days ago, but now you pretend that you can't remember."

The man will feel conflicted because she is clearly doing something nice for him with regard to the dinner. And he will also question himself about forgetting or not concentrating when she mentioned the dinner when she said she did.

Reframing

Gaslighters are very good at twisting the thoughts and experiences of the victim in favor of their narrative. This contributes to the victim questioning their reality and relying on the perspective of the abuser. Let's go back to the example of the woman who saw her partner at dinner with another woman. When confronted, the man can try to reframe the experience and twist the thoughts of the woman by saying something like, "We were both there and indeed I was having dinner with her. But surely, you are not suggesting that we shouldn't interact with other women or men just because we are seeing each other? I wouldn't do that to you."

Of course, the woman will quickly try to clarify that she is not against him having female interactions and then she questions whether she was reading too much into what she saw. He has succeeded in twisting her thoughts and making it seem like she is implying that she doesn't want him to have any interactions with other females. Because she says he is free to talk to other women, he will take advantage of this while always reminding her that she said she was okay with him having female friends.

Fake compassion

This is a very popular tactic, especially in the early days of gaslighting in a relationship. Since the victim is not yet under the abuser's thumb, he or she will try to claim everything they do is for the well-being of the victim. This tactic ingratiates the abuser to the victim and helps them gain the victim's trust. With time, they will begin to tell the victim what to do under the guise of being protective or having their best interests at heart.

In the beginning, the abuser will start by saying, "I don't want to tell you what to do, but I strongly care about you and I just want to make sure you are okay. If you ask me, you would be better off not being friends with X." As the relationship progresses and the victim can be controlled this phrase will change into, "I have always told you to put a stop to that friendship because I am just looking out for you. But you think I am trying to control you. Now look, she is coming between us." Fake compassion is a deadly tactic that is used to isolate the victim from friends and family.

Easy to spot warning signs that you are being manipulated by a gaslighter

You have proof of something yet they still deny it:

Gaslighters are focused on altering your reality, so even if you have proof of what they said, they will deny it and even accuse you of trying to alter their reality. They can be very believable in their denial and will pretend that they don't know what you are talking about to the extent that you begin to wonder if you are wrong.

They use your fears, failures, and doubts as ammunition:

When your partner uses negative and sometimes even positive aspects of your life to manipulate you, this is a gaslighting relationship. For example, they know how important a promotion, your family, your children, or your career is to you and they use this to manipulate you. They will tell you how unworthy you are because you failed to get that promotion or your career isn't progressing and so forth.

In most cases, gaslighters use the most intimate things you share with them to make you feel unworthy. These are among the first things they will attack, in order to control you and your response to them.

They constantly lie

They will lie about everything, usually either a lie here and there to support their narrative or undermine your credibility with yourself and others. These lies wear down the victim and, before long, it seems as though only the abuser sees things clearly in the relationship.

They occasionally use positive reinforcement

"See, that's not bad at all. You did that very well because you listened to what I said. Good job, honey." Using positive reinforcement throws the victim off-kilter and they see the man, woman, parent, or partner they once knew. This makes them feel that the abuser is not so bad. As long as the victim does what they are told, everything will be just fine. Looking closely at the action that prompted the positive reinforcement, you will notice that it serves the abuser.

They project their flaws onto their victim

The gaslighter is often dealing with unsavory issues, like infidelity, substance abuse, and violence, among other things. So, as a distraction from their own behavior, they will project it onto their victim. For example, if he or she is cheating, they will accuse the victim of cheating in order to draw attention away from their own infidelity.

They tell others that their victim is not stable

Maligning you to others is a tactic that a gaslighter will use so they can gain support for their actions. If they tell your mutual friend you have a bad temper, the next time you react to something they say in public in the presence of that mutual friend, it will reinforce the gaslighter's words and you look like the one with a problem. Soon enough, the gaslighter will tell you that even the mutual friend concurs you have a problem. That doesn't mean that the other person said that (remember gaslighters are blatant liars), but you are led to believe that others see you as problematic, as well.

Gaslighters know that confusion is the best way to disorient their victim and keep him or her in their clutches. Therefore, they are very strategic about sowing confusion in their relationship, while having the upper hand with the correct information. To achieve a good level of confusion, they will paint everyone related to the victim as a liar, so the victim is always relying on them for the truth.

It is crucial to be aware of gaslighting techniques, so you can start to identify them if they happen to occur in your relationship.

Questions to ask yourself to assess if you have a gaslighter in your life

As mentioned above, a gaslighting relationship is peppered with constant confusion and emotional turmoil. This is because what you see and what you hear from your loved one feeds two very different realities. You need an effective and efficient way to be able to tell whether you are in a relationship with a gaslighter. Introspection is important, but don't forget to also look at the other person's behavior. Here are some questions to get you started:

- Do you often wonder whether you are too sensitive because of the things your partner says? But yet you don't have this problem with other people?
- Is your personal definition of yourself something you identified or was it pointed out by your partner?
- Do you feel confused even about the most basic information or timeline of events?
- Do you have the tendency to second guess yourself since you entered into the relationship? To the extent of stifling your opinions because you are unsure of yourself?
- Are you always apologizing to the other person, even when you have not done anything that warrants an apology?
- Do you consider yourself lucky to have the other person, but you are still unhappy and you can't figure out why?
- Are you the excuse-maker in chief for the other person's actions?
- Do you live a double life because of their actions to avoid criticism? For example, do you act like you are living your dream life with the Glamour Gaslighter just to keep up appearances with friends, co-workers, and family members?
- Do you question your worth in your relationship or at work?
- Do you feel like you can't get anything right?
- Do you feel like there is something wrong with your relationship, but you can't point out what it is?
- Are you lying to your partner to avoid sarcastic responses, put-downs, and to maintain the peace in the relationship?

You will notice that all these questions tend to revolve around your reality, instincts, sanity, and feelings. They show you whether you have lost yourself to your partner. Also, note that these questions are very specific to your mental well-being.

Why do victims still choose to stay?

Gaslighting is a very painful reality to accept. Accepting that the person you trust and love and shared intimate moments with is trying to make you lose your mental stability isn't something that anyone wants to hear. In most cases, gaslighters have seen the signs mentioned above or they have been warned by friends and family or even the abuser's previous partner.

The victim needs to understand that it is not their fault and the gaslighting is a reflection of the abuser. In the words of Wayne Dyer, self-help book author, "How people treat you is their karma. How you react is yours." Victims of gaslighting may choose to stay in the relationship for a couple of reasons, including:

Societal expectations

Even though we live in a society where men and women are redefining how they want to live by living single lives or having open relationships, the majority of the population still holds on to the traditional sense of a relationship. This means that it still matters to many people to be in a monogamous relationship, sharing assets, children, and companionship for the rest of their lives.

These societal expectations make it hard for many victims to walk away from gaslighting relationships because they are afraid to lose their standing in society. They are also afraid to lose the feeling of being loved and attached to someone they care about, despite the fact that there is no love there. The fear of the stigma of divorce in some cultures is greater than the fear of living with an abusive partner.

It also doesn't help matters when society promotes a ride-or-die mentality. Even in love songs or romantic flicks, the woman, especially, will call herself the "ride-or-die chick." This mentality is typically not expected of men in society. This is a woman who will stand by their man through all manner of shenanigans.

Normalization of abuse

If the victim has lived in an abusive relationship for a long time, they may begin to normalize the behavior. Since gaslighting is an insidious and gradual form of abuse, the victim can slowly and unknowingly normalize the behavior or their partner by rationalizing it. Take, for example, an abuser who uses the fake compassion technique, in which they tell their victim they are only looking out for them or doing something for their good. The victim will come to associate the harmful behavior, like isolation or even physical violence, with love and care. This makes it hard for them to seek help because they no longer see anything wrong with what their partner is doing.

Physical danger

Gaslighters are capable of going to any lengths to keep their victim or keep their behavior a secret. The loss of power over their victim reinforces the gaslighter's feelings of insecurity and low self-esteem. They are likely to want to preserve their status in the abusive environment and also in society. As a result, they can become physically violent with the victim and may even go as far as killing them.

In some cases, the gaslighter will threaten to harm themselves if the victim leaves, putting the burden of their well-being on the victim. Who wants to be responsible for another human being's death, especially when you are already vulnerable and depleted yourself? Statistics from domestic environment organizations show that women are up to 70 times more likely to be killed within the next few weeks after leaving an abusive relationship. So, when a woman leaves a relationship, she has to create a safety plan to get out of reach of the abuser.

Eroded self-worth

The actions of the gaslighter over time will erode the self-esteem and self-worth of the victim. He or she is left feeling like they aren't good enough at anything or for anything. By eroding the victim's self-worth, the abuser makes the victim dependent on them to define who they are. And, since in many gaslighting relationships, the abuser makes the victim feel like there is no one who will love them because they are damaged goods, the person being gaslit will continue to stay.

Plus, it is hard to escape the pattern of control that has taken place over the years and has become a part of the victim's life. This is one of the reasons why a victim will probably go back to the abuser when he or she pleads for them to come back. Statistics show that a person in an abusive relationship will try to leave up to seven times before finally leaving for good.

The make-up honeymoon phase

Every so often in a gaslighting relationship, the victim catches a glimpse of the person they fell in love with and this is usually during an apology after an abusive situation. This is the typical cycle of abuse and it is aimed at getting their victim to let down their guard and minimize the abusive incident. The honeymoon stage is short-lived, however, as the abuser needs to maintain control of the victim and, to do this, they have to keep them feeling downtrodden.

During the make-up honeymoon period, the abuser is particularly attentive to the needs of the victim. They will buy them gifts, help with chores, and show love and affection. But they will still stay true to their gaslighting behavior by making the victim acknowledge how lucky they are to have them in their life and how things would be like that every day if only she or he behaved.

Remember the pattern of behavior of a gaslighter includes ingratiating themselves to their victim so they are blinded by the actions of love.

Hope for better

The victim always lives with the hope that the other person will change. This is one of the main reasons why they make excuses for the abuser. They believe that if things get better for the abuser, they will get better overall. This is especially true for people who are experiencing financial hardship or going through a life-altering situation, like an illness, loss of a loved one, or PTSD. Also, because of their love, they feel guilty leaving the other person at their most vulnerable time.

Religion

Victims who are deeply religious will find it hard to leave because it goes against their beliefs and religious values. In religions where separation or revelations of abuse can lead to ostracization, the victim will probably stay in the relationship and may even coerce those around her or him who know about the abuse (like the children) to maintain their silence.

Shared assets

Having children, property, and finances together makes it harder to make the decision to leave. In cases where there are children involved, the abuser may, over time, create a narrative for the children which favors them. The victim is therefore afraid of losing the affection of the children if they leave the relationship. Fear of losing financial stability, especially if the abuser is better off financially, is a major reason why victims stay. In friendships where gaslighting occurs, the victim is afraid of losing the mutual friends they have with the gaslighter. Or, if they live together, this may also be a reason to stay in the abusive friendship.

Empaths are the perfect partners for gaslighters

In the previous chapter, I highlighted the story of Greg, who had a type when it came to the women he chose and on whom his gaslighting tactics always worked. These were women who were trustworthy and empathetic towards others. Such people are known as empaths and their natural disposition makes them a prime target for gaslighters.

Empaths are defined as people with a high sense of awareness of their emotions and those of others around them. They are so in tune with these emotions, that they are keenly aware of others in their space and how they are doing, what they need, and their pain points. Do not confuse empaths with Highly Sensitive People (HSP), who tend to be mainly introverts. Empaths can be either extroverts or introverts. While empaths, like HSP, tend to want a deep and enriching inner life and have a strong desire to help others, they take it further by immersing themselves in the circumstance and experiences of others with the aim of finding ways to help. They will internalize someone else's pain and discomfort, feeling it as closely as their own.

Empaths are the complete opposite of narcissists. On the sensitivity spectrum, narcissists, sociopaths, and psychopaths are at the lowest end of the spectrum, Highly Sensitive People are in the middle section of the spectrum, and empaths are at the highest part of the spectrum. Narcissists are attracted to the nature and disposition of the empath because they exude the confidence, security, and love they so evidently lack. To control such powers and capabilities is alluring for someone who doesn't feel at the same level or at all. This is actually a parasitic relationship, where the abuser feeds off the goodness of their victim, depleting them while inflating their ego in the process.

Empaths need to understand their responses to fear, threats, stress, and uncertainty to be able to develop a healthy way to respond to gaslighting. The typical response of an empath in a gaslighting relationship is to try and fix the situation, rather than leave the abuser. They will try to diminish themselves, thinking that they are focusing on the bigger picture. Because they are so in tune with other people's feelings, they are willing to do all the work to make things work and narcissists use this quality to make them feel guilty when things don't go their way.

It is very important for empaths to understand that their role in the relationship is not to make the narcissist whole and happy. That is the responsibility of the narcissist to themselves. You may be the kindest, most helpful, and most patient person in their lives, but they won't change for you. They can only change for themselves and you have to let them do that. The gift of sensitivity is the first to be exploited by the gaslighter, which is why the victim always wonders, "Am I being too sensitive?"

Empaths embody a few distinct characteristics. Read them below to help you identify if you are one:

You internalize other people's emotions

This is the primary, classic trait of an empath who has the tendency to absorb other people's emotions. This ability to pick up on other people's emotions has long been the subject of debate and, what has emerged, is that people with high levels of empathy have very extremely active mirror neurons. This is the part of the brain which is able to read emotional cues from the people around you, letting you know how they are feeling. This is what makes you discern another person's joy, sadness, anger, or anxiety. Empaths are able to pick up on other people's emotional cues, like darting eyes to show anxiety, a downturn in the mouth, or a change in tone, helping them sense what the other person is feeling.

The depth of their feelings is so strong that catastrophic events seen on TV or heard on the radio can cause them a lot of distress. If they have lived through such an event in their past, this may even incapacitate them. An example of empaths in such situations include those who go to lay flowers, light candles, or hold a vigil at sites of terrorist attacks or other tragedies. These events so move the empaths that they will go to the place where they can feel closest to the victims and their families and make a gesture of love and care.

You go by vibes

The vibe in a room or emanating from other people matters to you. You can make a friend or not, depending on the vibe they emanate. Unfortunately, narcissists are very good at being pretentious and their original vibe can be deceptive. Empaths typically love nature and gardening because they get a sense of peace and are energized in this environment. Conversely, an atmosphere of conflict, chaos, and violence quickly saps an empath's energy and can cause you to become withdrawn.

Going back to the story of Kellie Sutton in chapter one, you will notice that she was described as happy, fun, and vibrant by her friends and family until she got into a relationship with Gane. Her environment caused her to change completely and withdraw so much that it was evident to those who knew her well. Empaths are unable to thrive in foul environments.

You are understanding

This is the reason why people turn to you for advice. You have a level head and have a lot of insight. Because of this, people are drawn to you, including some nasty characters who may want to take advantage of you. Empaths are also excellent listeners because they can put themselves in the other person's shoes and feel their emotions.

You love living things

Empaths love life and living creatures make them happy, so you will find most empaths have a pet, are parents, or are involved in a conservation effort of some kind, either for flora or fauna. Their reactions to either one of the above can seem over the top to other people, but for the empath, these creatures and plants *should* elicit such a reaction. The feelings of an empath are always turned way up compared to other people. It makes sense that empaths are attracted to careers in caregiving, like nursing, elder care, and other healing professions.

You can get easily overwhelmed

As mentioned, the feelings of empaths are highly pronounced, so when they feel both positive and negative emotions, they are susceptible to being overwhelmed. Perhaps this is the primary reason why the gaslighter can eventually tear down the victim's walls of empathy because the empath can feel the anger, irritation, and negative moods emanating from their abuser. This causes them to want to change themselves, conform, accept the alternative truth, and even accept abuse to make the relationship better.

You can detect lies

An empath is able to tell when people are lying because of a liar's subtle emotional cues. So, when an empath is lied to by a gaslighter, they can't easily come to terms with someone who says they love them but is blatantly lying to them. They rationalize the blatant lying by questioning their own reality or perception of events, especially when the gaslighter shifts them in that direction by saying things like, "That is not how I remember it."

You have a calming effect on people

Your voice and demeanor are calming and make the people around you calm down or look at a situation rationally. You will notice that your friends seek you out in moments of turmoil in their lives because they feel you are the level-headed friend. In the same vein, you can't see someone in pain and leave them unhappy. It may be inconvenient for you, but you will be there for your friend until they are fine.

CHAPTER FOUR:

Gaslighting in Intimate Relationships

Life with the charming gaslighter - The horrible truth

Fairytale love stories have given most people a false sense of romance, which is shattered when they begin having relationships and find frogs instead of their Prince Charming. But Alexa is a realist and she has never been that girl waiting for Prince Charming or to be swept off her feet. In fact, when her friends describe her, they all concur that she is a pragmatist, although she is also one of the most caring, loving, helpful, and thoughtful people in their circle of friends.

But when Nicholas came into her life, he seemed hell bent on showing her that the fairytale life existed and he was her Prince Charming. He wined and dined her, flew her to exotic places for holidays, lavished expensive gifts on her, was a gentleman to her, and a sweetheart to her mother. He was her greatest supporter when it came to her career as a cosmetic surgeon. She was pleasantly surprised after a string of cheating men in her life. Her friends were happy for her and her mom was finally thrilled to see her dating and thriving, which made the discrepancies she began to notice right after their wedding hard to share with them.

Since she had her own cosmetic surgery practice, with a small staff and a partner, she could travel with Nicholas during his business meetings all over the world. Plus, he liked having her next to him. He was lost without her and couldn't concentrate when he was away from her. Nicholas was a wealthy man and so he began to drop hints that she didn't need to work. He wanted a family and stability, so he suggested that she quit so that they could start a family.

She refused, of course, and that was the first day she saw the other side of Nicholas. They were having this discussion for the umpteenth time and she was once again explaining why she couldn't give up her career. Suddenly, he hurled his scotch glass across the room and, eyes blazing, turned to her and said, "You are nothing without me! Do you think Tabitha (her partner at the practice) wants you at the clinic? She knows you are not that good and she can do without you!"

Alexa was shocked at first and then she began to feel her anger rising within her. "That is a lie", she said quietly. Tabitha had been her best friend for over 15 years since high school and they had built the practice together from scratch 10 years ago. Nicholas abruptly got off the couch and, changing tactic, let his eyes brim with tears before saying in a hurt tone, "I am only doing this for your own good. I worked hard, so the woman I love can have all the luxuries in life and you continually turn down my loving gesture, like it means nothing to you. Why are you being so cruel to me?" With that, he stormed out of the house and she heard him getting into his car and driving away.

Alexa was unsure of what to feel. She was reeling at his attack, his disparaging manner about her work, and the reference to her best friend, thinking she wasn't good enough. Did Tabitha say something to him? Tabitha didn't like him from the beginning, but seemed to lay off attacking his character after he proposed, so she assumed her friend had come to like her husband eventually. But what was that comment about being cruel to him about? She felt bad that he thought she didn't appreciate the lifestyle he provided for her, but surely she could be appreciative and work at the same time? Sighing, she cleared the broken glass he had thrown across the room and settled on the sofa to wait for him and make things right. He may have overreacted, but he was coming from a place of love.

It was 5 am when Nicholas walked back into the house and, when she woke up to ask him if he was okay and where he had been, he walked right past her. The silent treatment continued for four days and, even when she apologized, he acted like he hadn't heard her. After several days of apologizing and pleading with him, he finally began to talk to her again. But at every turn, he would make a comment about how she should quit her job. The comments ranged from, "Look at how tired you are every day, just because of that practice" to "We could be so much happier if you would only quit your job and spend more time with me." Sometimes, she would find him outside her office waiting for her and he would say that he was lonely in the house without her. He insisted that she travel with him for his business meetings, wherever he went, effectively curtailing the time she spent at her practice. When she mentioned this to him, he replied, "I can see your priority in this relationship is your job and not us. We could be great, but you are ruining it for us by holding on to this job."

Alexa also talked to Tabitha about the comments he had made about her, but Tabitha hadn't even talked to Nicholas in months. In fact, the last time they spoke was the night of Alexa's engagement party, when she congratulated him and Alexa. According to Tabitha, her opinion of Nicholas hadn't changed, but she respected Alexa's decision and their friendship, which is why she backed off.

Six months into the marriage, Nicholas got Alexa a customized, top-of-the-range car, which he parked outside her workplace and waited to surprise her. Alexa walked out of her office laughing with Tim, the head nurse at the clinic and, on seeing her husband, walked over to say hi. Instead of a happy man wishing her a happy birthday and handing her the car keys, he barely smiled at her and tossed her the keys to the car. He hung around to see her friends and colleagues gush over the car and exclaim how lucky she is.

On the way home to prepare for the birthday party he was throwing for her, she was gushing over the car, but he barely said a word. Concerned, she asked him what was wrong and he replied by accusing her of being unfaithful. Shocked by the allegation, she asked him what he was talking about and he asked her who Tim was and how they knew each other. When she replied he was the head nurse at her clinic, he began to call her terrible names, insinuating that they were having an affair and that's why she was not willing to quit her job. Stunned, she sat in her seat quietly the rest of the way home.

They got ready for the party and left together without so much as a word between them. At the party, it was hard for Alexa to act like everything was okay, especially because Tim was there and he was a goofball. When receiving gifts, she could barely meet Tim's eyes and her hug was stiff when he handed her his gift. Mumbling her thanks, she moved on to the next gift, leaving Tim with a frown. She could hear him asking Tabitha if she was ok. She saw her mom and gladly made a beeline for her, giving her a warm hug and offering to take her coat. Her mom quietly said she wanted to see her in private for a minute. Wondering what was the matter, she followed her mother outside. "Hey mom, great to see you. Are you okay?" Her mother was never one for mincing words, so she got straight to the point. "Nicholas says you don't want to have a family. What's going on? I thought this is what you always wanted…a husband…children and a home?" "Unbelievable", Alexa muttered under her breath. "Mom, Nicholas wants me to quit my job and stay at home or travel with him. You know how hard I worked to get that clinic with Tabitha. I can't do that! But I never said I don't want a family. Why must I choose? Why can't I have both?" "He told me you refused to leave the practice and I must say I agree with him. He has everything you need and he is a great provider. He is financially stable for both of you, so why not follow his lead?"

Stunned, Alexa just stared at her mother. The older woman started to fidget under the stare and quickly cleared her throat to add, "Honey, I want you to be happy and you won't get anyone better than Nicholas. He adores you and just wants to make you happy. I think he has a point when he says you are paranoid about your independence. Please reconsider, because he is really hurting about this." Alexa felt deflated and the joy of her birthday flowed out of her. Standing in the warm night air, she started to feel invisible walls closing in.

The drive home was tense and she recalled the look on Tabitha's face when she shared her predicament during the party. Her friend looked horrified, not just at the thought of Alexa quitting the practice, but the support Nicholas was looking for from her mother. When they arrived in the house, Alexa was on the way to the bedroom when a subdued Nicholas called out, "Lexie, sweetheart, I am sorry I accused you and Tim of having an affair. It's just that I can't understand why you are so stubborn about letting me take care of you. Please, just give my proposal a chance and I promise you won't regret it."

"Did you talk to mom about us -- about this?" Alexa asked him. Flinching, he said, "Yes, I did. I was desperate and I thought she could help me talk to you. Your mom knows what I am trying to do here. If I were you, I would listen to her. You know she would never steer you wrong." Alexa could feel the fight draining out of her and she turned to walk away. She went to bed and fell into a disturbed sleep, which was interrupted by loud sobs. Waking up, she is startled to find Nicholas curled up in fetal position at the foot of their bed, loudly sobbing and promising to kill himself if she ever stopped loving him. "Why don't you want to make me happy? Just come and be with me or I swear I will go to the office and not come back one day. Promise me now. Promise you will leave that job and stay with me."

Despite her terror at what she was witnessing, Alexa calmed Nicholas down by placating him and promising she would quit by the end of the month, after she put her affairs in order. He returned to bed and held her tight for the rest of the night, almost like he was holding on to her for dear life. The next day, he seemed to be in a better mood and was more of his loving, jovial self. Alexa began to consider that perhaps she should give up the practice to let peace reign and avoid episodes like the one last night.

Two months later, worn out by the rollercoaster of emotions, Alexa finally quit and sold her share of the practice to Tabitha.

On her last day at work, she could barely stop crying, thinking about what she was giving up. When she got home, she made dinner and informed Nicholas that she was free of her work obligations, just like he wanted. She told him she never wanted him to feel or react the way he did on the night of her birthday party, where he threatened to take his own life over her decisions. Immediately Nicholas responded, "That's not what I said." "Sorry?" said Alexa. "I never said I would take my own life. You must be remembering it wrong. I said that you should promise not to leave me, but I am not suicidal. Maybe that's your thing." said Nicholas.

Alexa sat with a frown on her face, replaying the scene of her birthday, from the car gift to the party and the loud sobbing at night, and she could have sworn he said he would kill himself. That is why she was so worried in the first place and what prompted her to finally take the jump and leave her job. Nicholas was chewing his food and shaking his head saying, "You're crazy. That paranoia of yours is getting out of hand." When she insisted he said those words, he ordered her to stop trying to make him look crazy. He insisted that she was the one acting crazy by accusing him of wanting to kill himself. Alexa let it go, but she kept wondering if he was right.

Over the next three months after she quit her job, Nicholas became withdrawn and when he spoke to her it was an instruction rather than a conversation. He instructed her on what to wear, how to wear her hair, and even whom to talk to. He cut all communication in the house, so she couldn't call out and neither could someone call in. When she asked him why he did this, at first he pretended there was nothing wrong with the phone and she was being paranoid about it. Then, he pretended something was wrong with the phone company and he would sort it out. When she finally followed up with the company and found out their line was not working anymore because he stopped the service, she confronted him and he claimed to have done it for her sake. He knew she was talking to Tabitha every day and it wasn't helping her move on from her previous job and focus on starting a family.

Alexa's mother came by the house for dinner one night and commented about how frail and pale she was looking. "Is everything alright Lexie?" Alexa decided to open up to her mother and explain how Nicholas had changed. He was more controlling and didn't even want her to go grocery shopping alone. "He asked me to stop going to yoga and he even controls what I eat. Tabitha and the girls are not welcome here and Mom, I think I am going crazy because I swear he will say something and later deny ever saying it." As they were speaking, Nicholas walked into the room looking directly at his wife with an icy stare. But, when he turned to his mother-in-law, he gave her a doting, warm smile and a long hug.

"Hey Mom," he said. "You look good." Fixing himself a plate, he said, "Listen, I keep telling you Lexie is paranoid. Now she thinks I don't want her to have any friends. Why would I want that?" Alexa dropped her gaze when he looked at her and then she looked at her mom. Her mother was looking at her strangely and abruptly she asked her to help her serve the dessert she had brought for dinner. In the kitchen, Alexa's mother asked her directly, "Has Nicholas ever hit you?" "Nooo mom, it's not physical it's just...I can't explain it." said Alexa.

"Well, maybe you are just reading a lot more into his actions than you should, now that you are at home more. Like he said...why would he prevent you from seeing your friends? This is marriage, honey. You guys just need to understand each other."

Alexa tried to understand her husband, but the more she tried, the more she made no sense of his behavior. Two years into the marriage, they still didn't have children because Nicholas said he wanted everything to be perfect. When she questioned him about it, he would say, "We can get pregnant right now if you want, but with your paranoia, I don't think you would make a good mom." On his birthday, he sulked and when she asked him why he was mad, he complained about her present. "You give me the cheapest presents, which tells me you don't love me as much as I love you. If you did, you would invest in me and my happiness. We could be great together, but you just keep messing things up."

He no longer took her on his business trips because she didn't behave and was an embarrassment to him. One time during a dinner with some of his business partners, she engaged in conversation with an important member of the business delegation and he complimented Nicholas on having such an intelligent and charming wife. Immediately, he pulled her aside and told her to stop showing him up. On the way home, he exploded, saying, "This is exactly why I don't take you anywhere anymore. You just have to make a spectacle of yourself and make me look bad. You think he thought you were smart? He was just being polite. I can't have kids with someone like you." Alexa was now used to these outbursts, so she didn't flinch. Instead, she promised to be a better, quiet wife. At home, she wearily got out her clothes and into her pajamas, thinking to herself that she was so weary and alone.

The next day, she informed her husband that she needed to go and get a haircut. It was one of the things that she looked forward to, although he had started insisting that her hairdresser come to the house. At the hair salon, she bumped into Tabitha, whom she hadn't seen in close to 10 months. On seeing her friend, the tears started to stream down her face. Tabitha was shocked at how beaten her friend looked. She insisted on having a long lunch. While pushing her food around on her plate, Alexa told her friend everything that had been going on. Because Nicholas had taken away her phone and given her a phone with just his number and a few of his friend's numbers, she couldn't get in touch with anyone.

Alexa said she was afraid she was losing her mind, amid heart-wrenching sobs. Tabitha went across the street and bought her a phone and gave it to her to hide. "If you need me for anything, call me and I will come over, no matter what time of the day. Keep this safe, Alexa, this is your lifeline." They returned to the salon and had their hair done and, during that time, Tabitha could see fleeting glimpses of her vibrant friend when she smiled. "Why do you hide your smile behind your hand? You never used to do that," asked Tabitha. The veil of sadness immediately descended on her friend's face. "Nicholas doesn't like my smile because of my crooked teeth." What crooked teeth? Your teeth are perfect -- they always have been." At that moment, Tabitha realized what her friend was going through. She was being gaslit and she didn't even realize it! If she didn't do something, Alexa's life would be destroyed. But what can she do?

As they parted ways, Tabitha said a short prayer for her friend to be safe.

On arriving home, Alexa was confronted by a furious Nicholas. "I called the salon to talk to you since you conveniently left your phone behind and they said you had left with another woman. Who is she? Or is she a decoy for you to meet your lover? I knew you were not worth anything and that's why I can't have kids with you." Alexa tried to explain that it was Tabitha. "Ohhhh Tabitha! Was she picking you up so you could go and see Tim?" Alexa was so exhausted and drained, she just broke down in tears and let him continue to rant and hurl abuses at her. When it got too much, she ran into the bathroom and locked herself inside. She was just starting to compose herself when she heard the sound of an electrical appliance at the door. Not sure what was going on, she decided to wash her face before emerging. Suddenly, she saw the door teetering on its hinges. He was taking the door off at the hinges to get to her! She was terrified watching the door be dismantled and was sure she would die there today if he got to her. Instead, he calmly placed the door to the side after removing it and said to her, "I don't want there to be any barriers between us. This is me showing you that I love you."

That night, she sank into sleep, still disturbed by the events of the day, only to be woken up by the sound of glass shattering. She thought it was a burglar, so she reached out for Nicholas but he wasn't in bed. Tiptoeing downstairs, she whispered loudly, "Nicholas!" Then, she noticed the study door was open. She ran to it and found Nicholas lying in a heap, a glass of scotch shattered nearby and pills on his table and floor. She screamed and called 911. This was the third time he had done this. Nicholas was rushed to the hospital and his stomach pumped. When she went to visit him he looked at her sullenly and said, "Look what you made me do. I can't lose you. And if there is someone else, I won't ever let you be happy. If I can't have you, I won't let you have peace without me, even if it means I have to die and come back to haunt you."

As Alexa stood there looking at him, it struck her how much helplessness had overcome her. The nurse walked in and informed her that visiting hours are over. She leaned over him and kissed his forehead. "See you, Nicholas." "Come earlier tomorrow, so we can spend more time together," he said. As she walked out, she reached for a phone in her bag and dialed the only number in it. "Tabitha, please come and help me pack my stuff."

Alexa got a restraining order against Nicholas and filed for divorce. She relocated somewhere where Nicholas couldn't trace her, using the money from selling Tabitha her part of the clinic. Last she heard, Nicholas was on trial for domestic violence. Looking back on the three years she gave the man, she wondered what would have happened if she hadn't walked away. Would she be alive or dead? Thank god, she didn't have to find out. Alexa's mom walked up to Nicholas one day in the parking lot of a local grocery store and gave him a resounding slap on the face. "That is for breaking the most precious thing in my life."

7 stages of gaslighting in a relationship

Gaslighting is a persistent form of abuse that doesn't let up and is gradually done to the victim. When experienced in a mild form, there is a subtle shift in power in which the victim is always subjugated to the abuser.

When one experiences severe gaslighting, they can become completely disoriented from reality and be completely mind-controlled by the abuser. Cult leaders are known for employing severe gaslighting, which involves heavy mind control tactics to get their members to commit tragic acts, like killing themselves or even killing others, like in the case of the Charles Manson and the Manson family.

There are seven stages to gaslighting. Each builds on the previous and takes the level of manipulation up a notch higher.

Step 1: Exaggerate and lie

I have established that gaslighting is built on a foundation of lies. Like I said, without lies it is impossible to execute gaslighting. But to be effective in gaslighting, the lie needs a little exaggeration. The exaggeration is meant to establish different facts that mesmerize the victim into feeling that the story has too many details to be a lie. The better the embellishment, the more believable the story.

Gaslighters are masters at embellishing and spinning a new narrative around a story. For example, perhaps you both ran into one of your friends of the opposite gender and the interaction was public, but afterward, the gaslighter will introduce embellishments of how the interaction went, in order to support his or her narrative. If it was a friend who touched your shoulder while speaking to you, the gaslighter will declare that they were flirting with you and you didn't notice, but he or she can tell what the friend was trying to do. A simple, innocent meeting will go from being a fun interaction to something nefarious, supported by the exaggeration of the gaslighter. The victim is left wondering if there was something they missed and thanking the gaslighter for looking out their wellbeing.

They will also lie about you to other people in a bid to discredit you. For example, a gaslighting boss will lie about your performance and even blame you for mistakes made in the company, even when you have nothing to do with the responsible department. Facts and evidence may prove otherwise, but that doesn't mean they won't try to frame you, just to discredit you.

The lies are meant to breakdown the truth threshold of the victim and put the victim on the defensive. During this stage, you can expect to hear phrases like:

"Your department is a waste of resources because you don't get anything done. How do you justify your salary?"

"You wouldn't know the truth if it smacked you in the face. You can't remember even the most basic details of information, so I have to keep steering you right."

Step 2: Repetition

Donald Trump is known as the "Gaslighter in Chief" and one of his favorite tactics is the repetition of falsehoods until his base and others begin to believe his words to be true. For example, during one of his rallies, he pointed to the members of the press who were covering the event and called them "fake news". The crowd began to boo the press. The President of the United States called the media fake news, which his base believes. Formerly well-respected media houses, like CNN and BBC, have lost credibility with some members of the public.

But are these media houses really fake news? From their coverage, there is plenty of proof that their news is fact-checked and their sources are credible. In fact, media houses like CNN have fact-checked the president on some of his blatant lies and exaggerations proving the fake news source is in fact Donald Trump. But he has repeated the phrase so many times and used it to discredit credible sources of news and in the process established a pattern that is now used by dictators around the world. Dictators now call any unfavorable news fake news.

This is the perfect example of what happens when gaslighters repeat certain phrases. They become the alternative to the truth, but they are accepted by many as the real truth. In intimate relationships, the gaslighter uses words like "crazy", "paranoid", "sick", "unstable", and "insane" to describe their victim in public and this can cause friends, family, and even acquaintances to look at the "gaslightee" through those lenses.

The repetition of lies gives the gaslighter dominance over the conversation and keeps the victim on the constant defensive, which makes them appear unstable, even to themselves. Some victims will withdraw from conversations completely, in order to avoid being portrayed by their partner in this way, but the abuser will still use their silence to show how their condition is deteriorating. You can't win with a gaslighter.

Step 3: Escalation

Escalation typically occurs in a gaslighting relationship when the gaslighter is challenged, causing them to raise the bar. This is when one notices the gaslighter either getting violent, aggressive, or threatening to people around them. He or she will focus on people the victim values the most, like their children or elderly parents, threatening to cause harm to them or take the kids away.

Calling out a gaslighter on their lies makes them feel vulnerable and this causes them to want to regain dominance. To do this, they have to find something that will double down on the control over the victim, so they focus on things the victim loves. You can expect to hear phrases like:

"You know, this paranoia is why I think the kids are in danger around you. Who knows what you will say to them. I will take the kids away from you because you are a danger to them." Or,

"Your parents are better off without you since you are just becoming crazier and crazier. I will put them in a home and make sure you never cause them distress like this again. They also know you are crazy. Imagine what this is doing to them. You are a horrible daughter/son."

Remember that gaslighters do not play fair, so they have no shame using underhanded tactics on their victims. The escalation is meant to put fear into the victim and let them know they have no recourse for their situation. It creates a feeling of helplessness and constant anxiety. This is one of the reasons a victim stays in the relationship for years. They honestly believe they are protecting their loved ones by staying with the gaslighter and obeying him. Don't rock the boat and everything will be okay.

They may also get aggressive and abusive in the actions towards the victim. Physical abuse is not uncommon in gaslighting relationships.

Step 4: Wear out the victim

Wearing out the victim is a real strategy used by gaslighters. In the story of Alex and Nicholas, the latter constantly complained about his wife working and even used his mother in law to "talk some sense" into his wife. When she remained adamant, he threatened to kill himself, gave her the silent treatment, and emotionally blackmailed her into submission.

By constantly being on the offensive, the gaslighter keeps his or her victim on the defensive, which can be an exhausting state to be in, especially with someone you love. The fighting fatigue soon sets in and the victim doesn't want to be at constant odds with the other person.

The gaslighter can also wear out the victim by constantly attacking their responses to situations or their perception of events. Eventually, the victim begins to accept the narrative of their abusers because they become resigned to their fate and are filled with pessimism about the future. You must remember that the goal of the gaslighter is to break their victim and grind them into the ground, which will only happen by wearing them out with negativity.

Stage 5: Encourage a codependent relationship

The gaslighter needs their victim to become dependent on them, so they foster a relationship in which the victim looks to the abuser for verification of the reality she or he is experiencing. To create a codependent relationship, the abuser creates situations of constant insecurity, uncertainty, and anxiety in their victim. They dangle certain things in front of their victim, like starting a family, love, security, or even financial security, which puts the victim on strings to be played like a puppet any time the abuser feels like it. You will hear phrases like the following in this stage:

"I see that you are trying to behave, so I won't take the kids away from you. But you must promise me that you will be good because you know I have the power to take them from you."

"I have told you that your friends are just jealous of us. See how they want to make plans on the day I have planned our date night. You are better off without friends like that. Just you and me babe, we are enough for each other. We don't need anyone else."

For the codependency to take root, the victim must be marginalized from people who could show him or her the real definition of love and care. Exposing the victim to people who love them is counterproductive to what the gaslighter is trying to achieve. The victim must be made to believe that the abuser is the only person who has their best interests at heart. The codependent relationship is built on fear and lies and it allows the abuser to be the dominant partner in the relationship.

The gaslighter loves to play savior to the victim in the relationship, making the other person feel like they are the only safe place the victim has. Any codependent relationship is fraught with doubt and anxiety, not to mention confusion, and this one is no different. Unfortunately, only one person in the relationship feels this way.

Stage 6: False hope

This is the time that the manipulation is in full play. The gaslighter creates a scenario where they give the victim a sense of false hope that things will go back to the original love they shared or the stability that existed in the initial stages of their relationship. The false hope stage includes treating the victim with kindness and acting like the abuser really cares. Intimate dinners, gifts, and even gentle treatment is laid on thick for the benefit of the victim. But, just as suddenly as the kindness and romance came back, it will abruptly be withdrawn.

You see, the abuser gives false hope to throw the victim off-kilter and also to remind them that, just as easily as they can be loved, they can be discarded. During the period of false hope, which can last a day to a couple of days or maybe even a week, the abuser builds up the victim with the sole intention of tearing them down in such a destructive manner that they will be incapacitated by the letdown.

This is perhaps one of the most toxic parts of gaslighting, as the abuser intentionally inflicts psychological torture and torment. Not only do they know what they are doing in building false hope, but they try to make the victim feel guilty when they tear them down. At this stage, you will hear phrases like:

"Look at what you have done. It's your fault we are not happy. You see how hard I am trying to make us work and then you just go and try to show me up in public."

"What is wrong with you? Why can't you get what I am trying to do for us? If this doesn't work out, it is all your fault because God knows, I try."

"Why are you dressed like that? Do you expect me to go out with you looking like that? That's it. You clearly don't appreciate what I am trying to do here for you, so just go back upstairs and change. We aren't going out anymore."

Any cries by the victim to rectify the situation fall on deaf ears and the abuser is back in control, while the victim is left blaming themselves for ruining their chance at getting back their original love.

This tactic is used by the gaslighter anytime he or she sees the victim either unresponsive to their mind control game or showing some signs of resistance to the abuser's behavior. It is a very effective tactic in reminding the victim of who is the boss.

Step 7: Dominance

The ultimate goal of the gaslighter is to gain dominance and control over the victim. They do so in order to take advantage of the other person and, in some cases, have access to their valuables.

Dominance is achieved by having a constant and consistent flow of lies and mind games, including coercion. The abuser strives to keep the victim in a constant state of fear and doubt, which is why they will isolate them from their friends and family, who could give them perspective and reinforce their sanity. Dominance allows the abuser to exploit the victim at will and without any repercussions.

The love bombing tactic

Love bombing involves the gaslighter using over the top shows of affection to the victim in a bid to emotionally manipulate them. Besides the Intimidator Gaslighter, the Glamour Gaslighter and the Nice Guy Gaslighter typically use this tactic. It happens early in the relationship, in which the gaslighter manipulates the response of the victim by buying lavish gifts and taking him or her to expensive places for dinner or on vacation. There are signs that you are being love-bombed early in the relationship, including:

Saying what you want to hear

All of us have insecurities and when we share them with a love bombing expert, like a gaslighter, they will consistently say what they think you want to hear in order to inflate your ego or gain your affection. For example, maybe you hate the way your nose looks (we all have parts of our body that we don't like). The gaslighter will constantly tell you your nose is their favorite part of your body and, no, it doesn't look hawkish -- it looks regal. There is no genuine honesty in their compliment, instead, they serve the purpose of manipulating you.

Claiming you could do better

Beware of the partner who constantly tells you that you could do better because there is underlying insecurity in them. In the case of a gaslighter, they are trying to gain your sympathy and want to seem like they feel privileged and humbled that you chose them. Deep down, this is a manipulation tactic.

They might also begin to criticize your friends, career choice, colleagues, and even family members, saying you could do better. This is a ploy to ensure isolation from the people who love you, in order to enhance their manipulation. If your partner, early on in the relationship, starts suggesting that your friends or family don't have your best interest at heart but he/she does, they are trying to separate you from your support system. These claims are usually followed by a lavish gift or an expensive getaway, to make them look like they care about you.

They give expensive gifts

Now, receiving expensive gifts from a potential partner early on in a relationship is not a red flag in itself. But there are telltale signs that it is a love bombing tactic, especially if the giver makes a point to tell you how much the gift cost. Not only are they trying to impress you, they want to make you feel guilty when they don't get their way.

After all, they spent all that money on you and all they ask for is just your love and affection.

For the gaslighter, telling you how much they spent on you is their process of quantifying their investment in you and estimating your value as a person.

They lavish compliments

Gaslighters know that their victims want compliments. Remember, they know what you want to hear and they use compliments to condition you. Their complements are used to manipulate you into being what they need you to be. With time, their compliments shape you. For example, if the gaslighter tells you that you look good in black dresses, you will probably start wearing more black dresses in order to always look great to him. If they say you don't need makeup because your skin is flawless, you will probably stop using makeup in a bid to make them happy. This is conditioning you to make you the person they want to have in the future.

Public displays of affection

During the love bombing stage, the gaslighter loves public displays of affection. They will touch you, kiss you, and show warm body language in front of your loved ones. This is to prove to everyone that you guys are good together and he or she is into you. It sets you up to look like the offending party when you try to pull away from the person. Most victims are also taken in by the PDA and will believe it comes from a genuine place.

In return, they will expect you to return the affection by being obedient and listening to what they say. When they want to see you, they expect you to drop everything and show up. If you are unavailable, they take that as a rejection and typically have an extreme reaction to this. This introduces a pattern of extreme reactions, unmanageable expectations, and that walking on eggshells feeling.

CHAPTER FIVE:

Gaslighting in the Family

When parents are gaslighters, lives are lost

Suzie and her mother were close. They always had popcorn dates together when she was a kid and watched their favorite movies. They talked about the boys she liked as a teenager and talked on the phone every day of the week when she went to college. Her mom was a single parent and she was warm, fun, friendly, and beautiful. She also never spoke to her own mom, who was living in a different neighborhood but in the same city.

Growing up, Suzie's mother refused to take phone calls from her grandmother and Suzie only met and talked to the elderly woman twice or thrice in her life. She found out that her mother had a brother who passed away as a teenager from suicide. As she grew older, she found out that her mother blamed her grandmother for his death. During dinner at her mom's house one day, she broached the subject of her grandmother, asking about her and why her mom never spoke about her.

"I knew this day would come," said Suzie's mom. "Grab that bottle of wine and meet me in the den. I'll go get some pictures. It's time you met your uncle and your grandmother." In the den, Suzie's mom looked at a picture of a young man who looked like her and was holding her hand. In the picture, Suzie's mom was grinning at the young man, who looked down on her beaming. "This is your uncle, Tyler. He was so smart and kind and funny. Next to you, he was my favorite person in the whole world. He killed himself when I was 13 years old." This was the first time Suzie's mom had spoken about how her brother died.

"My mom was a pathological liar and mean as a rattlesnake and Tyler was her victim of choice. He was too sensitive and she destroyed him day by day until he couldn't take it anymore. She would lie to him about everything and lie about him, as well. She told him his girlfriend was cheating on him with his best friend and when he confronted the girl, he found out it wasn't true. They broke up and when my brother confronted my mom, she pretended she didn't say that and he must have heard her wrong. She always told him that he only needed her."

"My brother mentioned this to our grandfather, who asked mom. My mother said that my brother made up the whole cheating situation and is now blaming her. She said this in brother's presence and even added, 'You know how he is.' "One day we were grocery shopping and my mom slipped some eyeliner into my brother's backpack. He was arrested by the store security and my mother accused him of stealing it for one of his girlfriends. My brother denied it and she refused to get him out of jail that night, saying he needed to learn his lesson. I know it was her because I saw her do it, but I was too scared to tell anyone. My grandfather heard about the incident and asked my brother about it. My mom chimed in to the conversation, saying my brother was a liar and again adding, 'You know how he is."

Before long, my grandfather began to regard my brother as a troublemaker and my brother was so confused by what was happening, he began to withdraw into himself. There were many times when my mom called my brother names, like a liar, thief, good for nothing, dumb…the list was endless. My brother stopped hanging out with his friends because she would call his friends' parents and tell them he was a bad influence and was doing drugs and stealing. No one at school would come near my brother and he started to get bullied, really badly. He never told my mom about it, although he tried to tell my grandfather. Grandpa called mom and told her to go to school and find out what was happening. My mom told him not to bother because my brother was just looking for attention.

Two weeks later my brother slashed his wrists in the school bathroom. In his bag was a collection of notes from one of the school bullies telling him to kill himself. The note said that no one wanted him, not even his own mother. My brother never understood why mom hated him so much. My mother lost custody of me to my dad who took care of me and I haven't spoken to her since my brother was buried. She cried at my brother's funeral, vowing to find out what happened to her boy. But it was all for show. I never let you near her because she is a master gaslighter. I am grateful that I went to live with my dad because I think she would have done the same thing to me."

The toxic things that gaslighting parents can do

They dictate your likes and dislikes

This means that they tell the child what she or he likes or doesn't like. They say things like, "What do you mean you don't like baseball?" Or, "We are a family of meat-eaters. There is no place for vegetarians in this house." As a result, they force their preferences on the child.

They dismiss your feelings

"Stop crying!" Or, "Don't cry like a baby because you got hit during a game!" These are some of the phrases that parents use to dismiss sad or unhappy feelings. This conditions the child not to feel or show emotion, even when they are hurting. Eventually, the child learns to take their hurt out on something or someone else.

They minimize your achievements

Toxic families are characterized by bullying tactics in which the victim is downtrodden and their achievements are not validated. For example, if the child is great academically, the father might say, "Books don't matter in this world if you don't know how to take care of yourself." Or, "I don't care about straight As -- if you can't play ball, you are not a man." They will also make fun of your achievements, calling them silly and time-wasting.

They will label you

You might be called silly or paranoid or that you have a wild imagination. These labels are easy to put on kids because children are known to have imaginary friends or play most of the time. But in a gaslighting situation at home, it is meant to cast doubt on the child's reality.

If the child calls the gaslighter out on their behavior, the parent will label them rude, undisciplined, or a troublemaker, in order to make themselves feel better.

Gaslighting children

Gaslighting is a common occurrence in dysfunctional families and the gaslighter is typically the mother or the father of the child. Gaslighting is insidious in nature to anyone, but in children, it is especially devastating because the cycle of emotional abuse can continue even into adulthood. The children will also tend to choose gaslighters for their life partners.

The children stuck with gaslighting parents typically lose their confidence and they tend to have little to no integrity, through no fault of their own. When the child perceives the parent as the enemy, it is particularly traumatizing.

606

4 types of gaslighting in childhood and their effects

Even the most well-meaning parent can be a gaslighter without knowing it. If you give your child conflicting information that conscientiously contradicts the reality they saw, you have gaslit them. For example, your daughter or son walks in on you having a piece of chocolate and you have been saying all week that you are on a diet and are off sweets. When they ask you what you are eating and you say nothing after hurriedly swallowing the chocolate, you have gaslit your child.

Some parents like to call them white lies, but they are dangerous because they set up a precedent of alternative realities. If you do this frequently, your child can become conditioned to a skewed sense of perception.

Four types of childhood gaslighting

Double-bind gaslighting

This type of gaslighting parent was first identified in 1965 and it has been linked to schizophrenia and a personality disorder. The perfect example of double-bind gaslighting is when the parent tells the child they love them and can even be smothering in their love sometimes and, the next minute, the parent coldly rejects the child or inflicts corporal punishment.

The message is very confusing for the child, who feels loved one minute and unwanted the next. The effect of such gaslighting is that the child grows up unsure of their validity and they always question what others say to them. Questions like, "Am I worthy or not?" always plague them, especially in relationships, from life partners and friends to even at work.

Appearance focused gaslighting

In this type of gaslighting, the child is expected to uphold the status of the family by putting up appearances that everything is perfect, even when it is not. You will find that victims of sexual abuse by a family member have been gaslit in this way. Achievement focused parents also tend to engage in this type of gaslighting.

This type of gaslighting makes it difficult for the child to accept human weakness in themselves and others, as they grow up. It also makes it difficult to let other people in because of the fear of being vulnerable. The message in appearance focused gaslighting is that we must appear perfect and what happens in the family stays in the family. Your pain and reality don't matter.

Unpredictable gaslighting

In this type of gaslighting, the child is not sure how the parent will react to a situation. The same mistake is met by uncontrollable rage in some cases and, at other times, the parent is lucid and even gentle and understanding. Parents who are manic depressive or have a history of substance abuse are most likely to engage in this type of gaslighting.

The message to the child in this type of gaslighting is that you can never be stable. Anything can happen to you at any time. As a result, the child is not able to read people's characters and intentions as they grow older. This puts them at the risk of ending up with a similar abuser as a life partner.

Emotional negligence gaslighting

This type of gaslighting involves emotionally neglecting the child, although their physical needs are met. The parent will attack the child for showing emotion most of the time, saying things like "Don't you dare cry", "Suck it up" or, "I have no time for sensitive people."

The message to the child is that their emotions are irrelevant and they are not to be shared with anyone else. Such kids grow up feeling that they are lacking in a certain aspect of themselves and will seek people, like gaslighters, who will fulfill that side of them.

CHAPTER SIX:

Gaslighting in the Workplace

How working with a gaslighter nearly derailed a career

Macy had been working at one of the premier hotels in Dubai for over two years as a front office agent. Her work was exceptional and professional, which was proven by the guest interactions and accolades from the hotel brass. At the beginning of her third year in the same role, a new hotel manager was employed. The female boss took an instant dislike to Macy and, from their first interaction, was curt and short with her.

Thinking she may have done something to offend her, Macy set out to make things right. She asked for a sit-down and broached the subject by asking if there was anything the new manager had seen about her work that she felt Macy should improve. The manager launched into a litany of things she noticed about Macy that she should change, but none of them were based on her work, rather they were personal issues. "I don't like the way you wear your hair. Are you a natural blonde?" "Yes, I am" "Are you sure? Because it looks like you have bleached your hair. I have nothing against blondes. It's just that you look like you are trying to stand out and be noticed more. I think that is unprofessional." "I assure you that I am a natural blonde and my hair color is not a ploy to attract more attention to myself," said Macy. "Are you married?" asked the manager. "Not yet," replied Macy. "Mmmhhhh." said the manager, as if it all made sense now. With that, Macy was dismissed. She left wondering whether her hair color attracted more attention and if she looked like that's what she was trying to do.

About three weeks later, a colleague in the accounts office stopped Macy in the corridor to ask her what was wrong with her paperwork. "Nothing, as far as I know," replied Macy. "Why do you ask?" "Well, the hotel manager asked for all your paperwork dating back six months," said the colleague. "Why?" asked Macy. "I don't know why but she asked specifically for your paperwork and no one else's," said the other employee. That afternoon, she was summoned to the manager's office to find her paperwork neatly placed in a pile next to the manager.

I have been going through your work and I must say I am shocked you have lasted this long here," she began. Your paperwork is sloppy, you haven't attached supporting guest payment slips, and I don't see the relevant signatures on the credit card slips. How do you justify your salary? Do you think you are here to just look good?" Stunned, Macy finally found her voice to say "Sorry, I am confused here a little. No one in the accounts department raised any questions with me, so I am not sure what I have failed to do here. May I please see an example of the incomplete paperwork?" "Do you think I am making this up?" asked the manager. "I have tons of proof here. The accounts department also doesn't think you are competent. They all concur with me that your work is shoddy. I am putting you on six-month probation as I review your work. And, may I suggest that you consider a darker color for your hair so you are less conspicuous."

Macy stumbled out of the manager's office and went to the ladies' room to wash her face. "What is going on," she asked herself. She has been at the front desk for longer than anyone and her work has always been praiseworthy. Did the accounts department really believe her work was shoddy? Why didn't anyone say something? Maybe she had become complacent and wasn't giving her very best these days. She would make sure her work was impeccable.

For the next few months, she endured constant criticism, comparison, and even subtle bullying by the manager. So when a position opened up in another branch, she applied just to get out from under the thumb of her current boss. The manager heard about it and called the recruiting officer to "caution" him against offering the position to Macy. But since Macy was one of the last interviewees left standing, the recruiting officer scheduled a final interview with her nonetheless. Macy emerged as the best candidate, so the recruiter decided to have a candid conversation with her about her "reputation."

Macy, I am very impressed. You clearly are the best person for the job, but I have some concerns. To begin with, your boss got in touch with me and raised some concerns about your work. So, I asked the accounting office to share your paperwork with me and I honestly didn't find anything wrong with your work. A few mistakes here and there, but nothing that seems as major as your hotel manager tried to imply. Tell me about your relationship with the hotel manager at your branch." Macy decided to be honest with the recruiter about the relationship with her boss.

"I am certainly not surprised to hear this. This manager has become a notorious gaslighter, especially with female staff whom she feels threatened by. I would like to offer you the job and I would also like you to share your experience with the human resources director." It turned out that this manager had been gaslighting employees for years and most people were too afraid to lose their jobs to report her actions. The recruiter was one of her victims and she had decided enough is enough.

How to identify gaslighting at work

Gaslighting at work can be subtler because the abuser is more aware of their surroundings. He or she is usually a point of authority or a peer to the abuser, but junior staff can also be excellent gaslighters, especially if they are ambitious and eying a job opening with stiff competition. You can tell you are being gaslighted at work when you see telltale signs like:

- The gaslighter is spreading misinformation about you.
- You are the subject of gossip and blatant lies spread by one specific person.
- The gaslighter is very charming and witty around you.
- They try to get your contribution and then twist your words and use them against you.
- The gaslighter discredits you, leaving you feeling like you are not worthy.
- They make passive-aggressive comments about you under the guise of jokes or being friendly.

How common gaslighting tactics are used at work

Countering

This tactic involves the gaslighter questioning your memory of events, especially those that happened when you are together. For example, if you shared clients and were in a meeting together, they may question your notes and imply that what you wrote was inaccurate, only to write a report with the same version of events. When confronted, they will blatantly deny ever having changed the version of events, claiming you misunderstood what they said.

Withholding

The colleague or superior withholds pertinent information to your work, making it impossible for you to be effective at your job. They also withhold praise, even where it is due, with phrases like "That is what you are paid to do. There is nothing special about what you achieve."

Trivializing

If you close a deal or get a promotion, they find a way to trivialize the achievement. They may say "That is a minor achievement. At your age, I was on the fast track to becoming the company managing director." This leads the victim to think their ideas and input or achievements are not important.

Lying

Gaslighters at work will lie in order to paint their victim in a bad light. This works to their advantage because it casts doubt on their victim's competence. It also launches the victim into a state of anxiety and self-doubt.

Diverting

The gaslighter will divert attention from the subject of work to focus on the victim's emotional or private life. For example, Macy's manager shifted focus from the aim of the meeting, which was Macy looking for feedback about her work, to criticizing Macy's looks and style.

Phrases gaslighters use in the workplace

The following are common in a gaslighting work-related relationship:

- You need to concentrate.
- Don't you remember us discussing this yesterday?
- I always have to repeat myself because you can't remember stuff.
- If you could just learn how to listen, we wouldn't have this problem.
- You are being too sensitive.
- Stop being paranoid/irrational.
- You are too emotional.

- You read too much in my comments -- I am just trying to help.
- Can you hear what you just said? What does that say about you?
- Are you going through something at home? You are always behind on things.
- I only have these sorts of problems with you.
- You need to learn to take a joke. You are too thin-skinned.
- I am always reminding you of things because you have poor organization.
- I am hard on you because I like you.

The gaslighting boss and their tactics

They bad-mouth you

The gaslighting boss will find ways to bad-mouth you to other senior-level members of the company and your peers. This is a tactic to make you lose credibility with other members of the company, so when you make complaints, you don't have a friendly ear or support. They will also blatantly lie about you.

They move deadlines

A boss who gaslights their juniors makes unreasonable demands on them that he or she knows will cast the employee(s) in a bad light. For example, they will move a deadline up, knowing it will be impossible to produce the work within the new timeframe. And if asked why they moved the deadline, they may deny ever moving it.

They make insulting comments

This tactic falls under the diverting gaslighting technique. They will say something underhanded, like making a racist comment disguised as a joke. If you call them out about it, they will claim you are being too sensitive. They will say it in front of people and, when they face backlash, they will claim you misunderstood the comment or that everyone says it.

They exclude you

You are the one person missing the important team emails by accident, which impacts how you do your work. On the extreme end, the boss may even take credit for your ideas or work and exclude you from getting credit for your work. When you confront them, they will say there is no solo effort and it's always a team effort.

CHAPTER SEVEN:

Gaslighting in Friendships

A toxic friendship hidden in plain sight

Mike and Sam had been friends since they were in junior high. Every day after school, they would hang out in Mike's treehouse for hours on end, doing their homework, playing video games, and checkers. They were there for each other's first kisses and they talked about all their crushes. Nothing could separate them.

They applied to different colleges and so came their separation. Although the two friends visited each other, their visits became far and few in between. Three years after graduation, the two friends found themselves in the same city and bumped into each other during a morning coffee run. Mike thought the person ahead of him in the queue sounded familiar, so he stuck his head out from the back of the queue to see if it was who he thought it was. Sure enough, it was Sam.

Mike left the queue and followed his childhood friend as he walked out of the coffee shop, wrapping his arms tight around him and growling, "Give me your coffee, nice and slow." Alarmed, Sam turned around ready to punch his would-be assailant, but was instead met with the wide grin of his friend. "Ohhh...Mikey! Oh my God! What...How long has it been?" "Too long, my brother! I haven't seen you in over five years. How are you?" replied Mike. "I'm good, man - just grabbing my morning coffee on the way to work. I have a small tech startup, developing medical apps to help patients reach caregivers faster. How is your practice?" said Sam.

"You know the law. Everybody hates lawyers, but they sure love to keep us busy. How is Charlene and the kids?" asked Mike. "Everyone is fine. We would love to have you over for dinner. As a matter of fact, come over this Saturday, I am sure Charlene won't mind me making plans." Replied Sam, "That sounds great! Here is my business card. If you guys change your mind, let me know" said Mike.

The two friends rekindled their friendship and started hanging out more often. During their hangouts, Mike would always make underhanded jokes about Sam's race and his struggle with weight loss. It began with phrases like, "Put the fork down, otherwise you will go back to being known as 'Sam the Bubble.'" This was despite the fact that Sam was lean and fit as a whip. In fact, Mike was the chubbier of the two, but his references were to the bullying and teasing Sam experienced in junior high because of his weight.

During one of their conversations, he said, "You know your wife is a real mammy. She loves to take care of other people and makes a great presence in the house." Shocked, Sam looked at his friend and asked him, "What did you just say?" "You know, she has that nurturing character that is inherent in black women. I am sure she takes excellent care of you. Just look at you. It's a compliment bro! You know I am saying this because I love Charlene," replied Mike. For the rest of the evening, Sam was subdued and when he saw his friend off, his hug was lackluster. Should he tell Charlene what Mike said? She would lose her mind and confront him. Maybe Mike was just paying a compliment the best way he knew how, but why use a slavemaster's slang. He had known Mike all his life and the man didn't have an evil bone in his body. He choked it down to ignorance on his friend's part and decided that the next time they hung out, he would educate him.

The two friends played golf often and, on the days they played together, Mike had a nasty habit of counting the number of black people versus the number of white people on the course. "More and more black people are playing golf these days, I guess. After Tiger Woods, all of you thought you could do it. But you know, the only reason he even got in through the door was because he had a white, blonde wife. That is every black man's come up."

"What the hell are you talking about?" exploded Sam. "First, Tiger Woods is the greatest of all-time in golf. Second, my people don't need a 'come up' from any white man or woman. What has come over you with these racist comments?" Walking away from Mike, Sam replaced his club back in the bag, heaved it on to his shoulder and started off towards the golf cart. Mike caught up with Sam and said, "Why are you being so sensitive? I don't mean you. I respect you and I thought I could be myself around you. Why are you being emotional about this? We are friends and we can speak freely around each other. You are acting crazy."

The ride off the course was terse and the two men parted ways without saying anything. When Sam got home, his wife asked him what had transpired between him and Mike. "How did you know something happened?" he asked. "Well, Mike called me to tell me that you were acting funny, paranoid even. That you went off at him about him praising Tiger Woods and commenting about seeing more black people on the course, which he thought was great," Charlene explained. Sam let out a loud sigh and asked his wife to sit down. "Mike has been making some very disturbing comments about black people. He disparages me about my weight and, when I confront him about it, he says I am overreacting, being too sensitive, or that I am crazy. I know what he is saying and it's not right."

"I didn't want to tell you this, but Mike came over to my workplace the other day and he claimed he was worried about how you are behaving. He said you have been looking at other women when you two are together and even approached one woman to ask her for her number. He asked me not to tell you, so he could find proof for me. I didn't tell you because I was honestly shocked and it's been two days of me thinking about what to do with this information. But from what you have told me, I think Mike is gaslighting you."

Stunned, Sam sat silently for a while, staring straight ahead. Suddenly, he said, "Let's call him. If he tries and flips this on us, we know he is gaslighting us. Or, at least me." They phoned Mike, who picked up and said, "Hey buddy. Are you okay now? You overreacted back there. I was worried about you."

"Did you tell my wife I was looking at other women and approached someone for her phone number?" Asked Sam, quietly. "What...I...What are you talking about? I never said that. Charl..." Mike spluttered before being interrupted by Charlene. "Mike, are you saying I am lying about you coming to my office two days ago to tell me that you were concerned about Sam looking at other women and that he even solicited a number from one of them?" Charlene asked. "Charlene...honey...you must have misunderstood what I said. I never said that. What I was trying to tell you is that you should be careful to take good care of my friend because there are many women out there who would want a man like that. Remember, I even told you I would get you proof of how many women want him?"

Charlene and Sam looked at each other silently, as Mike continued to lie. "Guys...guys...are you there? Look, this has been a huge misunderstanding. I can come over right now and we can clear it up. I am on my way over. I'll bring some wine we can hash this out and have a great night," said Mike.

"Don't come near me or my family ever again. If I see you or hear that you have come near my wife or my kids, I will get a restraining order against you." Mike started sobbing on the other side of the line. "Don't do this bro. We can sort this out. I have nothing but love for you and your kids. Charlene is lying, man. You will come back to me one day when she dumps you and takes your kids. I know, I know."

Sam replaced the phone and called his sons downstairs. "Trey, Tyler, we have to tell you something. Uncle Mike is not welcome here anymore and you are not to have anything to do with him. Okay?" "Sure Dad", said Trey. "I didn't trust him anyway. He told Tyler that you and mom were fighting so bad that he was here to make sure you guys didn't get a divorce. He asked Tyler to tell him everything that was going on at home, so he could help you guys. When Tyler told me, I told him it was a lie, but we were afraid to tell you because he was your friend."

It turned out, Mike's wife had left him and taken his two daughters with her because of his gaslighting behavior. He picked up the habit in college and used it on multiple women he dated and some of his friends.

Signs of a toxic friendship

It is very important to discern when a friendship has become toxic. In some cases, the friendship is toxic from the beginning and in other cases, it gradually becomes toxic over time. Signs that a friendship has become toxic include:

Putting you down

A toxic gaslighting friend is more concerned with being right and having control over you than your best interests. In a healthy friendship, the feedback you receive is positive and uplifting, even motivating you. Corrections are made out of love, not out of malice. In a toxic friendship, the "friend" will play on your insecurities and even reinforce them in order to dominate you.

Exerting control

Speaking of dominating you, a toxic friendship tips the scales of balance to favor one person. The toxic friend will dictate where you go, what you do, and even influence how you dress or speak to them. By exerting control over you, they effectively take away your power to make your own choices and give themselves control over these choices.

Blame

We all make mistakes, but when the controlling person makes the problem about you and tries to exonerate themselves, leaving you with the blame, you are in a toxic friendship. Toxic friends will not take responsibility for their actions if they have negative results. You will be blamed for even the slightest issue that arises when you are in their presence.

Emotional blackmail

This tactic involves withholding support or affection to the victim in circumstances where they need it. Toxic friends give their love conditionally and their love is only based on what you can give them. If you aren't available to them, they will not return your call, pick up your calls, or reply to your texts. They want to teach you a lesson by not being available to you.

Humiliation

Friends like to rib each other and teasing is a special part of friendship, but toxic friends take this to another level with deliberate humiliation. They will even laugh at the expense of the victim. If a friend constantly tells cruel jokes about you or laughs at your expense, they are abusing your friendship. If you have raised this as a concern with your friend and they tell you that you don't have a sense of humor, this is not a good friend.

Unpredictability

An inconsistency in your friend's personality that makes them unpredictable should be a red flag. If they are acting like this more often than not, they have the potential of creating a toxic environment for your friendship. In this type of friendship, you are never able to relax completely.

Common gaslighting phrases toxic friends say:

- You are being too sensitive.
- If you were a good friend, you would notice...
- I am like this with everyone, not just you,
- I was just kidding.
- You have no sense of humor.
- It's good to learn to laugh at yourself.
- What would you do without me?
- I can criticize you because we are friends.
- You know you are being insecure right now.
- It's no big deal.
- It's your fault our friendship isn't better.

CHAPTER EIGHT:

The Language and Culture of a Gaslighting Society

Gaslighting culture today

The culture we live in is very quick to judge anyone whose reality isn't in line with what they believe should be a reality. For example, in the Trump era, anyone who doesn't subscribe to "Making America Great Again" is ill-informed or worse. The liberals are the crazies, the conservatives are too uptight, and anyone in between doesn't have the backbone to back the "winning horse". Here are some ways the current American discourse has contributed to gaslighting culture:

Ignoring minorities

Gaslighting is more prevalent in today's culture because we have marginalized many people whose identities or practices don't fit in the narrow definition of what we have normalized in society. From the LGBTQ community to different religious groups, races, and political ideologies, we have opened up people to being gaslit by denying that their rights and freedoms are as important as those of others.

These denials have destabilized whole communities, which in turn destabilizes the entire nation. As a result, skewed leadership, like that of Donald Trump and Vladimir Putin, has gained a foothold and their lies and deceptions are now considered the truth.

Labeling people

The culture today is all about labels. You are either a failure or a success, depending on where you live, whom you live with, and how independent you are from your family. This has led to people losing support systems, like parents and siblings, because they want to appear successful. Inevitably, when they fall into the hands of gaslighters, they are easily isolated from their families, leaving them completely vulnerable. Such labels are used to measure the worth of a person, but they provide a foothold for nefarious emotional behavior.

Denying credit where it's due

The culture today is very accommodating of cultural appropriation without understanding that not only do the appropriators take credit for what they didn't create, they also deny the real creators their due credit. This practice leaves the communities who originally created the trend disempowered. It wipes out and trivializes the historical human trauma associated with slavery and colonization. By denying the culture and encouraging appropriation, you are gaslighting an entire community. This makes it easy to gaslight individuals from that community in a new, systematic form of oppression.

Rewiring the past

This means feeding the current generation lies about what happened in the past. The gaslighters will try to erase the historical injustices by tweaking the narrative to favor their own. For example, the rewiring of how black people organized sit-ins and safe spaces has had a direct impact on the reception of Colin Kapernick's peaceful kneeling protest against the killing of young black men. Add the rewiring to the words of gaslighters like President Donald Trump and society becomes desensitized to the past and now looks at the protest as the problem.

The future of gaslighting society

Gaslighting in the future is going to focus on our children and we are sending a signal to them that messing with another person's mental health is an acceptable way of interacting with them. Incidences of bullying, where the bully even encourages the victim to kill themselves, have been on the rise and the bully usually has narcissistic tendencies. They believe that they are somehow better than their victims.

To destabilize this nefarious trajectory in human interactions, we need to start having conversations with our kids about gaslighting, what happens when you are gaslit, how to avoid it, and overcome it in relationships and friendships.

In order to combat gaslighting, we need to demand better from our leaders and others around us. It must not be business as usual when the president lies or gaslights an individual.

Gaslighting and social media

Gaslighting in social media is known as cloutlighting. Social media has become a place of business and personal interactions, but it can also be a place where you find the most nefarious form of gaslighting. It gives the gaslighter a larger audience when discrediting their victim and may even attract other gaslighters to the gaslighting party, with the victim as the main target.

Take, for example, a group of friends with one who is a gaslighter. She will arrange events and exclude her gaslighting victim then post pictures of herself with the other friends on social media, knowing that the victim will see it. If the victim asks why she was excluded, the gaslighter makes her look bad in front of the other friends, effectively discrediting her. If she doesn't ask, she constantly wonders what she did wrong to be excluded from the event. In such a scenario, it is very easy for the gaslighter to rope in the other friends and make them accomplices in the gaslighting. Soon, the victim's distress becomes a source of entertainment for the rest of the group and they don't know what is going on behind the scenes with the victim and the gaslighter.

Cloutlighting involves the exploitation of the victim on social media to shock and even sometimes entertain others. Have you ever seen a video of a man or woman who seems to be overreacting to a seemingly normal situation and it seems funny at the expense of the person in the video? Imagine for a minute that the person is in an abusive relationship and has just been gaslit. The abuser records him or her and posts it online. You have just seen a victim of cloutlighting. The abuser is looking for sympathy from viewers of the video and also to paint the victim in a poor light. Your nasty comment about the victim is used by the abuser to reinforce the emotional abuse currently taking place.

Familiar everyday phrases people use to gaslight others:

- You take things too personally.
- You can't take a joke.
- You are too sensitive.
- We talked about this, can't you remember?
- I have to repeat myself?
- Don't you think you are overreacting?
- You like to jump to the wrong conclusion.
- Can you hear yourself?
- Stop taking things so seriously.
- Why are you upset about a joke?

Harmful phrases that vicious gaslighters use to disarm people:

You are imagining things.

This phrase is supposed to make you doubt your perception of what you experienced. Once you start to doubt yourself, the gaslighter starts to take control.

It was a joke.

Using this phrase makes you look and feel like you are deficient in humor and you need to not read into what the gaslighter says. Even though the gaslighter says you should take the joke at face value, they actually want you to internalize the meaning of the joke and start doubting yourself.

You are always overreacting. You are too sensitive.

This phrase makes it look like your reaction to the gaslighter is flawed. The correct reaction is what they are asking of you, which is not to be too sensitive.

You need to lighten up or let this go

This is a very dismissive phrase that is supposed to trivialize your feelings and make them unimportant. It is used in public to devalue your worth in social circles.

You are crazy

This phrase is popular because it sets the victim up as unstable and gains sympathy for the abuser at the same time.

CHAPTER NINE:

The Long-Term Effects of Gaslighting

How victims feel and their state of mind during the process of gaslighting

The simple truth behind the way the victim of gaslighting feels is a loss of value. They tend to feel completely devalued and unworthy of their abuser, which is exactly what he or she wants them to feel. The state-of-mind cycle of a victim of gaslighting, as it happens, include:

Disbelief

The victim usually can't believe the shift in the abuser. They begin to feel they have to do more to restore the healthy balance that was there before. The very first time the gaslighting begins, they will make excuses for the abuser, believing that it's just a bump in the relationship.

Defense

The more the abuser comes down at the victim, the more he or she tries to break them, but in the beginning, there is still some fight left in the victim. They will push back at this point because the gaslighting hasn't completely overtaken them.

Depression

This stage quickly follows the defense stage because the victim may feel like she or he is not able to withstand the abuse and constant put-downs. At this stage, it feels like they are constantly doing things wrong and there is an unhappy environment in their personal space all the time, so they gradually sink into depression.

Coming out of depression is hard and this is the stage where the gaslighter begins to win. At this point, the abuser can't afford to let up their psychological torment, so they will isolate the person in order to have unchallenged access to them.

General effects and deep impact of gaslighting

There are several general effects of gaslighting to look out for in yourself or your loved one if you suspect gaslighting:

Second-guessing

Second-guessing is a direct result of eroded confidence since the abuser makes the victim feel like their judgment is flawed about everything. They constantly ask themselves if what they saw was real, or if they made the right decision.

Fear

There is a general aura of fear surrounding the victim of gaslighting. They are constantly afraid to make the abuser upset, afraid they will lose everything, afraid no one will believe them, and afraid to start all over again.

Constantly apologizing

The abuser always has the victim in defensive mode, so they are constantly sorry for their "flaws" which are breaking down the relationship. The victim can even begin to apologize for their existence, which means they are very delicate mentally and could harm themselves.

Depression

It is common for victims of gaslighting to become depressed and melancholy. Nothing rouses them from their fog of sadness and they constantly accept the abuse and put-downs from the gaslighter as their deserved reward.

Withholding information

Victims are usually conditioned to withhold information because the abuser tries to turn everyone against them. If they do not find support in the first person they tell, they may not ever feel like they can tell anyone else. Plus, there is a lot of shame still associated with all forms of abuse and the victims are usually the ones who feel the most ashamed.

Indecision

The victim will grapple with even the simplest decisions and look for someone to make them for him or her. This is because of their co-dependency on the abuser to make every decision. If he or she is not in the picture, they can become completely incapacitated in making the most basic decision.

Guilt

Some victims feel guilty talking about how bad their abuser is when he has been so good in the past. Friends and family may feel like they are being ungrateful or are gold diggers.

Emotional trauma and symptoms

It is important to recognize that victims of gaslighting have been traumatized in such deep ways that it will take years to undo the damage if it can even be undone. The majority of victims exhibit these trauma symptoms, which may be countered in time if identified early enough:

- Hypervigilance (anticipation of additional trauma).
- Flashbacks of painful events, which occur at any time of day or night.
- Heightened anxiety.
- Unpredictable mood swings.
- Mental confusion.
- Intrusive memories.

These are core symptoms that have taken years to develop and may be managed, but never really go away.

Cognitive dissonance

Like I said earlier, cognitive dissonance is the state of mind where one holds two different beliefs and one goes against the other, due to psychological stress. For victims of gaslighting, they believe that their very survival is dependent on their abuser and it is acceptable for the gaslighter to behave as he or she does. The anger and hate shown by the abuser are because he or she loves them and is protecting them against themselves.

For example, a woman in an abusive relationship hates the pain and abuse, but she is even more afraid of what she will face without him. After all, he loves her. They are willing to die rather than face life without the abuser, so they will defend his behavior from family and friends. In gaslighting, the victim tries to mute their cognitive dissonance to survive the internal conflict they feel. This helps them manage their primitive anxiety arising from the situation they find themselves in.

Unfortunately, during this time, they convince themselves that things are not that bad and when the abuser shows them some kindness, they believe things will get better. For victims of gaslighting, cognitive dissonance becomes a crutch they lean on to survive their hell.

How gaslighting in toxic relationships works to erode reality and sense of self

The gaslighter is always one step ahead of their victim in their game, meaning they have already planned ahead using these three steps to erode the reality and sense of self of their victim:

The idealization stage

In this stage, the gaslighter puts their best foot forward, effectively manipulating the victim into trusting them. The victim can do no wrong according to the narcissist, who will lavish them with attention and affection. This deludes the victim into believing she or he is in a loving relationship and makes them let down their guard.

The devaluation stage

During this stage, the gaslighter becomes cold and calculating towards the victim. She or he can do nothing right and is constantly showered with criticism in place of love. This launches the victim into depression and they increasingly try to make their abuser happy, with no success. They begin to feel unworthy and like a failure. This stage is extremely devastating because it can easily chart the pattern of future relationships.

The discarding stage

This is the period during which the abuser figures out how to discard the victim. They may walk out on them, have them committed for mental instability, or even have them killed. The most important thing is getting rid of them. The more the victim tries to hold on to the relationship, the more powerful and even crueler the abuser becomes. The gaslighter will always dangle the possibility of discarding their victim to make him or her cling on even more.

CHAPTER TEN

Proof of Gaslighting

Common gaslighting techniques you should know for when it hits you

Lies and denial

The one thing we have fully established is that a gaslighter is a liar. They will lie blatantly about anything and everything. The pattern of lies is used to condition their victim and establish themselves as his or her point of authority.

Projection

Gaslighting is characterized by the abuser projecting their own failings and insecurities onto the victim. If they are sloppy, they will blame the victim for being sloppy. If they struggle with keeping time, they will blame the victim for being constantly late when he or she is two minutes late. If they are cheating, they will accuse their victim of cheating to cover their actions.

Diverting

The gaslighter will divert the conversation by changing the entire subject and refusing to acknowledge the concerns of their victim. Sometimes, they will completely refuse to listen or respond to issues the victim raises.

Incongruence

This means that they don't mean what they say. The words coming from a gaslighter can be mismatched to their actions. They will say I love you, followed with unloving actions, like the silent treatment and cold looks or sulking.

Countering

Challenging the victim's memories and reality is a game to the gaslighter and they will play the game for as long as you are together. They love how you have to rely on them for information.

Isolation

When you notice your potential partner trying to drive a wedge between you and your loved ones, it is time to ask yourself why. Isolation is the key to effective gaslighting because it leaves the victim vulnerable to attack from the abuser without any support system.

The 5 steps of gaslighters: Learn how they do it

1. They use your fear against you

You have let the gaslighter in and they are now close to you and trusted. You confide in them and, instead of protecting you, they use your fears against you. For example, for the longest time, Americans have railed on and on about the deep state and the Washington swamp. Donald Trump has used these fears and concerns to gaslight the American people and every time he is taken to task, he says the deep state is after him because he is working for the Americans.

2. They act as if they know more about you than anyone

Every time you have an argument with a gaslighter, they will use something negative about your shortcomings against you. For example, if you are not good with finances, they will say, "You know

640

I know you better than anyone. You can't manage money. You are horrible at finances. That is why I am here to take care of stuff like that."

3. They normalize disrespect

During the stage where the abuser is trying to devalue the victim, he will normalize the disrespect every time she calls him out on it. For example, the man will say things like, "Can you hear yourself? You sound crazy." And the woman pushes back with, "Hey don't call me crazy." "Baby, learn to take a joke. I was just kidding," replies the man. Soon enough, he will be calling her crazy and she will accept it because he is just joking and she is being sensitive.

4. They question your commitment

By questioning your commitment, they are casting aspersions on the stability of the relationship. For example, they will demand something they know you can't do, like spend all your savings on their project, and when you don't, they become extremely sad and even threaten to end it or harm themselves.

5. They invest in negative affirmations

They make you doubt yourself by using negative statements as absolute truths about you. For example, the abuser will tell their victim, "I don't know how they haven't fired you from this job. You can barely handle your workload. You don't have what it takes."

Simple responses to smoke a gaslighter that gets them every time

Use the stare

Look at the person who made the comment for a long while, taking in their reaction. The uncomfortable mounting silence is usually enough to launch them into an apology or make them embarrassed. Try it and see the shame come over your would-be gaslighter. The stare is a great way to express disbelief in what the gaslighter is saying, every time you doubt their story.

Remember each mistake

A gaslighter is meticulous in remembering their victim's mistake, so make sure you remember theirs. If they slip up on a story they told you, make sure you call them out on it.

Intentionally misunderstand them

You can see the gaslighter is trying to feed you a bogus narrative and lie blatantly to you. Don't allow yourself to be swayed. Instead, act like you don't understand. For example, say something like, "I can't understand how we saw the same thing and you and I have different versions of it. Interesting how the human brain works. I know what I saw and I am sure you know what you saw. I can't change your mind and neither can you change mine. Let's just agree to disagree."

Do some countering of your own

You said you flushed the toilet and he says you didn't. But you were recording yourself singing as you use the loo. Provide the evidence and counter his or her lies. If he says he texted you to cancel plans and you know he didn't, ask him to show you the text. This lets him know you are on to his game. If something matters to you and the gaslighter tries to trivialize it, call him or her out on it immediately.

Quick comebacks for gaslighting scripts

Gaslighter: "I didn't say that."
Comeback: "You did and from now on I will start recording our conversations, so you can't deny your own words."

Gaslighter: "I look forward to dinner this Friday. Thanks for the invite."
Comeback: "I didn't invite you to dinner. I told you I have a soul cycle class with my friends."

Gaslighter: "I never confirmed that date"
Comeback: "Yes, you did. Here is your text confirming the date."

Gaslighter: "But you said you would help me pay for this stuff. How am I supposed to pay for it?"
Comeback: "I don't know. I never said I would help you pay for your clothes. I told you I may have some money and if I can, I will. This is not my responsibility."

Gaslighter: "Don't be so sensitive."
Comeback: "That is disrespectful. I don't tell you how to feel or act, so don't tell me how to feel."

Gaslighter: "Can't you take a joke?"
Comeback: "What was funny about this? Is it the part where you made fun of me in public or you told everyone my personal business?"

Gaslighter: "I texted you to cancel the date. Didn't you see my text?"
Comeback: "No, I didn't see any message. Show me the text."

Gaslighter: "You don't love me like I love you."
Comeback: "Look, I can only love you like I know how to love you. You do not set the standard of how to love."

Simple ideas to fight the effects of gaslighting

Confront

Do not let the gaslighter back you into submission when you know he or she is lying. It will definitely anger the abuser to see you push back, but it also tells them that you are no pushover. Take a minute and compose yourself, so you are very clear about what you are confronting. The responsive tactic will be to placate you and make you feel like you are overreacting.

Ask for an explanation

The gaslighter cannot explain their actions when asked to because they understand their nefarious nature. This puts them on the defensive and the responsive tactic is usually to get emotional and accuse you of not loving them or to blame you for a misunderstanding.

Prove yourself

If the gaslighter says you are not good at something and that is why they need to be there for you, point out instances where you have done that particular task well and excelled. It becomes harder for the gaslighter to criticize with no proof. And if they still want to argue, refuse, citing your proof.

Demand respect

The gaslighter will test your limits in terms of respect. Demand respect and end the relationship if none is forthcoming. Do not give the gaslighter a chance to become disrespectful because it will only go downhill from here.

A new skill to combat gaslighting

Mindfulness

Mindfulness is our basic human ability to stay in the present and be aware of our surroundings and our actions. The gaslighter will strive to alter your reality, but mindfulness will keep you in the present, able to counter any false narratives that they may try to spin.

Mindfulness gives you the confidence and ammunition to confront any situation. To cultivate mindfulness, you need to:

Build your gut instinct

Your gut instinct will never steer you wrong. Call it intuition if you will, but it tells you if a situation doesn't feel right. Gaslighting is based on lies, so trust your gut instinct if it tells you that you are being lied to.

Keep a journal

A gaslighter is an ever-changing animal, so keeping a journal that tells you what they said and when they said it and it will help you keep track of the facts. You may need to keep a journal in secret.

Meditate

The gaslighter likes to overpower you by calling you names and using put-downs to manipulate your mental health. Meditate and protect your mindfulness. Not only does this relax you, but it also gives you clarity.

Exercise

Easier said than done, but exercise will put your mind and body in sync. A healthy body and mind are harder for a gaslighter to control. The stress and PTSD from being around a gaslighter can be countered by taking some time to do yoga or Tai Chi.

FINAL WORDS

This book is meant to help you recognize and combat gaslighting before it takes root and has debilitating effects on yourself or your loved one. Gaslighting is a common occurrence that has gained momentum as a form of abuse and has been used for a long time to gain control over the victim. For some people, using gaslighting is a conscious decision, but there are some gaslighters who don't know that they are indulging in this behavior.

I've talked about gaslighting in the context of intimate relationships, family units, workplaces, and friendships. You should now be able to understand the approach of the gaslighter and what they want from their victim. I've also shed some light on how you can identify gaslighting in your life in any context.

The gaslighter personality is fraught with insecurities, fears, doubts, low self-worth, and low self-esteem. These character issues play a huge role in making the gaslighter a controlling, manipulative individual. Whether you are dealing with an aware or unaware gaslighter, the effect on the victim is the same.

It is crucial to know what type of gaslighter you're dealing with in order to be able to effectively see their patterns. The minute one becomes abusive and threatens you, this is an Intimidator Gaslighter. If you are dealing with a Jekyll and Hyde type of gaslighter, he or she fits the profile of a Good Guy Gaslighter. This type of gaslighter is perhaps the most insidious of all. The Glamour Gaslighter can be identified by his or her thoroughbred behavior, which they use to entrance you and eventually cause you to be beholden to them.

Self-examination is crucial in a relationship because you may be exhibiting gaslighting behavior, unknowingly. Some of the questions I've outlined can be instrumental in helping you identify if you are on the gaslighting spectrum and, if you are, how extreme are you? This book effectively helps you to understand all of the above and recognize the patterns.

The promise I made in this book was to give you all the information I could about gaslighting, to lay bare its intentions, and cite examples doing so. Using the examples and stories in the book, you can now identify gaslighting in your life and the lives of those around you and you can find a solution.

The biggest takeaway from this book should be that the victim of gaslighting is not at fault. You are dealing with an expert manipulator who has no scruples and doesn't play fair. Many victims show resilience and they are to be admired for their fighting spirit because a gaslighter doesn't go down without a fight. If you know someone who is being gaslit, remain as the constant in their lives, a safe haven for them, and always watch over them.

EXCLUSIVE GIFT

Hello! Thank you for purchasing this book. Here is your free gift. It's good and it's free!

This mini e-book will answer your questions about this rather controversial skill. It's controversial because it works!

Get ready to learn more about Conversational Hypnosis, simplified for easy and practical use.

Here are just a few of the many benefits of learning Conversational Hypnosis:

- Get your audience to warm up to you and be more open to your message
- Better sales tactics
- Create deeper connections with people
- Create positive change
- And more!

If you want to become a good hypnotic conversationalist, you better start learning the skill today and be a master tomorrow. All you have to do is access the secret download page below.

Open a browser window on your computer or smartphone and enter: <u>bonus.emorygreen.com</u>

You will be automatically directed to the download page.

Remember to influence the world with good intentions.

All the best,
Emory Green